# Privacy Solutions and Security Frameworks in Information Protection

Hamid R. Nemati
*The University of North Carolina at Greensboro, USA*

| Managing Director: | Lindsay Johnston |
| Editorial Director: | Joel Gamon |
| Book Production Manager: | Jennifer Yoder |
| Publishing Systems Analyst: | Adrienne Freeland |
| Assistant Acquisitions Editor: | Kayla Wolfe |
| Typesetter: | Erin O'Dea |
| Cover Design: | Nick Newcomer |

Published in the United States of America by
Information Science Reference (an imprint of IGI Global)
701 E. Chocolate Avenue
Hershey PA 17033
Tel: 717-533-8845
Fax: 717-533-8661
E-mail: cust@igi-global.com
Web site: http://www.igi-global.com

Library of Congress Cataloging-in-Publication Data

Privacy solutions and security frameworks in information protection / Hamid R. Nemati, editor.
    p. cm.
 Includes bibliographical references and index.
 Summary: "This book explores the areas of concern in guaranteeing the security and privacy of data and related technologies, including a range of topics in information security and privacy provided for a diverse readership ranging from academic and professional researchers to industry practitioners"-- Provided by publisher.
 ISBN 978-1-4666-2050-6 (hardcover) -- ISBN 978-1-4666-2051-3 (ebook) -- ISBN 978-1-4666-2052-0 (print & perpetual access) 1. Computer networks--Security measures. 2. Data protection. 3. Confidential communications. 4. Computers--Access control. I. Nemati, Hamid R., 1958-
 TK5105.59.P758 2013
 005.8--dc23
                            2012013064


British Cataloguing in Publication Data
A Cataloguing in Publication record for this book is available from the British Library.

The views expressed in this book are those of the authors, but not necessarily of the publisher.

# Table of Contents

# Detailed Table of Contents

**Chapter 1**

    *Devon Bennett, University of East London, UK*
    *Hamid Jahankhani, University of East London, UK*
    *Mohammad Dastbaz, University of East London, UK*
    *Hossein Jahankhani, University of East London, UK*

In developed economies, electronic communication infrastructures are crucial for daily public, private, and business interactions. Cellular systems are extensively used for business communications, private interaction, and in some cases, public information services, via such uses as mass SMS messaging. The Public Switched Telephone Network (PSTN) is at the core of all communications platforms. It was used primarily for voice communication purposes, but with current technological advances, this platform has been transformed from a voice to voice interface to a web enabled multimedia platform that provides commercial, business, and e-commerce services to the public. In response to the September 11, 2001, terrorist acts in New York City, the UK government introduced a policy of separating and transferring all emergency communication traffic from the PSTN to a digital public safety network based on the TETRA architecture. This paper extends the utilisation of the TETRA deployment by discussing a secure MANET hybrid solution for use in extreme situations as a short/mid-term EMS organisational communication platform for emergency and rescue operations.

**Chapter 2**

    *A. Bhattarai, University of Memphis, USA*
    *D. Dasgupta, University of Memphis, USA*

This paper studies the problems and threats posed by a type of spam in the blogosphere, called blog comment spam. It explores the challenges introduced by comment spam, generalizing the analysis substantially to any other short text type spam. The authors analyze different high-level features of spam and legitimate comments based on the content of blog postings. The authors use these features to cluster data separately for each feature using K-Means clustering algorithm. The authors also use self-supervised learning, which could classify spam and legitimate comments automatically. Compared with existing solutions, this approach demonstrates more flexibility and adaptability to the environment, as it requires minimal human intervention. The preliminary evaluation of the proposed spam detection system shows promising results.

## Chapter 3

*Ioana Lasc, University of Limerick, Ireland*
*Reiner Dojen, University of Limerick, Ireland*
*Tom Coffey, University of Limerick, Ireland*

Many peer-to-peer security protocols proposed for wireless communications use one-time shared secrets
for authentication purposes. This paper analyses online update mechanisms for one-time shared secrets.
A new type of attack against update mechanisms, called desynchronisation attack, is introduced. This
type of attack may lead to a permanent denial of service condition. A case study demonstrates the effectiveness of desynchronisation attacks against a security protocol for mobile satellite communications.
A new mutual authentication protocol for satellite communications, incorporating a resynchronisation
capability, is proposed to counter the disruptive effects of desynchronisation attacks. The new protocol has an esynchronisation phase that is initiated whenever desynchronisation is suspected. Thus, the
possibility of causing permanent denial of service conditions by mounting desynchronisation attacks
is eliminated. A security analysis of the proposed protocol establishes its resistance against attacks like
replay attacks, dictionary attacks, and desynchronisation attacks.

## Chapter 4

*Garry L. White, Texas State University – San Marcos, USA*
*Francis A. Méndez Mediavilla, Texas State University – San Marcos, USA*
*Jaymeen R. Shah, Texas State University – San Marcos, USA*

In the Web dependent world, companies must respect and protect individuals' information privacy.
Companies develop and implement corporate information privacy policies to comply with the domestic
and international information privacy laws and regulations. This paper investigates: (a) the approach
used by multinational and domestic companies to develop and implement corporate information privacy
policies; and (b) the perception of corporate managers/professionals toward information privacy legislation and secondary use of personally identifiable information (PII) that organizations collect. A survey
was conducted to collect data from corporate CEOs, managers, and technical professionals of national
and multinational companies. Findings indicate the following: 1) Views regarding the practicality and
effectiveness of information privacy legislations are similar for respondents from the national and
multinational companies. 2) Respondents are undecided about whether the privacy laws of the United
States and foreign countries are equally restrictive. 3) Multinational companies do not favor developing
and implementing uniform information privacy policies or different information privacy policies across
countries of operations. 4) Respondents strongly agreed that unauthorized secondary use of personal
information is unacceptable.

## Chapter 5

*Douglas M. Kline, University of North Carolina Wilmington, USA*
*Ling He, Saginaw Valley State University, USA*
*Ulku Yaylacicegi, University of North Carolina Wilmington, USA*

In this paper, user perceptions of information systems security are explored through a study of university
students. Server authentication, which is often ignored by users, clouded by system administrators, and
exploited by hackers, is explored in detail, as it significantly affects usability and requires user knowl-

edge and participation. The study also investigates the respondents' consistency, gender differences, and assessment of their own knowledge. Although users appear knowledgeable about security technologies, they rely more on peer opinion and reputation of web sites when making security decisions.

## Chapter 6

*Golam Kaosar, Victoria University, Australia*
*Xun Yi, Victoria University, Australia*

Frequent Path tree (FP-tree) is a popular method to compute association rules and is faster than Apriori-based solutions in some cases. Association rule mining using FP-tree method cannot ensure entire privacy since frequency of the itemsets are required to share among participants at the first stage. Moreover, FP-tree method requires two scans of database transactions which may not be the best solution if the database is very large or the database server does not allow multiple scans. In addition, one-pass FP-tree can accommodate continuous or periodically changing databases without restarting the process as opposed to a regular FP-tree based solution. In this paper, the authors propose a one-pass FP-tree method to perform association rule mining without compromising any data privacy among two parties. A fully homomorphic encryption system over integer numbers is applied to ensure secure computation among two data sites without disclosing any number belongs to themselves.

## Chapter 7

*Anirban Sengupta, Jadavpur University, India*
*Chandan Mazumdar, Jadavpur University, India*

As enterprises become dependent on information systems, the need for effective Information Security Governance (ISG) assumes significance. ISG manages risks relating to the confidentiality, integrity and availability of information, and its supporting processes and systems, in an enterprise. Even a medium-sized enterprise contains a huge collection of information and other assets. Moreover, risks evolve rapidly in today's connected digital world. Therefore, the proper implementation of ISG requires automation of the various monitoring, analysis, and control processes. This can be best achieved by representing information security requirements of an enterprise in a standard, structured format. This paper presents such a structured format in the form of Enterprise Security Requirement Markup Language (ESRML) Version 2.0. It is an XML-based language that considers the elements of ISO 27002 best practices.

## Chapter 8

*Cheng-Chi Lee, Fu Jen Catholic University, Taiwan*
*Min-Shiang Hwang, Asia University, Taiwan*
*I-En Liao, National Chung Hsing University, Taiwan*

Many cryptosystems have been developed to solve the problem of information security, and some approaches are based on the self-certified public key proposed by Girault. In Girault's scheme, the public key is computed cooperatively by both the system authority (SA) and the user. One of the advantages is that the public key is able to implicitly authenticate itself without any additional certificates. Another advantage is that the SA is not able to forge a public key without knowing the user's secret key. Despite the advantages of Girault's system, in this paper, the authors demonstrate that the system still suffers from two main weaknesses. As a result, the authors propose a slight improvement on Girault's system.

## Chapter 9

Design and Implementation of a Zero-Knowledge Authentication Framework for Java Card ......... 131

*Ahmed Patel, Universiti Kebangsaan Malaysia, Malaysia & Kingston University, UK*

*Kenan Kalajdzic, Center for Computing Education, Bosnia & Herzegovina*

*Laleh Golafshan, Department of Computer Engineering & IT, Science and Research Branch, Islamic Azad University, Fars, Iran*

*Mona Taghavi, Department of Computer, Science and Research Branch, Islamic Azad University, Tehran, Iran*

Zero-knowledge authentication protocols are an alternative to authentication protocols based on public key cryptography. Low processing and memory consumption make them especially suitable for implementation in smart card microprocessors, which are severely limited in processing power and memory space. This paper describes a design and implementation of a software library providing smart card application developers with a reliable authentication mechanism based on well-known zero-knowledge authentication schemes. Java Card is used as the target smart card platform implementation based on the evaluation of the Fiat-Shamir (F-S) and Guillou-Quisquater (G-Q) protocols under various performance criteria are presented to show the effectiveness of the implementation and that G-Q is a more efficient protocol.

## Chapter 10

E-Voting Risk Assessment: A Threat Tree for Direct Recording Electronic Systems ....................... 149

*Harold Pardue, University of South Alabama, USA*

*Jeffrey Landry, University of South Alabama, USA*

*Alec Yasinsac, University of South Alabama, USA*

Approximately 25% (according to http://verifiedvoting.com/) of voting jurisdictions use direct recording electronic systems to record votes. Accurate tabulation of voter intent is critical to safeguard this fundamental act of democracy: voting. Electronic voting systems are known to be vulnerable to attack. Assessing risk to these systems requires a systematic treatment and cataloging of threats, vulnerabilities, technologies, controls, and operational environments. This paper presents a threat tree for direct recording electronic (DRE) voting systems. The threat tree is organized as a hierarchy of threat actions, the goal of which is to exploit a system vulnerability in the context of specific technologies, controls, and operational environment. As an abstraction, the threat tree allows the analyst to reason comparatively about threats. A panel of elections officials, security experts, academics, election law attorneys, representatives from governmental agencies, voting equipment vendors, and voting equipment testing labs vetted the DRE threat tree. The authors submit that the DRE threat tree supports both individual and group risk assessment processes and techniques.

## Chapter 11

Intrusion Detection Algorithm for MANET ................................................................................. 163

*S. Srinivasan, Texas A&M International University, USA*

*S. P. Alampalayam, APS Technologies, USA*

Mobile ad hoc networks (MANET) present the opportunity to connect transient nodes to the internet without having central control. This very design supports new nodes to join and leave the network based on their proximity to the MANET. Concurrently, it creates many security challenges for authenticating nodes that are not present in a traditional wired network. Much of the existing work on MANET security has focused on routing and mobility. In this paper, the authors present an algorithm that considers the neighboring nodes' status to determine if a particular node is malicious or not. The authors used NS2 simulation tool to test the algorithm and present the results in the paper. The major benefits of this research work are in military applications.

## Chapter 12

*Mathew Nicho, University of Dubai, UAE*
*Hussein Fakhry, University of Dubai, UAE*

This paper analyses relevant IT governance and security frameworks/standards used in IT assurance and security to propose an integrated framework for ensuring effective PCI DSS implementation. Merchants dealing with credit cards have to comply with the Payment Card Industry Data Security Standards (PCI DSS) or face penalties for non-compliance. With more transactions based on credit cards, merchants are finding it costly and increasingly difficult to implement and interpret the PCI standard. One of the top reasons cited for merchants to fail PCI audit, and a leading factor in data theft, is the failure to adequately protect stored cardholder data. Although implementation of the PCI DSS is not a guarantee for perfect protection, effective implementation of the PCI standards can be ensured through the divergence of the PCI standard into wider information security governance to provide a comprehensive overview of information security based not only on security but also security audit and control. The contribution of this paper is the development of an integrated comprehensive security governance framework for 'information security' (rather than data protection) incorporating Control Objectives for Information and related Technology (COBIT), Information Technology Infrastructure Library (ITIL) and ISO 27002.

## Chapter 13

*Murthy V. Rallapalli, IBM and Stevens Institute of Technology, USA*

This article presents an alternate approach to effectively address the way privacy agreements are initiated through web services. In this new framework, the consumer and the service provider can mutually negotiate on the privacy terms. It contains a privacy model in which the transaction takes place after a negotiation between the service provider and the web user is completed. In addition, this framework would support various negotiation levels of the agreement lifecycle which is an important aspect of the dynamic environment of a B2C e-commerce scenario. A third party trusted agency and a privacy filter are included to handle privacy information of the web user. The author seeks to raise awareness of the issues surrounding privacy transactions and the potential ongoing impact to both service providers and clients as the use of web services accelerates.

## Chapter 14

*O. T. Arogundade, Chinese Academy of Sciences, China*
*A. T. Akinwale, University of Agriculture, Abeokuta, Nigeria*
*Z. Jin, Peking University, China*
*X. G. Yang, Chinese Academy of Sciences, China*

This paper proposes an enhanced use-misuse case model that allows both safety and security requirements to be captured during requirements elicitation. The proposed model extends the concept of misuse case by incorporating vulnerable use case and abuse case notations and relations that allows understanding and modeling different attackers and abusers behaviors during early stage of system development life cycle and finishes with a practical consistent combined model for engineering safety and security requirements.

The model was successfully applied using health care information system gathered through the university of Kansas HISPC project. The authors were able to capture both security and safety requirements necessary for effective functioning of the system. In order to enhance the integration of the proposed model into risk analysis, the authors give both textual and detailed description of the model. The authors compare the proposed approach with other existing methods that identify and analyze safety and security requirements and discovered that it captures more security and safety threats.

As the nation confronts a growing tide of security breaches, the importance of having quality data breach information systems becomes paramount. Yet too little attention is paid to evaluating these systems. This article draws on data quality scholarship to develop a yardstick that assesses the quality of data breach notification systems in the U.S. at both the state and national levels from the perspective of key stakeholders, who include law enforcement agencies, consumers, shareholders, investors, researchers, and businesses that sell security products. Findings reveal major shortcomings that reduce the value of data breach information to these stakeholders. The study concludes with detailed recommendations for reform.

While the rise of the Internet and the high speed networks made information easier to acquire, faster to exchange and more flexible to share, it also made the cybernetic attacks and crimes easier to perform, more accurate to hit the target victim and more flexible to conceal the crime evidences. Although people are in an unsafe digital environment, they often feel safe. Being aware of this fact and this fiction, the authors draw in this paper a security framework aiming to build real-time security solutions in the very narrow context of high speed networks. This framework is called ($\phi|\pi$) since it is inspired by the ele$\phi$ ant self-defense behavior which yields $\pi$ (22 security tasks for 7 security targets).

# Preface

In an increasingly digital society that relies heavily on Internet and mobile networks for every aspect of day-to-day life, security is a pressing concern. The sixteen chapters that follow represent the cutting edge of research and scholarship on IT security, as first witnessed in the *International Journal of Information Security and Privacy (IJISP)*. Within these pages, readers will find information on network security, modern encryption protocols, data analysis, and more.

The book begins with "A Secure Hybrid Network Solution to Enhance the Resilience of the UK Government National Critical Infrastructure TETRA Deployment" by Devon Bennett *et al.*, which describes how, in developed economies, electronic communication infrastructures are crucial for daily public, private, and business interactions. Cellular systems are extensively used for business communications, private interaction, and in some cases, public information services, via such uses as mass SMS messaging. The Public Switched Telephone Network (PSTN) is at the core of all communications platforms. It was used primarily for voice communication purposes, but with current technological advances, this platform has been transformed from a voice to voice interface to a web enabled multimedia platform that provides commercial, business, and e-commerce services to the public. In response to the September 11, 2001, terrorist acts in New York City, the UK government introduced a policy of separating and transferring all emergency communication traffic from the PSTN to a digital public safety network based on the TETRA architecture. This chapter extends the utilisation of the TETRA deployment by discussing a secure MANET hybrid solution for use in extreme situations as a short/mid-term EMS organisational communication platform for emergency and rescue operations.

Chapter 2, "A Self-Supervised Approach to Comment Spam Detection Based on Content Analysis" by A. Bhattarai and D. Dasgupta, studies the problems and threats posed by a type of spam in the blogosphere, called blog comment spam. It explores the challenges introduced by comment spam, generalizing the analysis substantially to any other short text type spam. The authors analyze different high-level features of spam and legitimate comments based on the content of blog postings. The authors use these features to cluster data separately for each feature using K-Means clustering algorithm. The authors also use self-supervised learning, which could classify spam and legitimate comments automatically. Compared with existing solutions, this approach demonstrates more flexibility and adaptability to the environment, as it requires minimal human intervention. The preliminary evaluation of the proposed spam detection system shows promising results.

Many peer-to-peer security protocols proposed for wireless communications use one-time shared secrets for authentication purposes. Chapter 3, "A Mutual Authentication Protocol with Resynchronisation Capability for Mobile Satellite Communications" by Ioana Lasc *et al.*, analyses online update mechanisms for one-time shared secrets. A new type of attack against update mechanisms, called desynchronisation attack, is introduced. This type of attack may lead to a permanent denial of service condition. A case study demonstrates the effectiveness of desynchronisation attacks against a security protocol for mobile satellite communications. A new mutual authentication protocol for satellite communications, incorporating a resynchronisation capability, is proposed to counter the disruptive effects of desynchronisation attacks. The new protocol has an esynchronisation phase that is initiated whenever desynchronisation is suspected. Thus, the possibility of causing permanent denial of service conditions by mounting desynchronisation attacks is eliminated. A security analysis of the proposed protocol establishes its resistance against attacks like replay attacks, dictionary attacks, and desynchronisation attacks.

In the Web dependent world, companies must respect and protect individuals' information privacy. Companies develop and implement corporate information privacy policies to comply with the domestic and international information privacy laws and regulations. Chapter 4, "Information Privacy: Implementation and Perception of Laws and Corporate Policies by CEOs and Managers" by Garry L. White *et al.*, investigates: (a) the approach used by multinational and domestic companies to develop and implement corporate information privacy policies; and (b) the perception of corporate managers/ professionals toward information privacy legislation and secondary use of personally identifiable information (PII) that organizations collect. A survey was conducted to collect data from corporate CEOs, managers, and technical professionals of national and multinational companies. Findings indicate the following: 1) Views regarding the practicality and effectiveness of information privacy legislations are similar for respondents from the national and multinational companies. 2) Respondents are undecided about whether the privacy laws of the United States and foreign countries are equally restrictive. 3) Multinational companies do not favor developing and implementing uniform information privacy policies or different information privacy policies across countries of operations. 4) Respondents strongly agreed that unauthorized secondary use of personal information is unacceptable.

"User Perceptions of Security Technologies," by Douglas M. Kline *et al.*, explores user perceptions of information systems security through a study of university students. Server authentication, which is often ignored by users, clouded by system administrators, and exploited by hackers, is explored in detail, as it significantly affects usability and requires user knowledge and participation. The study also investigates the respondents' consistency, gender differences, and assessment of their own knowledge. Although users appear knowledgeable about security technologies, they rely more on peer opinion and reputation of web sites when making security decisions.

Golam Koasar and Xun Yi, in "Secure Two-Party Association Rule Mining Based on One-Pass FP-Tree," explore Frequent Path tree (FP-tree), a popular method to compute association rules that is faster than Aprioribased solutions in some cases. Association rule mining using FP-tree method cannot ensure entire privacy since frequency of the itemsets are required to share among participants at the first stage. Moreover, FP-tree method requires two scans of database transactions which may not be the best solution if the database is very large or the database server does not allow multiple scans. In addition, one-pass FP-tree can accommodate continuous or periodically changing databases without restarting the process as opposed to a regular FP-tree based solution. In this chapter, the authors propose a one-pass FP-tree method to perform association rule mining without compromising any data privacy among two parties. A fully homomorphic encryption system over integer numbers is applied to ensure secure computation among two data sites without disclosing any number belongs to themselves.

In the next chapter, "A Mark-Up Language for the Specification of Information Security Governance Requirements," Anirban Sengupta and Chandan Mazumdar detail how, as enterprises become dependent on information systems, the need for effective Information Security Governance (ISG) assumes significance. ISG manages risks relating to the confidentiality, integrity and availability of information, and its supporting processes and systems, in an enterprise. Even a medium-sized enterprise contains a huge collection of information and other assets. Moreover, risks evolve rapidly in today's connected digital world. Therefore, the proper implementation of ISG requires automation of the various monitoring, analysis, and control processes. This can be best achieved by representing information security requirements of an enterprise in a standard, structured format. This chapter presents such a structured format in the form of Enterprise Security Requirement Markup Language (ESRML) Version 2.0. It is an XML-based language that considers the elements of ISO 27002 best practices.

"On the Security of Self-Certified Public Keys," by Cheng-Chi Lee *et al.* explains how many cryptosystems have been developed to solve the problem of information security, and some approaches are based on the self-certified public key proposed by Girault. In Girault's scheme, the public key is computed cooperatively by both the system authority (SA) and the user. One of the advantages is that the public key is able to implicitly authenticate itself without any additional certificates. Another advantage is that the SA is not able to forge a public key without knowing the user's secret key. Despite the advantages of Girault's system, in this chapter, the authors demonstrate that the system still suffers from two main weaknesses. As a result, the authors propose a slight improvement on Girault's system.

Zero-knowledge authentication protocols are an alternative to authentication protocols based on public key cryptography. Low processing and memory consumption make them especially suitable for implementation in smart card microprocessors, which are severely limited in processing power and memory space. Chapter 9, "Design and Implementation of a Zero-Knowledge Authentication Framework for Java Card" by Ahmed Patel *et al.*, describes a design and implementation of a software library providing smart card application developers with a reliable authentication mechanism based on well-known zero-knowledge authentication schemes. Java Card is used as the target smart card platform implementation based on the evaluation of the Fiat-Shamir (F-S) and Guillou-Quisquater (G-Q) protocols under various performance criteria are presented to show the effectiveness of the implementation and that G-Q is a more efficient protocol.

In the following chapter, "E-Voting Risk Assessment: A Threat Tree for Direct Recording Electronic Systems," Harold Pardue *et al.* explain that approximately 25% (according to http://verifiedvoting.com/) of voting jurisdictions use direct recording electronic systems to record votes. Accurate tabulation of voter intent is critical to safeguard this fundamental act of democracy: voting. Electronic voting systems are known to be vulnerable to attack. Assessing risk to these systems requires a systematic treatment and cataloging of threats, vulnerabilities, technologies, controls, and operational environments. This chapter presents a threat tree for direct recording electronic (DRE) voting systems. The threat tree is organized as a hierarchy of threat actions, the goal of which is to exploit a system vulnerability in the context of specific technologies, controls, and operational environment. As an abstraction, the threat tree allows the analyst to reason comparatively about threats. A panel of elections officials, security experts, academics, election law attorneys, representatives from governmental agencies, voting equipment vendors, and voting equipment testing labs vetted the DRE threat tree. The authors submit that the DRE threat tree supports both individual and group risk assessment processes and techniques.

S. Srinivasan and S.P. Alampalayam explore the security capabilities of Mobile ad hoc networks (MANETs) in "Intrusion Detection Algorithm for MANET." MANETs present the opportunity to connect transient nodes to the internet without having central control. This very design supports new nodes to join and leave the network based on their proximity to the MANET. Concurrently, it creates many security challenges for authenticating nodes that are not present in a traditional wired network. Much of the existing work on MANET security has focused on routing and mobility. In this chapter, the authors present an algorithm that considers the neighboring nodes' status to determine if a particular node is malicious or not. The authors used NS2 simulation tool to test the algorithm and present the results. The major benefits of this research work are in military applications.

Chapter 12, "An Integrated Security Governance Framework for Effective PCI DSS Implementation" by Mathew Nicho and Hussein Fakhry, analyses relevant IT governance and security frameworks/standards used in IT assurance and security to propose an integrated framework for ensuring effective PCI DSS implementation. Merchants dealing with credit cards have to comply with the Payment Card Industry Data Security Standards (PCI DSS) or face penalties for non-compliance. With more transactions based on credit cards, merchants are finding it costly and increasingly difficult to implement and interpret the PCI standard. One of the top reasons cited for merchants to fail PCI audit, and a leading factor in data theft, is the failure to adequately protect stored cardholder data. Although implementation of the PCI DSS is not a guarantee for perfect protection, effective implementation of the PCI standards can be ensured through the divergence of the PCI standard into wider information security governance to provide a comprehensive overview of information security based not only on security but also security audit and control. The primary contribution of this research is the development of an integrated comprehensive security governance framework for 'information security' (rather than data protection) incorporating Control Objectives for Information and related Technology (COBIT), Information Technology Infrastructure Library (ITIL) and ISO 27002.

Next, Murthy V. Rallapalli, in "A Privacy Agreement Negotiation Model in B2C E-Commerce Transactions," presents an alternate approach to effectively address the way privacy agreements are initiated through web services. In this new framework, the consumer and the service provider can mutually negotiate on the privacy terms. It contains a privacy model in which the transaction takes place after a negotiation between the service provider and the web user is completed. In addition, this framework would support various negotiation levels of the agreement lifecycle which is an important aspect of the dynamic environment of a B2C e-commerce scenario. A third party trusted agency and a privacy filter are included to handle privacy information of the web user. The author seeks to raise awareness of the issues surrounding privacy transactions and the potential ongoing impact to both service providers and clients as the use of web services accelerates.

The following chapter, "A Unified Use-Misuse Case Model for Capturing and Analysing Safety and Security Requirements" by O.T. Arogundade et al., proposes an enhanced use-misuse case model that allows both safety and security requirements to be captured during requirements elicitation. The proposed model extends the concept of misuse case by incorporating vulnerable use case and abuse case notations and relations that allows understanding and modeling different attackers and abusers behaviors during early stage of system development life cycle and finishes with a practical consistent combined model for engineering safety and security requirements. The model was successfully applied using health care information system gathered through the university of Kansas HISPC project. The authors were able to capture both security and safety requirements necessary for effective functioning of the system. In order to enhance the integration of the proposed model into risk analysis, the authors give both textual and detailed description of the model. The authors compare the proposed approach with other existing methods that identify and analyze safety and security requirements and discovered that it captures more security and safety threats.

As the nation confronts a growing tide of security breaches, the importance of having quality data breach information systems becomes paramount. Yet too little attention is paid to evaluating these systems. Chapter 15, "Evaluating the Quality and Usefulness of Data Breach Information Systems" by Benjamin

Ngugi, draws on data quality scholarship to develop a yardstick that assesses the quality of data breach notification systems in the U.S. at both the state and national levels from the perspective of key stakeholders, who include law enforcement agencies, consumers, shareholders, investors, researchers, and businesses that sell security products. Findings reveal major shortcomings that reduce the value of data breach information to these stakeholders. The study concludes with detailed recommendations for reform.

Finally, Hassen Sallay writes in "Wild-Inspired Intrusion Detection System Framework for High Speed Networks ($\varphi|\pi$) IDS Framework" that while the rise of the Internet and the high speed networks made information easier to acquire, faster to exchange and more flexible to share, it also made the cybernetic attacks and crimes easier to perform, more accurate to hit the target victim and more flexible to conceal the crime evidences. Although people are in an unsafe digital environment, they often feel safe. Being aware of this fact and this fiction, the authors draw a security framework aiming to build real-time security solutions in the very narrow context of high speed networks. This framework is called ($\varphi|\pi$) since it is inspired by the ele$\varphi$ant self-defense behavior which yields $\pi$ (22 security tasks for 7 security targets).

*Hamid R. Nemati*
*The University of North Carolina at Greensboro, USA*

# Chapter 1
# A Secure Hybrid Network Solution to Enhance the Resilience of the UK Government National Critical Infrastructure TETRA Deployment

**Devon Bennett**
*University of East London, UK*

**Mohammad Dastbaz**
*University of East London, UK*

**Hamid Jahankhani**
*University of East London, UK*

**Hossein Jahankhani**
*University of East London, UK*

## ABSTRACT

*In developed economies, electronic communication infrastructures are crucial for daily public, private, and business interactions. Cellular systems are extensively used for business communications, private interaction, and in some cases, public information services, via such uses as mass SMS messaging. The Public Switched Telephone Network (PSTN) is at the core of all communications platforms. It was used primarily for voice communication purposes, but with current technological advances, this platform has been transformed from a voice to voice interface to a web enabled multimedia platform that provides commercial, business, and e-commerce services to the public. In response to the September 11, 2001, terrorist acts in New York City, the UK government introduced a policy of separating and transferring all emergency communication traffic from the PSTN to a digital public safety network based on the TETRA architecture. This paper extends the utilisation of the TETRA deployment by discussing a secure MANET hybrid solution for use in extreme situations as a short/mid-term EMS organisational communication platform for emergency and rescue operations.*

DOI: 10.4018/978-1-4666-2050-6.ch001

# 1. INTRODUCTION

The ability for the emergency services to mobilise and organise efficient cross-communication platforms is critical in the delivery of a high quality service that is capable of coordinating the rescue effort in the most cost effective and efficient manner possible. This implies that the emergency services must be capable, under extreme circumstances, of quickly achieving a high-level of inter-services communications without the assurance of a fully operational telecommunications platform.

Over the last few years we have seen a number of natural disasters, where such incidents as the devastating floods in Worcestershire, UK, in both 1998 and 2007, the Sichuan earthquake in China in 2008 and the recent earthquake in the Italian city of L'Aquila in 2009. These disasters not only severely tested the national and international telecommunication infrastructures, but in some cases completely destroyed the communication infrastructure in the affected areas. Resulting in the inability of the emergency services to react and organise themselves; whilst managing the sense of panic and anxiety, which is commonplace amongst the general population in the disaster zone.

In 2001 the American city of New York found itself under an alternative extreme situation - a man-made political terrorist attack where the public voice and data communication infrastructure was severely compromised on 9/11, by the extreme demands put on the New York's PSTN. Research as clearly demonstrated that the inadequacies of the New York emergency radio communications infrastructure, was a major contributing factor to the loss of 120 New York fire-fighters (BWCS Consulting, 2002). Similar research both in the UK and Europe has found the old analogue radio networks demonstrated the same bandwidth inadequacies with congested airwaves, bad reception, and loss of signal (BBC News, 2002), during similar situations.

The governments of both Europe and the UK have taken these natural and man-made threats to their national communications infrastructure seriously and have developed systems to combat these types of threats; by the introduction of UK Critical National Infrastructure policy and the EU equivalent European Programme for Critical Infrastructure Protection (EPCIP). This was achieved by a policy of transferring all emergency communication from the PSTN services to a parallel digital TETRA based private mobile radio network and public access mobile radio network (ETSI, 2000).

The TETRA standard is a European wide standard for radio communications of the public safety and emergency services networks (ETSI, 1995), like GSM is the standard for mobile voice communication systems; TETRA is the equivalent standard and was developed by the European Telecommunications Standards Institute (ETSI, 2000).

# 2. TERRESTRIAL TRUNKED RADIO (TETRA) PUBLIC SAFETY NETWORKS

In the UK the TETRA system forms part of the UK government's strategic Critical National Infrastructure policy; this was developed after the 2001 terrorist incidents to provide a comprehensive solution to combat terrorist attacks on the countries electronic communications infrastructure. These new emergency services communications platforms are generally called Public Safety Networks and their initial objective is to achieve signal coverage across a country, homogenising the regional communications of that country, between the ambulance services, police services and the fire brigade. These systems are digital radio systems that are a vast improvement on the old analogue radio networks previously used by the emergency services.

TETRA is a modern digital private mobile radio (PMR) and public access mobile radio (PAMR) technology used exclusively for the police, ambulance and fire service and other national and public safety organisations (ETSI, 2007). The service was first deployed in 1997, but it was not until 2006 that the PMR and PAMR systems took an increased share of the market, this increased share can be directly attributed to the UK Critical National Infrastructure policy and the EU equivalent European Programme for Critical Infrastructure Protection (EPCIP), which adopted the TETRA standard for the rollout of the emergency services private mobile radio network (PMR) for all police, fire and ambulance service communications. Now the TETRA standard and services have been adopted by numerous countries outside the EU and is presently deployed in 88+ countries around the world. Interestingly the TETRA standard is not used in North America, but discussions are taking place to license the technology in the near future (Pandata Corp, 2009).

In Europe two of the best examples of public safety networks are the Motorola C2000 system in the Netherlands and the 02 Airwave system in the United Kingdom.

The 02 network is a secure digital radio network that supports intelligent networking, via Telsis® fastSSP intelligent switches installed in secured locations throughout the United Kingdom. They support QSIG signalling to route traffic via private circuits to airwave handsets anywhere in the UK (Telsis, 2004).

The 02 airwave intelligent networking platforms is one of the biggest emergency and public safety networks in Europe. It forms part of the United Kingdom's HMG Critical National Infrastructure, which is the largest of its kind in Europe. The UK's HMG Critical National Infrastructure was designed to cope with the excessive loads experienced during major incidents, where the conventional cellular and fixed wired telecommunication systems may fail due to traffic overloads.

In the UK the 02 airwave communications platform is owned by mm02 plc, which have out-sourced the core transmission network infrastructure to Cable & Wireless, for provision of its Ground Based Network (GBN). The Cable & Wireless /02 airwave network is a fixed line backbone core network, that consists of a mesh STM-4 link at 622Mbps, connecting seven core switching sites, that in turn connect over 100 police control rooms across the UK. Because this structure is a mesh it is highly resilient; if a switching site goes down then all the circuits to that site can be re-routed within minutes (Cable & Wireless Worldwide, 2004), via the mesh structure. Other benefits provided by this network are:

- The network is based on the TETRA standard.
- The radio network operates on the 380MHz to 400MHz band.
- It caters for speech, data, and image communications on the same infrastructure.
- All the radio sites are connected via an extensive ground based network, using Kilostream links.
- mmO2, as the service provider, procures, installs, maintains and manages the entire network via a number of network and service centres.

The 02 airwave network was originally rolled out to the police forces in the UK, and in March 2005 this process was completed. Allowing all the police forces in the UK to move from their outdated analogue radio systems, which were generally procured 'bespoke' for each force. To a fully digital and integrated state-of-the-art public safety network, that provides a wealth of new facilities:-

- Access to local and national databases leading to better and faster provision of information to Officers.
- Secure communications, contributing to combating crime and safeguarding information from unauthorised access by eliminating the use of analogue scanners operated by some criminals to listen into police radio traffic.

- High quality digital voice communication channels.
- One terminal acting as a radio, mobile telephone, and data terminal.
- Automatic Vehicle and Person location leading to quicker responses, more efficient use of resources and improved officer safety.
- Comprehensive Management Information enabling the best management of limited operational resources.
- Interoperability providing seamless voice, data and image communications, across the country and across organisational & geographical boundaries (Fife Constabulary, n.d.).

The rollout of the 02 airwave network to the police forces and the military police was so successful that a number of ambulance trusts, fire brigades, and county councils have moved to the 02 airwave network. This has become more crucial as the UK government will withdraw support of all of existing analogue VHF radio frequencies used by the emergency services, by the end of 2009.

A case study of successful TETRA deployment is the Shropshire Fire & Rescue service (Sepura, 2005), which migrated its old analogue radio communications system to the 02 airwave TETRA secured digital radio communication system, using the TETRA enabled Sepura in-vehicle mounted terminals and Sepura mobile handsets for mobile fire and rescue personnel. The Shropshire Fire & Rescue Service (SFRS) is situated in the largest landlocked county in the UK and has approximately 550 fire fighters, officers, and control room staff set across 33 fire stations in the county (Sepura, 2005). In addition the SFRS has over 80 fire and rescue vehicles each one has the Sepura in-vehicle TETRA terminals, with direct communication to one or other incident control room.

Because the SFRS has adopted the 02 airwave system, they have found that in addition to the increased voice communication clarity of the

digital system, when compared to the problems of the old analogue system. The 02 airwave system provides the facility for the Shropshire Fire & Rescue Service to talk directly to the police service, as all police forces in the UK have rolled out the 02 airwave system for their services use.

This inter-service cross communication platform is achieved by the Sepura handsets and terminals used across both services and the ability to define and setup 'talk-groups'. Talk-groups are used to provide inter-agency communication between the services and the secured nature of the 02 airwave TETRA platform means that the possibility of unauthorised persons eavesdropping is eliminated. In Shropshire these talk-groups have now been setup for specific fire-to-police communications, which are used in emergency incidents for emergency situation management and coordination between the fire and police services.

Another advantage provided to the SFRS is the Global Positioning System (GPS) services integrated in to the TETRA handset, which provides both the police and emergency services the ability to locate their personnel in adverse and dangerous emergency situations.

With this increase in intercommunications and the ability of the emergency services to construct cross-services talk-groups etc, it would appear the use of MANETs would be unnecessary as the 02 airwave system seems to provide all the necessary facilities to support the emergency services in any situation. This would be a short-sighted view as the 02 airwave system is a still primarily a fixed line backbone core network, which does provide resilience in its ability to reroute circuits via its mesh architecture to one of the seven core switching site across the country.

A good example of the vulnerabilities of the TETRA network can be seen by the tunnel fire which occurred 30 metres below ground in 2004 in the town of Manchester, UK. This underground fire caused two main BT telecommunications supply cables to be damaged; severing all voice and data communications to over 130,000 customers and affecting telecommunications service in a vast geographical area covering Cheshire, Merseyside, Lancashire and North Derbyshire (BBC News, 2004). One of the worst affected emergency services was the Manchester ambulance service, which found itself under extreme operational pressures as the tunnel fire had damaged its radio network; in this situation the Manchester ambulance service resorted to using commercial mobile phones to communicate with ambulance staff in the field, but were unable to receive any inward public 999 emergency calls until the fire was extinguished and communications could be rerouted to other switching stations. This case study demonstrates that these land line based systems are susceptible to network faults which make them vulnerable to outage, loss of facilities and services.

In the case of a major national disaster, as the recent earthquakes in Italy, China and Haiti, the telecommunications industry would not simply be in the process of trying to correct a fault, but could be in the midst of having to rebuild part or the entire communication infrastructure. A dynamic mobile communications platform such as the MANET could be one of the few methods of providing localised mission critical data communications, on the ground, in such situations.

## 3. MANET ARCHITECTURE AND ROUTING

A Mobile Adhoc NETwork (MANET) does not exhibit the same characteristics as a WLAN, where the all communications between client nodes are via Point-to-Point connections to a wireless access point (Geier, 1999). A MANET consists of a Peer-to-Peer network which is dynamically organised, with a continually changing topology or shape (Murthy & Manoj, 2004); within a defined geographical area. This is because a MANET environment leaves all the routing and authentication responsibilities to the client workstations in the network. A wireless local area network (WLAN)

does provide mobility but differs from a Mobile Ad-hoc Network in that it is primarily connected to a network access point (AP) that provides all the routing and authentication responsibilities of the network (Stallings, 2002). The AP is responsible for testing the connection status and signal quality and will handover to another AP as the device is moved from one AP range into another; this is not true of a mobile ad-hoc network.

Mobile Networks (MANET) have been around for some time but was exclusively used in the past for military purposes (DARPA, 1973). The roots of the mobile network technology can be traced back to the 1970s when the Defence Advanced Research Project (DARPA) introduced the Packet Radio Network (Jubin & Tornow, 1987), and in the 1980s the Survivable Adaptive Network (SURAN). These networks were designed for use in military situations under battle conditions and it was therefore necessary that these networks were resilient and would not share information with unauthorised personnel (Kahn, 1978).

This type of network was expected to be rapidly deployed without relying on a pre-existing fixed network infrastructure, under extreme conditions. This in practice meant that these relatively high-speed networks were integrating communications between different command levels, from the division to the brigades, on the move and in extremely short periods of time (Murthy & Manoj, 2004).

The modern/commercial term for this type of platform is the Mobile Ad-Hoc Network (MANET), where the commercial definition is such that a wireless ad-hoc network is a group of dynamic client nodes that has no infrastructure and are responsible for providing routing, authentication and security functions amongst themselves and within a given coverage area. The nodes in a MANET can dynamically join and leave a network frequently, and without warning, but should aim not to interfere with the other clients in the network. Finally the nodes in a MANET can be highly mobile and because of this a MANET environment has a continuously changing topology as links are constructed or broken dynamically (Haas et al., 2001). This definition becomes cloudy when the wireless device interacts with a fixed infrastructure either via RF frequency, cellular, or Satellite interface as all these facilities could be considered as providing wireless interfaces to a fixed environment and not the dynamically constructed network of an ad-hoc environment. The crucial objective of an ad-hoc network is the ability for client devices to take on trust and routing responsibilities with the ability to exchange information with other client devices when there is a complete absence of a client/server infrastructure has defined in a fixed environment.

As stated the nodes in a MANET exhibit nomadic behaviour by freely migrating within a coverage area and dynamically creating and tearing down associations with other nodes. It is these characteristics that differentiate a MANET from any other type of network, by rapidly and continuously changing its shape. In some cases nodes that have a common goal create formations together called clusters, where they are able to migrate together (Haas et al., 2001). In a MANET network if there is no direct link between the source and destination nodes a process called multi-hop routing is used.

Multi-hop routing is where packets are sent from one node to another; even in the case where a source node cannot directly connect to a destination node a packet can still be sent via the multi-hop process (Stallings, 2002). In Figure 1, we can see that source 'A' wants to send a packet to destination 'C', 'A' can communicate with 'B' but cannot communicate with 'C' directly. Source 'A' simply sends its packet to device 'B', which in turn forwards the packet on to its destination 'C'

The most difficult aspect of developing a MANET environment is the operation of the network when compared to the traditional wireless network, this is because there is no centralized entity in a MANET (Murthy & Manoj, 2004); and therefore there is no central component that can be used for routing and authentication. The potential for constant and rapid movement of the client nodes combined with the main weakness that all communication (i.e. Data, authentication, or encryption transmission) is carried over the wireless medium. Results in MANET's requiring distributed algorithms for routing and authentication function, as opposed to the traditional algorithms used on client/server WLAN's.

## 3.1 Routing Protocols for MANET's

In traditional networks routing protocols can be divided into two categories either proactive or reactive. Proactive routing protocols such as the traditional link-state or proactive distance-vector protocols learn the topology of the network by continuously exchanging topological information among the network nodes (Murthy & Manoj, 2004). With this process all nodes are constantly updated with the routing topology and when a route is required by a node it is immediately available. Because of this process of constantly updating the routing tables these protocols are sometimes referred to as table-driven routing protocols. The early proactive protocols that were used for ad-hoc networks were distance vector protocols based on the Distributed Bellman-Ford (DBF) algorithm (Perkins & Bhagwat, 2001). This did not work very well as distance vector protocols produce convergence and excessive control traffic overheads, resulting in slow transmission rates.

On the other side of the spectrum are the reactive routing protocols which are based upon a query / reply procedure. Reactive protocols do not attempt to continuously maintain the current topology of the network; instead when there is a requirement for a route a reactive protocol will invoke a procedure to find a route to its eventual destination. This procedure involves the protocol flooding the network with a route query, because of its operational manner these types of protocols are referred to as 'on-demand' protocols.

## 3.1 Proactive Routing Protocols (Table Driven)

The Destination Sequenced Distance-Vector (DSDV) routing protocol was one of the first routing protocols used for ad-hoc networks. It was an enhanced version of the Distributed Bellman-Ford (DBF) Distance Vector routing protocol, where each node maintains a table that contains the shortest distance and the first node on the shortest path to every other node on the network (Murthy & Manoj, 2004). DSDV combines incremental sequence numbers with table updates to prevent loops and to counter the count-to-infinity problem. Because DSDV is a table-driven protocol, every node on the network has a view on all routes to all destinations; as during regular intervals routing tables are exchanged between neighbours, by a process of flooding the network with routing updates (Perkins & Bhagwat, 2001).

DSDV provides two types of routing updates either an event-driven incremental update or a periodic full-table update. An incremental routing update consists of the protocol sending a single network data packet unit (NDPU), whereas a full-table update may contain multiple NDPUs. Generally an incremental update is used by a node when there are little or no changes to the topology; a full update is used when a node is aware that the local topology has changed significantly.

Routing table updates are initiated by a destination node that transmits an update next-hop table with a new sequenced number that is greater than the previous update. When a node receives this new next-hop table update from its neighbour it can perform two actions either to update its table to show the new destination, if the sequence number of the update is higher than the previous

*Figure 1. Multi-hop packet forwarding*

update. Or store the update to compare it against the multiple versions of the same updates from the neighbouring nodes, to determine the best metric, which could be the shortest number of hops or cheaper cost route. In addition to reduce the control message overheads DSDV provides a time-to-settle metric, which is an estimated settling time for each route to complete (Perkins & Bhagwat, 2001). Therefore a node will only send an update of a route to its neighbour if the settling time of the new route has expired and the route is the best option.

DSDV protocols require each node in an ad-hoc network to advertise to each of its neighbours its own routing tables by broadcasting its entries. Because of the nature of MANETs the entry lists may change quite dramatically, so it is important that the broadcasts are made often enough so that every mobile node can almost always locate every other node in the network (Murthy & Manoj, 2004). In addition each node in a DSDV enabled mobile network, must agree to relay data packets on request; this is extremely important in terms of determining the shortest path for a source route to its destination. DSDV also has the ability not to disturb mobile nodes that are in the 'sleep' mode and if a node is asleep then DSDV will still exchange information with all the other mobile nodes in the coverage area, even if the destination for the data is not within range for direct communication. Routing table update consists of the hardware address and the network address of the transmitting node within the header of the packet, plus a sequence number transmitted by the source node. As stated above routes with the more recent or higher sequence number are always preferred as the basis for updating the routing tables and making forwarding decisions. With the above mechanisms DSDV provides a vast improvement over the Bellman-Ford Distance Vector protocol, by eliminating route-looping, reducing control message overheads and increasing the speed of convergence.

## 3.2 Reactive Routing Protocols (On-Demand)

The dynamic source routing (DSR) protocol is an on-demand protocol, designed to reduce the control information overheads and therefore the bandwidth usage, by eliminating the requirement of the periodic table updates used in the table-driven protocols. DSR provides numerous efficiency improvements, such as the 'beaconless' protocol; which eliminates the need for the periodic 'hello' packets (beacon), generally used to notify a nodes neighbour of its presence in the network (Murthy & Manoj, 2004).

The DSR protocol enables each node on the network to keep a route cache that contains full paths to all known destinations. If a source requires a route to an unknown destination then it issues a 'RouteRequest' packet to flood the network. The destination node on receipt of the 'RouteRequest' packet, answers the source node by sending a 'RouteReply' packet back through the route that the request packet had traversed, delivering the correct routing information required.

The DSR routing protocol is also capable of identifying broken links and taking the necessary action to notify its neighbours (Johnson & Maltz, 1996). When an intermediate link identifies a broken network/route link it sends an error packet to the source node, which in some cases may initiate a new route discovery, if an alternative route is not readily available. Another efficiency improvement provided by the DSR protocol is the features mode; one such feature is the promiscuous mode, where a node will listen to routing broadcasts not intended for itself and updates its route cache accordingly. This is a great improvement as the

sharing of unintended broadcast, aid in keeping the network / routes updated without having to flood this information to all nodes on the network. Another DSR feature is the 'expanding ring search'; this is where a RouteRequest packet is sent with the maximum hop count and if the destination route cannot be found within the maximum hop count then the hop count can be increased until the destination is found.

DSR features also provide such facilities as 'packet salvaging', where correct route information can be extracted from route error packets and 'jitter' where adding a jitter packet increases the delay, but prevents the need for route reply storms. There are some disadvantages in using the DSR protocol, such as the considerable routing overheads involved in managing the source-routing mechanism, the use of 'stale' routing cache information which could cause route inconsistencies, during the route reconstruction phase (Murthy & Manoj, 2004). And the connection setup procedure takes longer to achieve than in the table driven protocols.

The DSR protocol works very well in static and low-mobility wireless networks, but the performance of this protocol degrades rapidly with the increase in nodes and mobility.

The Ad-Hoc on Demand Routing Protocol (AODV) is an improved routing protocol as it incorporates the destination sequence number techniques of the Destination Sequenced Distance Vector routing protocol (DSDV), it is still a on-demand routing protocol but it differs from DSR routing protocol in its routing management (Murthy & Manoj, 2004). The basic principle of the DSR protocol is source routing, where a RouteReply packet carries the complete path to the source node for data to be sent to the destination node. In AODV the source and the intermediate nodes store the next-hop information corresponding to each path.

The route construction process is very similar to the DSR process; the major difference is that AODV uses a destination sequence number to determine the most up to date path to the destination node (Murthy & Manoj, 2004). A node using the AODV protocol will only update its routing information if the destination sequence number of the received packet is greater than the last packet stored at the node. The main advantage of AODV is routes are established on demand (as with DSR), and it employs the use of destination sequence numbers to select the most current route. In addition when compared to DSR; AODV has much shorter connection setup times.

The main disadvantage is that unlike DSR, AODV employs the use of periodic beacons (hello packets), which results in an increase in overhead control traffic. Also intermediate nodes can lead to inconsistent routing information if the intermediate node has a sequence number higher than the source node.

## 4. HIERARCHICAL ROUTING FOR MANET ORGANISATION

MANET network behaviour exhibits a continuously changing topology as client nodes move in and out of the coverage area, for this reason some MANETs are organised in a hierarchical structure, where some client nodes are elected to be gateways between groups of MANETs. One such protocol that is able to provide this gateway function is the Cluster-Head Gateway Switch Routing Protocol.

The CGSR Protocol organises differently to other protocols discussed as it employs the use of a hierarchical network topology as opposed to the flat network topology of other table-driven routing protocols. In a CGSR structure nodes in a given coverage area, form themselves into clusters. Each cluster provides coordination functionality between all nodes in the cluster via a management node called a 'Cluster-head'. A cluster-head node is elected dynamically by employing a 'least cluster change' (LLC) algorithm (Murthy & Manoj, 2004). The LCC algorithm determines that a cluster-head node will only change its status if it comes into range of another cluster-head node that has a higher node ID or a higher connectivity algorithm, as shown in Figure 2.

In the cluster all routing between nodes in the cluster is managed by the cluster-head, therefore all member nodes in the cluster are able to be reached by the cluster-head node in a single hop. When routing information between clusters it is a node called a cluster gateway (Krishna et al., 1997) that provides this facility; a gateway is a node that is simultaneously a member of two clusters (Figure 3).

Clustering provides a mechanism for the allocation of bandwidth between clusters, which is a limited resource in ad-hoc networks; it achieves this by allowing different clusters to operate at different spreading codes (channels) on a CDMA system (Hollerung, 2004). Within a cluster it is

*Figure 2. Cluster-head status change (adapted from Krishna et al., 1997)*

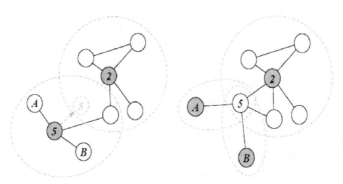

*Figure 3. Gateway for CGSR routing (adapted from Krishna et al., 1997)*

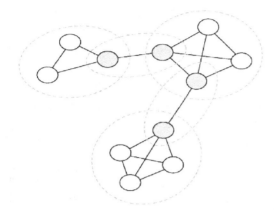

the cluster-heads responsibility to coordinate the channel access via the use of a 'token-based' protocol. This token-based scheduling is used within the cluster to manage access to the shared bandwidth, by all the members in the cluster. This bandwidth sharing is achieved by assigning access tokens to all member nodes in the cluster.

The CGSR routing protocol assumes all communications within a cluster passes through the cluster-head and any communication between clusters are routed via the cluster-gateways. A gateway could be considered to be a more sophisticated device has it is required to listen to multiple spreading codes that are in operation in the clusters to which the gateway is a member. Conflict at this stage can happen when a cluster-head node sends a token to a gateway over a spreading code when the gateway is tuned to another code. To avoid these situation gateways were developed to communicate simultaneously over two interfaces to avoid these types of inter-cluster communication conflicts (Krishna et al., 1997).

CGSR routing is based upon the DSDV routing protocol, where every member node maintains a routing table containing the destination cluster-head for every node in the network (Murthy & Manoj, 2004). In addition each member node maintains a routing table containing a list of next hop nodes for reaching every destination cluster.

When a node has packets to transmit it must first be issued with a token from the cluster-head, then obtain the destination cluster-head and the next-hop node from its cluster member routing table and the destination routing table, before it can transmit.

With its hierarchical routing capabilities CGSR provides many improvements to the flat network topology employed by other protocols. It enables a level of coordination between the clusters by electing Cluster-Head nodes and provides an increase in the utilisation of the available bandwidth. It also suffers from the problems of WRP and DSDV when used in a highly mobile environment, where the rate of change of cluster-heads increases greatly as the network grows (Murthy & Manoj, 2004). Also to elevate the problems of excessive gateway conflicts it is necessary to increase the number of interfaces which in term will increase the resource costs and finally because the power consumption at the cluster-head nodes are far higher than at the ordinary member nodes. There is a tendency for frequent changes of cluster-head nodes as these nodes are drained of power.

## CONCLUSION

The UK government has vastly improved its ability to protect the countries communication infrastructure by the introduction of the critical national infrastructure policy and the deployment of a TETRA based Public Safety Network that separates the emergency services communication platform from the commercial telecommunication infrastructure. This deployment has vastly improved the ability for the emergency services to communication effectively within the disaster zone as the TETRA system provides the emergency services with numerous benefits such as clear digital communication, digital integrated handsets, location awareness devices, digital images and seamless voice / data communications across other emergency services. This would not be possible pre-TETRA as the old analogue systems used by the emergency services were procured 'bespoke' which meant they were operating on different radio frequencies and as a result could not communicate with different divisions in the same service, much less achieve inter-service communications.

However even with these major improvements the government has still based its telecommunication infrastructure policy on a system that is still a fixed ground-based backbone cellular infrastructure that controls and manages its main connections and transmission of data via a number of switching station located on (under), the ground across the country. This does provide some systems integrity by having the ability to rerouted communications to sites that are not affected. But in situations where underground switching stations have been damaged, as demonstrated in Manchester, Lancashire and North Derbyshire in 2004 (BBC News, 2004). These switching stations can be made inoperable for hours and in some cases days, before services are effectively rerouted to other functioning switching stations.

In such extreme situations as hurricane Katrina in 2005; New Orleans, Louisiana, USA and floods in Gloucester, UK in 2007; both experienced varying degrees of extreme flooding across large geographical areas. Numerous earthquakes over the last few years across the globe in places such as Sichaun, China; L'Aquila, Italy and recently Haiti in the Caribbean, have demonstrated that natural disasters should be considered the major threat where movements in the ground could severely damage the ground based network resulting in the telecommunication infrastructure including the TETRA infrastructure, being completely inoperable.

It is in these extreme situations that it is necessary to provide the rescue workers and emergency services with a platform that will aid in the ability to mobilise and organise efficient cross communication procedures which is crucial to saving life and managing hysteria. In such cases mobile ad-hoc networking can be critical to the delivery of a high quality service that is capable of coordinating the incident / rescue effort in the most cost effective and efficient manner possible. The ability to utilise a number of laptops, PDA's and handheld devices to implement a dynamic network without the need for a fixed network infrastructure, to share biometric, database and

*Figure 4. Conceptual model for (last mile) emergency services localised MANET*

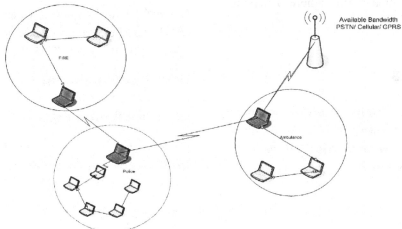

medical records would be invaluable in such situations. With the use of multi-hop routing protocols such as the cluster-head protocol; these short-term dynamically generated networks could be organised in a hierarchical structure to enable information sharing amongst emergency services personnel, in entirely flooded areas where the TETRA switching stations would be inoperable.

There are limitations to the utilisation of a MANET network and power is a major consideration, but it is possible to organise the network to utilise 'sleep' routines to save the power on the device, however a simple solution to power management is for the emergency services to connection the device to a electrical power generator or carry spare rechargeable power cells.

MANET's do have a number of advantages in disaster zones, where MANETs are able to utilise what little available cellular / GPS bandwidth that is present by bridging a connection to a cluster-head node and the (available) telecommunications interface; enabling data transfer between the EMS HQ and the rest of the nodes in a MANET network. Figure 4 presents a conceptual model for emergency services localised MANET.

There is still a great deal of work that needs to be undertaken before MANET's are seen as a viable addition to the emergency services communication platform, but as a short-term dynamic communication platform there is no better alternative.

## REFERENCES

Bhagyavati, S. W., & DeJoie, A. (2004, September 17-18). Wireless Security Techniques: An Overview. In *Proceedings of the InfoSecCD Conference 2004,* Kennessaw, GA.

Cable & Wireless Worldwide. (2004). *O2 Airwave appoints Cable & Wireless for bandwidth provision.* Retrieved from http://www.cw.com/media_events/media_centre/releases/2004/06_01_2004_59.html

Constabulary, F. (n.d.). *Home.* Retrieved from http://www.fife.police.uk

Consulting, B. W. C. S. (2002). *UK Emergency Services Voice Concerns Over Radio Systems in Face of September 11th Scale Disaster.* Retrieved from http://www.bwcs.com/news_detail.cfm

Corson, M. S., & Ephremides, A. (1995). A Distributed Routing Algorithm for Mobile Wireless Networks. *Wireless Networks, 1*(1), 61–81. doi:10.1007/BF01196259

ESTI. (1995). *Terrestrial Trunked Radio (TETRA).* Retrieved from http://www.etsi.org/WebSite/Technologies/TETRA

ESTI. (2002). *User Requirement Specification TETRA Release 2.* Retrieved from http://www.etsi.org/WebSite/Technologies/TETRA

ESTI. (2007). *ETSI TETRA (Terrestrial Trunked Radio) technology.* Retrieved from http://www.etsi.org/WebSite/Technologies/TETRA

Gafni, E., & Bertsekas, D. (1981). Distributed Algorithms for Generating Loop-free Routes in Networks with Frequently Changing Topology. *IEEE Transactions on Communications, 29*(1), 11–15. doi:10.1109/TCOM.1981.1094876

Geier, J. (1999). *Wireless LANs: Implementing Interoperable Networks.* New York, NY: Macmillan Technical Publishing.

Haas, Z. J. (2001). *The Interzone Routing Protocol (IERP) for Ad Hoc Networks. Internet Engineering Task Force (IETF).* MANET Working Group.

Haas, Z. J., Deng, J., Liang, B., Papadimitratos, P., & Sajama, S. (2001). *Wireless Ad-Hoc Networking*. Retrieved from http://www.ece.cornell.edu/~haas/wnl/html

Hansen, J. (2002). *802.11a/b A Physical Medium Comparison*. Retrieved from http://mobiledevdesign.com/hardware_news/radio_ba_physical_medium/

Hollerung, T. D. (2004). *The Cluster-Based Routing Protocol*. Paderborn, Germany: University of Paderborn.

Johnson, D. B., & Maltz, D. A. (1996). Dynamic Source Routing in Ad-Hoc Networks in Mobile Computing. In Imielinski, T., & Korth, H. (Eds.), *Mobile Computing* (pp. 153–181). Dordrecht, The Netherlands: Kluwer Academic Publishers. doi:10.1007/978-0-585-29603-6_5

Jubin, J., & Tornow, J. D. (1987). DARPA Packet Radio Networks. *Proceedings of the IEEE*, *75*(1), 21–32. doi:10.1109/PROC.1987.13702

Kahn, R. (1978). Advances in Packet Radio Technology. *Proceedings of the IEEE*, *66*, 1468–1496. doi:10.1109/PROC.1978.11151

Krishna, P., Vaidya, N. H., Chatterjee, M., & Pradhan, D. K. (1997). A cluster-based approach for routing in dynamic networks. *ACM SIGCOMM Computer Communications Review*, *27*, 49–65. doi:10.1145/263876.263885

Manoj, B. S., & Baker, H. (2007). Communications Challenges in Emergency Response. *Communications of the ACM*, *50*(3), 51–53. doi:10.1145/1226736.1226765

Motorola. (2001). *C2000 The Netherlands Digital Radio Networks for Public Safety*. Retrieved from http://www.motorola.com/governmentandenterprise/contentdir/en_GB/Files/CaseStudies/c2000.pdf

Murthy, C. S. R., & Manoj, B. S. (2004). *Ad Hoc Wireless Networks: Architecture and Protocols*. Upper Saddle River, NJ: Pearson Education-Prentice Hall.

Murthy, S., & Garcia-Luna-Aceves, J. J. (1996). An efficient Routing Protocol for Wireless Networks. *Mobile Networks and Applications*, *1*(2), 183–197. doi:10.1007/BF01193336

News, B. B. C. (1998). *Floods in Worcestershire*. Retrieved from http://news.bbc.co.uk/1/hi/uk/

News, B. B. C. (2004). *BT Manchester Tunnel Fire*. Retrieved from http://news.bbc.co.uk/1/hi/england/manchester/

News, B. B. C. (2007). *Floods in Herefordshire and Worcestershire*. Retrieved from http://news.bbc.co.uk/1/hi/uk/

News, B. B. C. (2009). *China Earthquake*. Retrieved from http://news.bbc.co.uk/1/hi/in_depth/asia_pacific/2008/china_quake/default.stm

News, B. B. C. (2009). *Earthquake L'Aquila, central Italy*. Retrieved from http://news.bbc.co.uk/1/hi/world/europe/

Schiller, J. (2003). *Mobile Communications* (2nd ed.). Reading, MA: Addison Wesley.

Sepura. (2005). *Sepura Case Studies – Lancashire Fire and Rescue*. Retrieved from http://www.sepura.com/case-studies-detail.php?caseid=9

Sepura. (2005). *Sepura Case Studies – Shropshire Fire and Rescue Service*. Retrieved from http://www.sepura.com/case-studies-detail.php?caseid=11

Sepura. (2005). *Sepura Case Studies – West Yorkshire Police*. Retrieved from http://www.sepura.com/case-studies-detail.php?caseid=12

Stallings, W. (2002). *Wireless Communications and Networks*. Upper Saddle River, NJ: Prentice-Hall.

Stallings, W. (2003). *Cryptography and Network Security*. Upper Saddle River, NJ: Pearson Education-Prentice Hall.

Telsis. (2004). *Critical Role for Telsis in 02 Airwave Network*. Retrieved from http://www.telsis.com/0218.htm

Telsis. (2005). *Telsis wins emergency services network expansion contract*. Retrieved from http://www.telsis.com/0297.htm

Tijssens, M. (2003). *Implementation of GRN's in Europe*. Retrieved from http://www.euro-police.com/pdf/tijssens.pdf

Walker, J., Cam-Winget, M., Housley, R., & Wagner, D. (2003). Security flaws in 802.11 data link protocols. *Communications of the ACM, 46*(5), 35–39. doi:10.1145/769800.769823

Wilson, J. (2005). *The Next Generation of Wireless LAN Emerges with 802.11n*. Santa Clara, CA: Intel.

*This work was previously published in the International Journal of Information Security and Privacy, Volume 5, Issue 1, edited by Hamid Nemati, pp. 1-13, copyright 2011 by IGI Publishing (an imprint of IGI Global).*

# Chapter 2
# A Self–Supervised Approach to Comment Spam Detection Based on Content Analysis

**A. Bhattarai**
*University of Memphis, USA*

**D. Dasgupta**
*University of Memphis, USA*

## ABSTRACT

*This paper studies the problems and threats posed by a type of spam in the blogosphere, called blog comment spam. It explores the challenges introduced by comment spam, generalizing the analysis substantially to any other short text type spam. The authors analyze different high-level features of spam and legitimate comments based on the content of blog postings. The authors use these features to cluster data separately for each feature using K-Means clustering algorithm. The authors also use self-supervised learning, which could classify spam and legitimate comments automatically. Compared with existing solutions, this approach demonstrates more flexibility and adaptability to the environment, as it requires minimal human intervention. The preliminary evaluation of the proposed spam detection system shows promising results.*

## 1 INTRODUCTION

Spam has evolved and expanded into different forms recently. Its initial root is the email domain. Blogs are becoming easy and popular targets for spammers due to the candidness with which people write their views and opinions. According to comScore (2009), the conversational media, which includes social networks and blogs, is the second highest growing category after games attracting around 75% web users with a growth rate of 7.1%. While this property has allowed it to increase its quantity tremendously, it also makes it easy to suffer from a serious problem of spam.

DOI: 10.4018/978-1-4666-2050-6.ch002

Spammers are taking advantage of free hosting of sponsored advertisements and hyperlinks. Spam is prevalent in the blogosphere in different forms, as described in the following section.

## 1.1 Spam Types in Blogosphere

### 1.1.1 Splogs

Splogs are spam blogs where the post itself is used to promote a product or a service. It is also used to entice users familiar with the service to exploit search-engine reputation of the hosted service; to attract traffic from "neighboring" blogs, etc. Additionally, free hosting services are the primary target for splogs due to the minimal cost of establishing one. A study reported at Google's official Enterprise blog (Google Enterprise, 2009) shows that overall spam volume growth during the first quarter of 2009 is the strongest since early 2008, increasing an average of 1.2% per day. Across the blogosphere at large, a study in 2007 found that 56% of blogs which sent update notifications to the weblogs.com2 ping server were splogs (Kolari, 2007).

### 1.1.2 Comment Spam

Such spams are posted to a blog in no relation to the blog topic for the sole purpose of promoting service or a site. Unlike splogs, comment spam has been targeted to all types of blogs which allow commenting. The popular Akismet blog spam is a classification service, which runs hundreds of tests on the comment received and Akismet classifies 82% of submitted messages as spam correctly (Akismet, n.d.).

### 1.1.3 Trackback Spam

This category of spam takes advantage of the trackback ping feature of popular blogs to get links from them. While the HTML internals of comment submission forms may be changed to confuse spam robots without affecting legitimate users, trackbacks are transmitted by an HTTP-based protocol with a fixed API. The trackback specification makes no mention of verification, allowing spammers to inject arbitrary URLs into a trackback ping message along with camouflaging text of the spammer's choosing. This has led to an abundance of trackback spam targeted at supporting blog software.

In this work, we only deal with short text-type spam just to narrow down the scope of our study. Spam comments are prevalent in blogs, WIKIs and all other online media where readers are allowed to freely post their comments. Blog comment spam is the act of posting comments to a publicly available blog which have nothing to do with the blog or post being commented on, and which are designed to direct users to other non-associated websites. There are several groups on the internet using blog spam in order to make money with advertising, click-throughs, adware installations and malware infections for stealing information (Valsmith, 2008). Comment spam generally contains hyperlinks to the spammers' websites. These messages not only annoy web users, but also pollute web pages and waste Internet bandwidth. Another attractive incentive for spammers to create spam comments is the huge number of (hundreds of millions) web searches being conducted every day. Thus unethical content providers would like do anything that is necessary to make their contents highly ranked than they really should be in their market place.

The open interactive environment that blogs provides makes it a target for misuse or abuse, the major being the unavailability of a filter to decipher whether a comment is a spam or not. Spammers avoid being blacklisted or being tracked by registering, generating random or using dynamic IP address. CAPTCHAs (Complete Automated Public Turing test to tell Computers and Humans Apart) have remained popular, and successful to some extent in spotting spammers. However, naively designed CAPTCHAs is solved by machine learning algorithms, and overly complicated CAPTCHAs place too much burden on visitors, and discourage them to write any comment. Other popular approach, Keyword filtering can be effective, however, this approach requires manual monitoring of a list of locked keywords, and it sometimes filters out legitimate comments as well.

## 1.2 Comment Spam vs. Email Spam

Email and comment spams share some common characteristics as well as a number of differences. While email spams are used solely to entice the reader to go to a site and/or to buy a product, comment spams are also targeted to exploit the search engines feature to mislead searches by increasing the search display of a particular page or site. There also exist many differences in attacks and defense profiles. Moreover, comment spammers can reach multiple readers with a single post whereas email spam has to be targeted to a particular email addresses. The effect of a comment spam is visible as anyone can see a comment in a blog as soon as it is posted whereas it's difficult to know whether an email spam got to the inbox of the receiver or was it filtered by a junk email filtering system. Another difference is that in most cases, email spams are accompanied by images of related products or words in order to bypass the email spam filter whereas this is not the case with comment spams as HTML <img> tags are

filtered from comments in most of cases. In general, email spam is relatively longer compared to comment spam, and it has systems that can attempt to authenticate senders based on SMTP server addresses. Also email spam has been studied for a long period with the availability of data corpus, however, comment spam are being researched only recently with limited availability of data.

## 1.3 Taxonomy of Spam

Table 1 summarizes major types of spam prevalent on the Internet as well as their sub-types and target types; in our work we are focusing on comment spam only.

## 2 HOW DOES THE EXPLOITS OCCUR THROUGH COMMENT SPAM?

In most cases, blog sites, bloggers, and commentators are not the primarily target of the spammer. However, the comments are used for the purpose of search engine optimization. The attackers use the openness of comment posting in the blogs to post their own links to different sites that the attacker wants to advertise, though some blogs are moderated and tries to remove spam.

For a comment spam attack to occur, initially a general blogger makes a post in the blog. The blog spammer on the other hand registers an account

*Table 1. Types of spam found on the web*

| Spam Types | Spam sub-types | Target types |
|---|---|---|
| Email Spam | | User directly targeted, phishing |
| Instant Messaging Spam | | User directly targeted |
| Web Spam | Search engine spam, body spam, title, meta-tag, anchor-text. URL cloaking (Gyongyi & Hector, 2005) | User directly targeted & ranking algorithm modified |
| Blog Spam | Spam blogs (Splogs), | User directly targeted & ranking algorithm modified |
| | Comment Spam | User directly targeted & ranking algorithm modified |
| | Trackback Spam | |

on the blog using a pseudo-random email address. Then the spammer starts posting comments on the blog post irrespective of the content or relevance. These comments will have catchy keywords along with the links to other websites. The keywords in the comments may have different purposes. One purpose is to increase the relevance of the comment in a search engine. Another purpose is to entice a reader to click through the provided link to a website which in turn may have active malwares running on them. The user is thus enticed to install a fake codec or any other fake software (Danchev, 2009). Once clicked, different bots are installed in the system unknowingly.

Various studies have shown that spammers continuously change the IP addresses and usernames making them difficult to traceback. According to PandaSecurity (Danchev, 2009), the social news site cybercriminals have made Digg.com as a good target to acquire legitimate traffic to their malware serving domains.

## 3 EXISTING WORKS ON COMMENT SPAM DETECTION

The initial research in spam detection was prevalent in emails, for example, Sahami, Dumais, Heckerman, and Horvitz (1998) used Naïve Bayes classifier to classify text-based emails. Drucker, Wu, and Vapnik (1999) evaluated Support Vector Machines (SVMs) to deal with spam. In 2001, Carreras and Marquez (2001) showed that AdaBoost is more effective than decision trees and Naïve Bayes. Zhang, Zhu, and Yao (2004) used link-spam as a feature and compared Naïve Bayes, Support Vector Machines and LogitBoost in their work. Email spam detection techniques basically depend on the analysis of the content sent through the email.

In late 1990s, spam started spreading in websites and blogs as the use of the Internet and the World Wide Web increased. Security researchers and venders also extended their works in genre

of spam like web-spam, blog-spam (known as splogs) and comment-spam. Accordingly, various web-spam filtering being explored both on content-based analysis and link-based analysis to detect the spam pages. Davison (2000) built a decision tree to identify link based web-spam to identify nepotistic links; Becchetti, Castillo, Donato, Leonardi, and Baeza-Yates (2005), used decision trees to identify link based web-spam, with features such as PageRank and trustRank. Drost and Scheffer (2005) used SVM to classify web spam with content and link based features, and Ntoulas, Najork, Manassee, and Fetterly (2006) built decision trees to classify web-spam with content based features. In 2005, Umbria (2005) highlighted that the blogosphere has increasing facing the problem of various spam. Gyongyi and Hector (2005) produced a spam taxonomy discussing different types of spam, their techniques of spam generation, techniques of hiding spam and their target algorithms on the web etc. Kolari, Java, Finin, Oates, and Joshi (2006) used SVM models based on local features like bag of words and N-gram features and link-based features to detect splogs. Han, Ahn, Moon, and Jeong (2006) proposed a collaborative filtering method for combating hyperlink spam which relies on manual identification of spam and share this information through a network of search. Provos, McNamee, Mavrommatis, Wang, and Modadugu (2007) identified the mechanism used to inject malicious content on web pages, and illustrates the current state of malware on the web.

Mishne (2006) developed language models for the blog posts, blog comments and pages linked by comments where comments were classified based on disagreements of the language model. Cormack, Gomez, and Sanz (2007) conducted in-depth analysis on filtering of short messages. They evaluated different content-based filtering systems implementing algorithms like Naïve Bayes, Support Vector Machines, Dynamic Markov Compression and Logistic Regression using bag-of-words, orthogonal sparse bigram features and compression model-based approach for short text message, blog-spam and email summary information. Table 2 summarizes various approaches exist for spam detection in blogs and other short comments as these are directly related to our work.

Most of these comment spam detection works used supervised models where an initial set of training data has to be provided to build the detection system. Once the system is built, it can then be used to detect future comment spam. This method, however, has its own advantages and disadvantages: with the historical training dataset, the detection system can achieve high accuracy provided that the spam comments remain fairly similar. But spam comments are constantly changing their anatomy making them hard to detect. Thus, the supervised system is unable to adapt with new kind of spam. Moreover, the initial cost of manually classifying the training data is also high. In such a scenario, an unsupervised or self-supervised approach has to be incorporated.

Also in content-based analysis, the features generally used were bag-of-words, *n*-gram combinations, specific tags present on the webpage, etc. While in document classification, these features helped to accurately classifying and clustering documents but in short text spam classification such representations did not produce better results. Thus in this work, we use seven unique aspects to distinguish spam and legitimate comments and classify them based on self-supervised learning.

## 4 COMMENT SPAM CHARACTERISTICS

To analyze blog spam characteristics and to evaluate our detection system, we used the corpus created by Mishne and Carmel (2005). This corpus contains approximately 50 random blog posts with 1024 comments posted. All the posts contain a mixture of spam and legitimate comments. Comments in the corpus were manually classified and reported to have 332 legitimate comments and the rest are spam. Spam excerpts shown in the following sections for illustration are taken from the Mishne and Carmel dataset (2005).

*Table 2. Existing techniques for blog spam detection*

| Spam Targets | Existing works (citations) | Features used to detect spam | Methods used for spam detection | Best Detection Rates |
|---|---|---|---|---|
| Blog Comments | Mishne and Carmel (2005) | Bag of words | KL-Divergence | 83% accurate |
| Blog Posts | Kolari et al. (2006) | N-gram, Bag of words from text and anchor with binary and tf-idf weighting | Support Vector Machine (SVM) | 0.9 Area Under Curve (AUC) |
| Blog Posts | Han et al. (2006) | Manual and trust based approaches | Collaborative Sharing | 80% accurate |
| Short Text (sms, blog comments, email summary) | Cormack et al. (2007) | Bag of words expanded based on its occurrence position in the text, Orthogonal bigrams | Dynamic Markov Compression (DMC), Support Vector Machines (SVM), Logistic Regression (LR) | 0.95 AUC |
| Blog Posts | Ishida (2008) | Keywords, hyperlinks | Transition based filtering | ~53% accurate |
| Blog Comments | Romero, Garcia-Valdez, and Alanis (2010) | Bag of words with tf-idf weighting | Standard Naïve Bayes, K Nearest Neighbors, Neural Networks, Support Vector Machines | 84.61% accurate |
| Blog comments | Huang, Jiang, and Zhang (2010) | Comment length, Similarity, KL-Divergence, popular words ratio | SVM, Naïve Bayes, Decision Trees(c4.5) | 92.86 accurate |

We first describe different features that are used to analyze spam and legitimate comments. We consider a legitimate comment as a non-spam comment which is also called ham comment. While spam comments are usually generated automatically, we will show that with the proper selection of features it is possible to capture different characteristics which can better differentiate a spam from the ham.

## 4.1 Post-Comment Similarity

Spammers use computer-generated scripts to produce myriads of spam for posting in blogosphere. However, in most cases these automated spam comments are not related to the context of the posting. We analyze the coherence of the comments compared to the blog post where legitimate comments are expected to have more coherent phrases compared to spam.

Figure 1 illustrates a spam comment which is not related to the context of the post. This type of spam is difficult for human analyst to differentiate as it looks very much like a legitimate comment. It is to be noted that some legitimate comments also do not have coherent words or sentences. Therefore, relying on post-comment similarity alone is not a good approach. However, it can help in the overall detection of spam when combined with other features. The post-comment similarity value is calculated by taking inner product of all representative words in the post and comment, and then normalizing it with the length of comment. The post-comment similarity for a post $P_j$ and comment $C_k$ can be expressed as follows:

*Figure 1. Example of a comment spam which is not related to the context of the blog (adapted from Mishne & Carmel, 2005)*

> Hi, I just wanted to say thank you guys! I really like your site and I hope you'll continue to improving it.

$$Similarity(P_j, C_k) = \frac{\vec{P_j} . \vec{C_k}}{|P_j||C_k|} =$$

$$\frac{\sum_{i=1}^n w_{i,j} w_{i,k}}{\sqrt{\sum_{i=1}^n w_{i,j}^2} \sqrt{\sum_{i=1}^n w_{i,k}^2}}$$

Here, $w_{i,j}$ is the frequency of words occurring in the blog post. Since blog comments are relatively short compared to other documents, most of the time the weight is assumed as 1. We plotted a graph to analyze the behavior of spam and legitimate comments based on their similarity to the posts (Figure 2).

Here, the front horizontal axis represents the similarity of a comment (labeled with unique ID) to a post with scale 0 to 1. A spamicity value of 1 represents a spam comment whereas a 0 represents a legitimate comment. The distribution indicates that most of the comment spam has similarities less than 0.0833 to the posts excluding some outliers whereas legitimate comments have higher similarity values. The average post-comment similarity of spam comments was 0.018, whereas the average post-Comment similarity of legitimate comments was found to be 0.073.

One of the obvious extensions to our work would be to add synonymous or hyponymous words both in the post and in comment (using tools like WordNet) to increase the accuracy of this feature in detecting spam comments.

## 4.2 Word-Duplication

A careful analysis of spam comments revealed that some spam comments use repeated words to attract search engines whereas a legitimate comment is often a continuous flow of context-related text. As most blog comments are short in nature, same word rarely repeats in a legitimate comment. Motivated by this idea, we analyzed the behavior of blog comments based on their word repetition pattern.

*Figure 2. Distribution of spam and legitimate comments based on post-comment (spam comments with spamicity=1)*

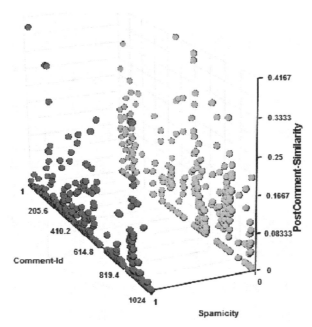

Word redundancy in our context is defined as follows:

$$Word\ Redundancy\ Ratio = \\ 1 - \frac{Number\ of\ unique\ words\ in\ the\ comment}{total\ number\ of\ words\ in\ the\ comment}$$

Figure 3 shows an example of a spam comment where words are repeated multiple times. Figure 4 depicts the distribution of comments based on word redundancy ratio in the dataset (Mishne & Carmel, 2005) used for analysis. The distribution indicates that legitimate comments have fairly low word-redundancy compared to spam comments which have a redundancy ratio as high as

0.9. The average redundancy ratio for legitimate comments was found to be 0.098 whereas it was 0.265 for spam comments.

## 4.3 Number of Anchor texts

The text that appears in HTML between <a...> and </a> tags are referred to as anchor texts. These texts basically create a link to another page which can be reached by clicking the hyperlink. Web crawlers usually follow these links iteratively to explore web pages on the Internet. Since most comment spams are intended for web crawlers as opposed to human, these comments try to include many anchor texts pointing to spammer sites in order to increase their page ranking in search engines. An

*Figure 3. Example of a spam comment which has redundant words in it (adapted from Mishne & Carmel, 2005)*

Get a Generic Viagra alternative at Cheap Generic ViagraGet a Cheap Generic Viagra alternative at Cheap Generic Viagra

Comments posted by: Cheap Generic Viagra at March 11, 2005 09:27 PM

*Figure 4. Distribution of spam and non-spam comments based on word redundancy ratio*

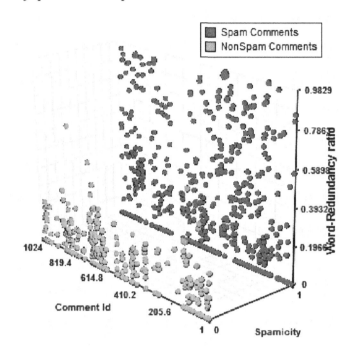

example of spam comment with several anchor texts is shown in Figure 5.

Our analysis of comments based on anchor text count shows (Figure 6) that almost all legitimate comments have 3 or less anchor texts whereas spam comments were found to have as many as 233 anchor texts in the dataset (Mishne & Carmel, 2005). This clearly indicates that the anchor text count can be a good feature/indicator to detect spam and ham comments. The average anchor-text count in spam comments was 6.35 whereas for legitimate comments, it was 0.14.

## 4.4 Noun Concentration

One of the main goals of spammers is to increase the ranking of spam pages by search engine optimization. Most auto-generated spam comments are filled either by some keywords in the form of noun-phrase chunks without the formation of a complete sentence or some hyperlinks to keep the crawler searching. These spam comments are expected to have a higher concentration of

noun-phrases compared to other word/phrase categories like verbs, prepositions, etc. Moreover, ham comments are more likely to express an idea using grammatical sentences or phrases. Figure 7 shows an example of such concentration of noun in spam comments. We used OpenNLP (Carreras & Marquez, 2001) tools to extract sentences from the blog postings and part-of-speech tags for the sentences.

Noun-Concentration is calculated using the following formula:

*Figure 5. Example of a spam comment containing lots of URLS (adapted from Mishne & Carmel, 2005)*

hold em http://texas-hold-em.musicbox1.com/ online poker online poker http://online-poker.musicbox1.com/ phentermine phentermine http://phentermine.musicbox1.com/ interest only

*Figure 6. Distribution of spam and non-spam comments based on number of anchor texts*

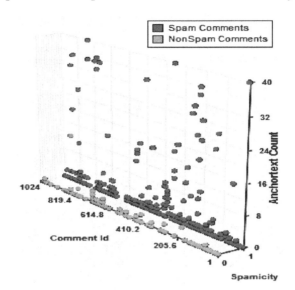

$$NounConcentration =$$

$$\frac{No.\ of\ noun\ phrases\ present\ in\ the\ comment}{total\ No.\ of\ words\ in\ the\ comment}$$

Figure 8 depicts the distribution of spam and legitimate comments in blogs (Mishne & Carmel, 2005). This analysis shows that legitimate comments almost always have a noun-phrase concentration less than 0.4 whereas for spam comments, the concentration was found to be as high as 0.7. Although there may have spam comments with a low noun-phrase concentration, we can always filter a group of spam comments which have high noun-concentration. The average noun-concentration for legitimate comments was

found to be 0.196 whereas for spam comments it was approximately 0.26.

## 4.5 Stopwords Ratio

Using a similar explanation as that of noun phrase concentration, we hypothesized that legitimate sentences tend to have a fairly balanced stopwords ratio compared to spam comments (Figure 9).

In our analysis, the stopwords ratio is calculated as:

$$Stopwords\ Ratio =$$
$$\frac{Number\ of\ stopwords\ present\ in\ the\ comment}{total\ number\ of\ words\ in\ the\ comment}$$

Again, the distribution of spam/legitimate comments based on the stopword ratio is shown in Figure 10. Here the legitimate comments almost always have a stopwords ratio in the range 0.3 to 0.61; where spam comments have wide variation in the stopwords ratios. Clearly, as indicated by the graph, comments with a lower stopwords

*Figure 7. An example of a comment spam which has high noun-concentration (adapted from Mishne & Carmel, 2005)*

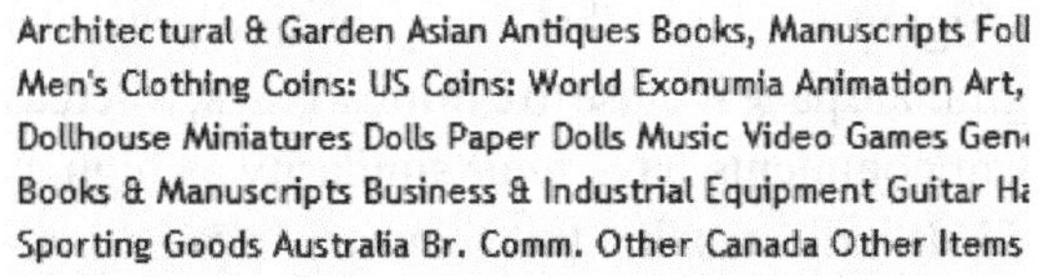

Architectural & Garden Asian Antiques Books, Manuscripts Foll
Men's Clothing Coins: US Coins: World Exonumia Animation Art,
Dollhouse Miniatures Dolls Paper Dolls Music Video Games Geni
Books & Manuscripts Business & Industrial Equipment Guitar Ha
Sporting Goods Australia Br. Comm. Other Canada Other Items

*Figure 8. Distribution of spam and non-spam comments based on noun concentration*

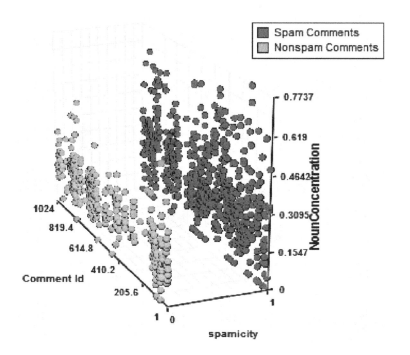

ratio are more likely to be spams than with high stopwords ratio.

## 4.6 Number of Sentences

Some spam comments tend to be relatively longer as they try to add a lot of anchor-texts and jargon keywords. Figure 11 shows the distribution of the number of sentences in spam and legitimate comments. The average number of sentences in spam comments was found to be 5.7 whereas it was 4.08 for legitimate sentences. The maximum count of sentences in a comment spam was found to be 233 in the corpus whereas the maximum

*Figure 9. Example of a comment spam where there is no stopword (adapted from Mishne & Carmel, 2005)*

Football betting football betting line online football betting college football betting football betting odds Pro football betting nfl football betting ncaa football

count of a legitimate spam was found to be 23. It illustrates that the sentence count is not so informative for the dataset (Mishne & Carmel, 2005) we used. Despite this fact, we believe this feature may play an important role in a scenario where there exist significant spam contents with a relatively high count of sentences.

## 4.7 Spam Similarity

The spam similarity of any comment is expressed as

$$SpamSimilarity(C_k) = \frac{\sum_{i=1}^{n} w_{k,i}}{i}$$

Here we summarize the distribution of the comments based on their spam-similarity.

Figure 12 shows that the spam similarity of a legitimate page is close to 0 in most cases, whereas spam comments have their similarity as high as 0.55. It indicates that this feature is a good indicator for the detection of spam comments. The average spam-similarity of a legitimate comment was 0.011714 whereas for spam comments, it was found to be 0.096.

## 4.8 Feature Correlation

In order to realize the correlation of different features we considered (discussed above), we calculated Pearson correlation between each features and thus obtain the following statistics (Table 3).

The statistics show that all the features have a correlation value of less than 0.5. Thus we considered all the features for the purpose of spam detection. The most correlated features are the hyperlink count and sentence count with value 0.84915. Since the sentence detector assumes each hyperlink as a sentence, the increase in the hyperlink count causes the increase in the sentence count. Thus the correlation value shows that one of the features can be ignored without losing substantial the discrimination ability of the proposed system.

## 5 SELF-SUPERVISED SPAM DETECTION ARCHITECTURE

Figure 13 depicts the basic concept of our self-supervised model for spam detection. We briefly define our method in two major steps. The step involves generating a training set (annotation for a portion of corpus) from raw data with self extracted methods. The second step involves using standard supervised machine learning algorithms to classify more documents in the corpus. We describe each of the stage in the following subsections.

## 5.1 Extraction of Training Data and Preprocessing

As an initial step, the posts and the comments are extracted from the blogs (Mishne & Carmel, 2005). Since simple extraction of keywords cannot perform classification/clustering, we designed seven high-level features such as post-comment similarity, word redundancy ratio, number of anchor texts, noun concentration, stopwords

*Figure 10. Distribution of spam and non-spam comments based on stopwords ratio*

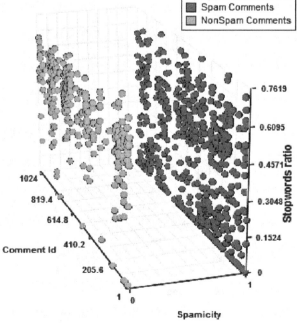

*Figure 11. Distribution of spam and non-spam comments based on sentence count*

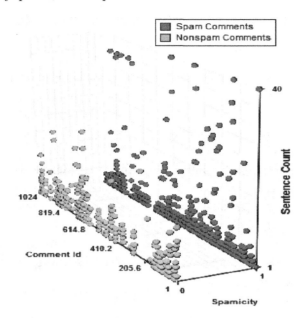

ratio and number of sentences (as described in section 4). The extracted comments and posts are preprocessed (such as tokenizing, stemming, stopwords removal, etc.) and grammatical shallow parsing was also done to extract noun-phrases[1].

After preprocessing data, we calculated all the feature values for each comment; however, the stopwords ratio was calculated directly from the raw data without any preprocessing.

*Figure 12. Distribution of spam and non-spam comments based on spam-similarity of the comment*

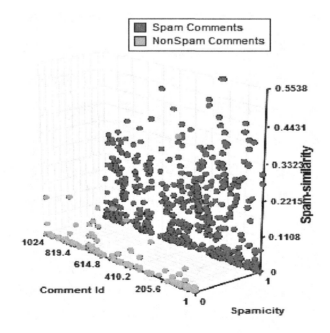

After calculating these high dimensional features, the task is then to use the dataset to form two clusters based on each feature separately. Since we are considering seven features, we would thus have fourteen clusters, one spam and the other non-spam. For the clustering purpose, we chose to use popular K-Means[2] (Hartigan, 1975) clustering algorithm. This algorithm is very simple to understand and converges very fast. Besides it also fits very well to our method as it essentially needs a pivot point for spam and non-spam comments. We will discuss the details about the usage of this pivot point in the later section. In the K-Means clustering algorithm, given a set of observations ($x_1$, $x_2$,...,$x_n$), where each observation is a $d$-dimensional real-valued vector, then $k$-means clustering bundles the vectors in $k$ partitions ($k<n$) $S=\{S_1, S_2,...,S_k\}$ so as to minimize the intra-cluster distance, and maximize the inter-cluster distance.

Mathematically, the expression can be written as follows:

$$\arg\min_{\mathbf{S}} \sum_{i=1}^{k} \sum_{\mathbf{x}_j \in S_i} \left\| \mathbf{x}_j - \boldsymbol{\mu}_i \right\|^2$$

where $\mu_i$ is the mean of $S_i$ (Hartigan, 1975; MacQueen, 1967).

Where $K$ is the number of centroids representing each cluster. In our case k=2 i.e. one for spam and the other for non-spam. These centroids are initially placed as far from each other as possible to confirm that the results are not biased. In the next step, for each comment, we calculate the distance of data-points to each of the centroids. After associating all comment data-points to one or other centroids, the centroid values are re-calculated as the centers of all the data-points associated in the cluster. The center is the average of all the points in the cluster—that is, its coordinates are the arithmetic mean for each dimension over all the points in the cluster. This process is repeated until the centroid stops changing.

The algorithm can be summarized as follows:

1. Select K initial points (considered as centroids for each cluster) in the space represented by vectors that are to be clustered.
2. Associate each vector point to the cluster that has closest centroid.
3. Recalculate the centroid of each of the K clusters (by taking the mean of all assigned vectors). These become new centroid values.

*Table 3. Correlation of features used in our spam detection system*

|  | Comment Similarity | Compression Ratio | Stopwords Ratio | Sentence Count | Word Count | Noun Concentration | Hyper-link Count |
|---|---|---|---|---|---|---|---|
| Comment Similarity | 1 |  |  |  |  |  |  |
| Comp Ratio | -0.19281 | 1 |  |  |  |  |  |
| Stopwords Ratio | 0.25791 | -0.4075 | 1 |  |  |  |  |
| Sentence Count | -0.05684 | 0.43475 | -0.1401 | 1 |  |  |  |
| Word Count | -0.00500 | 0.51676 | -0.0303 | 0.495208 | 1 |  |  |
| Noun Concentration | -0.142519 | 0.58569 | -0.5167 | 0.336608 | 0.3366 | 1 |  |
| Hyperlink Count | -0.093023 | 0.48731 | -0.2269 | 0.849146 | 0.4986 | 0.303844 | 1 |

*Figure 13. System framework for self-supervised spam detection model*

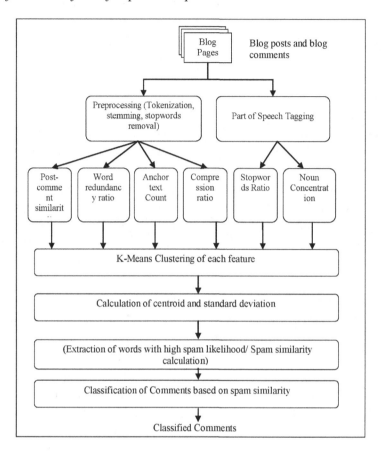

4.  Repeat Steps 2 and 3 until the centroids no longer move. This produces a separation of the vectors into groups which has minimal intra-cluster distance and maximum inter-cluster distance.

We used the SimpleKMeans Clustering algorithm provided in Weka (n.d.) and cluster the datasets (Mishne & Carmel, 2005) to get two centroids for spam and non-spam. Table 4 shows the centroids for each feature along with the standard deviation in spam and non-spam classification.

Thus, after obtaining the centroid for each feature, we use these values as threshold for the classification methodology based on co-training (Drucker et al., 1999). The co-training assumes that a problem can be seen from different aspects. With the same principle, we visualize a com-

ment in a blog in six different perspectives such as post-comment similarity, word-duplication, noun-concentration, stopwords-ratio, number of sentences and number of hyperlinks. Now, the process can be seen as a two step process.

Each instance of a comment can be defined in the following form based on co-training instance $X$ in an instance space as

$$X = X_1 \times X_2 \ldots \ldots \ldots X_n$$

The variables $X_1 \ldots X_n$ represent unique high dimensional features for the instance such as post-comment similarity, noun-concentration, stopwords ratio etc. For each feature, a threshold value is defined that essentially separates spam and non-spam space in the model. The centroid and the standard deviation values come into play at this point. The threshold values for each feature are obtained with the following equation.

Threshold(fx) = mean(fx)+
standardDeviation(fx)

Here, $f_x$ is one of the high dimensional features and mean indicate the corresponding centroid obtained from K-means clustering along with standard deviation as shown in Table 3. Since there are only two clusters, the potential spam and non-spam clusters can be easily identified with simple intuition. Simple intuition suggests that the post-comment similarity is high for a legitimate comment compared to spam comment. Similarly, other value distributions and potential clusters are shown in Table 3. Thus, with the threshold values, we can now work towards the first stage of our classification methodology.

Any instance $(X)$ is classified spam if its value lies in the spam space, and can be expressed as:

Spamicity(X) = f(X_1) ⫫ f(X_2) ⫫ ...............
f(X_n)

This process is explained in more detail in our previous work (Bhattarai, Rus, & Dasgupta, 2009). This method provides us with a set of potential spam comments. Thus at the second stage, we extract simple bag of words features from this set which are then filtered with stopwords removal, stemming, tokenization, etc. The weight for each feature is assigned as:

$$w = \frac{\text{frequency of current feature word of interst}}{\text{maximum frequency of feature word in the corpus}}$$

With the calculated weight *(w)* of each word in the potential spam corpus, in the second iteration, we then use this weight for each word to calculate the spam similarity for each comment in the corpus. This process refines the classification in two stages thus confirming high precision and recall without the need of a pre-classified spam corpus. This makes the system more resilient to evolving spam tricks and wordings. We use the following formula to calculate the spam similarity of each document.

$$spam\ similarity = \frac{\sum_{i=1}^{n} w_{k,i}}{i}$$

With the adjustment of this spam similarity value, we can maintain our need of either high precision or high recall. A higher value of spam similarity will enforce the system to be more precise while reducing recall whereas a modest value of spam similarity will have a high recall system with a compromise in precision. The tradeoff of precision and recall with changing spam similarity is illustrated in our previous work (Bhattarai et al., 2009). Since this step aims to generate a

*Table 4. Centroids and standard deviation of data points for different features*

| | | Comment Similarity | Compression Ratio | Stop-word Ratio | Sentence Count | Word Count | Noun Concentration | Hyper-links Count |
|---|---|---|---|---|---|---|---|---|
| Spam | Mean/ Mode | 0.0156 | 0.3976 | 0.0777 | 8.5649 | 80.38 | 0.33 | 11.1043 |
| | Std Dev. | 0.0474 | 0.3321 | 0.0989 | 23.9426 | 159.2 | 0.1501 | 33.5056 |
| Non-Spam | Mean /Mode | 0.048 | 0.0969 | 0.4926 | 3.1854 | 48.66 | 0.1808 | 0.2092 |
| | Std Dev. | 0.0751 | 0.1168 | 0.1145 | 2.8926 | 60.86 | 0.0756 | 0.5201 |

*Table 5. Comparison of data-points division in actual and observed cases based on spam/non-spam behavior*

|  | Observed | Actual |
|---|---|---|
| Spam | 631 | 692 |
| Non-Spam | 393 | 332 |

training corpus for our second step, we chose a high threshold value to classify comments. These comments classified as spam now serve as a training data.

## 5.2 Standard Supervised Classification

Using the training data generated with the method in the previous section, we now use standard methods to classify blog comments. In our previous work (Bhattarai et al., 2009), we compared different algorithms such as Naïve Bayes, Support vector machines (SVM), neural networks, Logistic Regression, Decision Trees, etc. work (Bhattarai et al., 2009). The comparison indicated that decision tree (J48) performed the best for the dataset used. We thus employed our new method with decision tree (J48).

Table 5 shows the number of comments clustered in each spam and non-spam clusters in the observed and actual case. While the numbers in the clusters shows the accuracy of the observed system as high as (631/692= 91%), the real data

needs further analysis as few spam comments are clustered in non-spam clusters and non-spam comments are clustered in spam clusters.

Table 6 shows the accuracy, precision, recall and F-measure of the developed self-supervised system along with existing supervised systems, where these measures are defined as follows:

$$Accuracy = \frac{\# \, of \, correctly \, classified \, ins \tan ces}{Total \, number \, of \, ins \tan ces}$$

$$Recall = \frac{\# \, of \, detected \, spam \, comments}{\# \, of \, spam \, documents}$$

$$Precision = \frac{\# \, of \, detected \, spam \, documents}{\# \, of \, detected \, documents}$$

$$F - Measure = \frac{2 * Recall * Precision}{Recall + Precision}$$

Thus, from the Table 6, we obtain an accuracy of 71.58% with a relatively high recall of approximately 98%. The self-supervised method achieves a near perfect recall with a compromise in the precision compared to previous self-super-

*Table 6. Performance comparison of the self-supervised system*

| Classifying Algorithms | Accuracy | Precision | Recall | F-Measure |
|---|---|---|---|---|
| Naïve Bayes Classifier | 71.94% | 94% | 62% | 75% |
| Support Vector Machine (SMO) | 83% | 88% | 78.7% | 87% |
| Neural Network (Multilayer Perceptron) | 83% | 87% | 88% | 87% |
| Logistic Regression | 84% | 88% | 88% | 88% |
| Decision Tree (J48) | **86%** | **90%** | 88% | **89%** |
| Self Supervised Decision Tree (J48) | *71.58* | *71.45* | ***98.28*** | *82.54* |

vised decision tree method. However, the self-supervised method has an added advantage of not requiring human expertise. This is a great plus point since human expertise needs substantial knowledge of the domain to define threshold values. Other existing work performed by Mishne and Carmel (2005) shows a false negative rate of 6.5% in the best case and 21.5% in the baseline case along with a false positive rate of 11.5% and 21.5% respectively. However, in these cases the authors have also analyzed the target page which introduces a huge amount of overhead in the system making a practical system really slow. Another existing work in the same dataset, performed by Cormack et al. (2007) also shows the best Area-Under-Curve (AUC) of 1.0673 with expanded features in the Bogofilter which implements method to combine the features in a Bayesian filter. However, these systems require a direct supervision (a training data for the system to work) making the system not so flexible. Moreover, the size of the dataset is also not representative to make a trustful comparison of the methods employed. Thus, in this work, we emphasize on the proposed self-supervised model rather than the result accuracy to show that systems can be built which can work without any supervision to detect spam.

## 6 CONCLUSION

We applied self-supervised learning to develop a spam detection system which utilizes unique spam characteristics. This work is inspired and extended the work done by Mishne and Carmel (2005) and our previous work (Bhattarai et al., 2009). The prototype system has appeared to be more flexible than most supervised spam detection systems which depend primarily on pre-classified data. Most of the features we used are equally applicable to any other short text type spam (like twitter spam) detection system. The observed results show that even with a self-supervised system, we were able to obtain an accuracy of approximately 71% in detecting spam comments. Although the accuracy of the system is not as good as the existing supervised systems, our system is flexible and can be integrated to existing systems. Such an approach will help to obtain an overall higher accuracy rate as the comment pattern changes. Since the dataset (Mishne & Carmel, 2005) we used for evaluation is relatively small, future work will use larger datasets for measuring the performance of the system. While existing methods are failing miserably to deal with increasingly sophisticated spam, we will need more flexible approaches to alleviate the situation. Moreover, we believe that the proposed system can also be used to detect twitter spamming as similar tricks are being used by spammers for retweets (Richmond, 2009).

## REFERENCES

Akismet. (n.d.). *Home*. Retrieved from http://akismet.com/

Assis, F. (2006). A text classification module for Lua – the importance of the training method. In *Proceedings of the 15th Text Retrieval Conference*, Gaithersburg, MD.

Becchetti, L., Castillo, C., Donato, D., Leonardi, S., & Baeza-Yates, R. (2005). Link-based Characterization and Detection of Web Spam. In *Proceedings of the 2nd International Workshop on Adversarial Information Retrieval on the Web (AIRWeb)*, Seattle, WA.

Bhattarai, A., Rus, V., & Dasgupta, D. (2009, March). Characterizing Comment Spam in the Blogosphere through Content Analysis. In *Proceedings of the Symposium on Computational Intelligence in Cyber Security (CICS), IEEE Symposium Series on Computational Intelligence (SSCI 2009)*.

Blum, A., & Mitchell, T. (1998). Combining Labeled and Unlabeled Data with Co-Training. In *Proceedings of the 11th Annual Conference on Computational Learning Theory*.

Bratko, A., Cormack, G. V., Filipič, B., Lynam, T. R., & Zupan, B. (2006). Spam filtering using statistical data compression models. *Journal of Machine Learning Research, 7*, 2673–2698.

Carreras, X., & Marquez, L. (2001). Boosting trees for anti-spam email filtering. In *Proceedings of RANLP01: 4th International Conference on Recent Advances in Natural Language Processing.*

Castillo, C., Donato, D., Becchetti, L., Boldi, P., Leonardi, S., Santini, M., & Vigna, S. (2006). A reference collection for web spam. *ACM SIGIR Forum, 40*(2). comScore. (2009). *The Comscore Data Passport - first half 2009.* Retrieved from http://www.comscore.com/press_events/presentations_whitepapers/2009/comscore_data_passport_-_first_half_2009

Cormack, G. V., Gomez, J. M., & Sanz, E. P. (2007). Spam Filtering for short messages. In *Proceedings of the 16th ACM Conference on Information and Knowledge Management (CIKM 2007).*

Danchev, D. (2009). *Massive comment spam attack on Digg.com leads to malware.* Retrieved from http://blogs.zdnet.com/security/?p=2544

Davison, B. D. (2000). Recognizing Nepotistic Links on the Web. In *Proceedings of the AAAI 2000 Workshop on Artificial Intelligence for Web Search,* Austin, TX.

Davison, B. D., & Wu, B. (2005). Identifying link farm pages. In *Proceedings of the 14th International World Wide Web Conference (WWW),* Chiba, Japan.

Drost, I., & Scheffer, T. (2005). Thwarting the nigritude ultramarine: Learning to identify link spam. In *Proceedings of the ECML 2005 Conference.*

Drucker, H., Wu, D., & Vapnik, V. (1999). Support vector machines for spam categorization. *IEEE Transactions on Neural Networks, 10*(5), 1048–1054. doi:10.1109/72.788645

Google. (2005). *Nofollow.* Retrieved from http://googleblog.blogspot.com/2005/01/preventingcomment-spam.html

Google Enterprise. (2009). *Spam Data and Trends.* Retrieved from http://googleenterprise.blogspot.com/2009/03/spam-data-and-trends-q1-2009.html

Gyongyi, Z., & Hector, G. (2005). Web Spam Taxonomy. In *Proceedings of the Adversarial Information Retrieval on the web (AIRWeb) Conference* (pp. 39-47).

Han, S., Ahn, Y. Y., Moon, S., & Jeong, H. (2006). Collaborative Blog Spam Filtering Using Adaptive Percolation Search. In *Proceedings of the WWW2006 Conference,* Edinburgh, UK.

Hartigan, J. A. (1975). *Clustering Algorithms.* New York, NY: Wiley.

Hearst, M. A., Hurst, M., & Dumais, S. T. (2008). What Should Blog Search Look Like. In *Proceedings of the 2008 ACM Workshop on Search in Social Media,* Napa Valley, CA.

Huang, C., Jiang, Q., & Zhang, Y. (2010). Detecting comment spam through content analysis. In *Proceedings of the 2010 International Conference on Web-age Information Management.*

Ishida, K. (2008). Extracting spam blogs with co-citation clusters. In *Proceedings of the WWW 2008 Conference.*

Jindal, N., & Liu, B. (2007, May 8-12). Review Spam Detection. In *Proceedings of the WWW 2007 Conference,* Banff, AB, Canada.

Kolari, P. (2007). *Detecting Spam Blogs: An Adaptive Online Approach.* Unpublished doctoral dissertation, University of Maryland, Baltimore County.

Kolari, P., Java, A., Finin, T., Oates, T., & Joshi, A. (2006). Detecting Spam Blogs: A Machine Learning Approach. In *Proceedings of the AAAI 2006 Conference.*

Ku, L., Liang, Y., & Chen, H. (2006). *Opinion Extraction, Summarization and Tracking.* Menlo Park, CA: American Association for Artificial Intelligence.

MacQueen, J. B. (1967). Some Methods for classification and Analysis of Multivariate Observations. In *Proceedings of 5th Berkeley Symposium on Mathematical Statistics and Probability* (pp. 281-297).

Miller, G. (1995). WordNet: a lexical database of English. *Communications of the ACM, 38,* 39–41. doi:10.1145/219717.219748

Mishne, G. (2006). Multiple Ranking Strategies for Opinion Retrieval in Blogs. In *Proceedings of the TREC 2006 Conference.*

Mishne, G., & Carmel, D. (2005). Blocking blog spam with language model disagreement. In *Proceedings of the AIRWeb 2005 Conference.*

Ntoulas, A., Najork, M., Manassee, M., & Fetterly, D. (2006). Detecting Spam Web Pages through Content Analysis. In *Proceedings of the WWW 2006 Conference,* Edinburgh, UK.

OpenNLP. (2010). *Home.* Retrieved from http://opennlp.sourceforge.net/

Provos, N., McNamee, D., Mavrommatis, P., Wang, K., & Modadugu, N. (2007). The Ghost in the Browser Analysis of Web-based Malware. In *Proceedings of the 1st Conference on Hot Topics in Understanding Botnets.*

Raymond, E. S., Relson, D., Andree, M., & Louis, G. (2004). *Bogofilter.* Retrieved from http://bogofilter.sourceforge.net

Richmond, R. (2009). *More Scamming and Spamming on Twitter.* Retrieved from http://gadgetwise.blogs.nytimes.com/2009/06/11/more-scamming-and-spamming-on-twitter/

Romero, C., Garcia-Valdez, M., & Alanis, A. A. (2010). Comparative Study of Blog Comments Spam Filtering with Machine Learning Techniques. In *Studies in Computational Intelligence* (Vol. 312, pp. 57-72).

Sahami, M., Dumais, S. D., Heckerman, E., & Horvitz, A. (1998). Bayesian approach to filtering junk e-mail. In *Proceedings of the AAAI Workshop on Learning for Text Categorization.*

Technorati. (2008). *State of the Blogosphere.* Retrieved from http://technorati.com/blogging/state-of-the-blogosphere/

Umbria. (2005). *Spam in the blogosphere.* Retrieved from http://www.umbrialistens.com/consumer/showWhitePaper

Valsmith, A. C. (2008). *Inside the Malicious world of Blog Comment Spam.* Retrieved from http://www.offensivecomputing.net/?q=node/800

Webb, S., Caverlee, J., & Pu, C. (2007). Characterizing Web Spam Using Content and http session Analysis. In *Proceedings of the 4th Conference on Email and Anti-Spam.*

Weka. (n.d.). *Weka 3: Data Mining Software in Java.* Retrieved from http://www.cs.waikato.ac.nz/ml/weka/

Wikipedia. (n.d.). *Search engine optimization.* Retrieved from http://en.wikipedia.org/wiki/Search_engine_optimization

Zhang, L., Zhu, J., & Yao, T. (2004). An evaluation of statistical spam filtering techniques. *ACM Transactions on Asian Language Information Processing, 3*(4), 243–269. doi:10.1145/1039621.1039625

## ENDNOTES

1. OpenNLP (2010) chunker was used to extract noun phrases.
2. SimpleKMeans implemented in Weka (n.d.) toolkit was used for the work.

*This work was previously published in the International Journal of Information Security and Privacy, Volume 5, Issue 1, edited by Hamid Nemati, pp. 14-32, copyright 2011 by IGI Publishing (an imprint of IGI Global).*

# Chapter 3
# A Mutual Authentication Protocol with Resynchronisation Capability for Mobile Satellite Communications

**Ioana Lasc**
*University of Limerick, Ireland*

**Reiner Dojen**
*University of Limerick, Ireland*

**Tom Coffey**
*University of Limerick, Ireland*

## ABSTRACT

*Many peer-to-peer security protocols proposed for wireless communications use one-time shared secrets for authentication purposes. This paper analyses online update mechanisms for one-time shared secrets. A new type of attack against update mechanisms, called desynchronisation attack, is introduced. This type of attack may lead to a permanent denial of service condition. A case study demonstrates the effectiveness of desynchronisation attacks against a security protocol for mobile satellite communications. A new mutual authentication protocol for satellite communications, incorporating a resynchronisation capability, is proposed to counter the disruptive effects of desynchronisation attacks. The new protocol has an esynchronisation phase that is initiated whenever desynchronisation is suspected. Thus, the possibility of causing permanent denial of service conditions by mounting desynchronisation attacks is eliminated. A security analysis of the proposed protocol establishes its resistance against attacks like replay attacks, dictionary attacks, and desynchronisation attacks.*

DOI: 10.4018/978-1-4666-2050-6.ch003

## INTRODUCTION

Wireless communications are being driven by the need to provide network access for mobile or nomadic computing devices. The increase of available services using these wireless devices requires users to trust the employed communication networks with highly sensitive information. Security protocols are one of the most critical elements in enabling the secure communication and processing of information. Basic security protocols allow agents to authenticate each other, to establish fresh session keys for confidential communication and to ensure the authenticity of data and services (Dojen, Lasc, & Coffey, 2008). Building on such basic security protocols, more advanced services like non-repudiation, fairness, electronic payment and electronic contract signing are achieved. The design of such security protocols should be robust enough to resist attacks, such as replay attacks, parallel session attacks or type-flaw attacks. Additionally, the possibility of interfering with communication on physical channels by jamming needs to be considered as it can affect the security at the application layer (Gansler & Binnendijk, 2005). Denial of Service (DoS) attacks are a common form of cross-layer attacks (Radosavac, Benammar, & Baras, 2004), which can be achieved in two ways (Peng, Leckie, & Ramamohanarao, 2007): Firstly, an attacker can interact continuously with the targeted system to prevent service availability. In this case, the DoS condition disappears when the malicious interaction ends. Secondly, an attacker can interact with the targeted system for only a limited time to achieve a permanent denial of service condition. In this case the DoS condition remains until some corrective measures are taken.

Many peer-to-peer security protocols proposed for wireless communications use one-time shared secrets for authentication purposes (Lee, Chang, Hwang, & Chong, 2009; Chen, Lee, & Chen, 2008; Tseng, 2007; Chang & Chang, 2005; Lee & Yeh, 2005). These secrets are used by the owning principals to prove their identity in a protocol

session. Additionally, the same protocol run establishes a new instance of the shared secret that will be used in the next session. The messages of the protocol that establish the new shared secret are referred to as the update mechanism. These update mechanisms serve two purposes: Firstly, the generation of a new instance of the shared secret and, secondly, agreement on the same new shared secret by all communicating parties. Thus, update mechanisms aim to ensure synchronous storage of the shared secret by all principals at the end of each protocol run.

In this paper, online update mechanisms for shared secrets are analysed. This analysis reveals a new form of attack against security protocols employing update mechanisms. As these new attacks aim to desynchronise the communicating parties on their stored shared secret, we term them desynchronisation attacks. A successful desynchronisation attack disables the affected parties from authenticating each other in future protocol runs. Thus, by mounting a desynchronisation attack, the intruder can cause a permanent DoS condition. As an example, a case study is performed on a protocol for mobile satellite communications that aims at providing mutual authentication between a mobile user and the Network Control Centre (NCC). This case study reveals two desynchronisation attacks that exploit the weaknesses in the update mechanism employed by the protocol. Subsequently, the targeted users are denied access to the communication service and a permanent denial of service condition is reached that persists even after the jamming ends.

To counter the disruptive effects of desynchronisation attacks, a new mutual authentication protocol with resynchronisation capability is proposed that confirms synchrony of the stored shared secrets. If desynchronisation is detected a resynchronisation phase is initiated that re-establishes synchrony between the communicating parties. Thus, the possibility of affecting the security at application layer by interfering with the communication on physical channels is eliminated. A security analysis of the proposed protocol establishes its resistance against attacks such as replay attacks, dictionary attacks and desynchronisation attacks.

## ONLINE UPDATE MECHANISMS OF SHARED SECRETS

Providing mutual authentication based on shared secrets is a common feature in security protocols (Bargh et al., 2004), where the communicating parties involved prove their identity by showing possession of the shared secrets. To avoid freshness issues, such as compromise of long-term session keys, replay attacks etc., security protocols use dynamic shared secrets, where the secrets are renewed in an online update mechanism.

Online update mechanisms have two goals: Firstly, the generation of new instance of the shared secret. Secondly, the agreement of all communicating parties on this new instance as the current shared secret. Consequently, update mechanisms aim to ensure a synchronous storage of the same shared secret by all principals at the end of each protocol run as outlined in Figure 1: When entering a protocol session, the two parties store one instance of the shared secret (the old secret) and at completion of the session they store the updated instance of the shared secret (the new secret).

## STRUCTURE OF SECURITY PROTOCOLS EMPLOYING AN UPDATE MECHANISM

Security protocols use update mechanisms to establish new instances of shared secrets. A successful run of such a protocol ensures mutual authentication of both principals by proving possession of the current shared secret to each other. Further, a new shared secret is agreed upon that will be used in the subsequent protocol run.

Update mechanisms using a pre-determined chain of shared secrets can be used to minimise the computational burden on the communicating parties. Security protocols that use such online update mechanisms have the structure outlined in Figure 2: A chain of shared secrets is initially established in a one-time registration phase and can facilitate multiple (i.e. N) authentication phases, where each phase uses consecutive values from the chain. At every $N^{th}$ authentication phase the end of the chain is reached. The update phase is then entered to establish a new chain of shared secrets.

The details of the authentication phase are outlined in Figure 3. The user computes the new shared secret $\theta_{i+1}$ and sends its authentication request to the server using both its current shared secret $\theta_i$ and the new secret $\theta_{i+1}$. Authenticity of the user is evaluated by the server by comparing the received $\theta_i$ against its own stored secret. If

*Figure 1. Synchrony of shared secrets provided by an update mechanism*

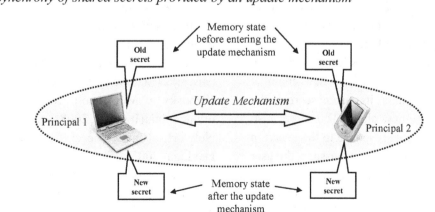

*Figure 2. Structure of security protocols employing an update mechanism for shared secrets*

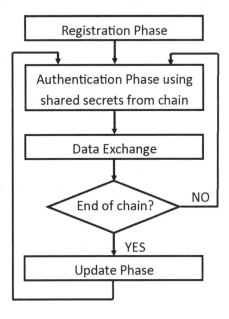

and updates its current secret to the first value $\theta_1$ of the new chain.

Frequently, the pre-determined chain of shared secrets is implemented by a backward hash chain built from a seed and a one-way collision-resistant hash function $h$. The seed can be a session key or any other secret material, such as a random number. The $m^{th}$ element of the hash chain is computed with the formula $h^m(seed)$, where $m$ iterates from N+1 down to 1 and $h^m()$ denotes $m$ applications of the hash function $h$. Thus, in the first authentication phase the seed is hashed N+1 times to obtain the first instance of the shared secret $\theta_1 = h^{N+1}(seed)$. In general the authentication token $\theta_i$ is computed by $h^{N+1-i}(seed)$.

## DESYNCHRONISATION ATTACKS AGAINST UPDATE MECHANISMS

Online update mechanisms for shared secrets aim to ensure generation and distribution of new instances of the shared secret between the communicating parties. As shown in the previous section, the principals executing an update mechanism do not update their data simultaneously. Instead, the local update of the shared secrets happens asynchronously as shown in Figure 4. An update mechanism is thus not an atomic operation, but a sequential process that relies on successful delivery of all outgoing messages to ensure synchrony of shared secrets after a protocol run.

However, the loss of messages due to accidental interference or jamming is a common threat in wireless environments (Xu, Trappe, Zhang, & Wood, 2005), for example in GSM and WLAN networks (Stahlberg, 2000), low power networks (Brodsky & McConnell, 2009), satellite communications (Ippolito, 2008) and Wireless Sensor Networks (Law, Hoesel, Doumen, Hartel, & Havinga, 2005). If messages that are part of the update mechanism are lost, the update mechanism may fail. As a consequence, principals may be desynchronised on their shared secrets as outlined

these values match, the server locally updates its stored secret from $\theta_i$ to $\theta_{i+1}$ and sends its response to the user. On successful authentication of the server's response message, the user also updates its stored current secret to $\theta_{i+1}$. As shown, the two principals do not update their data simultaneously: the server replaces the old value ($\theta_i$) with the new one ($\theta_{i+1}$) before issuing the response message and the user does it after receiving the message from the server.

At the $N^{th}$ authentication phase the update phase is entered, where the server generates a seed for a new chain of shared secrets. Analogous to the authentication phase, the server authenticates the user on the value of the contained shared secret $\theta_N$. Subsequent to successful authentication, the server generates a seed for a new chain of shared secrets and updates its current secret to the first value $\theta_1$ of the new chain. The server also includes this seed in its response to the user. On receipt of the server's response message, the user verifies its authenticity by comparing the received $\theta_N$ against its stored instance of $\theta_N$. If these match, the user accepts the new chain of shared secrets in Figure 5. This constitutes a weakness of the update mechanism that might be exploited in a new attack. As such an attack desynchronises the principals on their stored shared secrets, we call these attacks desynchronisation attacks. A successful desynchronisation attack causes a permanent DoS condition.

The structure of a desynchronisation attack against an authentication phase of a protocol using an online update mechanism is outlined in Figure 6. In such an attack, the authentication phase initiates as normal: The user sends its request to the server, who in turn authenticates the request, updates its shared secret and sends its response to the user. However, if the response message is not delivered successfully to the user due to interference of an attacker, then the server and the user are desynchronised on their shared secrets: while the user still stores $\theta_i$, the server has updated to $\theta_{i+1}$. The user's next authentication request will fail, as it is again based upon $\theta_i$, while the server expects a request based upon $\theta_{i+1}$. Thus, a desynchronisation attack has been successfully mounted that causes a permanent Denial of Service condition.

Alternatively, an attacker can interfere in the same manner with the update phase. To prevent such attacks, corrective measures need to be built into an update mechanism that enables the communicating parties to recover from an asynchronous state.

Both these desynchronisation attacks are directed at individual mobile users that prevent the affected user(s) from using the satellite system even after the jamming has stopped. Any future authentication requests initiated by the affected user(s) will fail, as the server is not aware of the asynchronous state and therefore interprets the request as a replay attack using an old shared secret.

## REALISING THE PRESENTED DESYNCHRONISATION ATTACKS IN A SATELLITE COMMUNICATION SYSTEM

The presented desynchronisation attacks are based on jamming a single mobile user's downlink to stop messages reaching the mobile user. Such jamming can be achieved with a low-power jammer. Information on the feasibility of jamming a handset's uplink and downlink in a satellite-based communications system is presented in Lee and Marshall (1994), United States General Account-

*Figure 3. Authentication phase structure*

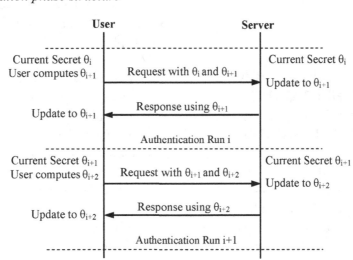

*Figure 4. Local update in the authentication phase*

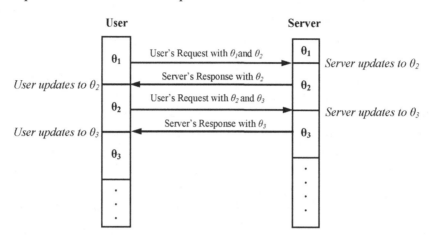

ing Office (2002), Rausch (2006). The attack can also be realised by jamming the NCC's messages on the uplink from the gateway to the LEO. As the NCC serves multiple mobile terminals simultaneously, this affects all the mobile users executing an authentication or mobile update phase with the NCC at the time the jamming occurs. Corresponding to the previous attack, all the affected mobile users are out of synchronisation with the NCC and any of their subsequent authentication requests will be denied by the NCC. While attacking a gateway's uplink is more difficult than jamming a mobile user's downlink, the feasibility of such attacks has been presented in Gansler and Binnendijk (2005), United States General Accounting Office (2002), and Rausch (2006).

## CASE STUDY: NEW DESYNCHRONISATION ATTACKS AGAINST AN AUTHENTICATION PROTOCOL FOR MOBILE SATELLITE COMMUNICATIONS

Chang and Chang proposed a mutual authentication protocol (Chang & Chang, 2005) - hereafter referred to as the CC protocol - for mobile satellite communication systems, such as Iridium (Hartleid & Casey, 1993). These communication systems

offer advanced mobility services (Comparetto & Ramirez, 1997; Chini, Giambene, & Kota, 2010). The CC protocol was designed for the network architecture outlined in Figure 7 and aims to provide authentication between a mobile user and the Network Control Centre (NCC) within a LEO satellite communication system. Mobile users are interconnected directly through LEO satellite links, while communication between satellites and the NCC is managed by Gateways.

The CC protocol follows the structure presented in Figure 2 and is composed of three phases: registration, mobile authentication and mobile update. A second version for the mobile update phase was also proposed that provides for perfect forward secrecy preservation. For the analysis presented in this paper, we regard these update phases as equivalent.

- **The Registration Phase:** A new mobile user U is first registered by the gateway: U and the NCC are provided with U's secret permanent identity, U's temporary identity, the secret shared session key and the number of times (N) that the mobile user can access the service before an update phase is required.

- **The Authentication Phase:** The authentication phase is performed by U and NCC prior to any communication. By using a hash chain to create the authentication token, the same credentials/secrets are used a fixed number of times (N). Once this number has been reached, the update phase is entered.

- **The Mobile Update Phase:** On the $N^{th}$ authentication, U and NCC enter the mobile update phase. The NCC generates and issues a new session key and a new temporary identity for the user to be used for the next N authentications.

## ANALYSIS OF THE CC PROTOCOL

The notations used describe protocols throughout this paper are presented in Table 1.

The CC protocol employs an update mechanism for shared secrets with a structure as discussed (cf. Figure 2). Initially the mobile user registers with the LEO. After the registration phase, whenever the mobile user wants to access the satellite service, it emits an authentication request to the NCC using the next authentication token from a chain. If all the available authentication tokens in the chain have been used, U and NCC enter the update phase. When this phase has been completed the two parties have established a new hash chain and they can re-enter the authentication phase.

The authentication process between the authentication server NCC and the mobile user U in this protocol is based on proving possession of the current value of the authentication token P. U obtains P by hashing the concatenation of K with its permanent and temporary identities $ID_U$ and $TID_U$:

$$P = H^{N-(j-1)}(K \parallel ID_U \parallel TID_U)$$

The index N-(j-1) indicates the number of times that the expression $(K \parallel ID_U \parallel TID_U)$ is hashed to obtain the current value of the authentication token P. Thus, initially the value of P is $H^N(K \parallel ID_U \parallel TID_U)$ and it evolves toward $H(K \parallel ID_U \parallel TID_U)$ as the protocol proceeds.

While U performs the hashing of $(K \parallel ID_U \parallel TID_U)$ every time it enters an authentication or update phase, the NCC stores the value of H(P) and updates this value after each successful completion of the authentication or update phase. In contrast, U only stores the index N-(j-1) for hashing the expression $(K \parallel ID_U \parallel TID_U)$ and computes P when entering the authentication or update phase.

*Figure 5. Asynchronous shared secrets after a failed update mechanism*

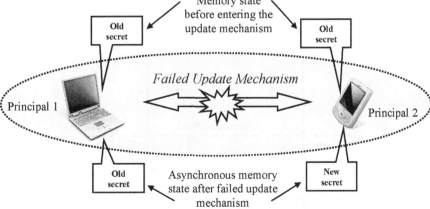

The CC protocol considers the update mechanism as an atomic operation and, thus, it is unable to handle desynchronisation of authentication tokens. However, as principals update their shared secrets asynchronously, the update mechanism is a sequential process. Consequently, the CC protocol is susceptible to desynchronisation attacks. If some messages do not reach their destination, then the authentication phase or the update phase is interrupted and the protocol reaches an undefined state as shown in Figure 8. Loss of messages can happen either by unintended interference or intentionally as a result of a jamming attack by an intruder. Jamming of messages can be achieved with a low-power jammer (Mahoney et al., 1999; Felstead & Keightley, 1995; Lee & Marshall, 1994).

In case where an undefined state is reached, the mobile user can resend the request or it can move to the next level in the chain. Both options present an opportunity to mount a desynchronisation attack. The desynchronisation attacks presented below assume that the user will resend the request. Alternatively, if the user moves to the next level in the chain, corresponding attacks can be mounted. Attempting to resynchronise by re-starting the protocol from the registration phase is not feasible, as any practical registration phase is based on delivery of some hardware device (e.g. smart card).

## DESYNCHRONISATION ATTACK ON THE AUTHENTICATION PHASE

In the authentication phase of the CC protocol, NCC and U update their shared secret information in the following way:

- The NCC updates its shared secret before sending message 4.
- U updates its shared secret after receiving message 5.

If message 5 (LEO -> U) of the authentication phase of the protocol does not reach the mobile user U, e.g. through jamming by an attacker (see Figure 9), the NCC has already updated the secret shared data, while U hasn't updated yet. Thus, they operate asynchronously on the hash value used to authenticate each other, e.g. they are at different levels in the hash chain. Consequently, when U resends the request for authentication, this request will be rejected by the NCC as it does not match the data stored locally in its table. The NCC considers this legitimate request as an

*Figure 6. Attack structure*

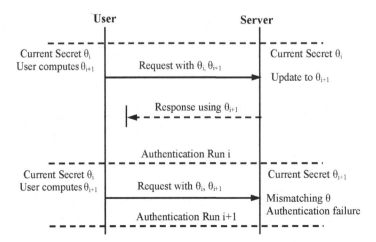

attempt by an intruder to replay an old captured request message.

## DESYNCHRONISATION ATTACK ON THE MOBILE UPDATE PHASE

In the mobile update phase of the CC protocol, NCC and U update their shared secret information in the following way:

- The NCC updates its shared secret before sending message 4.
- U updates its shared secret after receiving message 5.

The desynchronisation attack on the mobile update phase is outlined in Figure 10, where F1 and F2 represent the expressions $H(R'\|P') \oplus K'$ and $H(R'\|P') \oplus H(K'\|TID_U')$ respectively.

The consequence of this attack is loss of synchronisation between U and NCC on:

- The authentication token P
- The shared secret key K
- The user's temporary identity $TID_U$

As a result, U and NCC operate on different hash chains. Thus, when U resends the request for authentication, this legitimate request will be rejected by the NCC.

## A MUTUAL AUTHENTICATION PROTOCOL WITH RESYNCHRONISATION CAPABILITY

The attacks presented in the previous sections highlight the possibility of affecting the security of protocols at application layer by interfering with the communication on physical channels. In this section a new security protocol for satellite communications is proposed. This protocol provides mutual authentication between a mobile

*Figure 7. A LEO communications system*

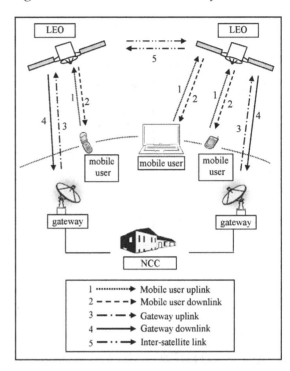

user and the network control centre. Additionally the new protocol possesses a resynchronisation capability to counter the disruptive effects of desynchronisation attacks. The structure of the new protocol is shown in Figure 11.

The proposed protocol confirms synchrony between U and NCC at each authentication phase and update phase. Further, the resynchronisation phase enables the parties to recover from a desynchronised condition. Therefore, the protocol ensures that U and NCC are always able to reach a synchronous state.

## REGISTRATION PHASE

The proposed registration phase stores the initial shared secrets in a smart card or directly in the mobile device. In addition to any information required by the service provider the smart card contains $(ID_U, TID_U, K, N)$ while the NCC (service

*Table 1. Notations used throughout the paper*

| U | The mobile user |
|---|---|
| LEO | Low Earth Orbit Satellite |
| NCC | Network Control Centre |
| $ID_U$, $ID_{LEO}$ | User/LEO permanent identity |
| $TID_U$ | User temporary identity |
| K | Secret key shared by U and NCC |
| K', $TID_U$' | Shared secret key/Temporary user identity newly generated by NCC |
| P | Authentication token |
| H(.) | One-way collision-resistant hash function |
| $\oplus$ | XOR function |
| $\|$ | Concatenation operator |

provider) stores the corresponding value ($ID_U$, $TID_U$, $ID_{LEO}$, $H^{N+1}(K\|ID_U\|TID_U)$, N).

## MOBILE AUTHENTICATION PHASE

The mobile authentication phase of the protocol is detailed in Figure 12. The authentication phase differentiates between legitimate authentication requests (messages 1, 2, 3, 4a, 5a) and illegitimate authentication requests (messages 1, 2, 3, 4b, 5b).

After receiving the authentication request in the first message the mobile user responds with $TID_U$, $H(P) \oplus P$, $P \oplus H(R)$ where $P = H^{N-(j-1)}(K\|ID_U\|TID_U)$. When LEO receives U's response it appends its own identity $ID_{LEO}$ to the message and forwards it to the NCC. In message 3, if $ID_{LEO}$ is legal the NCC will lookup $TID_U$ to retrieve ($ID_U$, $TID_U$, $ID_{LEO}$, $H^{N+1-(j-1)}(K\|ID_U\|TID_U)$, (N-(j-1))). Subsequently the NCC computes the following components:

$$R' = H^{N+1-(j-1)} (K\|ID_U\|TID_U) \oplus (H(P) \oplus R)$$

$$P' = H(R') \oplus (P \oplus H(R))$$

$$H(P')$$

The NCC then checks if $H(P')$ equals $H^{N+1-(j-1)}(K\|ID_U\|TID_U)$. If the check holds, the NCC updates the corresponding entry in the lookup table to ($ID_U$, $TID_U$, $ID_{LEO}$, P', (N-j)). In message 4a NCC sends $H(R'\|P')$, $ID_{LEO}$, $TID_U$ to LEO. LEO then forwards $TID_U$, $H(R'\|P')$ to U in message 5a of the protocol. U verifies the validity of the equation: $H(R\|P) = H(R'\|P')$. If this proves to be true, U accepts that NCC is authentic and updates the stored secret data to ($ID_U$, $TID_U$, K, (N-j)).

On the other hand, if the NCC receives an incorrect authentication request, it responds with a resynchronisation challenge (Messages 1, 2, 3, 4b and 5b). This resynchronisation challenge contains $H(P_{NCC}\|TID_U)$, $H(P_{NCC}) \oplus R_{NCC}$, where $P_{NCC}$ is the NCC's currently stored authentication token, $R_{NCC}$ is a newly generated random number and $TID_U$ is the user's temporary identity.

On receiving a resynchronisation challenge, the mobile user compares the received $P_{NCC}$ with the remaining $P_U$ values in the chain. If a match is found, the mobile user advances to the resynchronisation phase. On the other hand, if no match is found the resynchronisation request is deemed illegitimate and the same authentication request is resent.

## MOBILE UPDATE PHASE

Analogous to the authentication phase, the mobile update phase in Figure 13 also distinguishes between legitimate (Messages 1, 2, 3, 4a and 5a) and illegitimate authentication tokens (Messages 1, 2, 3, 4b and 5b). On receiving message 3 the NCC generates new data $TID_U$' and K'. If the received authentication token is correct, the NCC sends the updated $TID_U$' and K' via the LEO to the user. However, to counter the disruptive effects of any jamming attacks, the NCC stores the old value $H^2(K\|ID_U\|TID_U)$ until the first legitimate authentication request including the new data is received from U, which proves that U has updated successfully. Meanwhile, any illegitimate authentication request is treated as an unsuccessful mobile update request.

On detecting an illegitimate authentication token, the NCC assumes the mobile user is still operating on the old hash chain. Therefore, the resynchronisation challenge issued by NCC contains the last hash value from the old chain $(H^2(K\|ID_U\|TID_U))$. On receiving a resynchronisation challenge, the mobile user compares the received $P_{NCC}$ with its current authentication token $P_U$. If these match the mobile user enters the resynchronisation phase. On the other hand, if these values do not match the resynchronisation request is deemed illegitimate and the same mobile update request is resent.

## RESYNCHRONISATION PHASE

The resynchronisation phase presented in Figure 14 ensures communication can continue from a safe state if synchronisation of the hash chain is lost between mobile users and the NCC. The resynchronisation phase differentiates between resynchronising the authentication phase (Messages 1, 2, 3a and 4a) and resynchronising the mobile update phase (Messages 1, 2, 3b and 4b).

In the resynchronisation phase, U issues the authentication message $TID_U$, $P_{NCC} \oplus H(R_U)$, $H(P_{NCC}\|R_{NCC}) \oplus R$, where $P_{NCC}$ is the agreed hash value, $R_U$ is a newly generated random number by U and $R_{NCC}$ is the random number received from the NCC in the resynchronisation request.

On receiving this authentication message, the NCC checks that $R_{NCC}$ and $H(P_{NCC})$ have the correct values. If any one of these values is incorrect, the message is considered illegitimate and the NCC resends the previous resynchronisation challenge, where the random number $R_{NCC}$ is newly generated. Otherwise, the resynchronisation phase continues as follows:

In case of resynchronisation of the authentication phase, the NCC computes $H(R_U'\|P_{NCC}')$ and sends it via the LEO to the mobile user. On receiving message 4a, U checks $H(R_U\|P_U)$ equals $H(R_U'\|P_{NCC}')$. If this is true the mobile user updates its secret data from $(ID_U, TID_U, K,$

*Figure 8. Reaching undefined states in the CC protocol*

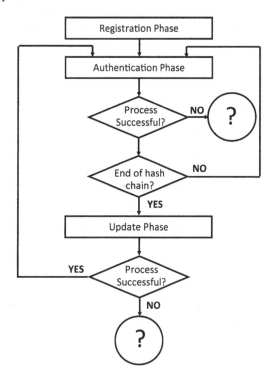

*Figure 9. A desynchronisation attack against authentication phase*

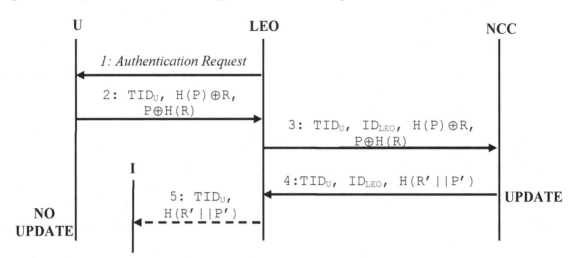

m) to $(ID_U, TID_U, K, i)$, where m is U's level in the hash chain before resynchronisation and i is NCC's level in the hash chain.

In case of resynchronisation of the mobile update phase, the NCC computes $H(R_U'\|P_{NCC}')$ $\oplus K'$ and $H(R_U'\|P_{NCC}') \oplus H(K'\|TID_U')$ and sends it via the LEO to the mobile user. On receiving message 4b, U retrieves K' from $H(R_U'\|P_{NCC}') \oplus$ K' using the stored $H(R_U\|P_{NCC})$. U recalculates the expression $H(K'\|TID_U')$ to confirm integrity

of the $TID_U'$. If the integrity is established, U updates its table to $(ID_U, TID_U', K', N)$.

## SECURITY ANALYSIS OF THE PROPOSED PROTOCOL

In the situation in which all the messages are successfully delivered, the security of the proposed protocol is equivalent to the CC protocol (Chang & Chang, 2005). The following security analysis

*Figure 10. A desynchronisation attack against mobile update phase*

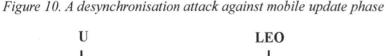

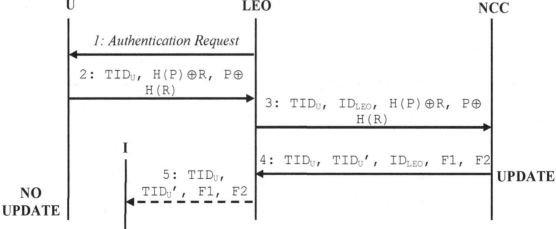

*Figure 11. Structure of the mutual authentication protocol with resynchronisation capability*

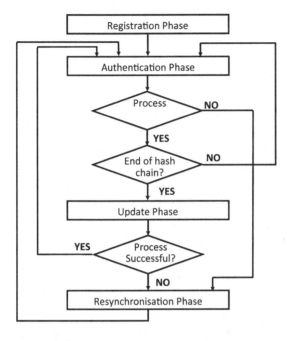

of the proposed protocol establishes the effectiveness of the protocol when messages are lost by unintended interference or by a deliberate attack.

## TRIGGERING THE RESYNCHRONISATION PROCESS

The NCC has the responsibility of issuing the resynchronisation challenge with its current data and the resynchronisation adjustments are left to the mobile user. This approach is chosen as activating the resynchronisation process has a significant impact on the performance of the entire communication system. Further, the NCC serves multiple users and performs other complex tasks, such as call routing and call management functions and it should not be overly burdened with additional resynchronisation tasks.

## REPLAY ATTACKS

- **Replaying an Old Resynchronisation Challenge on Behalf of NCC:** An attempt by an intruder to replay an old resynchronisation challenge to mislead the mobile user into modifying its position in the hash chain will fail, as the user will search for the received $P_{NCC}$ of the resynchronisation challenges within the remaining authentication tokens $P_U$ in the chain. If this value is not found, then the user will ignore the resynchronisation request.

- **Replaying an Old Answer to a Resynchronisation Challenge on Behalf of U:** In the resynchronisation phase, the mobile device sends the random number $R_{NCC}$ in message 1, where $R_{NCC}$ is received from NCC in the resynchronisation challenge. Replaying message 1 of the resynchronisation phase would be unsuccessful, as the NCC discards messages with incorrect $R_{NCC}$ values.

- **Replaying NCC's Response in the Resynchronisation Phase:** NCC's response in the resynchronisation phase contains the random number $R_U$ submitted by mobile user U, who uses this value to establish freshness of the response. Thus, replayed messages can be identified and discarded.

## FORGING A RESYNCHRONISATION CHALLENGE

An attacker may also attempt to forge the resynchronisation challenge by replacing the last component $H(P_{NCC}) \oplus R_{NCC}$ with another custom value. This will fail as the mobile user will search for the received $P_{NCC}$ of the resynchronisation challenges within the remaining authentication tokens $P_U$ in the chain. If this value is not found, then the user will ignore the resynchronisation request.

## DICTIONARY ATTACKS

The mobile user generates a new random number $R_U$ for message 1 in the resynchronisation challenge, rather than using the random number R used in the message 2 of the current authentication phase. This prevents a dictionary attack using the fields $P \oplus H(R)$ and $P_{NCC} \oplus H(R_U)$ of these two messages.

## DESYNCHRONISATION ATTACKS

As detailed previously, there are two messages in the CC protocol vulnerable to desynchronisation attacks: the last message in the authentication phase and the last message in the mobile update phase. These vulnerabilities have been countered by introducing a resynchronisation phase. Once the jamming is stopped, this new phase will ensure that the two parties are resynchronised.

If an intruder jams either of these two messages, NCC and U are temporarily desynchronised, as the NCC advances through the hash chain, while U remains at the current level. However, on the next authentication attempt by the user, the NCC will detect desynchronisation and will issue a resynchronisation challenge, which leads to synchronised secret data shared by NCC and U.

## CONCLUSION

The increased transmission of sensitive information over wireless networks drives the need for improved security protocols. Many peer-to-peer security protocols proposed for wireless communications employ online update mechanisms to facilitate the use of one-time shared secrets. These update mechanisms serve two purposes: Firstly, the generation of a new instance of the shared secret and, secondly, agreement on the same new shared secret by all communicating parties.

In this paper, the use of online update mechanisms for the generation and distribution of shared secrets was analysed. The presented analysis revealed a new form of attack (which we call desynchronisation attacks) against security protocols employing such update mechanisms. These new attacks desynchronise the shared secrets stored by communicating peer principals thereby causing a permanent DoS condition. A case study demonstrated the mounting of two desynchronisation attacks against a mutual authentication protocol for mobile satellite communications. As a consequence of the attacks, the targeted users are

*Figure 12. The authentication phase*

```
1. LEO -> U: Authentication request
2. U -> LEO: TID_U, H(P)⊕R, P⊕H(R)
3. LEO -> NCC: TID_U, H(P)⊕R, P⊕H(R),ID_LEO

4.a. NCC->LEO: TID_U, ID_LEO, H(R'||P')
5.a. LEO -> U: TID_U, H(R'||P')

4.b. NCC -> LEO: DENY MESSAGE + RESYNC. CHALLENGE: TID_U, ID_LEO,
                 H(P_NCC||TID_U), H(P_NCC)⊕R_NCC
5.b. LEO -> U: DENY MESSAGE + RESYNC. CHALLENGE: TID_U,
                 H(P_NCC||TID_U), H(P_NCC)⊕R_NCC
```

*Figure 13. Mobile update phase*

```
1. LEO -> U: Authentication request
2. U -> LEO: TID_U, H(P)⊕R, P⊕H(R)
3. LEO -> NCC: TID_U, H(P)⊕R, P⊕H(R), ID_LEO

4.a. NCC -> LEO: TID_U, TID_U', ID_LEO, H(R'||P')⊕K',
                         H(R'||P')⊕H(K'||TID_U')
5.a. LEO -> U: TID_U, TID_U', H(R'||P')⊕K',
                  H(R'||P')⊕H(K'||TID_U')

4.b. NCC -> LEO: DENY MESSAGE + RESYNC.CHALLENGE:
                         TID_U, ID_LEO, H(P_NCC||TID_U), H(P_NCC)⊕R_NCC
5.b. LEO -> U: DENY MESSAGE + RESYNC. CHALLENGE: TID_U,
                  H(P_NCC||TID_U), H(P_NCC)⊕R_NCC
```

denied access to the communication service and a permanent denial of service condition is reached that persists even after the interference ends.

To counter the disruptive effects of desynchronisation attacks, a new mutual authentication protocol with resynchronisation capability was proposed. The new protocol provides mutual authentication between a mobile user and the satellite Network Control Centre. Additionally, the protocol has a resynchronisation phase that is initiated by the NCC whenever it suspects desynchronisation with a mobile user. This resynchronisation phase re-establishes synchrony between the communicating parties. Thus, the possibility of causing a permanent DoS condition by mounting a desynchronisation attack is eliminated. A security analysis of the proposed protocol established its resistance against attacks such as replay attacks, dictionary attacks and desynchronisation attacks.

## ACKNOWLEDGMENT

This work was funded by the Irish Research Council for Science, Engineering and Technology (IRCSET Embark Initiative) and Science Foundation Ireland - Research Frontiers Programme (SFI RFP07CMSF 631).

*Figure 14. Resynchronisation phase*

```
1. U -> LEO: TID_U, P_NCC⊕H(R_U), H(P_NCC||R_NCC)⊕R_U
2. LEO -> NCC: TID_U, ID_LEO, P_NCC⊕H(R_U), H(P_NCC||R_NCC)⊕R_U

3.a. NCC -> LEO: TID_U, ID_LEO, H(R_U'||P_NCC')
4.a. LEO -> U: TID_U, H(R_U'||P_NCC')

3.b. NCC -> LEO: TID_U, TID_U', ID_LEO, H(R_U'||P_NCC')⊕K',
                         H(R_U'||P_NCC')⊕H(K'||TID_U')
4.b. LEO -> U: TID_U, TID_U', H(R_U'||P_NCC')⊕K',
                  H(R_U'||P_NCC')⊕H(K'||TID_U')
```

# REFERENCES

Bargh, M. S., Hulsebosch, R. J., Eertink, E. H., Prasad, A., Wang, H., & Schoo, P. (2004). Fast authentication methods for handovers between IEEE 802.11 wireless LANs. In *Proceedings of the 2nd ACM International Workshop on Wireless Mobile Applications and Services on WLAN Hotspots* (pp. 52-60).

Brodsky, J., & McConnell, A. (2009, January 21-22). Jamming and interference induced Denial of Service attacks on IEEE 802.15.4 based wireless networks. In *Proceedings of the SCADA Security Scientific Symposium,* Miami Beach, FL.

Chang, Y. F., & Chang, C. C. (2005). An efficient authentication protocol for mobile satellite communication systems. *ACM SIGOPS Operating Systems Review, 39,* 70–84. doi:10.1145/1044552.1044560

Chen, T. H., Lee, W. B., & Chen, H. B. (2009). A self-verification authentication mechanism for mobile satellite communication systems. *Computers & Electrical Engineering, 35*(1), 41–48. doi:10.1016/j.compeleceng.2008.05.003

Chini, P., Giambene, G., & Kota, S. (2010). A survey on mobile satellite systems. *International Journal of Satellite Communications and Networking, 28*(1), 29–57.

Comparetto, G., & Ramirez, R. (1997). Trends in mobile satellite technology. *IEEE Computer, 30*(2), 44–52.

Dojen, R., Lasc, I., & Coffey, T. (2008, August 28-30). Establishing and Fixing a Freshness Flaw in a Key-Distribution and Authentication Protocol. In *Proceedings of the IEEE 4th International Conference on Intelligent Computer Communication and Processing,* Cluj-Napoca, Romania.

Felstead, E. B., & Keightley, R. J. (1995, November 7). Robustness capabilities of transponded commercial satellite communications. In *Proceedings of the IEEE Military Communications Conference (MILCOM 95),* San Diego, CA (Vol. 2, pp. 783-787).

Gansler, J. S., & Binnendijk, H. (Eds.). (2005). *Information assurance: Trends in vulnerabilities, threats and technologies.* Washington, DC: National Defense University, Center for Technology and National Security Policy.

Hartleid, J. E., & Casey, L. (1993, June). The Iridium system personal communications anytime, anyplace. In *Proceedings of the 3rd International Mobile Satellite Conference,* Pasadena, CA (pp. 285-290).

Ippolito, L. J. Jr. (2008). *Satellite communications systems engineering: atmospheric effects, satellite link design and system performance.* New York, NY: Wiley. doi:10.1002/9780470754443

Law, Y. W., Hoesel, L., Doumen, J., Hartel, P., & Havinga, P. (2005). Energy-efficient link-layer jamming attacks against wireless sensor network MAC protocols. In *Proceedings of the 3rd ACM Workshop on Security of Ad hoc and Sensor Networks,* Alexandria, VA (pp. 76-88).

Lee, J. W., & Marshall, V. A. (1994, October). Maximum capacity prediction and anti-jamm performance analysis for commercial satellite communication systems. In *Proceedings of the IEEE Military Communications Conference (MILCOM94),* Fort Monmouth, NJ (pp. 506-510).

Lee, T. F., Chang, S. H., Hwang, T., & Chong, S. K. (2009). Enhanced Delegation-Based Authentication Protocol for PCSs. *IEEE Transactions on Wireless Communications, 8*(5), 2166–2171. doi:10.1109/TWC.2009.070032

Lee, W. B., & Yeh, C. K. (2005). A new delegation-based authentication protocol for use in portable communication systems. *IEEE Transactions on Wireless Communications, 4*(1), 57–64. doi:10.1109/TWC.2004.840220

Mahoney, T., Kerr, P., Felstead, B., Wells, P., Cunningham, M., Baumgartner, G., & Jeronim, L. (1999, October 31-November 3). An investigation of the military applications of commercial personal satellite-communications systems. In *Proceedings of the IEEE Military Communications Conference (MILCOMM 1999)* (Vol. 1, pp. 112-116).

Peng, T., Leckie, C., & Ramamohanarao, K. (2007). Survey of network-based defense mechanisms countering the DoS and DDoS problems. *ACM Computing Surveys, 39*(1). doi:10.1145/1216370.1216373

Radosavac, S., Benammar, N., & Baras, J. S. (2004, March 17-19). Cross-layer attacks in wireless ad hoc networks. In *Proceedings of the Conference on Information Sciences and Systems,* Princeton, NJ.

Rausch, H. (2006). Jamming commercial satellite communications during wartime: an empirical study. In *Proceedings of the 4th IEEE International Workshop on Information Assurance* (pp. 109-118).

Stahlberg, M. (2000). Radio jamming attacks against two popular mobile networks. In H. Lipmaa & H. Pehu-Lehtonen (Eds.), *Proceedings of the Helsinki University of Technology Seminar on Network Security and Mobile Security.*

Tseng, Y. M. (2007). A heterogeneous-network aided public-key management scheme for mobile ad hoc networks. *International Journal of Network Management, 17,* 3–15. doi:10.1002/nem.603

United States General Accounting Office. (2002). *Critical Infrastructure Protection: Commercial Satellites Should Be More Fully Addressed.* Washington, DC: Author.

Xu, W., Trappe, W., Zhang, Y., & Wood, T. (2005). The feasibility of launching and detecting jamming attacks in wireless networks. In *Proceedings of the 6th ACM International Symposium on Mobile Ad Hoc Networking & Computing,* Urbana-Champaign, IL (pp. 46-57).

*This work was previously published in the International Journal of Information Security and Privacy, Volume 5, Issue 1, edited by Hamid Nemati, pp. 33-49, copyright 2011 by IGI Publishing (an imprint of IGI Global).*

# Chapter 4
# Information Privacy:
## Implementation and Perception of Laws and Corporate Policies by CEOs and Managers

**Garry L. White**
*Texas State University – San Marcos, USA*

**Francis A. Méndez Mediavilla**
*Texas State University – San Marcos, USA*

**Jaymeen R. Shah**
*Texas State University – San Marcos, USA*

## ABSTRACT

*In the Web dependent world, companies must respect and protect individuals' information privacy. Companies develop and implement corporate information privacy policies to comply with the domestic and international information privacy laws and regulations. This paper investigates: (a) the approach used by multinational and domestic companies to develop and implement corporate information privacy policies; and (b) the perception of corporate managers/professionals toward information privacy legislation and secondary use of personally identifiable information (PII) that organizations collect. A survey was conducted to collect data from corporate CEOs, managers, and technical professionals of national and multinational companies. Findings indicate the following: 1) Views regarding the practicality and effectiveness of information privacy legislations are similar for respondents from the national and multinational companies. 2) Respondents are undecided about whether the privacy laws of the United States and foreign countries are equally restrictive. 3) Multinational companies do not favor developing and implementing uniform information privacy policies or different information privacy policies across countries of operations. 4) Respondents strongly agreed that unauthorized secondary use of personal information is unacceptable.*

DOI: 10.4018/978-1-4666-2050-6.ch004

## INTRODUCTION

The emergence of social networking and cloud computing, and enhancements in the Internet and Web technologies have significantly increased the use of the Web by businesses and individuals. Increase in the use of the Web and global e-commerce together with the advances in online data collection technologies and online marketing techniques have created potential threats to consumers' information privacy that are invisible to many users (Camp, 1999; Pedley, 2002; Zhang et al., 2007). Using sophisticated automated data collection technologies, companies now collect, store, and transfer across the borders ever more personally identifiable information (PII) in electronic form, often without individuals' knowledge, which has significantly increased information privacy concerns (Cassini et al., 2008). Collecting PII about individuals without their knowledge is not fair. Further, one of the consequences of the use of global information infrastructure developed to support global e-commerce is that companies can almost instantaneously move individuals' personal data collected by them across national jurisdictions. This is easy as unlike physical goods, data freely flows across national jurisdictions without any checks. Although, the free flow of information is one of the most essential requirements for the economic growth of an organization (Oz, 1994), flow of individuals' PII across national jurisdictions substantially increase individuals' concerns regarding information privacy and expose companies to criminal liability (Gilbert, 2008). Transborder data flows makes it difficult to deal with information privacy problems as the majority of the existing privacy laws do not address this issue. This has resulted in information privacy to become one of the most critical issues of international concern that threatens the growth of global e-commerce (Stephens, 2007; Zuckerman, 2001; Chandran et al., 1987).

Results of a study by Ranganathan and Ganapathy (2002) indicated that information privacy concerns have a significant impact on the purchasing intent of consumers. Individuals' are concerned regarding their information privacy when they use the Web. A consumer survey revealed that almost 61% of the Internet users refuse to shop online due to concerns regarding information privacy (Ryker et al., 2002). To alleviate consumers' information privacy concerns and build consumer trust online, most companies develop information privacy policies and post them on their websites. To be effective in alleviating individuals' privacy concerns, these policies must explicitly state what data the company collects, and how the company will use the collected data. A survey by Milne and Culnan (2004) found that 66.3% of online users who read the information privacy policy posted on a company's website, but did not understand how their personal information will be used by the company, did not use the website to make any purchases. This result clearly suggests that online users are concerned regarding companies making unauthorized secondary use of their personal information, and sharing and selling it to business partners without obtaining prior authorization from them.

This research is a follow-up study to Shah et al. (2007) to investigate the approach used by multinational and domestic companies to develop and implement corporate information privacy policies, and the perception of corporate managers/professionals towards the information privacy legislations and unauthorized secondary use of PII collected by organizations. For this study, targeted survey participants were CEOs and managers of multinational and domestic companies. The remainder of the paper is organized as follows: The following section contains background discussion regarding global information privacy, and the two possible solutions available to companies to deal with the patchwork of global information privacy laws. The main objectives of this research are presented in the Research Objectives section. It is followed by the Survey Method section, which contains discussion regarding the survey conducted to collect data for this research. Next, results of this study are presented in the Results section. The Discussion section contains discussion regarding the findings of this research, and Possible Dependence Structure section contains discussion regarding the exploratory analysis performed using classification tree analysis. Finally, the Conclusion section mainly contains discussion about the need for developing unified global information privacy regulations.

## BACKGROUND

Warren and Brandeis (1890) defined an individual's right to privacy as "the right to be left alone". Information Privacy is defined as the right of an individual or business to determine what, when, how, and how much information regarding them should be divulged to others (Grandinetti, 1996; Martin, 1973; Udo, 2001; Westin, 1967). Individuals typically believe that they own their personal information, and view protection of information privacy as an important issue. However, cultural and legislative differences across countries tend to affect these beliefs.

Invasion of individuals' information privacy may occur due to unauthorized collection, disclosure, and/or secondary use of individuals' PII (Wang et al., 1998). To protect individuals' information privacy, most countries have information privacy laws. However, the effectiveness of national information privacy laws seems to have diminished with the emergence of the Internet and e-commerce as they do not recognize national jurisdictions. Managing individuals' information privacy when PII flows across countries is difficult and complicated because of the differences in the information privacy laws across countries (Zuckerman, 2001).

"Different countries have different views about privacy of computerized data due to different attitudes about the role of government and commerce" (George, 2004, pp.167-168). What is legal in one country may be illegal in another country. This has resulted in considerably different information privacy laws across countries around the globe (Wugmeister et al., 2007). The outcome of these differences in information privacy laws across countries is that the collection, compilation, use, disclosure, and transfer of PII by a company is governed by a complex patchwork of domestic and foreign information privacy laws. For example, there are 51 different sets of data protection regimes in the U.S.A., and Canada has different federal and provincial information privacy laws (Frauenheim, 2006; Gilbert, 2008). This is an important issue from a business perspective, as multinational companies have to understand these differences in information privacy laws across the countries in which they do business to ensure that their corporate information privacy policies comply with all the applicable information privacy laws.

In the absence of global standards and legislation for information privacy, how can multinational companies cope with the differences in the information privacy laws in different countries in which they do business? Multinational companies usually select one of the following two possible solutions: 1) implement the most restrictive "one size fits all" information privacy policy that is used across all countries in which the company does business; or, 2) implement different information privacy policies that comply with the specific information privacy regulations of the different countries in which the company does business. Further, should companies use the PII they collect only for the purpose for which it was collected, and not share or sell it without prior authorization from individuals? These are important questions concerning information privacy and good corporate behavior, thus deserve to be investigated.

## RESEARCH OBJECTIVES

The main objectives of this research study are as follows: 1) explore how national and multinational companies view and comply with information privacy regulations across different countries in which they do business; 2) determine how corporate managers and technical professionals view US information privacy laws; and, 3) discover corporate managers' and technical professionals' perceptions regarding the secondary use and unauthorized sale of PII collected by companies. The term multinational company is defined as a company that does business in other countries in addition to where it is incorporated. The specific questions that are the focus of this study are as follows:

1.  Do national and multinational companies have similar views regarding information privacy legislations' practicality and effectiveness? The null hypothesis #1 is: Views regarding information privacy legislations' practicality and effectiveness are the same for national and multinational companies (survey items 1-5).
2.  Does the U.S.A. have the most restrictive information privacy laws when compared to other countries? The null hypothesis #2 is: Survey respondents view U.S.A. and foreign information privacy laws to be equally restrictive (survey item 9).
3.  Do multinational companies implement uniform information privacy policies across different countries in which they do business? It is cheaper and less error prone to implement uniform information privacy policies across the countries of operation. This approach may require multinational companies to implement the most restrictive information privacy policy across the countries of operation. The null hypothesis #3a is: Survey respondents have no opinion regarding foreign information privacy laws'

impact on the corporate information privacy policies (survey item 6). The null hypothesis #3b is: Multinational companies do not favor either the use of uniform information privacy policies or different information privacy policies across different countries in which they do business (survey items 7 and 8).

4.  Do corporate professionals have an opinion regarding the use of an individual's PII for other purpose than what it was collected for? This will indicate corporate professionals' view about who owns the collected PII, the collector or the individual. The null hypothesis #4 is: Survey respondents have no opinion regarding secondary use of PII (survey items 10-13).

## SURVEY METHOD

The subjects for this study were corporate managers and technical professionals from national and multinational companies. An e-mail requesting participation in the survey for this study was sent to corporate managers and technical professionals who subscribed to the World Trade magazine. This resulted in a total of 10,000 potential subjects. The survey instrument for this study consisted of four parts and sixteen survey questions. The four parts of the survey instrument dealt with the following:

1.  Information privacy laws in the U.S.A.
2.  Survey of multinational corporations regarding implementation of information privacy policies across countries of operation.
3.  Secondary use of PII.
4.  Demographic questions.

The first thirteen questions in the survey covering the first three parts used a five-level Likert scale. Each survey question was rated by selecting Strongly Disagree (1), Disagree (2), Undecided (3), Agree (4), or Strongly Agree (5). The three demographic questions requested information about the type of business, the position of the respondent, and if the respondent contributed towards the development of corporate information privacy policies. Survey respondents were not required to provide their name or their company's name in order to maintain anonymity.

The survey instrument was distributed via e-mail to World Trade subscribers. Each e-mail contained a brief message explaining the purpose of the study and a hyperlink to the Web-based survey. The survey instrument was designed to ensure easy access and minimal amount of time to complete it. It was available to the respondents on the survey website for ten days. At the end of the survey period there were 177 valid responses. The response rate was approximately 1.77%. Data collected from this survey was analyzed using SPSS statistical software and R language (R Development Core Team, 2009).

## DATA ANALYSIS METHODOLOGY

Five-level Likert scales were used to record responses from a sample of 177 respondents. In this Likert scale, a response of 3 indicates indecisiveness. Thus a response of 3 is being considered as a response that does not carry a strong opinion or any information about the opinion of the respondent about the statement in question. The purpose is to detect statistically significant departures from "undecided" for a measure of the "typical" response to each item. Concerning such "typical measures", it is believed that robust measures of central tendency and robust measures of variability best describe the data obtained from the five-level Likert scale used (Higgins, 2004; Gibbons, 1993). Thus, the median response is used to describe the central tendency of the responses. Several measures of dispersion around the median are used in order to assess the variability of the responses: the mean absolute deviation from the median response (equation 1: $MAD_{median}$);

the median absolute response (equation 2: $MAD_{robust}$); and, the coefficient of variation relative to the median (equation 3: $CV_{robust}$) (Peña, 2002).

$$MAD_{median} = \frac{\sum |x_i - \bar{X}_M|}{n}; \qquad (1)$$
where $\bar{X}_M$ is the median

$$MAD_{robust} = Median\left(|x_i - \mathbf{1}\bar{X}_M|\right); \qquad (2)$$
where $\bar{X}_M$ is the median, $\mathbf{1}$ is $n \times 1$ vector of 1's

$$CV_{robust} = \frac{Median\left(|\mathbf{X} - \mathbf{1}\bar{X}_M|\right)}{Median\left(\mathbf{X}\right)}; \qquad (3)$$
where $\bar{X}_M$ is the median,
$\mathbf{X}$ is the $n \times 1$ vector of values

Three main types of analysis were performed on these items: estimation and inference using nonparametric bootstrap intervals, correspondence analysis, and classification tree analysis. Nonparametric bootstrap was used to determine the 95% bootstrap intervals for the median responses. These intervals were generated using 1,000 resamples for each item, a reasonable size to estimate the sampling distribution for the median response (Efron & Tibshirani, 1993). A Chi-square test for independence was used to determine if the distribution of responses to items were independent from the position held by the respondent (i.e., CEOs, managers and technical). For those cases in which enough evidence was found to reject the hypothesis that responses were independent from position, a correspondence analysis was performed. Correspondence analysis was used to map response patterns to items dealing with secondary use of PII collected by the company and the type of positions these individuals held in their companies: technical position, managerial position, or CEO position. Finally, classification trees were used to select variables that reduce the variability in responses. The main purpose is to reveal possible dependence structures among the variables being explored. Plausible explanations for these dependence structures are provided. It is essential to bear in mind that this is an exploratory analysis and that any evidence of a dependence structure should be treated with caution, considering the possibility that the findings are spurious. However, dependence structures found in this study will be used as a starting point for future research.

## RESULTS

The demographic data presented in Table 1 indicate that respondents represented a range of industries, with almost 29% of the respondents from the Manufacturing sector. Approximately 60% (107) of the respondents were from multinational companies, and the remaining 40% (70) were from national companies (see Table 2). The majority of the survey respondents consisted of individuals who were involved with the development of information privacy policies in their organizations, and were knowledgeable about the corporate information privacy policies. Of all the respondents, 88% were decision makers, and 75% contributed to the development of corporate information privacy policies.

Statistics presented in Table 3 indicate that the relative variability in responses for all respondents is small for survey item #6: Laws of other countries impact your overall corporate information privacy policies, and for survey items related to secondary use of information (survey items 10 through 13). Relative to the other survey items, there seems to be higher variability in responses

*Table 1. Demographic data of respondents, n = 177*

| |
|---|
| **Business Type of Respondents** |
| Manufacturing 28.8% Consulting 14.7% Distribution 8.5% |
| Construction 1.7% Transportation 6.8% Financial 5.1% |
| Communication 3.4% Retail 13.6% Health Care 2.8% |
| Government 1.7% Other 13.0% |
| **Position Type of Respondents** |
| Technical 11.9 % Management 42.9 % CEO 45.2 % |
| **Respondents contributed to Privacy Policies** |
| YES 75% NO 18% Undetermined 7% |

*Table 2. Company type frequencies and percentages*

| |
|---|
| National company 70 40% |
| Multinational company 107 60% |

to survey questions related to the effectiveness of information privacy laws, information privacy lawsuits, heterogeneity of implementation, restrictiveness of policies and US laws (survey items 3, 5, 7, 8 and 9, respectively).

Ninety-five percent bootstrap intervals for the median response were obtained using non-parametric bootstrap techniques (see Table 4). Median responses were in agreement with items related to the US law privacy policy (survey item 1), practicality of the existing US privacy laws (survey item 2), and foreign laws (survey item 6); evidence of strong agreement on all items related to the requirement of individuals' authorization for the secondary use or sale of personal information (survey items 10 through 13). In general, relatively large variability in responses was found for items 1, 2, 3, 4, 5, 7, 8, and 9, as evidenced from the robust coefficient of variation (see $CV_{robust}$ in Table 3). This is evidence of the diversity in opinion about the issues to which those items relate (see MAD in Table 3). Furthermore, internal consistency was found among items related to the secondary use of the personal information (survey items 10 through 13; Cronbach alpha = 0.65; n = 177).

*Table 3. Central tendency and variability of responses*

| Item # | Item | Median | MAD(median) | MAD(robust) | CV(robust) |
|--------|------|--------|-------------|-------------|------------|
| 1 | US Law Privacy Policy | 4 | 0.8807 | 1 | 0.25 |
| 2 | Practicality of Law | 4 | 0.9661 | 1 | 0.25 |
| 3 | I. Privacy Laws Effectiveness | 2 | 0.9379 | 1 | 0.5 |
| 4 | Tech Implementation | 4 | 1.0452 | 1 | 0.25 |
| 5 | Lawsuits | 3 | 0.9718 | 1 | 0.33 |
| 6 | Foreign Laws | 4 | 0.7048 | 0 | 0 |
| 7 | Heterogeneous Implementation | 3 | 1.0099 | 1 | 0.33 |
| 8 | Restrictive Policies | 3 | 0.8854 | 1 | 0.33 |
| 9 | US Laws Restrictive | 3 | 0.7358 | 1 | 0.33 |
| 10 | Secondary Use Authorization | 5 | 0.2542 | 0 | 0 |
| 11 | Secondary Use not Allowed | 5 | 0.3107 | 0 | 0 |
| 12 | Never Sell Personal Information | 5 | 0.3446 | 0 | 0 |
| 13 | Never Sell Unless Authorized | 5 | 0.1241 | 0 | 0 |

*Table 4. Estimated median responses*

| Item # | Item | Median | 95% Boostrap Interval |
|--------|------|--------|------------------------|
| 1 | US Law Privacy Policy | 4 | [4, 4] |
| 2 | Practicality of Law | 4 | [4, 4] |
| 3 | I. Privacy Laws Effectiveness | 2 | [2, 2] |
| 4 | Tech Implementation | 4 | [3, 4] |
| 5 | Lawsuits | 3 | [3, 3] |
| 6 | Foreign Laws | 4 | [4, 4] |
| 7 | Heterogeneous Implementation | 3 | [2, 4] |
| 8 | Restrictive Policies | 3 | [2, 3] |
| 9 | US Laws Restrictive | 3 | [3, 3] |
| 10 | Secondary Use Authorization | 5 | [5, 5] |
| 11 | Secondary Use not Allowed | 5 | [5, 5] |
| 12 | Never Sell Personal Information | 5 | [5, 5] |
| 13 | Never Sell Unless Authorized | 5 | [5, 5] |

## Results for Research Objective Question #1

The first question of this study was to answer the following: Do national and multinational companies have similar views regarding information privacy legislations' practicality and effectiveness?

Not enough evidence was found to support that the views regarding the practicality and effectiveness of information privacy legislations are any different for respondents from the national and multinational companies (see ANOVA in Table 5).

The responses to survey items 1, 2, and 3 were significantly skewed (see Table 6, std error = 0.183). Analysis of responses to survey items 1

*Table 5. One-way ANOVA for survey items 1-5 between national and multinational companies*

| ANOVA | | | | | |
|---|---|---|---|---|---|
| | Sum of Squares | df | Mean Square | F | Sig. |
| usa affect comp<br>Between Groups<br>Within Groups<br>Total | .125<br>226.233<br>226.358 | 1<br>174<br>175 | .125  1.300 | .096 | .757 |
| usa pri laws pra<br>Between Groups<br>Within Groups<br>Total | 1.773<br>267.448<br>269.220 | 1<br>175<br>176 | 1.773  1.528 | 1.160 | .283 |
| pri laws eff<br>Between Groups<br>Within Groups<br>Total | .129<br>265.091<br>265.220 | 1<br>175<br>176 | .129<br>1.515 | .771 | .085 |
| pri laws eff & eco<br>Between Groups<br>Within Groups<br>Total | 2.638E-02<br>261.341<br>261.367 | 1<br>175<br>176 | 2.638E-02<br>1.493 | .018 | .894 |
| imped internet oper<br>Between Groups<br>Within Groups<br>Total | 1.478E-02<br>263.963<br>263.977 | 1<br>175<br>176 | 1.478E-02<br>1.508 | .010 | .921 |

and 2 show evidence that corporate decision makers believe U.S.A. legislations affect their companies' corporate information privacy policies, and that these laws are practical. However, when considering the global nature of the Internet, these decision makers disagree that current information privacy laws are effective (see survey item 3 in Tables 4 and 6). This is consistent with the global nature of the Internet. National laws are effective within a judicial boundary, but have little value outside the judicial boundary, as they cannot be enforced.

The skewness towards agreement for item 4 was not significant. The 95% bootstrap interval does not discard agreement with the idea that there are technologies available to implement information privacy laws effectively and economically (see survey item 4 in Tables 4 and 6). The decision makers were undecided regarding whether or not the information privacy lawsuits involving the Internet impeded their company's Internet operations (see survey item 5 in Tables 4 and 6).

## Results for Research Objective Question #2

The next research question was to find out if the U.S.A. had the most restrictive information privacy laws when compared to other countries. Survey item 9, in Table 7, was developed to address this question. The skewness coefficient for the distribution of responses to item #9 is not significant (Table 7, std error = 0.061). The responses centered on undecided (see Table 4). At the 0.05 significance level, not enough evidence was found to reject hypothesis #2. Therefore, the evidence supports that survey respondents are undecided regarding whether the U.S.A. and foreign information privacy laws are equally restrictive or not.

## Results for Research Objective Question #3

Survey item 6 was developed to elicit responses from survey respondents regarding whether foreign information privacy laws had any influence

*Table 6. Views regarding information privacy legislation, practicality, and effectiveness (n=177)*

1. Internet legislations by the U.S.A. government affect your company's privacy policies.
(Mean 3.78, Median 4.00, Mode 5. Skewness -.639, std error for skewness .183. Trend was to AGREE)
2. Information privacy laws in the U.S.A. are practical.
(Mean 3.58, Median 4.00, Mode 4. Skewness -.533, std error for skewness .183. Trend was to AGREE)
3. Considering the global nature of the Internet, current information privacy laws are effective.
(Mean 2.58, Median 2.00, Mode 2. Skewness +.595, std error for skewness .183. Trend was to DISAGREE)
4. Technologies are available to effectively and economically implement information privacy laws.
(Mean .343, Median 4.00, Mode 4. Skewness -.282, std error for skewness .183. Trend was to AGREE)
5. Information privacy lawsuits involving the Internet impede Internet operations.
(Mean 2.99, Median 3.00, Mode 2. Skewness +.209, std error for skewness .183. Trend was UNDECIDED)

*Table 7. Views of companies that do business in other countries*

6. Laws of other countries impact your overall corporate information privacy policies.
(Mean 3.58, Median 4.00, Mode 4. Skewness -.553, std error of skewness .236. Trend was to AGREE)
7. Your company implements different information privacy policies across different countries.
(Mean 3.05, Median 3.00, Mode 4. Skewness -.076, std error of skewness .240. Trend was UNDECIDED)
8. Your company implements across countries the most restrictive policies as defined by the most restrictive laws of one country.
(Mean 2.91, Median 3.00, Mode 2. Skewness +.245, std error of skewness .246. Trend was UNDECIDED)
9. The U.S.A. has the most restrictive privacy laws when compared to other countries.
(Mean 2.91, Median 3.00, Mode 3. Skewness +.061, std error of skewness .235. Trend was UNDECIDED)

on the corporate information privacy policies. The responses to item #6 were significantly skewed (Table 7, std error = 0.236). The 95% bootstrap interval shows evidence of a median response for item 6 of agreement (see survey item 6 in Table 4). At the 0.05 significance level, enough evidence was found to reject hypothesis #3a. Therefore, survey respondents agree that information privacy laws of countries in which they do business affects their company's corporate information privacy policies.

Do multinational companies implement uniform information privacy policies across different countries in which they do business? Analysis of responses to survey items 7 and 8 indicate that the respondents do not know how best to deal with the differences in the information privacy laws across the countries of operation. The responses to items 7 and 8 were not statistically significantly skewed (Table 7, std errors: 0.240 and 0.246 respectively). The 95% bootstrap intervals do not rule out the possibility that the median responses for both items reflect indecisiveness. Overall, not enough evidence was found to reject hypothesis #3b.

Therefore, in general, multinational companies do not favor implementation of uniform information privacy policies over the implementation of different information privacy policies across countries in which they do business.

## Results for Research Objective Question #4

Do corporate professionals have an opinion regarding the use of an individual's PII for any other purpose than what it was originally collected for? The 95% bootstrap intervals for the median responses to items 10, 11, 12, and 13 indicate strong agreement with all the items (see Tables 4 and 8). The dispersion of the responses is relatively small for these survey items, as assessed by the measures of dispersion in Table 3. The skewness coefficients for the distribution of responses to items #10 to #13 were significant (std errors: 0.183 for all items). At the 0.05 significance level, enough evidence was found to reject hypothesis #4. Therefore, survey respondents do have an opinion regarding the secondary use of PII. These

*Table 8. Sub-survey \* on secondary use of personal information*

10. Companies should NOT use personal information for any purpose unless it has been authorized by the individuals who provided the information.
(Mean 4.75, Median 5.00, Mode 5. Skewness -2.992, std error of skewness .183. Trend was STRONGLY AGREE)

11. When people give personal information to a company for some reason, the company should never use the information for any other reason.
(Mean 4.69, Median 5.00, Mode 5. Skewness -2.890, std error of skewness .183. Trend was STRONGLY AGREE)

12. Companies should never sell the personal information in their computer databases to other companies.
(Mean 4.75 Median 5.00, Mode 5. Skewness -2.374, std error of skewness .183. Trend was STRONGLY AGREE)

13. Companies should never share personal information with other companies unless it has been authorized by the individual who provided the information.
(Mean 4.88, Median 5.00, Mode5. Skewness -4.351, std error of skewness .183. Trend was STRONGLY AGREE)

*\* These four items are adapted from Smith, H. J., Milberg, S. J., & Burke, S. J. (1996). Information Privacy: Measuring Individuals' concerns about Organizational Practices. MIS Quarterly, 20(2), 167-196.*

results indicate that the survey respondents are in strong agreement that an individual's PII must not be used for any other purpose or sold to anyone unless the individual authorizes it. Respondents strongly agreed that unauthorized secondary use of personal information is unacceptable. This result indicated that business managers and CEOs have respect for customers' and employees' information privacy. These corporate decision makers probably believe that individuals own their personal information, which should be used only for the purpose for which it was collected. Further, personal information should not be sold or shared with business partners without prior authorization from individuals owning the PII.

## DISCUSSION

The ubiquitous access and global connectivity of the Internet has made it easy to quickly access and share information, and move it across national boundaries. This has increased the probability of compromising individuals' information privacy. Although countries have enacted information privacy laws to protect individuals' information privacy, the jurisdictions of such national laws are limited to within the boundaries of the country. Multinational companies have to tread carefully through the maze created by the proliferation of information privacy laws, and address the differ-

ences in the information privacy laws of different countries and states in which they do business. They carry the burden of safeguarding consumers', employees', and businesses' information privacies across the various countries of operation, in accordance with each country's information privacy laws. Dealing with such a patchwork of national information privacy laws is expensive for businesses. An alternative available to deal with these differences in information privacy laws across different countries is to develop and implement uniform corporate information privacy policies across all countries in which the company does business.

Result of this study suggested that corporate managers are almost equally split between developing and implementing uniform corporate information privacy policy based on the most restrictive information privacy laws of the countries in which they do business; and developing and implementing different information privacy policies to satisfy the information privacy laws of each country in which the company operates. This result differed from the results of a past research study in which respondents indicated that multinational companies tend to develop and implement uniform information privacy policy based on the most restrictive information privacy policy across the countries in which they do business, a "one size fits all" approach (Shah et al., 2007). This seems to be a better alternative than implementing different information privacy policies in different countries, as it is more efficient and cost-effective. This difference in the results may be due to the differences in the type of respondents for these two studies. In Shah et al. (2007) study, 49% of the respondents were technical professionals, 12% were CEOs, and 42% of the companies did business in foreign countries. In this study, CEOs constituted 45% of all the respondents, while only 12% of the respondents were technical professionals. Further, almost 60% of the respondents represented multinational companies that did business outside the USA. Thus, in this study, there was a much larger percentage of respondents who were decision-makers involved with the development of their company's information privacy policies, and those who represented multinational companies. These differences in the respondent populations of the two studies may have resulted in these differences in the results.

There were similarities between results of these two studies. Results of both these research studies did indicate the following:

1.  Laws of other countries in which the company operates does have impact on the overall corporate information privacy policies;
2.  Information privacy laws in the U.S.A. are practical;
3.  Due to the global nature of the Internet, current information privacy laws are NOT effective; and
4.  Technologies are available to effectively and economically implement information privacy policies that comply with the information privacy laws and regulations.

Results of this study suggest that corporate managers are concerned with the unauthorized secondary use, and unauthorized sharing and sale of customers' and employees' personal information. Advancements in information technology have made it easier to support internal secondary use of consumers' personal information and to share this information with business partners. Due to this, there seems to be a general notion that companies tend to share consumers' personal information with their business partners without individuals' consent (Pratt and Conger, 2009), however, this may not be completely true. Results indicate that respondents were in strong agreement against the unauthorized secondary use and unauthorized sale of personal information collected by a company. Correspondence analysis of responses to survey item 11 regarding the secondary use of personal information revealed a marginally significant difference ($\chi^2$ = 8.0012, p-value = 0.0900) among responses from respondents holding technical positions, managerial positions, and CEOs. Figure 1 shows that respondents holding technical positions (triangle 1) and managerial positions (triangle 2) answered Agree or Strongly Agree to survey item #11 relatively more often than respondents who were CEOs. This result suggests that managers and technical personnel, who deal more directly with individuals' personal information, have a stronger view against the secondary use of personal information than CEOs, who are more focused on company's bottomline. This could imply that CEOs may allow or even push managers to make secondary use of personal information if such use of customers' PII is beneficial to company's bottomline, competitiveness, and/ or supports operationalization of corporate strategies. Typically, increase in competitive pressure may compel companies to collect more PII, and use it for secondary purpose, such as analyzing collected PII to understand consumers' online behavior (Dhillon & Moores, 2001). This may be the reason why companies such as Facebook and Palm were reported to be involved in extensive collection, secondary use, and sharing of users' PII with their business partners without prior authorization from users (Boorstin, 2009; McAllister, 2009).

Correspondence analysis of responses to survey item #12 related to unauthorized sale of personal information showed a marginally sig-

*Figure 1. Correspondence diagram, item #11*

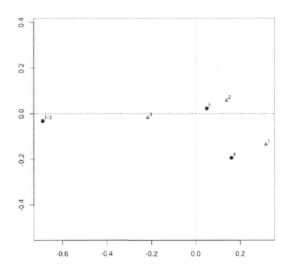

**Legend:** The *dots* represent responses to item #11.
The *triangles* represent type of position of the respondent
(1: Tech; 2: manager; 3: CEO).

nificant difference ($\chi^2 = 9.3622$, p-value = 0.0540) among responses from respondents holding technical positions, managerial positions, and CEOs. Figure 2 shows that respondents holding technical positions (triangle 1) and managerial positions (triangle 2) seem more in agreement with survey item #12 than respondents who were CEOs (triangle 3). This result suggests that managers and technical personnel who deal more directly with indviduals' personal information have stronger propensity against unauthorized sale of personal information than CEOs who are more focused on company's profits. CEOs seem to have a different mindset regarding information privacy than managers and technical personnel, which is reflected in the terse statement by Sun Microsystem's former CEO Scott McNealy: "You have zero privacy anyway. Get over it" (Fitzgerald, 2009). Such attitude of many CEOs towards individuals' information privacy violates the social contract between the individual customer/user and the organization. From a social contract perspective, when individuals provide PII to an organization, they expect the organization to uphold its side of

the social contract by maintaining privacy of their information (Dhillon & Moores, 2001). If the organization does not uphold its social contract then individuals' trust in the organization will decline.

## POSSIBLE DEPENDENCE STRUCTURES

Classification tree analysis was used to explore possible dependence structures between variables and to identify possible sources of the variability in the responses. Results revealed that responses to the statement about the US Internet legislations affecting company's information privacy policies (survey item #1) were associated with responses to the statement about the laws of other countries having an impact on the company privacy policies (survey item #6) and the type of business (survey item #14). Respondents from government, transportation, communication, and construction companies mostly agreed or strongly agreed that US Internet legislations affected their company's

*Figure 2. Correspondence diagram, item #12*

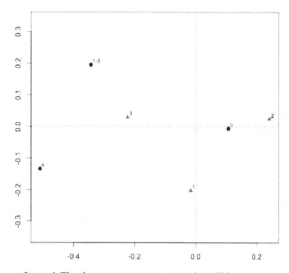

**Legend:** The *dots* represent responses to item #11.
The *triangles* represent type of position of the respondent
(1: Tech; 2: manager; 3: CEO).

information privacy policies, given that they agreed that laws of other countries also have an impact on their company's privacy policies. This result suggests that both, the US Internet legislations and privacy laws of other countries affect information privacy policies of multinational companies in the transportation, communication, and construction sectors, and government agencies. Transportation companies such as airlines typically store significant amount of PII about domestic and international customers, and their travel within and outside the US. Similarly, communications companies store PII regarding customers and their domestic and international phone calls. Thus, these companies' information privacy policies are more likely to be affected by information privacy laws of other countries in addition to the US privacy laws.

Respondents agree with the practicality of US information privacy laws (survey item #2), given that they believe that laws of other countries do not impact their company's information privacy policies (survey item #6) and that they also strongly believe that current information privacy laws are

ineffective (survey item #3). Respondents working for multinational companies who disagreed with the effectiveness of information privacy laws (survey item #3) tend to strongly disagree with the practicality of US information privacy laws (survey item #2). These results reveal a clear dichotomy regarding the perception of the practicality of US information privacy laws. However, even respondents who believed that US information privacy laws are practical indicated that due to the global nature of the Internet these laws are ineffective. This clearly suggests that it is important for governments to work together to create global information privacy laws that are effective across national jurisdictions. In the Internet age, development of unified global information privacy laws and coordinated implementation of these privacy laws seem to be the only way to make information privacy laws effective.

Results indicated that on the one hand the respondents who believed that technologies are not available to effectively and economically implement information privacy laws (survey item #4) also believed that information privacy lawsuits impede Internet operations of companies (survey item #5). On the other hand, CEOs and managers who strongly agreed that technology is available to effectively and economically implement information privacy laws also believed that information privacy lawsuits impede Internet operations of companies. This suggests that CEOs and managers are cognizant of the fact that even with the availability of technology to effectively and economically implement information privacy laws; it is easy to violate information privacy laws if the electronic PII collected by an organization is not properly secured and protected from inappropriate use. Any such violation of information privacy laws can result in a lawsuit against the company, thus making them more wary about Internet operations. It is further noticed that respondents who held technical positions were uncertain regarding whether or not information privacy lawsuits involving the Internet impede Internet operations of companies. These respondents tend to agree that technologies are available to effectively and economically implement information privacy laws. These results suggest that an individual's position type (technical or management) affects an individual's perception regarding the availability of technology to effectively and economically implement information privacy laws, and whether lawsuits involving the Internet impede Internet operations of a company or not.

There were respondents who believed that information privacy lawsuits do not impede Internet operations of companies who also believed that technologies are not available to effectively and economically implement information privacy laws. This implies that there are individuals who believe that unavailability of technology to effectively and economically implement information privacy laws may increase the chances of information privacy lawsuits to occur, however, this will not impede Internet operations of companies. Many companies will risk information privacy

lawsuits, but they will move forward with their Internet operation as it may be a critical part of their business operations. Results also suggest that the perception regarding whether information privacy lawsuits involving the Internet impede Internet operations of companies depends on the type of business for which an individual works.

Respondents from multinational companies seemed to be aware of information privacy laws of other countries. All respondents from multinational companies agreed that laws of other countries affect the overall corporate information privacy policies of their companies (survey item #6). Respondents from multinational companies who believed that their company implements across all countries of operation the most restrictive information privacy policy as defined by the most restrictive laws of a country (survey item #8), also believed that information privacy lawsuits involving the Internet do not impede Internet operations (survey item #5).

Respondents from multinational companies who believed that their company implemented across all countries of operation the most restrictive information privacy policy as defined by the most restrictive laws of one country (survey item #8), also believed that their company does not implement different information privacy policies across different countries (survey item #7). These results validate the clarity and consistency of these two survey items.

Irrespective of what the US and foreign information privacy laws permit, respondents who believed that individuals' personal information should not be shared with other companies unless authorized by individuals who provided the information (survey item #13) and that it should never be used for any purpose other than what it was collected for (survey item #11), also believed that companies should not make unauthorized secondary use of personal information (survey item #10).

## CONCLUSION

In conclusion, managers, CEOs, and technical personnel perceived that the information privacy laws of foreign countries in which their company operates affect their company's overall corporate information privacy policies. They perceived that information privacy laws in the U.S.A. are practical, but are not effective due to the global nature of the Internet. Results also indicate that CEOs, managers, and technical personnel have strong ethics regarding unauthorized secondary use of personal information. Almost all respondents indicated that unauthorized selling and sharing of personal information collected by companies is unacceptable. However, in practice, there are companies that share and/or sell consumers' PII they collect without obtaining explicit prior authorization from individuals. These companies believe that the PII they collect belongs to them (Fitzgerald, 2009).

As information privacy laws across countries are not consistent, it is difficult and expensive for multinational companies and e-commerce businesses to ensure that their corporate information privacy policies comply with the patchwork of information privacy laws of various countries. Multinational companies are required to navigate through myriad of information privacy laws across countries in which they do business, thus, they typically expend hundreds of thousands of dollars to develop and implement information privacy policies (Frauenheim, 2006). As global business and e-commerce continue to increase, more and more personal information will routinely cross international borders. In order to ensure that information privacy is maintained even with the growth of e-commerce and transborder data flow without significant increase in the cost and complexity of developing and implementing corporate information privacy policies, corporations such as Google have proposed creation of unified global information privacy regulations to regulate transborder flow of personal information

(Kirk, 2007). The idea of creating a unified set of information privacy regulations across countries involved in global trade may be feasible as the Organisation for Economic Co-operation and Development (OECD) has indicated that there is a widespread international support for the use of fair information practices (Peslak, 2006; Malman, 2000). Development of a unified global information privacy policy seems to be a logical move, as it will simplify development and implementation of global corporate information privacy policies, and it will provide a consistent legislative platform to effectively deal with the growth of transborder flow of personal information. As efforts are channeled towards the development of unified global information privacy policies, it is necessary to ensure that these policies are not open to multiple interpretations as it can impede its adoption and implementation (Barnett, 2008). Results of study by Nam et al. (2006) suggested that it is essential for governments to develop and implement comprehensive legislations to preserve consumers' information privacy.

Irrespective of whether unified global information privacy policies are developed or not, it is imperative for companies to carefully address information privacy concerns, and focus on developing and implementing appropriate information privacy policies that control how PII is collected, processed, used, shared and transferred across national boundaries. This is essential to avoid non-compliance with any applicable national and foreign information privacy laws, which could result in unwanted sanctions and criminal liability, and tarnish a company's reputation (Frauenheim, 2006; Gilbert, 2008). Further, explicitly stating in company's information privacy policy, what, when and how PII collected by the company will be used will alleviate customers' anxiety regarding improper secondary use and sharing of their PII. This will have a positive impact on customers' perception of the company, which will potentially result in increased willingness of consumers to disclose their PII to the company. Many companies such as Wal-Mart have recognized the importance of properly managing consumers' information privacy expectations. These companies have modified their information privacy policies and practices to provide consumers more control over the collection and use of their PII. This shift in corporate attitude towards individuals' information privacy is reflected in Wal-Mart's chief privacy officer Zoe Strickland's comment – "We want to provide customers with more control over their own data, which is a big topic today for relationships with customers and their privacy" (Weier, 2009).

## REFERENCES

Barnett, J. (2008). The Impact of Privacy Legislation on Patient Care. *International Journal of Information Security and Privacy, 2*(3), 1–17. doi:10.4018/jisp.2008070101

Boorstin, J. (2009). *Facebook sued on privacy concerns*. Retrieved from http://www.cnbc.com/id/32458206/

Camp, L. (1999). Web security and privacy: An American perspective. *The Information Society, 15*(4), 249–256. doi:10.1080/019722499128411

Cassini, J., Medlin, D., & Romaniello, A. (2008). Laws and Regulations Dealing with Information Security and Privacy: An Investigative Study. *International Journal of Information Security and Privacy, 2*(2), 70–82. doi:10.4018/jisp.2008040105

Chandran, R., Phatak, A., & Sambharya, R. (1987). Transborder Data Flows: Implications for Multinational Corporations. *Business Horizons, 30*(6), 74–83. doi:10.1016/0007-6813(87)90055-3

Dhillon, G., & Moores, T. (2001). Internet Privacy: Interpreting Key Issues. *Information Resources Management Journal, 14*(4), 33–37. doi:10.4018/irmj.2001100104

Efron, B., & Tibshirani, R. (1993). *An Introduction to the Bootstrap*. Boca Raton, FL: Chapman & Hall/CRC.

Fitzgerald, M. (2009). The privacy paradox. *CIO*, 26-33.

Frauenheim, E. (2006). Many U.S. multinationals doing little to meet overseas employee data privacy rules. *Workforce Management, 85*(9), 48–51.

George, J. F. (2004). *Computers in Society: Privacy, Ethics, and the Internet*. Upper Saddle River, NJ: Pearson-Prentice Hall.

Gibbons, J. D. (1993). *Nonparametric statistics: an introduction*. Newbury Park, CA: Sage Publications.

Gilbert, F. (2008). Is your due diligence checklist obsolete? Understanding how information privacy and security affects corporate and commercial transactions. *The Computer & Internet Lawyer, 25*(10), 13–18.

Grandinetti, M. (1996). Establishing and maintaining security on the Internet. *Sacramento Business Journal, 13*(25), 22.

Higgins, J. J. (2004). *An introduction to modern nonparametric statistics*. Pacific Grove, CA: Thomson/Brooks/Cole.

Kirk, J. (2007). *Google calls for global online privacy standard*. Retrieved from http://www.infoworld.com/article/07/09/14/Google-calls-for-global-online-privacy-standard_1.html

Malman, S. (2000). Memes and corporate identities in the telecommunication sector. In *Proceedings of the XIII Biennial Conference of the International Telecommunications Society (ITS 2000)*. Retrieved from http://www.its2000.org.ar/conference/malman.pdf

Martin, J. (1973). *Security, Accuracy, and Privacy in Computer Systems*. Englewood Cliffs, NJ: Prentice-Hall.

McAllister, N. (2009). *Developers should learn from the Palm Pre's privacy mistakes.* Retrieved from http://www.infoworld.com/d/developer-world/developers-should-learn-palm-pres-privacy-mistakes-529

Milne, G. R., & Culnan, M. J. (2004). Strategies for reducing online privacy risks: Why consumers read (or don't read) online privacy notices. *Journal of Interactive Marketing, 18*(3), 15–29. doi:10.1002/dir.20009

Nam, C., Song, C., Lee, E., & Park, C. (2006). Consumers' Privacy Concerns and Willingness to Provide Marketing-Related Personal Information Online. *Advances in Consumer Research. Association for Consumer Research (U. S.), 33*(1), 212–217.

Oz, E. (1994). Barriers to international data transfer. *Journal of Global Information Management, 2*(2), 22–29.

Pedley, P. (2002). Data protection for intranets and web sites. *Business Information Review, 19*(3), 41. doi:10.1177/026638202401093608

Peña, D. (2002). *Análisis de datos multivariantes.* Madrid, Spain: McGraw-Hill/Interamericana de España.

Peslak, A. R. (2006). Internet privacy policies of the largest international companies. *Journal of Electronic Commerce in Organizations, 4*(3), 46–62. doi:10.4018/jeco.2006070103

Pratt, J., & Conger, S. (2009). Without Permission: Privacy on the Line. *International Journal of Information Security and Privacy, 3*(1), 30–44. doi:10.4018/jisp.2009010103

R Development Core Team. (2009). *R: A language and environment for statistical computing.* Vienna, Austria: R Foundation for Statistical Computing.

Ranganathan, C., & Ganapathy, S. (2002). Key Dimensions of Business-to-Consumer Websites. *Information & Management, 39*(6), 457–465. doi:10.1016/S0378-7206(01)00112-4

Ryker, R., Lafleur, E., McManis, B., & Cox, K. C. (2002). Online Privacy Policies: An Assessment of the Fortune E-50. *Journal of Computer Information Systems, 42*(4), 15–20.

Shah, J., White, G., & Cook, J. (2007). Privacy Protection Overseas as Perceived by USA Based I.T. Professionals. *Journal of Global Information Management, 15*(1), 68–81. doi:10.4018/jgim.2007010104

Smith, H. J., Milberg, S. J., & Burke, S. J. (1996). Information Privacy: Measuring Individuals' concerns about Organizational Practices. *Management Information Systems Quarterly, 20*(2), 167–196. doi:10.2307/249477

Stephens, D. O. (2007). Protecting personal privacy in the global business environment. *Information Management Journal, 41*(3), 56–59.

Udo, G. (2001). Privacy and security concerns as major barriers for e-commerce: a survey study. *Information Management & Computer Security, 9*(4), 165–174. doi:10.1108/EUM0000000005808

Wang, H., Lee, M., & Wang, C. (1998). Consumer Privacy Concerns about Internet Marketing. *Communications of the ACM, 41*(3), 63–70. doi:10.1145/272287.272299

Warren, S., & Brandeis, L. (1890). The right to privacy. *Harvard Law Review, 4*(5), 193–220. doi:10.2307/1321160

Weier, M. (2009, July 20). Wal-Mart change hints at data-driven marketing. *InformationWeek, 10.*

Westin, A. (1967). *Privacy and Freedom.* New York, NY: Atheneum.

Wugmeister, M., Retzer, K., & Rich, C. (2007). Global solution for cross-border data transfers: Making the case for corporate privacy rules. *Georgetown Journal of International Law, 38*(3), 449–498.

Zhang, X., Sakaguchi, T., & Kennedy, M. (2007). A cross-cultural analysis of privacy notices of the Global 2000. *Journal of Information Privacy & Security, 3*(2), 18–36.

Zuckerman, A. (2001). Order in the courts? *World Trade, 14*(9), 26–29.

*This work was previously published in the International Journal of Information Security and Privacy, Volume 5, Issue 1, edited by Hamid Nemati, pp. 50-66, copyright 2011 by IGI Publishing (an imprint of IGI Global).*

# Chapter 5
# User Perceptions of Security Technologies

**Douglas M. Kline**
*University of North Carolina Wilmington, USA*

**Ling He**
*Saginaw Valley State University, USA*

**Ulku Yaylacicegi**
*University of North Carolina Wilmington, USA*

## ABSTRACT

*In this paper, user perceptions of information systems security are explored through a study of university students. Server authentication, which is often ignored by users, clouded by system administrators, and exploited by hackers, is explored in detail, as it significantly affects usability and requires user knowledge and participation. The study also investigates the respondents' consistency, gender differences, and assessment of their own knowledge. Although users appear knowledgeable about security technologies, they rely more on peer opinion and reputation of web sites when making security decisions.*

## MOTIVATION

Successful security mechanisms depend on user participation. At best, users are seen as the weakest link in the chain of events that must occur for secure communications (Gross & Rosson, 2007). At worst, users are seen as "the enemy" of system administrators, actively working against security mechanisms (Adams & Sasse, 1999). Understanding users' perception of security mechanisms can help us use technical mechanisms better, and improve the overall security of systems. System security is only as strong as the weakest link (Scheier, 2000).

The security mechanisms used on the internet are made up of a number of technologies that encrypt/decrypt and authenticate. Encryption/decryption involves scrambling/unscrambling data that is transmitted to prevent understanding of intercepted data. Authentication involves verification of the identity of the participants in the communication. Authentication is ideally

DOI: 10.4018/978-1-4666-2050-6.ch005

2-way: the user is authenticated by the system, and the system is authenticated by the user. User authentication is typically accomplished with a username and password, while system authentication is typically accomplished through a digital certificate. (Many other technologies exist, but these are the de facto standard mechanisms.)

The technologies involved are:

- **HTTPS (Hypertext Transfer Protocol, Secure):** The protocol that web browsers use to communicate securely with a web server.
- **SSL (Secure Sockets Layer):** The network protocol that accomplishes encryption on the media, which enables a web browser to communicate securely.
- **Digital Certificates:** Digital keys that are used to verify the identity of a participant.
- **Certifying Authority:** An organization (such as Thawte, Verisign, Geotrust) that certifies the identity of a web site by issuing a digital certificate.

The above technologies interact to accomplish secure communication between two participants (typically a user and a system.) In order for the communication to be secure, these conditions must be satisfied:

1. The user has been authenticated by the system.
2. The system has been authenticated by the user.
3. The communication is encrypted.

Condition 1 above, is the concern of the system and system administrators, and is standard policy and practice in most secure environments. Condition 2 above is the sole responsibility of the user, and requires that the user confirm the identity of the server they are communicating with, i.e., is it the server they intend to exchange data with? Users can authenticate servers by inspection of the connection details: the URL, the digital certificate, etc. Condition 3 above is a cooperative effort between the server and the user's client program, e.g., web browser. In some cases, the server can force a secure connection, but this is only effective if Condition 2 is satisfied. In cases where the server does not enforce a secure connection, the user needs to verify that the protocol in use is encrypted, and change if necessary, e.g., switch from an http connection to https. This study is mainly concerned with conditions 2 and 3, since these are conditions that require user participation. Consider the following combinations in Table 1.

The matrix in Table 1 represents all the possible combinations of false and real systems, false and real users, and encryption status. Encrypted communication between the "real" user and "real" system is the ideal situation. This is shown in the upper left most cell of the matrix, and labeled (1). The remaining combinations are numbered for ease of reference.

The items of concern to this study are bolded (2, 5, and 6). These items require awareness and knowledge on the part of the user to verify that the system that they are communicating with is the real system, and that the information they are sending is being encrypted. Item 2 is the classic server spoofing attack on users where the user is tricked into believing that the server is real. Once the username and password is transmitted to the false system, the hackers can log in to the real system using the user's credentials. Item 5 is where the user and server are real, but the communication can be intercepted. Item 6 is the combination of the two.

Many users rely mainly on the "system" they are communicating with to ensure secure communication. This may be due to the belief that security is a technical issue that is not in their control. This of course ignores the many variations on "soft hacks" or "social engineering" that are the basis of most confirmed security compromises. System Administrators (SA) also tend to focus on the technical issues: authentication of the user, and encryption. SAs tend to ignore the system authentication portion. Security compromises that occur through lack of system authentication (items 3 and 7) are usually thought to be out of the control of the SA, but may be ultimately tracked to server spoofing (items 2 and 6). Therefore, it behooves the SA to use well-recognized, standard mechanisms for server identification and educate users to verify server identities.

The primary research questions of this project are:

1.   What is the level of awareness of SSL and HTTPS?
2.   What is the level of understanding of SSL and HTTPS?
3.   How do the awareness and understanding of SSL and HTTPS affect user's behavior online?

These questions are important to securely participating in electronic commerce. Without an awareness and understanding of basic security technologies, users are susceptible to common security threats as shown in Table 1, items 2, 5, and 6. Question 3 addresses whether awareness and understanding actually impact behavior. User behavior also impacts system administrators, since a user who falls prey to a server spoof gives their authentication information away, which leads to compromising the real server.

These are important to e-commerce in a broad sense; not only are monetary transactions at risk, but all communications between a user and a server. Using a university as a typical organization,

here are some examples of secure connections that are at risk: email, university portal, grades, and other personal information.

## BACKGROUND

Security research breaks down into two major areas: technical and human factors. Technical research falls mainly in the realm of "computer security" while human factors falls into the realm of "human computer interaction". The relatively new area of "information security" recognizes the importance of both computer security and human factors. Much research has been done on the technical aspects of security mechanisms, while the human factors are less well examined (Dourish, Grinter, Delgado de la Flor, & Joseph, 2004). Technical aspects of security are typically designed to be secure, and have either provable or quantifiable qualities. The human factors typically require a qualitative analysis and empirical studies to evaluate.

The literature recognizes that the major weakness in security is the user (Smith, 2003), and that users do not necessarily understand the security mechanisms (Whitten & Tygar, 1999). Additional research shows that a variety of issues can affect user's trust of a web site, including "look-and-feel", download times, security policy statements, and too many or too few advertisements (Turner et al., 2001). Other research focuses on the usability issues of secure systems (Whitten & Tygar, 1998), and indicates that stronger security mechanisms such as browser pop-up security warnings and

*Table 1. Matrix representing all possible combinations of false and real systems*

| | | System | |
|---|---|---|---|
| | | **Real** | **False** |
| **User** | **Real** | Encrypted (1) Unencrypted (5) | Encrypted (2) Unencrypted (6) |
| | **False** | Encrypted (3) Unencrypted (7) | Encrypted (4) Unencrypted (8) |

enforcing strong passwords can inhibit the usability of systems.

There is limited research that directly straddles the human computer interaction and computer security areas. Papers that touch on both areas range from shoulder-surfing (Tari, Ozok, & Holden, 2006) to consumer behavior centered on trust (Nilsson, Adams, & Herd, 2005) and privacy (Conti & Sobiesk, 2007). The gap in the research is widely recognized (Ye, Yuan, & Smith, 2005; Dourish et al., 2003; Adams & Sasse, 1999; Brodie et al., 2005; Greenwald et al., 2004), but not often studied directly.

Adams and Sasse (1999) administered a web-based survey related to password usage. They concluded that users generally did not know how to judge the strength of a password, and that password policies are not always compatible with work practices. Dourish et al. (2004) studied attitudes and practical issues around security. One main conclusion is that age affects attitudes and compliance with security measures, with younger respondents having a higher level of trust in the technologies. Friedman et al. (2002) report results from an open-ended questionnaire, concluding that users are largely unable to correctly identify a secure connection. Finally, Gross and Rosson (2007) administered a survey measuring concern about security and privacy threats, finding that users can distinguish between security/privacy threats and general computer concerns.

It is generally recognized that there are trade-offs involved in implementing secure systems. The usability/security trade-off is most commonly referred to (e.g., DeWitt & Kuljis, 2006). This reflects some of the common security policies that attempt to increase security through dictating user policy, e.g., password policies. A policy that requires, for instance, very long passwords decreases the likelihood of the password being cracked by technical means, but may be less convenient, since the user must remember a longer password, and it takes longer to type. In addition, the policy may ultimately be less secure, since the user may be more likely to write the password down and place it in close proximity to the machine, increasing the likelihood that the password is obtained by non-technical means.

As a result of the usability issues, it is not uncommon for systems to subvert the standard https, "hide" the https connection within HTML frames, or use a non-standard, less-commonly-accepted, encryption technology. These steps can improve usability, since they eliminate the need for the user to authenticate the server; the users are asked to "trust us, the server is secure." However, the user is then not able to authenticate the server. In general, the "trust us" paradigm reduces the awareness of the security measures, and plays into the hands of spoofers. It also trains the users to avoid authenticating the servers they access, and ultimately makes users and systems more vulnerable.

This study is exploratory in nature, and does not state a priori hypotheses. It is meant to begin the exploration of user perceptions in the realm of security. However, we are interested in some basic questions. Firstly, should researchers spend effort on this area of research? Secondly, what are some high-level observations that can be made to direct research in this area? Thirdly, are there demographic or other factors that might affect users' perceptions in this area?

## RESEARCH METHODS

The study will consists of a background survey, covering online activities, perceptions, and practices. Survey participants for this study consisted of students of a university from undergraduate level introduction to information systems sections.

The survey consists of the following sections:

- **Demographic information:** Age, gender

- **Basic technological literacy:** Frequency of computer use, online experience, etc.
- General usage
- **Importance of security mechanisms:** An https connection? A certifying authority logo? Inspect a digital certificate?
- Usage of security mechanisms
- Password habits

The survey instruments included both likert-type scales and open-ended questions. Since this study is exploratory in nature, data analysis consisted of univariate measures on the entire sample and by sub-groups as called for, as well as cross tabulations.

The survey was administered anonymously in the Fall semester of 2006. The course through which the survey was given is taken by all business majors, generally during the sophomore or junior years. Some students were given incentive to take the survey (extra credit) but none were penalized if the survey was not completed, and many of the respondents took the survey without incentive. The survey resulted in 135 usable responses, with 45% males, with 89% between the ages of 17 and 22, the rest older.

The survey sample was mainly one of convenience: a set of college students currently enrolled in an introductory Information Systems course. The main biases we expect from this demographic, compared with the general population, are: 1) a relatively high technological sophistication, and 2) a relatively high level of trust in technology (Dourish et al., 2004). With relatively high technical sophistication, this sample might be better able to assess security risks than the general population. However, this sample also tends to trust technology more, which might lead passing over security assessment. We attempt to control for the first concern by asking self-reported general technical knowledge. The second concern must be qualitatively considered when drawing conclusions from the results.

## RESULTS

We first asked a question to gauge respondents' general level of technical sophistication. Table 2 gives the responses for respondents' view of their own general technical knowledge. Interestingly, the self-reported general knowledge level does not fit a normal distribution, with more respondents viewing their general knowledge as above average. This may be relatively accurate, considering the demographic of the sample, i.e., young college students.

We next asked about their general usage of various technologies: web browsing, email, chat, internet phone, online banking (transferring funds, checking balances), and online billpay. It was not surprising that 92% used a web browser on a daily basis, and 93% used email on a daily basis. Table 3 shows the likert-type scale that was used to measure usage with regard to Chat. These results were somewhat surprising: 75% use chat daily or every few days, and only 10% never use chat.

Table 3 also shows the usage of internet phone. By this we mean services such as Skype, where a microphone and webcam are used, rather than services such as Vonage, where traditional phones are connected to broadband connections. Clearly, this technology is not being adopted by this demographic. Online banking appears to have been adopted by the majority, but the frequency of use varies significantly. Online billpay is not as well-adopted as online banking, but more than half use the service, however infrequently. This is as expected considering the sample of students. As

*Table 2. General knowledge*

| Rating | Response % |
|---|---|
| Well below average | 0% |
| Below average | 7% |
| Average | 60% |
| Above Aveage | 30% |
| Well Above Average | 3% |

*Table 3. Service usage*

| Frequency | Web Browsing | Email | Chat | Internet Phone e.g., Skype | Online Banking | BillPay |
|---|---|---|---|---|---|---|
| Every day | 86% | 90% | 47% | 4% | 20% | 5% |
| Every few days | 11% | 9% | 15% | 1% | 26% | 5% |
| About once a week | 2% | 0% | 6% | 1% | 21% | 5% |
| Several times per month | 0% | 0% | 7% | 4% | 14% | 16% |
| Several times per year | 1% | 1% | 5% | 5% | 7% | 19% |
| Never | 0% | 0% | 19% | 84% | 12% | 48% |

these students enter the work force, based on their adoption of online banking, we expect that online billpay will be adopted.

We next asked a series of questions about their consumer behavior online. This, we felt, was a usage that concerned security since it entailed online payments, potentially involving entities other than their bank.

Column 1 of Table 4 shows the frequency of purchases of tangible products from a well-known online merchant, e.g., Walmart.com. Only 13% of the respondents have never done this, with most making purchases several times per year.

Table 4 also shows the frequency of purchases of electronic products, such as audio or video files from a well-known online merchant, e.g., Itunes.com. Notice that 10% of respondents made these purchases once a week or more, but 43% also never made this kind of purchase. This is an interesting contrast with tangible products. It seems that consumers of intangible products

become heavier consumers in comparison with tangible products. In general, however, more people were willing to buy tangible products online than intangible products.

The last two columns of Table 4 show consumer-to-consumer transaction frequencies. Clearly, fewer individuals were making sales to other individuals. However, 61% of individuals had bought from another individual on the internet.

Table 5 shows the numbers of accounts, usernames, and passwords of respondents. Clearly, people use the same username for multiple accounts, but they also use common passwords across multiple accounts, which can be a security risk. Another question asked if they used stronger or weaker passwords for different accounts: 46% said yes. This is a good indicator, in that respondents are aware that all passwords are not equally secure.

We next asked a series of questions regarding how they judge the security of a web site. We first

*Table 4. Consumer behavior*

| Frequency | Tangible product, Well-Known Merchant | Digital product, Well-known Merchant | Purchase from individual | Sell to individual |
|---|---|---|---|---|
| Every day | 1% | 1% | 0% | 1% |
| Every few days | 0% | 5% | 0% | 2% |
| About once a week | 2% | 4% | 1% | 0% |
| Several times per month | 17% | 10% | 6% | 2% |
| Several times per year | 67% | 37% | 54% | 19% |
| Never | 13% | 43% | 39% | 76% |

*Table 5. Numbers of accounts and passwords*

|  | Number of Accounts | Number of Usernames | Number of Passwords |
|---|---|---|---|
| none | 1% | 1% | 1% |
| 1-5 | 54% | 85% | 87% |
| 6-10 | 30% | 12% | 11% |
| 11-20 | 13% | 2% | 1% |
| Over 20 | 3% | 0% | 0% |

asked how important each item was on this scale: (Very Unimportant, Unimportant, Neutral, Important, Very Important). Then we asked how often they used that feature on this scale: (Never, Almost Never, Sometimes, Almost Always, Always). Table 6 summarizes the responses for this series of questions. The reported Importance in this table is the percentage that responded as important or very important. The Usage reported in this table is the percentage that responded as almost always or always. Clearly, there is a difference between known importance and compliance with people's own knowledge. Surprisingly, more respondents judge site reputation as more important than the browser lock, protocol, URL, and digital certificate. The items are reported in, roughly, level of sophistication or awareness. We see that as the methods require more technical

sophistication, both the importance and usage decline.

In addition to reporting the responses above, we have also performed cross-tabulations to shed more light on user perceptions. The cross-tabulations focus on user consistency, gender biases, and the effect of knowledge on compliance. Table 7 reports the cross-tabulations for the user consistency with respect to inspection of the URL of a web site. This reports the same data from Table 6 in another manner. The table gives the percentage of responses for each combination of importance and usage. For instance, the cell in the upper left indicates that 15% of the respondents consider verifying the URL as very important and in practice, they always verify the URL. The bolded items in the diagonal would be considered "consistent", in that their practice is in line with

*Table 6. Importance and usage of security items*

| Item | Importance | Usage |
|---|---|---|
| **Reputation**<br>the reputation of the web site that you are accessing | 84% | 61% |
| **Peer**<br>friends' level of trust of the website | 76% | 49% |
| **Browser Lock**<br>the lock icon/picture that appears at the bottom of the browser window | 66% | 38% |
| **Protocol**<br>http vs. https | 43% | 30% |
| **URL**<br>verifying the URL of the site you are at | 57% | 42% |
| **Cert**<br>verifying the digital certificate of the site you are at | 46% | 23% |

*Table 7. URL inspection consistency crosstab*

| | | Actual Practice | | | | | |
|---|---|---|---|---|---|---|---|
| | | **Always** | **Almost Always** | **Sometimes** | **Almost Never** | **Never** | **Don't Know What This Is** |
| Importance | Very Important | 15% | 2% | 3% | 1% | | 2% |
| | Important | 3% | 15% | 13% | 3% | 2% | |
| | Neutral | | 5% | 15% | 7% | 1% | 5% |
| | Unimportant | | 2% | | 2% | 1% | |
| | Very Unimportant | 1% | | | 1% | 1% | |
| | Don't Know what this is | | | | | | 2% |

how important they consider URL verification. In general, users are fairly consistent, with 48% on the diagonal (excluding "don't know"). If we add in the "near" diagonal, we see that 32% more responding in a "fairly" consistent manner. Respondents in the upper right cells (10%) exhibit risky behavior in that they consider the mechanism important, but do not use it. Respondents in the lower left (3%) exhibit risk-averse behavior. The URL inspection crosstab is representative of the other crosstabs related to consistency.

To more examine more deeply the inconsistencies between knowledge and usage, we construct a "consistency" metric from likert-scale survey responses. First, the likert-scale responses within

each individual were scored according to Table 8. (Note that responses where the user has no knowledge of the security mechanism are thrown out.) This is equivalent to scoring Actual Practice values (Always, Almost Always, ..., Never) as (5, 4, ..., 1), and Importance values (Very Important, Important, ..., Very Unimportant) as (5, 4, ..., 1), then subtracting Importance from Actual Practice. Large positive numbers can be interpreted as "very optimistic" or "trusting" users who recognize the importance of a security mechanism, but do not use it. Large negative numbers can be interpreted as "very pessimistic" or "untrusting" users who regularly use security mechanisms even the ones they don't perceive as important. Users whose

*Table 8. Likert-scale consistency metric construction*

| | | Actual Practice | | | | | |
|---|---|---|---|---|---|---|---|
| | | **Always** | **Almost Always** | **Sometimes** | **Almost Never** | **Never** | **Don't Know What This Is** |
| Importance | Very Important | 0 | 1 | 2 | 3 | 4 | NA |
| | Important | -1 | 0 | 1 | 2 | 3 | NA |
| | Neutral | -2 | -1 | 0 | 1 | 2 | NA |
| | Unimportant | -3 | -2 | -1 | 0 | 1 | NA |
| | Very Unimportant | -4 | -3 | -2 | -1 | 0 | NA |
| | Don't Know what this is | NA | NA | NA | NA | NA | NA |

*Table 9. Consistency metric t-tests by security mechanism*

| Security mechanism | Mean | N | Stddevn | t-value |
|---|---|---|---|---|
| Reputation | 0.53 | 134 | 0.82 | 7.48 |
| Peer | 0.51 | 134 | 0.83 | 7.08 |
| Browser Lock | 0.45 | 106 | 0.79 | 5.87 |
| Protocol | 0.48 | 96 | 0.85 | 5.55 |
| URL | 0.31 | 119 | 1.00 | 3.40 |
| Cert | 0.84 | 95 | 1.08 | 7.57 |

responses all score as zero could be interpreted as appropriately consistent between knowledge and usage.

Based on the consistency metric scored as in Table 8, we use t-tests for the null hypothesis that the consistency metric is greater than zero (i.e., one-tailed). Table 9 summarizes t-tests on the consistency metric by security mechanism. Note that all t-values are significant with p-values < 0.0005. Although this consistency metric is difficult to interpret in an absolute manner, it appears that users are generally "optimistic" or "trusting" with regard to the security technologies. This is consistent with the observations of Dourish et al. (2003), who concluded that younger people are generally more trusting of technology. In a relative sense, it appears that users are most consistent with regard to verifying the URL, but least consistent with regard to verifying the Digital Certificate. In general, the URL is much easier to inspect than the Digital Certificate, so users comply more with URL inspection than Digital Certificate inspection.

We were also able to perform cross tabulations to examine the effect of gender on usage of technologies that have security-related issues. Table 10 shows chat usage frequency by gender. The survey had 55% female respondents and 45% male respondents. The numbers show the percentage of each gender's responses, e.g., the percentage of females that use chat every day is 49%. Chat usage is reflective of the other usages, so we report only the single table here. In general, there do not appear to be significant gender differences, although there is a larger percentage of males that never use chat.

Table 11 shows how frequently users inspect for a secure protocol (https) contrasted by how they view their own technical knowledge. The columns indicate the users' self-reported general computer knowledge. Notably, no respondents viewed their computer knowledge as "well below

*Table 10. Chat usage by gender*

| Usage Frequency | Female | Male |
|---|---|---|
| Every day | 49% | 47% |
| Every few days | 15% | 16% |
| About once a week | 7% | 4% |
| Several times per month | 7% | 4% |
| Several times per year | 4% | 7% |
| Never | 16% | 22% |
| No response | 2% | 2% |

average", so the column is not shown here. The rows indicate how often the user inspects the protocol. We see that, in general, inspection of the protocol correlates with self-reported computer knowledge. However, 17% of respondents who consider themselves above average do not know what a secure protocol is, and 23% of average users do not know a secure protocol. This perhaps confirms their self-assessment, but is also worrisome.

## CONCLUSION

The results reported above shed some light on user behavior, but what do the results say about the level of awareness and understanding of SSL and HTTPS? Table 6 speaks to these issues best. The items that indicate awareness are "Browser Lock", "Protocol", "URL", and "Cert". The browser lock would indicate, in a graphical manner, an encrypted connection. Protocol is a non-graphical manner to verify encryption. Inspection and verification of the URL is one part of authenticating the server, the other part being inspection and verification of the digital certificate.

From responses in Table 6, we can see that less than half of respondents consider the digital certificate important, and less than 25% actually inspect the certificate on a regular basis. This is worrisome, but to some extent understandable. A

digital certificate is somewhat technical in nature, and is not readily apparent to the user, taking some extra awareness and effort to inspect. In some situations, the browser may report a conflict between URL and digital certificate, but these messages are often over-ruled by the user based on other factors: reputation, peers' trust, etc.

In general, respondents use "soft" authentication, relying on site reputation or peer trust more than technical authentication. This may be perceived as adequate as long as users limit their activities purchasing from well-known merchants (Table 4). However, without server authentication, "soft" authentication practitioners are ripe for site spoofing attacks. Furthermore, we see that users are engaging in a variety of activities (Tables 3 and 4), and tend to use common passwords across multiple accounts.

This exploratory research should provide the motivation for future research that is more descriptive and prescriptive in nature. Descriptive studies could observer directly users' usage of web sites, personal password management, and mental models of security mechanisms. Surveys of system administrators might shed light on their views and policies with regard to system authentication. Prescriptive research might examine the effects of differing password policies or browser security messages.

Clearly, there is a disconnect between knowledge and practice, which needs further explora-

*Table 11. Protocol inspection by self-reported knowledge*

|  | **Well Above Average** | **Above Average** | **Average** | **Below Average** |
|---|---|---|---|---|
| Always | 25% | 15% | 14% | 0% |
| Almost Always | 50% | 17% | 16% | 11% |
| Sometimes | 25% | 20% | 26% | 11% |
| Almost Never | 0% | 22% | 12% | 0% |
| Never | 0% | 7% | 6% | 0% |
| Don't know what this is | 0% | 17% | 23% | 78% |
| No response | 0% | 2% | 2% | 0% |
| Total | 100% | 100% | 100% | 100% |

tion. Perhaps users perceive the risks as very low compared to the inconveniences associated with the security technologies. Or perhaps users have over-rated their technological sophistication and knowledge of the security technologies. With a student sample, it might be useful to perform a pre/post survey where user behavior is evaluated before and after covering security technologies.

Based on the consistency metrics, some security mechanisms such as URL verification are used more regularly than others (e.g., Digital Certificate verification). This could be explained partially by the usability/security trade-off, but improvements may be feasible in the human computer interface to improve usability without sacrificing security. Another explanation might be that users do not perceive the risks and consequences of security failures to be significant enough to warrant the extra inconvenience.

A better understanding of how users perceive the basic security mechanisms of the internet will enable organizations to develop better systems and security policies. We anticipate that future studies could involve user perceptions of other security mechanisms such as firewalls, password selection and policies, and personal digital certificates. Hopefully, this exploratory study will lead to a model of user perception of security and its technologies.

## REFERENCES

Adams, A., & Sasse, M. A. (1999). Users are Not the Enemy: Why users compromise computer security mechanisms and how to take remedial measures. *Communications of the ACM, 42*(12), 41–46.

Brodie, C., Karat, C., Karat, J., & Feng, J. (2005, July 6-8). Usable Security and Privacy: A Case Study of Developing Privacy Management Tools. In *Proceedings of the Symposium on Usable Security and Security (SOUPS)*, Pittsburgh, PA (pp. 35-43).

Conti, G., & Sobiesk, E. (2007, July 18-20). An Honest Man Has Nothing to Fear: User Perceptions on Web-based Information Disclosure. In *Proceedings of the Symposium on Usable Privacy and Security (SOUPS),* Pittsburgh, PA (pp. 112-121).

De Paula, R., Ding, X., Dourish, P., Nies, K., Pillet, B., Redmiles, D., et al. (2005, July 6-8). Two Experiences Designing for Effective Security. In *Proceedings of the Symposium on Usable Privacy and Security (SOUPS)*, Pittsburgh, PA (pp. 25-34).

DeWitt, A., & Kuljis, J. (2006). Is Usable Security an Oxymoron? *Interaction, 13*(3), 41–44.

Dourish, P., Grinter, R. E., Delgado de la Flor, J., & Joseph, M. (2003). Security in the Wild: User Strategies for Managing Security as an Everyday, Practical Problem. *Personal and Ubiquitous Computing, 8*, 391–401.

Fogg, B. J., Soohoo, C., Danielson, D., Marable, L., Stanford, J., & Tauber, E. R. (2002). *How Do People Evaluate a Web Site's Credibility? Results from a large study.* Retrieved from http://www.consumerwebwatch.org/pdfs/stanfordPTL.pdf

Friedman, B., Hurley, D., Howe, D., Felten, E., & Nissenbaum, H. (2002, April 20-25). Users' conceptions of risks and harms on the web: a comparative study. In *Proceedings of CHI 2002*, Minneapolis, MN (pp. 746-747).

Greenwald, S. J., Olthoff, K. G., Raskin, V., & Ruch, W. (2004). The User Non-Acceptance Paradigm: INFOSEC's Dirty Little Secret. In *Proceedings of the 2004 Workshop on New Security Paradigms*, Hunts Point, NS, Canada (pp. 35-43).

Gross, J. B., & Rosson, M. B. (2007, March 30-31). Looking for Trouble: End-User Security Management. In *Proceedings of the 2007 Symposium on Computer Human Interaction for the Management of Information Technology*, Cambridge, MA (Vol. 10).

Gross, J. B., & Rosson, M. B. (2007, July 18-20). End User Concern about Security and Privacy Threats. In *Proceedings of the Symposium on Usable Privacy and Security (SOUPS),* Pittsburgh, PA (pp. 167-168).

Hardee, J. B., West, R., & Mayhorn, C. B. (2006). To Download or Not to Download: An Examination of Computer Security Decision Making. *Interaction, 13*(3), 32–37.

Hassell, L., & Wiedenbeck, S. (2004). *Human Factors and Information Security* (Tech. Rep.). Philadelphia, PA: Drexel University. Retrieved from http://clam.rutgers.edu/~birget/grPssw/hasselSue.pdf

Moores, T. T., & Dhillon, G. (2003). Do Privacy Seals in E-Commerce Really Work? *Communications of the ACM, 46*(12), 265–271.

Nilsson, M., Adams, A., & Herd, S. (2005, April 2-7). Building Security and Trust in Online Banking. In *Proceedings of the CHI 2005 Conference,* Portland, OR (pp. 1701-1704).

Schneier, B. (2000). *Secrets & Lies: Digital Security in a Networked World.* Indianapolis, IN: John Wiley.

Singh, S., Cabraal, A., Demosthenous, C., Astbrink, G., & Furlong, M. (2007, April 28-May 3). Password Sharing: Implications for Security Design Based on Social Practice. In *Proceedings of the CHI 2007 Conference,* San Jose, CA (pp. 895-904).

Smith, S. W. (2003). Humans in the Loop: Human-Computer Interaction and Security. *IEEE Security & Privacy, 1*(3), 75–79.

Tari, F., Ozok, A. A., & Holden, S. H. (2006, July 12-14). A Comparison of Perceived and Real Shoulder-surfing Risks between Alphanumeric and Graphical Passwords. In *Proceedings of the Symposium On Usable Privacy and Security (SOUPS),* Pittsburgh, PA (pp. 56-66).

Turner, C. W., Zavod, M., & Yurcik, W. (2001, November). Factors that affect the perception of security and privacy of e-commerce web sites. In B. Gavish (Ed.), *Proceedings of the 4th International Conference on Electronic Commerce Research (ICER-4),* Dallas, TX (Vol. 2, pp. 628-636).

Whitten, A., & Tygar, J. D. (1998). *Usability of Security: A Case Study* (Tech. Rep. No. CMU-CS-98-155). Pittsburgh, PA: Carnegie Mellon University.

Whitten, A., & Tygar, J. D. (1999, August 23-26). Why Johnny Can't Encrypt: A Usability Evaluation of PGP 5.0. In *Proceedings of the 9th USENIX Security Symposium,* Washington, DC.

Ye, E. Z., Yuan, Y., & Smith, S. (2002). *Trusted Paths for Browsers* (Tech. Rep.). Hanover, NH: Dartmouth College, Department of Computer Science. Retrieved from http://www.cs.dartmouth.edu/~pkilab/demos/spoofing

Yurcik, W., Sharm, A., & Doss, D. (2002, March). False Impressions: Contrasting Perceptions of Security as a Major Impediment to Achieving Survivable Systems. In *Proceedings of the IEEE/CERT/SEI 4th Survivability Workshop,* Vancouver, BC, Canada. Washington, DC: IEEE Computer Society.

*This work was previously published in the International Journal of Information Security and Privacy, Volume 5, Issue 2, edited by Hamid Nemati, pp. 1-12, copyright 2011 by IGI Publishing (an imprint of IGI Global).*

# Chapter 6
# Secure Two-Party Association Rule Mining Based on One-Pass FP-Tree

**Golam Kaosar**
*Victoria University, Australia*

**Xun Yi**
*Victoria University, Australia*

## ABSTRACT

*Frequent Path tree (FP-tree) is a popular method to compute association rules and is faster than Apriori-based solutions in some cases. Association rule mining using FP-tree method cannot ensure entire privacy since frequency of the itemsets are required to share among participants at the first stage. Moreover, FP-tree method requires two scans of database transactions which may not be the best solution if the database is very large or the database server does not allow multiple scans. In addition, one-pass FP-tree can accommodate continuous or periodically changing databases without restarting the process as opposed to a regular FP-tree based solution. In this paper, the authors propose a one-pass FP-tree method to perform association rule mining without compromising any data privacy among two parties. A fully homomorphic encryption system over integer numbers is applied to ensure secure computation among two data sites without disclosing any number belongs to themselves.*

## 1 INTRODUCTION

Data mining, often referred as the major part in knowledge discovery in database (KDD) is the process of discovering knowledge for decision making in business by utilizing patterns or models existed in data. Data mining has been one of the hot research areas for at least last two decades.

Data mining process is a challenging work because of many reasons, such as various kind of knowledge is required for different databases and administrations, in many cases data sources are distributed, format of the data is diversified (e.g., text, audio, video, image, etc.), privacy preservation of the data, efficiency of the mining process, presentation of the outcome, etc. Some

DOI: 10.4018/978-1-4666-2050-6.ch006

of the applications of data mining includes but not limited to: advertising, bioinformatics, customer relationship management (CRM), database marketing, fraud detection, e-commerce, health care services, manufacturing, process control, sports and entertainment, telecommunications, web applications, etc.

Association rule mining (ARM) first introduced in 1966 (Hajek, Havel, & Chytil, 1966) is one of the straightforward data mining process which can be further computed in various methods such as Apriori (Agrawal & Srikant, 1994), FP-tree (Han, Pei, & Yin, 2000), Eclat (Zaki, 2000), One-attribute-rule, etc. FP-tree is a method to compute association rule mining (ARM) which was first proposed by Han et al. (2000) and Han, Pei, Yin, and Mao (2004). FP-tree based solution is advantageous than Apriori based solution in some cases due to following reasons:

- Apriori technique requires multiple scanning of database in each iteration. FP-tree requires two scans only. One scan generates frequent items and second scan generates a FP-tree from which frequent itemsets can be generated.
- Apriori technique generates enormous number of candidate itemsets in each iteration which require lot of computation. FP-tree does not create such candidate itemsets.

Ensuring data privacy is a compulsory requirement before integrating data to be mined. Definition of privacy itself varies from context to context. In the age of information technology the definition of privacy may be referred as the right of concealing one's information and have control over the information in some extent (Ackerman, Cranor, & Reagle, 1999; Cockcroft & Clutterbuck, 2001). Another definition for information privacy (Victorian Government, Department of Human Service, 1999) is "Information privacy

refers to a group of related rights regarding an individual's control over the collection, use, release, and disposal of their personal information. Personal information is information which allows an individual to be identified, and it can appear in any form (for example, sound, image, text, biological-based) and be recorded in any medium (for example, print or electronic)". Most countries have established privacy acts to preserve data privacy. This privacy can be achieved in basic two ways - statistical method and cryptographic method. Cryptographic method is capable to maximize both privacy and accuracy by the cost of high mathematical computation.

Homomorphic encryption system is most successfully used in preserving privacy in ARM algorithm. Original homomorphic cryptosystems, such as RSA (Rivest, Shamir, & Adleman, 1978), El Gamal (1985), Benaloh (Clarkson, 1994), and Paillier (1999), fully homomorphic encryption for integers (Dijk, Gentry, Halevi, & Vaikuntanathan, 2010), etc., are used in various privacy preserving ARM algorithms. A homomorphic encryption based secure two-party computation technique is used in preserving privacy in ARM in Ouyang and Huang (2006). Homomorphic encryption based association rule mining algorithm is also proposed in Kantarcioglu and Clifton (2004) which minimizes the information sharing with minimum mining overhead. Paillier cryptosystem based homomorphic encryption system and semi-trusted mixer based privacy preserving distributed association rule mining algorithm is proposed in Yi and Zhang (2007).

There are various other techniques in preserving privacy in ARM algorithms too. Luo, Zhao, and Le (2009) in survey on privacy preserving ARM algorithm has divided privacy preserving techniques into three classes - heuristic-based, reconstruction-based, and cryptography-based. Data perturbation techniques (Evmievski, Gehrke, & Srikant, 2003; Rizvi & Haritsam, 2002) which, basically propose a technique to estimate association rules from perturbed data which are very much close to the original data. Data sanitization is a technique to remove sensitive information from the data such a way that sensitive association rules cannot be generated from the data. Such technique is proposed in Atallah, Elmagarmid, Ibrahim, Bertino, and Verykios (1999). Sensitive association rule hiding technique is proposed in Dasseni, Verykios, Elmagarmid, and Bertino (2001) as well. It prevents sensitive association rules to be disclosed. The generation of sensitive rules is also prevented by hiding corresponding frequently large itemsets in the datasets. Data blocking concept in association rule mining algorithm is proposed in Saygin, Verykios, and Clifton (2001) and Saygin, Verykios, and Elmagarmid (2002). Sensitive data is randomized before sharing and combined together from different parties to mine association rules in Evmievski, Srikant, Agrawal, and Gehrke (2002). Privacy preserving association rule mining for vertically partitioned database is proposed in Vaidya and Clifton (2002) with some weaknesses in terms of leakage of privacy. Zhong (2007) proposes more privacy preserving ARM techniques both for vertically and horizontally partitioned database.

Though FP-tree based solution is more efficient than Apriori based solution, applying privacy requirement in Apriori is simpler and more feasible than FP-tree based solutions. Preserving privacy in FP-tree based solution is apparently impractical in spite of its being efficient. Moreover, Su and Sakurai (2008) have proposed some privacy preserving solution in FP-tree. But these solutions disclose some intermediate mining results. In this paper we propose a one-pass FP-tree based privacy preserving association rule mining algorithm which works for two parties possessing horizontally partitioned databases. Our proposed solution does not disclose any intermediate mining result.

The organization of the paper is as follows: Section 2 discusses about some background knowledge relating to the topic of the paper. Sec-

tion 3 and Section 4 discuss the model definition and the proposed solution respectively. Section 5 discusses the analysis of the solution and finally Section 6 concludes the paper.

## 2 BACKGROUND

In this section some background knowledge relating to the topic of the paper is discussed.

### 2.1 Association Rule Mining

Association rule mining (ARM) is a popular and efficient way to discover correlations (known as rules) among variables in a large database. Based on interestingness, ARM is capable to discover some knowledge from huge transactional data which is apparently intelligible. As for an example, an ARM algorithm may discover a rule {sugar, flour}..{yeast} from a supermarket transactional data which implies that if a customer buys sugar and flour then most probably he will buy yeast too. If this correlation is revealed to the supermarket authority, they may put all these three items in same aisle which may make the supermarket more shopping-friendly to customers.

Let us consider, in a distributed data mining environment collective database DB is subdivided into $DB_1$, $DB_2$, ..., $DB_N$ in distributed

*Figure 1. A simple secure multiparty computation (SMC) model showing private inputs and public output of the participants*

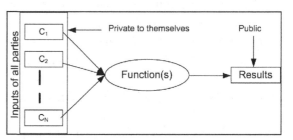

*Figure 2. 4-bit two's complement numbers' representation with sign bit or most significant bit (MSB)*

| MSB | | | | | MSB | | | | |
|---|---|---|---|---|---|---|---|---|---|
| 0 | 0 | 0 | 0 | =0 | 1 | 0 | 0 | 0 | =-8 |
| 0 | 0 | 0 | 1 | =1 | 1 | 0 | 0 | 1 | =-7 |
| 0 | 0 | 1 | 0 | =2 | 1 | 0 | 1 | 0 | =-6 |
| 0 | 0 | 1 | 1 | =3 | 1 | 0 | 1 | 1 | =-5 |
| 0 | 1 | 0 | 0 | =4 | 1 | 1 | 0 | 0 | =-4 |
| 0 | 1 | 0 | 1 | =5 | 1 | 1 | 0 | 1 | =-3 |
| 0 | 1 | 1 | 0 | =6 | 1 | 1 | 1 | 0 | =-2 |
| 0 | 1 | 1 | 1 | =7 | 1 | 1 | 1 | 1 | =-1 |

data sites $S_1$, $S_2$, ..., $S_N$ respectively. I= $\{i_1, i_2, ..., i_m\}$ is the set of items where each transaction T $\subseteq$ I. Typical form of an association rule is X $\Rightarrow$ Y, where X $\subseteq$ I, Y $\subseteq$ I and X $\cap$ Y=$|$ . Then two parameters are important to maintain minimum support and confidence of the rule where,

- **Support s of X $\Rightarrow$ Y:** It is the probability of a transaction in DB contains both X and Y.

- **Confidence c of X $\Rightarrow$ Y:** It is the probability of a transaction containing X will contain Y too.

Usually it is the interest of the data vendor to find all association rules having support and confidence greater than or equal to a minimum pre-set threshold value. Let us consider the definition of support and confidence for another instance of an association rule $AB \Rightarrow C$:

*Table 1. Sample transactions with frequent items in order*

| TID | Items | Frequent items (ordered) | TID | Items | Frequent items (ordered) |
|---|---|---|---|---|---|
| 1 | A,B,C | B,C,A | 11 | B,C | B,C |
| 2 | A,B,P | B,A,P | 12 | P,B,C | B,C,P |
| 3 | P,O,A,B,C | B,C,A,P | 13 | D,Q,P | P |
| 4 | D,C | C | 14 | E,B,C | B,C |
| 5 | X,Y,Z | $\phi$ | 15 | Y,Z | $\phi$ |
| 6 | X,P,A,B,C | B,C,A,P | 16 | X,Q,R | $\phi$ |
| 7 | T,P,Q | P | 17 | B,C | B,C |
| 8 | A,B,D | B,A | 18 | A,B | B,A |
| 9 | X,Y,Z | $\phi$ | 19 | A,B,C | B,C,A |
| 10 | A,B,T,P,Q | B,A,P | 20 | A,B,C | B,C,A |

*Table 2. Frequency of each item*

| Item | Frequency | Item | Frequency |
|------|-----------|------|-----------|
| A | 9 | B | 13 |
| C | 10 | D | 3 |
| O | 1 | P | 6 |
| Q | 4 | R | 1 |
| T | 2 | X | 4 |
| Y | 3 | Z | 2 |

$$Support_{AB \Rightarrow C} = s = \frac{\sum_{i=1}^{sites} SupportCount_{ABC_i}}{\sum_{i=1}^{sites} DatabaseSize_i} \quad (1)$$

$$Support_{AB} = \frac{\sum_{i=1}^{sites} SupportCount_{AB_i}}{\sum_{i=1}^{sites} DatabaseSize_i} \quad (2)$$

$$Confidence_{AB \Rightarrow C} = c = \frac{Support_{AB \Rightarrow C}}{Support_{AB}} \quad (3)$$

More detail on association rule mining process can be found in Han and Kamber (2006) and Tan, Steinbach, and Kumar (2006).

## 2.2 Secure Multiparty Computation

Privacy preserving data mining in distributed settings utilizes the concept of secure multi-party computation (SMC) proposed first by Yao (1982). Using SMC several participants can compute some common functions of their inputs without revealing individual input. At the end of the computation each party does not learn anything more than its own input and the resultant output. Let us consider $c_1$, $c_2$, ..., $c_N$ are inputs of $N$ parties. SMC computes a function F $\{c_1, c_2, ..., c_N\}$ without revealing any $c_i$ to any party. A two party computation (e.g., millionaire problem) is

a special case of SMC. A simple SMC scenario is depicted in Figure 1.

## 2.3 Two's Complement Number

Two's complement of a number is considered as the negative of the number. It can be determined by subtracting itself from a large number (must be power of two). Let us say, the number is $X$ with $N$ bits then its two's complement is equal to $2^N - X$. Two's complement can be computed in another method - two's complement of $X = \bar{X} + 1$ where $\bar{X}$ represents binary NOT operation on $X$. Figure 2 illustrates 4-bits two's complement numbers.

Two's complement concept is used in implementing subtractor in computer architecture. $X - Y$ can be computed by adding $X$ with two's complement of $Y$. That is $X - Y = X + \bar{Y} + 1$.

## 2.4 FP-Tree Based ARM Process

This section discusses the FP-tree based ARM process in the light of first proposed papers (Han et al., 2000, 2004) on FP-tree. A brief description of FP-tree is as follows:

Let us consider a transactional database $DB$ consists of transactions $T_1$, $T_2$, ..., $T_n$ where each transaction consists of some items $I = \{a_1, a_2, ..., a_k\}$. Minimum required support and confidence thresholds are $s_{min}$ and $c_{min}$ respectively. FP-tree generates complete set of

*Figure 3. FP-tree for first two transactions*

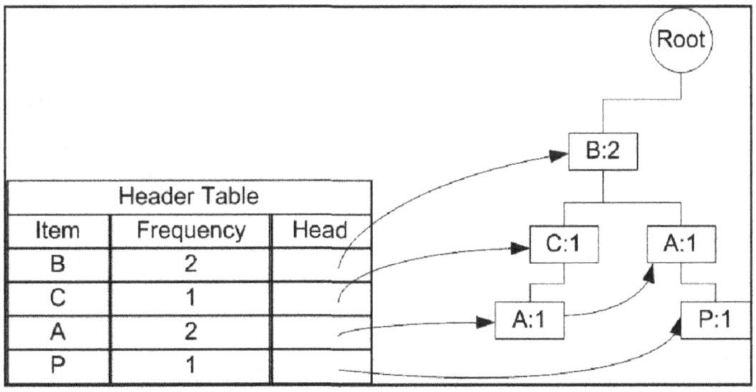

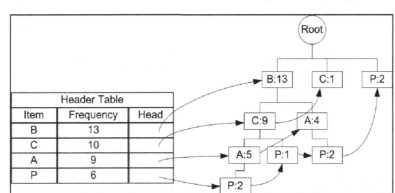

frequent patterns from the centralized database *DB* in three major stages - (1) FP-tree construction (2) Mining frequent pattern using FP-tree and (3) Association rule computation. Let us consider following example which would clarify how the basic FP-tree algorithm works.

*FP-tree example:* Let us consider the database *DB* consists of some set of transactions with their ordered frequency items (items with frequency more than the threshold) listed in Table 1.

Frequency of all items are listed in Table 2.

One scan of *DB* reveals the list of frequent items - $[(B:13),(C:10),(A:9),(P:6)]$, ordered by frequency counts. Items are accompanied with their frequency. Now the root of the FP-tree is created with empty (null) subtree. Each transaction is scanned again to create branches of the tree. As for example, for the first transaction - path

$[(B:1),(C:1),(A:1)]$ is created. In second transaction - path $[(B:2),(A:2),(P:1)]$ is created. Now the FP-tree with the header is depicted in Figure 3.

Thus, after completion of all the transactions, the formed FP-tree is shown in Figure 4.

Now let us consider items in the header table from the bottom (*P* in the example). Paths to *P* are $[B,C,A,P:2]$, $[B,C,P:1]$, $[B,A,P:2]$ and $[P:2]$. Only node leads to *P* with minimum support (in this case it is 5) is - *B*. Therefore, $[B,P:5]$ is considered as frequent. Similarly with the consideration of *A*, *C* and *B* we can compute $[C,A:5]$ and $[B,C,A:5]$, $[B,A:9]$ and $[B,C:9]$ respectively. If 1-itemset is also considered, we get the full list of frequent itemsets as follows:

*Figure 4. FP-tree for the example*

$[(B : 13), (C : 10), (A : 9), (P : 6), (BP : 5),$
$(CA : 5), (BCA : 5), (BA : 9) and (BC : 9)].$

## 2.5 Fully Homomorphic Encryption System

Homomorphic encryption is a special form of encryption where one can perform a specific algebraic operation on the plain-text by performing the same or different operation on the cipher-text. If $X$ and $Y$ are two numbers and $E$ and $D$ denotes encryption and decryption function respectively, then homomorphic encryption holds following condition for an algebraic operation such as '+':

$$D[E(X) + E(Y)] = D[E(X + Y)] \qquad (4)$$

Most homomorphic encryption systems, such as RSA (Rivest et al., 1978), El Gamal (1985), Benaloh (Clarkson, 1994), Paillier (1999), etc., are capable to perform only one operation. But fully homomorphic encryption system can be used for many operations (such as addition, multiplication, division, etc.) at the same time. Very recently proposed fully homomorphic cryptosystem (Dijk et al., 2010) has the ability to perform both addition and multiplication over the ciphertext and these operations are represented in plaintext. Hence, a untrusted party is able to operate on private or confidential data, without the ability to know what data the untrusted party is manipulating. Following two subsections (2.5.1 and 2.5.2) briefly discuss how this cryptosystem works for both binary and integer numbers respectively.

## 2.5.1 Fully Homomorphic Encryption for Binary Numbers

The fully homomorphic scheme (Dijk et al., 2010) is a simplification of an earlier work involving ideal lattices (Gentry, 2009). It encrypts a single bit (in the plaintext space) to an integer (in the ciphertext space). When these integers are added

and multiplied, the hidden bits are added and multiplied (modulo 2). The symmetric version of the encryption function is given by $c = m' + pq$, where $p$ is the private key, q is chosen randomly, and $m'$ has the same parity (or evenness) as the message $m \in \{0, 1\}$. The decryption is simply $(c \quad mod \quad p) mod \quad 2$, which recovers the bit. Hence, when we add or multiply the ciphertext, the message is manipulated accordingly.

Using the symmetric version of the cryptosystem, it is possible to construct an asymmetric version. The asymmetric version is far more useful to the association rule application, since another party must be able to encrypt in order to use the homomorphic property of the cryptosystem. The following functions define the asymmetric version of the cryptosystem (Dijk et al., 2010).

- $KeyGen(\lambda)$ :
  - Choose a random n-bit integer as the private key.

Using the private key, generate the public key as $x_i = pq_i + 2r_i$ where $q_i$ and $r_i$ are chosen randomly, for $i = 0, 1, ..., \tau$. Relabel so that $x_0$ is the largest.

*Figure 5. Displays the carry bit operation*

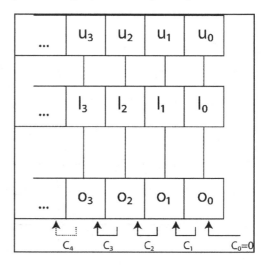

*Figure 6. One-pass FP-tree model*

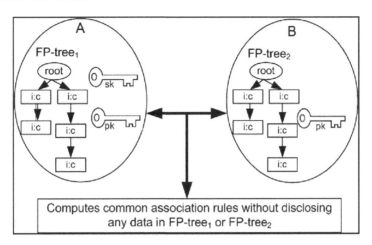

- *Encrypt$(pk, m \in \{0,1\})$:*
  - Choose a random subset $S \subseteq \{1, 2, ..., \tau\}$ and a random integer $r$, and output

$$c = (m + 2r + 2\sum_{i \in S} x_i)(\mod \quad x_0).$$

- *Decrypt$(sk, c)$:*
  - Output
    $$m = (c \quad mod \quad p) mod \quad 2$$

This asymmetric version still achieves the same level of correctness as the symmetric version. Addition and multiplication correctness is shown in Equations 5 and 6 respectively.

$$c_1 + c_2 = m'_1 + m'_2 + pq' \qquad (5)$$

$$c_1 \cdot c_2 = m'_1 \cdot m'_2 + pq' \qquad (6)$$

The $m'$ component of the encryption represents the message, and is referred to as the noise of the encryption. As long as this noise stays below the threshold equation $| m'_1 \cdot m'_2 | < \frac{p}{2}$, Equations 5 and 6 will work. It follows that adding and mul-

tiplying integer ciphertext is reduces to performing the binary XOR and AND gates on the plaintext. Hence, it is possible to construct very complicated binary circuits to evaluate on the data, without exposing the actual data. More details regarding implementation can be found in the original paper (Dijk et al. 2010).

## 2.5.2 Fully Homomorphic Encryption for Integers

The association rule mining algorithms does not operate on binary data, however. They operates on values in the integer space. Hence we need to extend the underlying cryptosystem to accommodate integer numbers. This is achieved by representing the integer as a binary vector and encrypting each bit. For instance, an 8-bit integer $z$ can be encrypted as shown in Equation 7, using the encryption function from the asymmetric version of the fully homomorphic encryption scheme.

$$E_{pk}(z) =$$
$$[E_{pk}(v_7), E_{pk}(v_6), E_{pk}(v_5), E_{pk}(v_4),$$
$$E_{pk}(v_3), E_{pk}(v_2), E_{pk}(v_1), E_{pk}(v_0)], where \ z \in \mathbb{Z}$$
$$(7)$$

Using this format it is possible to encrypt two integers and apply binary AND and XOR to each

*Algorithm 1. Comparison of two integers (M and N) without privacy concern*

$input : integers\ M, N$

$output : R\big(One\ bit\ output.\ If\ R{=}0\ then\ M{\geq}N\ else\ M{<}N.\big)$

**Begin**

$\qquad Y \leftarrow M + \bar{N} + 1$

$\qquad$ /* Subtraction of M and N gives the clue about their relative size. Two's complement of a number is equivalent to the negative of the same number. Therefore, Y = M-N.*/

$\qquad R \leftarrow Y\ AND\ 2^{n-1}$

$\qquad$ **return** $MSB(R)$ /* returns the *most significant bit (MSB)* of R. This is actually is the sign bit of the subtracted result*/

**End**

respective encrypted binary value, with the consequence of the homomorphic property of the encryption scheme. Let us consider two integers $u$ and $l$, which can be represented as binary numbers $u = \big[u_{n-1}, u_{n-2}, \ldots, u_i, \ldots, u_0\big]$ and $l = \big[l_{n-1}, l_{n-2}, \ldots, l_i, \ldots, l_0\big]$ respectively. Computer architecture implements the carry bit to perform regular addition (Brookshear, 2005) and therefore the homomorphic encryption must satisfy this requirement.

Since all homomorphic arithmetic is performed modulo 2, it is possible to satisfy this requirement. The carry bit can be calculated using the following expression in Equation 8, starting with the least significant bit.

$$c_i = (l_i \wedge u_i) \vee ((l_i \oplus u_i) \wedge c_{i-1}) \qquad (8)$$

Where $l_i$ and $u_i$ refer to the lower and upper binary vector respectively, $\wedge$ and $\vee$ represent AND and OR respectively, and $c_i$ representing the carry bit. The carry bit is initially zero $c_0 = 0$. In this expression the binary OR $\vee$ is represented by $(p \oplus q) \oplus (p \cdot q)$ where $\oplus$ and $\cdot$ refer to XOR and AND operations respectively. This substitute is needed because binary OR is not directly available as part of the homomorphism of the cryptosystem. The output bit for that position in the binary vector is calculated using Equation 9.

*Algorithm 2. Secure comparison of two encrypted integers (M and N)*

$input : ciphertexts\ \alpha, \beta$

$output : \bar{R}$ (One bit encrypted output. If R = $D_{sk}(\bar{R})$ = 0 then M ≥ N else M < N)

**Begin**

$\qquad \bar{\beta} \leftarrow HomXOR(\alpha, E_{pk}(2^n - 1))$ /* Binary negation of α */

$\qquad \bar{Y} \leftarrow HomAdd(\alpha, \bar{\beta})$ /* Homomorphic addition of α and $\bar{\beta}$ */

$\qquad \bar{Y} \leftarrow HomAdd(\bar{Y}, E_{pk}(1))$

$\qquad \bar{R} \leftarrow HomAND\big(\bar{Y}, E_{pk}\big(2^{n-1}\big)\big)$

$\qquad return\ MSB(\bar{R})$

**End**

*Algorithm 3. Secure comparison of two fractional numbers*

$input: ciphertext\,\alpha, \beta, threshold\,\gamma$

$output: \overline{R}$   (One bit encrypted output. If $R = D_{sk}\left(\overline{R}\right) = 0\,then\,\dfrac{\alpha}{\beta} \geq \gamma, else\,\dfrac{\alpha}{\beta} < \gamma$ )

**Begin**

$\quad \eta \leftarrow number\,of\,digits\,in\,\gamma\,after\,decimal$

$\quad \varepsilon \leftarrow \gamma\,X\,10^n$

$\quad TempAlpha \leftarrow 0$

$\quad for\,i = 1\,to\,10^n\,do$

$\qquad TempAlpha \leftarrow HomAdd(TempAlpha, \alpha)$

$\qquad\qquad$ /*iterative addition to avoid multiplication*/

$\quad end\,for$

$\quad TempBeta \leftarrow 0$

$\quad for\,i = 1\,to\,\varepsilon\,do$

$\qquad TempBeta \leftarrow HomAdd(TempBeta, \beta)$

$\qquad\qquad$ /*iterative addition to avoid multiplication*/

$\quad end\,for$

$\quad \dot{R} \leftarrow HomComparison\left(TempAlpha, TempBeta\right)$

$\quad return\,MSB(\overline{R})$

**End**

$$output_i = l_i \oplus u_i \oplus c_{i-1} \qquad (9)$$

Using Equation 9, it is possible to add any two n-bit integers represented as binary vectors. This is illustrated in Figure 5.

## 3 MODEL DEFINITION

Let us consider two parties or data sites $A$ (Alice) and $B$ (Bob) want to compute their common association rules privately from their combined horizontally partitioned database $DB_1$ and $DB_2$ respectively, where $DB = \{DB_1 \bigcup DB_2\}$. They have common list of items $I = \{i_1, i_2, ..., i_n\}$ where each transaction $T \subseteq I$. Both $A$ and $B$ agree to generate all association rules with a minimum support and confidence threshold value, from their combined database ($DB$) privately. In this paper

we propose a solution to this problem. Both $A$ and $B$ would generate their own one-pass FP-tree and later on they would share or combine the trees with preserving privacy.

Let us also assume the fully homomorphic encryption system discussed in previous section is used in exchanging numeric values among $A$ and $B$ securely. $A$ has both public and secret keys $pk$ and $sk$ respectively. $B$ uses $pk$ to encrypt its secret values. $B$ is never required to decrypt any result. Figure 6 depicts the proposed model.

## 4 PROPOSED SOLUTION

This section presents a secure computation technique to preserve data privacy and how a one-pass FP-tree is formed from database within a site. Finally privacy preserving frequent itemset generation technique is discussed in this section.

*Algorithm 4. One-pass FP-tree formation*

$input : DB; T; I$

$output : FP - tree$ (it contains item counts in each node and a header table to store pointer to each item)

**Begin**

$root \leftarrow null$ /*initialize the root of the tree*/

$for\, i = 1 to |DB| do$

    $flag \leftarrow 1$

    $for\, j = 1 to |T_i| do$

        $count\left(HeaderTable\left[T_i\left[j\right]\right]\right) \leftarrow count\left(HeaderTable\left[T_i\left[j\right]\right]\right) + 1 fd$

        /* Increments the count in header table*/

        $if\, T_i\left[j\right] \in L\left[j\right] and\, flag = 1 then$

        /* L represents the level of the tree. Each item's position in the transaction have a corresponding position of the level of the tree*/

        $pointer\left(HeaderTable\left[T_i\left[j\right]\right]\right) \leftarrow last\, node\, in\, the\, branch$

    $else$

        $flag \leftarrow 0$ /* A new branch is necessary. Once this segment is arrived, rest of the items in Ti fall under the new branch and loop is needed to be broken*/

        $start\, a\, new\, branch\, at\, level\, i + 1$

        /* A new branch is created whenever rest of the items of Ti does not match the path*/

        $pointer\left(HeaderTable\left[T_i\left[j\right]\right]\right) \leftarrow last\, node\, in\, the\, branch$

        $j \leftarrow |T_i|$

    $end\, if$

    $end\, for$

$end\, for$

**End**

## 4.1 Secure Computation

Preserving privacy in combining one-pass FP-trees require some fully homomorphic functions which are needed to be developed. This section presents such functions based on the fully homomorphic cryptosystem discussed in Section 2.5. Mechanism of comparing two numbers (both integer and fractional) with preserving privacy is discussed

here too. We proposed these Secure Multiparty Computation (SMC) techniques (especial case of two parties) in Kaosar, Paulet, and Yi (2011).

### 4.1.1 Homomorphic Function Abstraction

Using the basic fully homomorphic cryptosystem discussed in Section 2.5, it is possible to define

*Table 3. Transactions in $DB_1$ possessed by party A*

| TID | Items | Sorted Items | TID | Items | Sorted Items |
|-----|-------|--------------|-----|-------|--------------|
| 1 | A,B,C | A,B,C | 11 | B,C,P | B,C,P |
| 2 | A,B,P | A,B,P | 12 | P,B,C | B,C,P |
| 3 | P,O,A,B,C | A,B,C,P | 13 | D,Q,P | D,P,Q |
| 4 | D,C | D,C | 14 | E,B,C | B,C,E |
| 5 | X,Y,Z | X,Y,Z | 15 | Y,Z | Y,Z |
| 6 | X,P,A,B,C | A,B,C,P,X | 16 | X,Q,R | Q,R,X |

some functions in terms of $n$-bit integers. The encryption and decryption functions for (abstracted) integers are as follows.

- $E_{pk}(i)$ : Encrypts a $n$-bit integer $i$ using the public key $pk$, returning a encrypted $n$-bit integer $c$ as ciphertext.
- $D_{sk}(c)$ : Decrypts a $n$-bit integer $c$ using the private key $sk$, returning a plaintext $n$-bit integer $i$.

The purpose of these functions is to convert an integer between the plaintext and ciphertext. Due to the abstraction of binary bits into integers, it will assist the creation of a higher level protocol. The functions for such a protocol are defined next.

- **Homomorphic Binary AND Operation:**
  - $HomAND(x, y)$ : Receives two encrypted $n$-bit integers $x$ and $y$, and returns a third encrypted $n$-bit integer $z$. The output is calculated bit-by-bit using the homomorphic property, that is

$z_j = x_i ANDy_i$, where $AND$ is evaluated using Equation 6, for $i = j$.

- **Homomorphic Binary XOR:**
  - $HomXOR(x, y)$ : Receives two encrypted n-bit integers $x$ and $y$, and returns a third encrypted n-bit integer $z$. The output is calculated bit-by-bit using the exclusive OR property of the homomorphic encryption, that is $z_j = x_i XORy_i$, where XOR is evaluated using Equation 5, for $i = j$.

- **Homomorphic Addition:**
  - $HomAdd(x, y)$ : Receives two encrypted n-bit integers $x$ and $y$ and returns a third n-bit integer $z$. Where $z_i$ is calculated using Equations 9 and 8 for the current column and carry bit calculation, respectively. Figure 2 illustrates this double calculation of carry bit and column bit for each bit of the integer.

*Table 4. Transactions in $DB_2$ possessed by party B*

| TID | Items | Sorted Items | TID | Items | Sorted Items |
|-----|-------|--------------|-----|-------|--------------|
| 7 | T,P,Q | P,Q,T | 17 | B,C | B,C |
| 8 | A,B,D | A,B,D | 18 | A,B | A,B |
| 9 | X,Y,Z | X,Y,Z | 19 | A,B,C | A,B,C |
| 10 | A,B,T,P,Q | A,B,P,Q,T | 20 | A,B,C | A,B,C |

*Figure 7. One-pass FP-tree in party A*

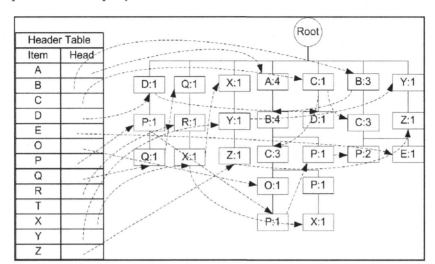

## 4.1.2 Privacy Preserving Comparison for Two Integers

This segment of the section proposes a solution to compute privacy preserving comparison between two numbers. Let us consider two integer numbers $M$ and $N$. This proposed technique compares $M$ and $N$ and determines whether $M$ is equal or less than or greater than $N$ without revealing the value of $M$ or $N$ themselves.

Let us, consider the first version of the algorithm (Algorithm 1) which performs the comparison without preserving the privacy. This basic technique can be found in many computer architecture books such as Harris and Harris (2007).

With the consideration of fully homomorphic functions- $HomXOR$, $HomAdd$ and $HomAND$ derived in Section 2.5; this proposed solution would do the same comparison as in Algorithm 1 with preserving privacy. Let us say Alice and

*Figure 8. One-pass FP-tree in party B*

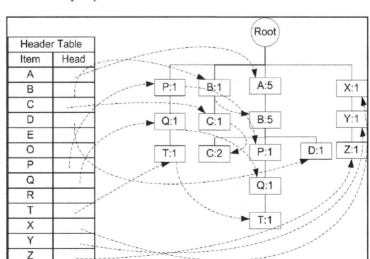

*Figure 9. Frequency matrix for item P*

Frequency Matrix for P — Count of P in that path

| Path | A | B | C | D | E | O | P | Q | R | T | X | Y | Z |
|---|---|---|---|---|---|---|---|---|---|---|---|---|---|
| DP | 0 | 0 | 0 | 1 | 0 | 0 | 1 | 0 | 0 | 0 | 0 | 0 | 0 |
| ABCOP | 1 | 1 | 1 | 0 | 0 | 1 | 1 | 0 | 0 | 0 | 0 | 0 | 0 |
| ABCP | 1 | 1 | 1 | 0 | 0 | 0 | 1 | 0 | 0 | 0 | 0 | 0 | 0 |
| ABP | 1 | 1 | 0 | 0 | 0 | 0 | 1 | 0 | 0 | 0 | 0 | 0 | 0 |
| BCP | 0 | 1 | 1 | 0 | 0 | 0 | 2 | 0 | 0 | 0 | 0 | 0 | 0 |

Count of P is multiplied to form $P^{FM}$

| Path | A | B | C | D | E | O | P | Q | R | T | X | Y | Z |
|---|---|---|---|---|---|---|---|---|---|---|---|---|---|
| DP | 0 | 0 | 0 | 1 | 0 | 0 | 1 | 0 | 0 | 0 | 0 | 0 | 0 |
| ABCOP | 1 | 1 | 1 | 0 | 0 | 1 | 1 | 0 | 0 | 0 | 0 | 0 | 0 |
| ABCP | 1 | 1 | 1 | 0 | 0 | 0 | 1 | 0 | 0 | 0 | 0 | 0 | 0 |
| ABP | 1 | 1 | 0 | 0 | 0 | 0 | 1 | 0 | 0 | 0 | 0 | 0 | 0 |
| BCP | 0 | 2 | 2 | 0 | 0 | 0 | 2 | 0 | 0 | 0 | 0 | 0 | 0 |

Encryption is performed on all entries before transmission

| | | | | | | | | | | | | |
|---|---|---|---|---|---|---|---|---|---|---|---|---|
| $E_{pk}(0)$ | $E_{pk}(0)$ | $E_{pk}(0)$ | $E_{pk}(1)$ | $E_{pk}(0)$ | $E_{pk}(0)$ | $E_{pk}(1)$ | $E_{pk}(0)$ | $E_{pk}(0)$ | $E_{pk}(0)$ | $E_{pk}(0)$ | $E_{pk}(0)$ | $E_{pk}(0)$ |
| $E_{pk}(1)$ | $E_{pk}(1)$ | $E_{pk}(1)$ | $E_{pk}(0)$ | $E_{pk}(0)$ | 1 | $E_{pk}(1)$ | $E_{pk}(0)$ | $E_{pk}(0)$ | $E_{pk}(0)$ | $E_{pk}(0)$ | $E_{pk}(0)$ | $E_{pk}(0)$ |
| $E_{pk}(1)$ | $E_{pk}(1)$ | $E_{pk}(1)$ | $E_{pk}(0)$ | $E_{pk}(0)$ | $E_{pk}(0)$ | $E_{pk}(1)$ | $E_{pk}(0)$ | $E_{pk}(0)$ | $E_{pk}(0)$ | $E_{pk}(0)$ | $E_{pk}(0)$ | $E_{pk}(0)$ |
| $E_{pk}(1)$ | $E_{pk}(1)$ | $E_{pk}(0)$ | $E_{pk}(0)$ | $E_{pk}(0)$ | $E_{pk}(0)$ | $E_{pk}(1)$ | $E_{pk}(0)$ | $E_{pk}(0)$ | $E_{pk}(0)$ | $E_{pk}(0)$ | $E_{pk}(0)$ | $E_{pk}(0)$ |
| $E_{pk}(0)$ | $E_{pk}(2)$ | $E_{pk}(2)$ | $E_{pk}(0)$ | $E_{pk}(0)$ | $E_{pk}(0)$ | $E_{pk}(2)$ | $E_{pk}(0)$ | $E_{pk}(0)$ | $E_{pk}(0)$ | $E_{pk}(0)$ | $E_{pk}(0)$ | $E_{pk}(0)$ |

Bob have their secret numbers encrypted $\alpha \leftarrow E_{pk}(M)$ and $\beta \leftarrow E_{pk}(N)$ respectively. Secure comparison between $\alpha$ and $\beta$ is proposed in Algorithm 2.

In summary; a function can be defined - $HomComparison(\alpha, \beta)$ which would compare two encrypted integers and returns an encrypted one bit result $R'$ which can be decrypted only by the owner of the secret key (in this case - Alice). If $R = D_{sk}(R') = 0$ then $M \geq N$ else $M < N$.

### 4.1.3 Privacy Preserving Comparison for Fraction Numbers

In the comparison of support and confidence of an itemset and an association rule respectively, it is necessary to compare two fractional numbers. The general form of both cases is to determine whether $\frac{\alpha}{\beta} \geq \gamma$ is true, where both $\alpha$ and $\beta$ are encryption of two integers. $\frac{\alpha}{\beta} \geq \gamma$ can be simplified as follows:

$$\frac{\alpha}{\beta} \geq \gamma \equiv \alpha \geq \gamma \times \beta \equiv \alpha \times 10^{n} \geq \gamma \times \beta \times 10^{n}$$

$$\equiv \alpha \times 10^{n} \geq \varepsilon \times \beta$$

Where, $n = $ number of digits in $\gamma$ after decimal points and $\varepsilon = \gamma \times 10^{n}$

We propose Algorithm 3 to perform the comparison securely.

In summary; a function can be defined - $HomFractionComparison(\alpha, \beta, \gamma)$ which determines whether $\dfrac{\alpha}{\beta} > \gamma$ is true or not. If

$$R = D_{sk}(R') = 0 \text{ then } \frac{\alpha}{\beta} \geq \gamma, \text{ else } \frac{\alpha}{\beta} < \gamma$$

## 4.2 One-pass FP-tree Formation

Unlike regular FP-tree, the one-pass FP-tree considers all items regardless of their frequency. One-pass FP-tree is a compact expression of all transactions of the database. Items in the transactions are sorted alphabetically. Algorithm 4 forms a one-pass FP-tree for any party with database $DB$, set of items $I$ and the set of transactions $T \subseteq I ::$

*Example:* Let us consider two horizontally partitioned transactional databases $DB_1$ and $DB_2$ for $A$ and $B$ respectively. Transactions in the da-

tabase are alphabetically sorted and are illustrated in Table 3 and Table 4, respectively.

One-pass FP-tree formed out of these transactions is illustrated in Figures 7 and 8.

## 4.3 Privacy Preserving Frequent Itemset Generation from One-Pass FP-Tree

Two parties $A$ and $B$, having their own private one-pass FP-tree want to compute common frequent itemsets without disclosing their FP-trees. Both $A$ and $\underline{B}$ encrypts their secret values using $pk$. $A$ sends her encrypted secret values to $B$. Though $B$ possesses encrypted data, he cannot decrypt since he does not have the secret key $sk$ of $A$. $B$ performs all operations on encrypted data and send the outcome to $A$ without decrypting the result.

*Algorithm 5. Frequent itemset generation from FP-tree securely*

$input\,of\,A : FP - tree$
$input\,of\,B : FP - tree$
$output : Large\,itemset\,(L)$
**Begin**
$L \leftarrow \Phi$
$Both\,Alice\big(A\big)\,and\,Bob\big(B\big)$
    $for\,all\,I_i \in I\,do$
        $Alice\big(A\big)$
               $M_A \leftarrow E_{pk}\left(I_i^{FM}\right)$
               `/* Encrypts its frequency matrix for item` $I_i$`*/`
               $SendToB\big(M_A\big)$
        **Bob(B)**
               $M_B \leftarrow E_{pk}\left(I_i^{FM}\right)$
               `/* Encrypts its frequency matrix for item` $I_i$`*/`
               $L\bigcup FindFrequentItems(I_i, M_A, M_B)$
               `/* FindF requentItems extracts all frequent itemsets from` $I_i$`.`
               `This function is defined in Algorithm 6*/`
    $end\,for$
**End**

*Algorithm 6. Computing frequent itemsets from frequent matrices [FindFrequentItems()]*

$input\,of\,B : M_A, M_B, \pi, s, \rho$

```
/* Dimension of both M_A and M_B is nXm and nXm0 respectively. ρ is the item for which frequent
itemsets are to be determined.*/
```

$output$ : Large itemsets (l)

**Begin**

**Bob(B)**

    $sum\left[1...n\right] \leftarrow 0$

    $for\,i = 1\,to\,n\,do$

        $temp \leftarrow 0$

        $for\,j = 1\,to\,m\,do$

            $temp \leftarrow temp + M_A\left[i\right]\left[j\right]$

```
                    /* Homomorphic addition (as discussed in previous sections)*/
```

        $end\,for$

        $for\,j = 1\,to\,\dot{M}\,do$

            $temp \leftarrow temp + M_B\left[i\right]\left[j\right]$

```
                    /* Homomorphic addition (as discussed in previous sections)*/
```

        $end\,for$

        $sum[i] \leftarrow temp$

        $temp \leftarrow 0$

$End\,for$

$for\,i = 1\,to\,n\,do$

        $temp \leftarrow 0$

```
        /* Function CompareCipherWithP lain is defined in Algorithm 7*/
```

        $if\left(CompareCipherWithPlain\left(sum\left[i\right];s\right) = 1\right)and\left(I_i \neq \rho\right)then$

            $l \leftarrow l\bigcup\left\{I_i, \rho\right\}$

            $temp \leftarrow temp + 1$

            $TempFrequent[temp] \leftarrow I_i$

```
            /* Store all frequent items to check whether 3 or more itemsets are possible
            to form.*/
```

        $end\,if$

$end\,for$

$if\,temp \geq 2\,then$

        $\delta \leftarrow Generate\,all\,possible\,p - itemsets\,containing\,\rho\,where\,\rho \geq 3$

        $Do\,all\,itemsets\,in\,\delta\,have\,same\,value\,in\,M_A\,and\,M_B\,?$

        $if\,yes\,then$

            $l = l\bigcup\delta$

        $end\,if$

        $end\,if$

        $return\,l$

**End**

*Algorithm 7. Compare a ciphertext with a number [CompareCipherWithPlain()]*

$input: c, \beta$
$output: Returns\, 1\, if\, c \geq \beta$
**Begin**
**Bob** $\left( B \right)$
    $SendToA\left( c, \beta \right)$
**Alice** $\left( A \right)$
    $\alpha \leftarrow D_{sk}(c)$
    `/* Homomorphic secure comparison (as discussed previously)*/`
    $if\, \alpha \geq \beta\, then$
        $return\, 1$
    $else$
        $return\, 0$
    $end\, if$
**End**

On the other hand $A$ is only able to decrypt the final result which she transmits back to $B$ too.

*Frequency matrix:* Both $A$ and $B$ generates frequency matrix and encrypt it before sharing. Number of columns in matrix is equal to the number of items ($n$) and number of rows is equal to number of times a particular item appears in the FP-tree (let us say $m$). Therefore the matrix dimension is $n \times m$. As for example in Figure 7, item $P$ occurs 5 times (therefore, $m = 5$). For each path from a particular item to the root in FP-tree there will be one entry in the matrix. If an item is present in the path, its corresponding entry in the row becomes 1 otherwise 0. Entry for the particular item itself is equal to the count of the item. Let us assume $I_i^{FM}$ denotes as the frequency matrix for item $I_i$ and $E_{pk}(I_i^{FM})$ denotes encrypted frequency matrix which is formed by encrypting each entry of $I_i^{FM}$ by the public key $pk$ of $A$. As for example frequency matrix for item $P$ in Figure 7 is illustrated in Figure 9.

Algorithm 5 illustrates how $A$ and $B$ securely generate frequent itemsets from their FP-trees.

Following initialization operations are performed between $A$ and $B$ once at the beginning:

$$A : D_1 \leftarrow E_{pk}(| DB_1 |)$$
$$SendToB(D_1)$$

$$B : D_2 \leftarrow E_{pk}(| DB_2 |)$$
$$\pi' \leftarrow HomAdd(D_1, D_2)$$

## 5 ANALYSIS

- **Privacy Preservation:** In our proposed solution scheme Alice ($A$) is the owner of secret and public key $sk$ and $pk$ respectively. Alice does not send any data to Bob ($B$) but encrypted by her own public key ($pk$). No one but Alice herself can recover her data. Therefore, the privacy of Alice is secured by the security assumption of the encryption system of Dijk et al. (2010) (approximate-GCD problem). On the other hand Bob encrypts his data using same public key ($pk$) and performs operations on its own cipher-text and Alice's cipher-text.

Bob then discloses the result of the operations (Bob cannot decrypt) to Alice which is only one bit in length (one bit encrypted result of secure comparison operation). The privacy of Bob's data depends on whether Alice can learn anything about Bob's data from the result sent by Bob. Since it is only one bit, Alice cannot learn anything about Bob's inputs.

- **Performance analysis:** To analyze the theoretical performance between the proposed solution and regular FP-tree let us consider following parameters:
  - N Total number of transactions
  - N Total number of different items
  - $\eta$ Average number of items in a single transaction
  - $\iota$ No of items frequent in the database
- **Database scan:** In case of FP-tree the number of times to scan the database is $2N$ as opposed to $N$ in the case of the proposed solution.
- **Length of the tree:** Among $n$ items, $\iota$ items are frequent and $\eta$ items are present in a path. Therefore average length or level of tree in FP-tree is $\dfrac{\iota \times \eta}{n}$. In case of the proposed solution it is $\eta$.
- **Number of branches of the tree:** In case of FP-tree, only frequent items are considered in the tree which are already sorted alphabetically. Therefore in average case

the number of branches in FP-tree is $\dfrac{\iota!}{!(\iota - \dfrac{\iota \times \eta}{n})}$. In case of the proposed solution it is $\dfrac{n!}{!(n - \eta)}$. is summarized in Table 5.

From the performance study it is observed that in some aspects (such as average number of branches of the tree and memory to store the tree) the regular FP-tree based algorithm performs better than the proposed solution. But in some circumstances FP-tree is not suitable whereas the proposed solution can work perfectly such as (1) where the database does not allow multiple scan (e.g., stream of real time data) (2) where preservation of privacy is a requirement such as in distributed settings and (3) where the database changes continuously or periodically. Moreover it should be also noted that, the size of the tree does not depend on the size of database. Therefore for a large database, the proposed solution would perform better since it require single scan. The proposed algorithm can easily be extended for multiparty settings. In that case two of all the parties are required to work similarly as party A and party B work in the case of this proposed solution with an assumption that party A and B would not collude each other.

*Table 5. Comparison of FP-tree and one-pass FP-tree algorithms*

| Evaluation Criteria | FP-tree | Proposed solution |
|---|---|---|
| Number of database scan | 2N | N |
| Average length of tree | $\dfrac{\iota \times \eta}{n}$ | $\eta$ |
| Average number of branches | $\dfrac{\iota!}{(\iota - \dfrac{\iota \times \eta}{n})!}$ | $\dfrac{n!}{(n - \eta)!}$ |

# 6 CONCLUSION

From the performance study, though it is observed that regular FP-tree based algorithm performs better than the proposed solution, in some cases proposed solution performs better. Such cases are: (1) where the database does not allow multiple scan (e.g., stream of real time data) and (2) where preservation of privacy is a requirement in distributed settings. Moreover it should be also noted that, the size of the tree does not depend on the size of database. Therefore for a large database the proposed solution would perform better since it require single scan. Moreover, one-pass FP-tree can accommodate continuous or periodically changing databases without restarting the process from the very beginning as opposed to the regular FP-tree based solution. Only additional transaction(s) can be appended in the tree or some transactions can be deducted from the tree anytime it is required. The proposed algorithm can easily be extended for multiparty settings too with an assumption - any two parties among all participants do not collude each other.

# ACKNOWLEDGMENT

This research contribution was supported and funded by Australian Research Council (ARC) Discovery Project (DP0770479) – "Privacy Protection in Distributed Data Mining".

# REFERENCES

Ackerman, M. S., Cranor, L. F., & Reagle, J. (1999). Privacy in e-commerce: examining user scenarios and privacy preferences. In *Proceedings of the 1st ACM Conference on Electronic commerce (EC '99)* (pp. 1-8). New York, NY: ACM.

Agrawal, R., & Srikant, R. (1994, September). Fast algorithms for mining association rules. In *Proceedings of the 20th International Conference on Very Large Data Bases,* Santiago, Chile (pp. 487-499).

Atallah, M., Elmagarmid, A., Ibrahim, M., Bertino, E., & Verykios, V. (1999). Disclosure imitation of sensitive rules. In *Proceedings of the 1999 Workshop on Knowledge and Data Engineering Exchange (KDEX '99)* (p. 45). Washington, DC: IEEE Computer Society.

Brookshear, J. G. (2005). *Computer Science: An Overview*. Reading, MA: Addison Wesley.

Clarkson, J. B. (1994). Dense probabilistic encryption. In *Proceedings of the Workshop on Selected Areas of Cryptography* (pp. 120-128).

Cockcroft, S., & Clutterbuck, P. (2001). Attitudes towards information privacy. In *Proceedings of the 12th Australasian Conference on Information Systems*.

Dasseni, E., Verykios, V. S., Elmagarmid, A. K., & Bertino, E. (2001). Hiding association rules by using confidence and support. In *Proceedings of the 4th International Workshop on Information Hiding (IHW '01),* Pittsburgh, PA (LNCS 2137, pp. 369-383).

Dijk, M. V., Gentry, C., Halevi, S., & Vaikuntanathan, V. (2010). Fully homomorphic encryption over the integers. In *Proceedings of the Eurocrypt 2010 Conference* (pp. 24-43).

El Gamal, T. (1985). A public key cryptosystem and a signature scheme based on discrete logarithms. In *Proceedings of the Advances in Cryptology Conference (CRYPTO 84)* (LNCS 196, pp. 10-18).

Evmievski, A., Gehrke, J., & Srikant, R. (2003). Limiting privacy breaches in privacy preserving data mining. In *Proceedings of the 22nd ACM SIGMOD-SIGACT-SIGART Symposium on Principles of Database Systems*, San Diego, CA (pp. 211-222). New York, NY: ACM.

Evmievski, A., Srikant, R., Agrawal, R., & Gehrke, J. (2002). Privacy preserving mining of association rules. In *Proceedings of the 8th ACM SIGKDD International Conference on Knowledge Discovery and Data Mining*, Edmonton, AB, Canada (pp. 217-228). New York, NY: ACM.

Gentry, C. (2009). Fully homomorphic encryption using ideal lattices, In *Proceedings of the 41st Annual ACM Symposium on Theory of Computing*, Bethesda, MD (pp. 169-178). New York, NY: ACM.

Hajek, P., Havel, I., & Chytil, M. (1966). The GUHA method of automatic hypotheses determination. *Computing, 1*, 293–308. doi:10.1007/BF02345483

Han, J., & Kamber, M. (2006). *Data Mining Concepts and Techniques* (2nd ed.). Amsterdam, The Netherlands: Elsevier.

Han, J., Pei, J., & Yin, Y. (2000). Mining frequent patterns without candidate generation. In *Proceedings of the 2000 ACM SIGMOD International Conference on Management of Data*, Dallas, TX (pp. 1-12). New York, NY: ACM.

Han, J., Pei, J., Yin, Y., & Mao, R. (2004). Mining frequent patterns without candidate generation: A frequent-pattern tree approach. *Data Mining and Knowledge Discovery, 8*(1). doi:10.1023/B:DAMI.0000005258.31418.83

Harris, D., & Harris, S. (2007). *Digital Design and Computer Architecture: From Gates to Processors*. San Francisco, CA: Morgan Kaufmann.

Kantarcioglu, M., & Clifton, C. (2004). Privacy-preserving distributed mining of association rules on horizontally partitioned data. *IEEE Transactions on Knowledge and Data Engineering, 16*(9), 1026–1037. doi:10.1109/TKDE.2004.45

Kaosar, M. G., Paulet, R., & Yi, X. (2011, January 17-20). *Secure two-party association rule mining.* Paper presented at the Australasian Information Security Conference (AISC 2011), Perth, WA, Australia.

Luo, Y., Zhao, Y., & Le, J. (2009). A survey on the privacy preserving algorithm of association rule mining. In *Proceedings of the 2009 2nd International Symposium on Electronic Commerce and Security (ISECS '09)* (Vol. 1, pp. 241-245).

Ouyang, W., & Huang, Q. (2006). Privacy preserving association rules mining based on secure two-party computation. In *Intelligent Control and Automation* (LNCIS 344, pp. 969-975).

Paillier, P. (1999). Public-key cryptosystems based on composite degree residuosity classes. In *Proceedings of the Advances in Cryptology Conference (Eurocrypt 1999)*, Prague, Czech Republic (pp. 223-238).

Rivest, R. L., Shamir, A., & Adleman, L. (1978). A method for obtaining digital signatures and public-key cryptosystems. *Communications of the ACM, 21*(2), 120–126. doi:10.1145/359340.359342

Rizvi, S. J., & Haritsa, J. R. (2002, August 20-23). Maintaining data privacy in association rule mining. In *Proceedings of the 28th International Conference on Very Large Data Bases*, Hong Kong (pp. 682-693).

Saygin, Y., Verykios, V. S., & Clifton, C. (2001). Using unknowns to prevent discovery of association rules. *SIGMOD Record, 30*(4), 45–54. doi:10.1145/604264.604271

Saygin, Y., Verykios, V. S., & Elmagarmid, A. K. (2002). Privacy preserving association rule mining. In *Proceedings of the 12th International Workshop on Research Issues in Data Engineering: Engineering E-Commerce/E-Business Systems (RIDE'02),* San Jose, CA (p. 151). Washington, DC: IEEE Computer Society.

Su, C., & Sakurai, K. (2008). A distributed privacy-preserving association rules mining scheme using frequent-pattern tree. In C. Tang, C. Ling, X. Zhou, N. Cercone, & X. Li (Eds.), *Advanced Data Mining and Applications* (LNCS 5139, pp. 170-181).

Tan, P. N., Steinbach, M., & Kumar, V. (2006). *Introduction to Data Mining.* Upper Saddle River, NJ: Pearson Education.

Vaidya, J., & Clifton, C. (2002). Privacy preserving association rule mining in vertically partitioned data. In *Proceedings of the 8th ACM SIGKDD Conference,* Edmonton, AB, Canada (pp. 639-644). New York, NY: ACM.

Victorian Government, Department of Human Service. (1999). *Information Privacy Principles.* Melbourne, VIC, Australia: Author.

Yao, A. C. (1982). Protocols for secure computations. In *Proceedings of the 23rd Annual Symposium on Foundations of Computer Science,* Chicago, IL (pp. 160-164). Washington, DC: IEEE Computer Society.

Yi, X., & Zhang, Y. (2007). Privacy-preserving distributed association rule mining via semi-trusted mixer. *Data & Knowledge Engineering, 63*(2). doi:10.1016/j.datak.2007.04.001

Zaki, M. J. (2000). Scalable algorithms for association mining. *IEEE Transactions on Knowledge and Data Engineering, 12,* 372–390. doi:10.1109/69.846291

Zhong, S. (2007). Privacy-preserving algorithms for distributed mining of frequent itemsets. *Information Sciences, 177*(2), 490–503. doi:10.1016/j.ins.2006.08.010

*This work was previously published in the International Journal of Information Security and Privacy, Volume 5, Issue 2, edited by Hamid Nemati, pp. 13-32, copyright 2011 by IGI Publishing (an imprint of IGI Global).*

Chapter 7

# A Mark-Up Language for the Specification of Information Security Governance Requirements

**Anirban Sengupta**
*Jadavpur University, India*

**Chandan Mazumdar**
*Jadavpur University, India*

## ABSTRACT

*As enterprises become dependent on information systems, the need for effective Information Security Governance (ISG) assumes significance. ISG manages risks relating to the confidentiality, integrity and availability of information, and its supporting processes and systems, in an enterprise. Even a medium-sized enterprise contains a huge collection of information and other assets. Moreover, risks evolve rapidly in today's connected digital world. Therefore, the proper implementation of ISG requires automation of the various monitoring, analysis, and control processes. This can be best achieved by representing information security requirements of an enterprise in a standard, structured format. This paper presents such a structured format in the form of Enterprise Security Requirement Markup Language (ESRML) Version 2.0. It is an XML-based language that considers the elements of ISO 27002 best practices.*

## INTRODUCTION

An enterprise information system consists of assets (Information Assets, Software Assets, Hardware Assets, and Service Assets) and their inter-connections. These assets may contain vulnerabilities (ISO/IEC, 2005), which can be exploited by threats (ISO/IEC, 2005), to cause breach of security parameters (like confidentiality, integrity, and availability). An enterprise should ensure that all its users (both external and internal) are provided with a secure information systems

DOI: 10.4018/978-1-4666-2050-6.ch007

environment. This is possible only when senior management of an enterprise identifies the need for the establishment of an effective Information Security Governance (ISG) mechanism. ISG is defined as "the establishment and maintenance of the control environment in an enterprise to manage the risks relating to the confidentiality, integrity and availability of information and its supporting processes and systems" (Brotby, 2006; Moulton & Coles, 2003).

ISG requirements of an enterprise depend on several factors. Though the major determinant is the business goal, the operational context, technology used, organizational structure and network connectivity also play important roles in determining the approach towards ISG. Information Security needs of an enterprise are not static, but depend on the dynamics of operation, changing business goals, changes to legal framework, changes to risk perception, etc. Hence, ISG is not a one-time affair; it is a continuous process of analysis, design, implementation, monitoring and adaptation to changing information security needs. In many enterprises, the changes encountered are frequent. Moreover, even for a medium-sized enterprise, the number, and complexity, of assets and their inter-connections are usually huge. The management of such a complex and dynamic process needs structured representation of enterprise security requirements specification documents, and their automatic analysis and generation with interoperable features.

In this paper, the design of Enterprise Security Requirement Markup Language Version 2.0 (ESRML 2.0) is presented. It is an XML (W3C, 2003) based structured language for specifying enterprise information security requirements to facilitate the automatic analysis, design and governance of Enterprise Information Security. This was first introduced in Sengupta and Mazumdar (2010). It has been subsequently enhanced and is being described in this paper in detail. ESRML 2.0 is based on ISO 27002 Best Practices for Information Security Management (ISO/IEC, 2005). Security standards consolidate and specify best practices for achieving desired information security goals. In order to successfully implement ISG in an enterprise, it is important to adopt relevant information security best practices (Williams, 2001). ISO 27002 is one of the most widely accepted international standards that specifically address ISG issues of an enterprise (Solms & Solms, 2009). It provides detailed guidelines on how a secure management framework should be implemented, and how it should demonstrate compliance with laws, regulations, and standards (these are the principal requirements of ISG). It consists of eleven security clauses. They are: Security Policy, Organization of Information Security, Asset Management, Human Resources Security, Physical and Environmental Security, Communications and Operations Management, Access Control, Information Systems Acquisition, Development and Maintenance, Information Security Incident Management, Business Continuity Management, and Compliance. Under each clause, there are certain security objectives to be fulfilled. Each objective can be attained by a number of controls. These controls may prescribe management measures like guidelines and procedures, or some security infrastructure in the form of tools and techniques.

Rest of this paper is organized as follows. First, a survey of related work is given. Then, the design of ESRML 2.0 is presented. After that, the usefulness of ESRML 2.0 is described. Finally, the paper concludes with a brief description of WISSDOM (Web-Enabled Information System Security Design and Operational Management) tool suite that has been implemented using ESRML 2.0. A Sample Security Requirement Specification using ESRML 2.0 has been included in the Appendix.

## RELATED WORK

Paul Williams (2001) discussed the role of information security within a corporate governance framework. He stated that the four basic outcomes of ISG should be (i) alignment of investment in information security with the enterprise strategy and risk profile, (ii) a standard set of security practices with provision for continuous improvement, (iii) risk management, and (iv) performance measurement techniques. Moulton and Coles (2003) stated that ISG can provide a better framework to meet business requirements and to manage risks within an enterprise. It can help to communicate more effectively within the enterprise as well as with external parties, including regulators. They suggested a control environment for ISG, where (i) an enterprise level information risk is identified, (ii) responsibilities for managing that risk are assigned, and (iii) controls are implemented to mitigate the risk. Julia Allen (2005) stated that ISG means viewing adequate security as a non-negotiable requirement of being in business. She identified risk management, checking for regulatory compliance and performance measurement as the pillars of ISG.

For successful implementation of ISG in a dynamic enterprise environment, it is imperative that its processes are automated and controlled. In order to automate the processes of ISG, a structured representation of enterprise information security requirements is needed. Extensible Markup Language (XML) provides a means for such structured representation. A few existing XML languages in the domain of security applications are described below.

SAML (Security Assertion Markup Language) (OASIS, 2008) is an XML standard that allows a user to log on once for affiliated but separate Web sites. SAML is designed for business-to-business (B2B) and business-to-consumer (B2C) transactions. SAML defines how identity and access information is exchanged and lets organizations convey security information to one another without having to change their own internal security architectures. But SAML can only communicate information. How to use that information is where XACML (Extensible Access Control Markup Language) (OASIS, 2005) comes in. The language, which uses the same definitions of subjects and actions as SAML, of-

fers a vocabulary for expressing the rules needed to define an organization's security policies and make authorization decisions. Security Services Markup Language (S2ML) (OASIS, 2001) is aimed to create a common language for sharing security information about transactions and end users between companies engaged in online B2B and B2C transactions. The S2ML specification addresses three main areas of security services: authentication, authorization, and entitlement/ privilege. IDMEF (Intrusion Detection Message Exchange Format) (OASIS, 2004b) defines data formats and exchange procedures in XML for sharing information of interest to intrusion detection and response systems, and to the management systems which may need to interact with them. AVDL (Application Vulnerability Description Language) (OASIS, 2004a) aims at creating an XML definition for exchanging information about the security vulnerabilities of applications exposed to networks. The EDXL (Emergency Data eXchange Language) (OASIS, 2006) is a growing suite of specific message standards developed by emergency practitioners in a project sponsored by the Department of Homeland Security's Disaster Management E-Gov Initiative. EDXL messages are designed for IP (Internet Protocol) data communications between all emergency professions. EDXL is compatible with most existing and planned networks and data systems at the federal, state, local and tribal levels. The goal of EDXL project is to facilitate emergency information sharing and data exchange across local, state, tribal, national and non-governmental organizations of different professions that provide emergency response and management services. EDXL will accomplish this goal by focusing on the standardization of specific messages (messaging interfaces) to facilitate emergency communication and coordination, particularly when more than one profession is involved.

None of the languages described above cater to the ISG needs of an enterprise. Roy, Barik, and Mazumdar (2004) devised an Enterprise Security Requirement Markup Language (ESRML) that helped specify enterprise information security requirements in compliance with ISO 17799:2000 standard (ISO/IEC, 2000). Later, this was updated to comply with the requirements of ISO 27002 (ISO/IEC, 2005) that would take care of ISG needs of an enterprise. This was introduced as ESRML 2.0 in (Sengupta & Mazumdar, 2010). It was subsequently enriched based on feedback from practical implementations; in this paper, this enhanced and current version of ESRML 2.0 is presented.

## DESIGN OF ESRML 2.0

The different entities of ESRML 2.0, which are important for specifying security requirements of an enterprise, are

- Managerial Vulnerabilities
- Environmental Threats
- Information Systems
- Physical Network Structure
- Assets
  - Individual asset information
  - Security Class of individual assets
  - Security Concern (threat(s) to individual assets and vulnerabilities exploited)
- Users
- Access control to assets

These entities are in accordance with the requirements of ISO 27002. The root element of the specification is Requirement. It consists of two sub-elements, viz. AssetRegister and NetworkStructure. Clause Asset Management of ISO 27002 mandates that an enterprise must contain an inventory of all its assets, along with information about their owners and custodians. This inventory is referred to as an asset register. The element AssetRegister takes care of this requirement. It also contains information regarding access control lists of all assets, which is mandated by the Access

Control clause of ISO 27002. Finally, the element NetworkStructure specifies the physical network structure of the enterprise. This is mandated by the Communications and Operations Management clause of ISO 27002.

The element AssetRegister contains sub-elements ManagerialVulnerability, EnvironmentalThreat, Information System, and ServiceAssets. The element NetworkStructure consists of sub-elements InterConnection and IntraConnection. The detailed structures of these elements are described in subsequent sections.

## Managerial Vulnerabilities

Element ManagerialVulnerability describes different vulnerabilities that are exploited by the threats perceived by an enterprise. Each vulnerability is described by an element Vulnerability, which is a sub-element of the ManagerialVulnerability element. Each Vulnerability element has the following attributes

- **id:** Unique identifier of the vulnerability exploited.
- **name:** Name of the vulnerability exploited.
- **severity:** Severity value of individual vulnerability; value range is {very low, low, medium, high, very high}.

## Environmental Threats

Element EnvironmentalThreat contains information regarding threats perceived by an enterprise as a whole. Each perceived threat is described by an element Threat, which is a sub-element of the EnvironmentalThreat element. Each Threat element has the following attributes

- **id:** Unique identifier of the threat.
- **name:** Name of the threat.
- **loc:** Likelihood of occurrence of individual threat; possible values are {very low, low, medium, high, very high}.

## Information Systems

The network structure of an enterprise can be visualized as being composed of Information Systems (IS). An IS is the smallest indivisible part of the network. In the simplest case, it can be just a single server, or a workstation or router, switch, etc. It can also be a cluster of such components. Whatever be the case, it must satisfy the following properties:

- Its constituent components perform the same business activity.
- ISs cannot overlap and one cannot encompass another.

The element InformationSystem contains information regarding the information systems of an enterprise. It consists of 2 sub-elements: no_of_IS and ISInformation. The element no_of_IS contains a count of the total no. of ISs in an enterprise. The element ISInformation contains the details regarding an IS. So, if, for instance, there are 2 information systems in an enterprise, then the element ISInformation will appear twice in the specification. Its sub-element is HardwareAsset which, in turn, has sub-elements SoftwareAsset, and InformationAsset. These, together, contain details regarding the assets of an enterprise.

Figure 1 shows a snapshot of the XML tag structure describing an information system.

## Assets

In order to correctly specify the information security measures of an enterprise, different assets contained within it have to be known in advance. Assets may be of different types viz., hardware, software, information, and service assets (ISO/IEC, 2005). Hardware assets consist of Computing Systems, Communication Links (Network connections and backbone technologies) and IT sites (sites in which IT systems are installed or which are used for IT operations). Software assets

comprise of applications and programs (automated and manual) that process information. Information assets pertain to input, processed, output and stored data. Service assets comprise of computing and communications services and general utilities, e.g., heating, lighting, power, and air-conditioning.

As described in the preceding section, in ES-RML 2.0, the element ISInformation consists of sub-element HardwareAsset which, in turn, has sub-elements SoftwareAsset, and InformationAsset. Service assets are specified separately with the help of the element ServiceAssets, which is not a part of the element InformationSystem. The element ServiceAssets consists of sub-element ServiceAsset. The element ServiceAsset contains details regarding a service asset. So, if, for instance, there are 2 service assets in an enterprise, then the element ServiceAsset will appear twice in the specification. Each of these elements will have respective set of attributes. In addition to this, each of the asset elements (HardwareAsset, SoftwareAsset, InformationAsset, and ServiceAsset) will contain sub-elements pertaining to Security Class, Asset-specific threats and vulnerabilities, and an Access Control List. All of these elements are described in the following sections.

## Hardware Assets

The HardwareAsset element describes an individual hardware asset. The attributes of this element are

- **id:** Unique identifier of each hardware asset.
- **name:** Name of the hardware asset.
- **owner:** Owner of the hardware asset.
- **custodian:** Custodian of the hardware asset (person responsible for daily maintenance of the hardware).
- **type:** Type of hardware asset; possible values are {server/workstation /router, etc.}.
- **typeid**: Unique identifier denoting the hardware asset type.

- **vendor:** Vendor of hardware asset.
- **model:** Model of hardware asset.
- **price**: Price of the hardware asset.
- **mobility:** Mobility of a hardware asset specifies whether or not it can be taken off-premise.
- **ISname:** Name of the information system in which the hardware asset is located.
- **no_of_s**: No. of software assets installed in the hardware asset.
- **no_of_info**: No. of information assets residing in the hardware asset.

## Software Assets

As software assets are installed in hardware assets, the entire element SoftwareAsset will be a child element of the element HardwareAsset. The attributes of SoftwareAsset element are

- **id:** Unique identifier of the software asset.
- **name:** Name of the software asset.
- **owner:** Owner of the software asset.
- **custodian:** Custodian of the software asset.
- **type:** Type of the software asset; possible values are {OS, Server software, Application software, etc.}.
- **typeid**: Unique identifier denoting the software asset type.
- **subtype:** Sub-type of the software asset; possible values are {Microsoft Windows XP Prof., Fedora Core 7, etc.}.
- **subtypeid:** Unique identifier denoting the software asset sub-type.
- **vendor:** Vendor of the software asset.
- **version:** Version of the software asset.
- **price**: Price of the software asset.
- **mobility:** Mobility of a software asset specifies whether or not it can be taken off-premise.
- **ISname:** Name of the information system in which the software asset is located.

- **hname:** Name of the hardware asset where the software asset is installed.

## Information Assets

As information assets are contained within hardware assets the entire element InformationAsset will be a child element of the element HardwareAsset. The attributes of InformationAsset element are

- **id:** Unique identifier of the information asset.
- **name:** Name of the information asset.
- **owner:** Owner of the information asset.
- **custodian:** Custodian of the information asset.
- **type:** Type of information asset; possible values are {Database, File, Program Source, Libraries, System Documentation, etc.}.
- **typeid**: Unique identifier denoting the information asset type.
- **price**: Price of the information asset.
- **mobility:** Mobility of a information asset specifies whether or not it can be taken off-premise.
- **ISname:** Name of the information system in which the information asset is located.
- **hname:** Name of the hardware asset where the information asset is installed.

## Service Assets

The ServiceAsset element describes an individual service asset (e.g., air-conditioner, heating equipment, etc.). The attributes of this element are

- **id:** Unique identifier of each service asset.
- **name:** Name of the service asset.
- **owner:** Owner of the service asset.
- **custodian:** Custodian of the service asset.
- **type:** Type of service asset; possible values are {air-conditioner, UPS, fire-extinguisher, etc.}.

- **typeid**: Unique identifier denoting the service asset type.
- **vendor:** Vendor of service asset.
- **model:** Model of service asset.
- **price**: Price of the service asset.
- **mobility:** Mobility of a service asset specifies whether or not it can be taken off-premise.
- **ISnamelist:** Names of the information systems (comma-separated) which the service asset serves.
- **hnamelist:** Names of the hardware assets (comma-separated) which the service asset serves.
- **no_of_IS**: No. of information systems served by the service asset.
- **no_of_h**: No. of hardware assets served by the service asset.

## Security Class

Security of an asset can be compromised in different ways. There can be no security without confidentiality (Stoneburner, 2001). This ensures that information is accessible only for reading by authorized users; in other words this ensures that unauthorized users do not intercept, copy, or replicate information. At the same time integrity (Stoneburner, 2001) is necessary so that only authorized users are able to modify assets and transmitted information. Availability (Stoneburner, 2001) ensures that information is available to authorized users when needed and also the ability to recover quickly and completely in the event of an interruption in service. Also information is not secure without authentication, which ensures that the origin of a message or electronic document

*Figure 1. XML tag structure of information system*

```
<InformationSystem>
    <no_of_IS>2</no_of_IS>
    <ISInformation id="1" name="abc1" no_of_hardwareasset="2">
        <HardwareAsset id="1" ISname="abc1" name="AS" type="Server" owner="SAS" custodian="SAS"
vendor="SS" model="SSS" price="222" typeId="14" mobility="" no_of_s="1" no_of_info="1">
            ---
            ---
        <SoftwareAsset id="1" ISname="icra1" hname="AS" name="S1" type="Multimedia"
owner="SAS" custodian="SAS" vendor="as" version="as" price="222" typeId="21" SubTypeId="27"
mobility="N" subtype="Adobe Illustrator 8.0">
            ---
            ---
        </SoftwareAsset>
            ---
            ---
        <InformationAsset id="1" ISname="icra1" name="sdf" type="Personnel Files" owner="SAS"
custodian="sad" price="333" typeId="64" mobility="N" hname="AS">
            ---
            ---
        </InformationAsset>
            ---
            ---
        </HardwareAsset>
            ---
            ---
    </ISInformation>
    <ISInformation id="2" name="abc2" no_of_hardwareasset="1">
        ---
        ---
    </ISInformation>
        ---
</InformationSystem>
```

*Figure 2. XML tag structure of Software Asset*

```
---
---
<SoftwareAsset id="1" ISname="abc1" hname="AS" name="S1" type="Multimedia" owner="SAS"
custodian="SAS" vendor="as" version="as" price="222" typeId="21" SubTypeId="27" mobility="N"
subtype="Adobe Illustrator 8.0">

    <SecurityClass cVal="2" iVal="2" aVal="2" auVal="2" liVal="2" lcVal="N"/>

    <SoftwareAccessControlList>
        <Subject ISname="abc1" hname="AS" subname="User" r="Y" w="Y" d="Y" e="Y" m="N" a="N" />
    <SoftwareAccessControlList/>

    <SoftwareThreat>
        <AccidentalThreat name="Denial of Service" loc="Low" id="35"/>
        <AccidentalThreat name="Authentication Failure" loc="Low" id="23"/>
        <AccidentalThreat name="Information Leakage" loc="Low" id="24"/>
    </SoftwareThreat>

    <SoftwareThreat>
        <DeliberateThreat name="Malicious Code" loc="Low" id="41"/>
        <DeliberateThreat name="Denial of Service" loc="Low" id="43"/>
        <DeliberateThreat name="Password Leakage" loc="Low" id="25"/>
        <DeliberateThreat name="Information Leakage" loc="Low" id="26"/>
        <DeliberateThreat name="Physical Attack" loc="Low" id="37"/>
        <DeliberateThreat name="Hacking" loc="Low" id="27"/>
    </SoftwareThreat>

    <SoftwareVulnerability>
        <Vulnerability id="7" name="Bad password handling" severity="Low"/>
        <Vulnerability id="8" name="Uncontrolled copying of proprietary information or software"
severity="Low"/>
        <Vulnerability id="9" name="Bugs in Software" severity="Low"/>
    </SoftwareVulnerability>
</SoftwareAsset>
```

is correctly identified, with an assurance that the identity is not false. Non-repudiation ensures that neither the sender nor the receiver of a message will be able to deny the transmission. This factor is crucial to e-commerce. Without it an individual or entity can deny that he, she, or it is responsible for a transaction that he, she, or it is therefore, not financially liable. The Legal and Contractual attribute of an asset specifies the security requirements regarding the set of statutory and contractual requirements that an enterprise, its trading partners, contractors and services providers have to satisfy. It is important, for example, for the control of proprietary software copying, safeguarding of enterprise records, or data protection, and vital that the implementation, or absence, of security controls in each of the information

systems do not breach any statutory, criminal or civil obligations, or commercial contracts. Loss Impact can be identified as a monetary estimate or some other intangible impact such as loss of customer confidence, competitive advantage or the enterprise's reputation.

The SecurityClass element describes the security attributes of each asset. The attributes of this element are

- **cVal:** Confidentiality value of the asset (for all four types of asset); possible values are {1,2,3,4,5}.
- **iVal:** Integrity value of the asset (for all four types of asset); possible values are {1,2,3,4,5}.

- **aVal:** Availability value of the asset (for all four types of asset); possible values are {1,2,3,4,5}.
- **auVal:** Authenticity value of the asset (for all four types of asset); possible values are {1,2,3,4,5}.
- **nrVal:** Non-repudiation value of the asset (only for information asset); possible values are {Y, N}, which stands for Yes/No.
- **lcVal:** Legal and contractual value of the asset (for all four types of asset); possible values are {Y, N}, which stands for Yes/No.
- **liVal:** Loss-impact value of the asset (for all four types of asset); possible values are {1,2,3,4,5}.

Figure 2 shows the SecurityClass element for a software asset.

## Security Concern

Security concern for each individual asset describes the set of vulnerabilities and the set of threats exploiting those vulnerabilities. It is denoted by HardwareThreat and HardwareVulnerability elements for a hardware asset, SoftwareThreat and SoftwareVulnerability elements for a software asset, InformationThreat and InformationVul-

nerability elements for an information asset, and ServiceThreat and ServiceVulnerability elements for a service asset. Threats can be accidental (unintentional) or deliberate (intentional). These are denoted by sub-elements AccidentalThreat and DeliberateThreat. Each AccidentalThreat and DeliberateThreat element has the following attributes

- **id:** Unique identifier of the threat.
- **name:** Name of the threat.
- **loc:** Likelihood of occurrence of individual threat; possible values are {very low, low, medium, high, very high}.

Each HardwareVulnerability (or, SoftwareVulnerability or, InformationVulnerability, or, ServiceVulnerability) element has the following attributes

- **id:** Unique identifier of the vulnerability exploited.
- **name:** Name of the vulnerability exploited.
- **severity**: Severity value of individual vulnerability; value range is {very low, low, medium, high, very high}.

Figure 2 shows threats and vulnerabilities for a software asset.

*Figure 3. XML tag structure of physical network structure*

```
<NetworkStructure>
    <InterConnection>
        <Connection sISname="abc1" snode="AS" dISname="abc2" dnode="AS3" linktype="Ethernet"
protocol="TCP/IP" speed="10MBPS" connectivityTypeId="1"/>
        ---
        ---
    </InterConnection>
    ---
    ---
    <IntraConnection>
        <Connection ISname="abc1" snode="AS" dnode="AS1" linktype="Ethernet" protocol="TCP/IP"
speed="10MBPS" connectivityTypeId="1"/>
        ---
        ---
    </IntraConnection>
</NetworkStructure>
```

*Figure 4. Services of WISSDOM*

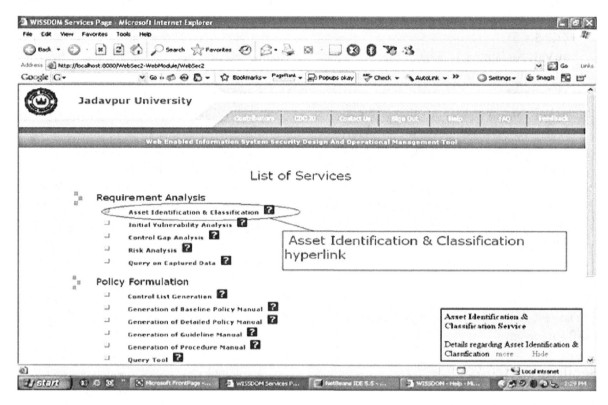

## Users

Users of enterprise assets are generally grouped into classes which are termed "user-groups". These user groups are hierarchical in nature. Permissions to access specific assets are assigned to user-groups. A user inherits the access rights of the user group/user sub-group to which it is assigned. Similarly, a user sub-group inherits the access rights of the user group of which it is part. If a user is assigned an access right that is in conflict to one that it has inherited, then the assigned access right overrides the inherited one. One user can be assigned to multiple user-groups; in such a scenario, the assigned user groups should not have access permissions that are in conflict to each other. In some enterprises, conflicting user-groups are assigned to a user, but they are not "active" simultaneously. It is separately specified as Principles of least privilege and Separation of Duty (Gligor, Gavrila, & Ferraiolo, 1998).

Besides access rights, a user may have certain privileges which are as follows:

1. **Create user:** This privilege allows a user to create other users in a hardware asset.
2. **Remove user:** This privilege allows a user to remove users from a hardware asset.
3. **Grant:** This privilege allows a user to grant access rights to subjects.
4. **Revoke:** This privilege allows a user to revoke access rights from subjects.

To ensure security, inheritance of privileges is not allowed.

The element User contains information regarding users of assets and their access permissions. As users are defined in some hardware asset (denoted by a unique user-id), the entire element User will be a child element of the element HardwareAsset. Each User has the following attributes

- **name**: Name of the user.
- **r**: Whether the user has read permission on the hardware asset; possible values are {Y, N}, which stands for Yes/No.
- **w**: Whether the user has write permission on the hardware asset; possible values are {Y, N}, which stands for Yes/No.
- **d**: Whether the user has delete permission on the hardware asset; possible values are {Y, N}, which stands for Yes/No.
- **e**: Whether the user has execute permission on the hardware asset; possible values are {Y, N}, which stands for Yes/No.
- **m**: Whether the user has modify permission on the hardware asset; possible values are {Y, N}, which stands for Yes/No.
- **a**: Whether the user has append permission on the hardware asset; possible values are {Y, N}, which stands for Yes/No.

- **cu**: Whether the user can create other users in the hardware asset; possible values are {Y, N}, which stands for Yes/No.
- **ru**: Whether the user can remove other users from the hardware asset; possible values are {Y, N}, which stands for Yes/No.
- **gr**: Whether the user can grant access permissions to subjects on objects (software and information assets) of the hardware asset; possible values are {Y, N}, which stands for Yes/No.
- **re**: Whether the user can revoke access permissions from subjects on objects (software and information assets) of the hardware asset; possible values are {Y, N}, which stands for Yes/No.

*Figure 5. Hardware asset details*

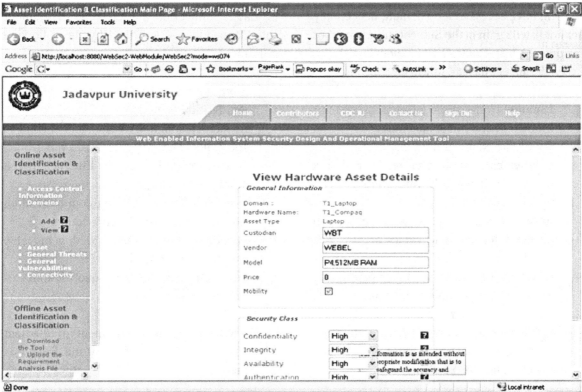

## Access Control

To specify proper infrastructure of an enterprise the access permissions to different assets have to be known in advance, which forms part of the security requirement specification. Every asset has its own set of access permissions, where rights to various subjects are specified.

The HardwareAccessControlList (or, SoftwareAccessControlList or, InformationAccessControlList or, ServiceAccessControlList) element captures information regarding the different access controls to different assets of the entire enterprise. Access permission(s) are referenced by corresponding asset(s). Each set of access permissions corresponding to some asset is a sub-entity of that asset. Element Subject, which is a sub-element of HardwareAccessControlList (or, SoftwareAccessControlList or, InformationAccessControlList or, ServiceAccessControlList) element, defines the list of subjects that have access to the corresponding asset. In case of a hardware asset, the users defined under its User element have access to it by default; hence, they are not listed again in the Subject sub-element of HardwareAccessControlList element.

Each Subject has the following attributes

- **ISname**: Name of the information system.
- **hname**: Name of the hardware.
- **subname**: Name of the subject.
- **r**: Whether the subject has read permission on the asset; possible values are {Y, N}, which stands for Yes/No.
- **w**: Whether the user has write permission on the asset; possible values are {Y, N}, which stands for Yes/No.
- **d**: Whether the user has delete permission on the asset; possible values are {Y, N}, which stands for Yes/No.
- **e**: Whether the user has execute permission on the asset; possible values are {Y, N}, which stands for Yes/No.

- **m**: Whether the user has modify permission on the asset; possible values are {Y, N}, which stands for Yes/No.
- **a**: Whether the user has append permission on the asset; possible values are {Y, N}, which stands for Yes/No.

Figure 2 shows the access control list for a software asset.

## Physical Network Structure

This entity describes the physical network structure of an enterprise. The connectivity of various hardware components within each information system (Intra-connection) and the connectivity between various information systems themselves (Inter-connection) describe the element NetworkStructure. Thus, the above two, i.e., IntraConnection and InterConnection, form the two sub-elements of NetworkStructure. Each type of connectivity contains various Connection sub-elements.

Each Connection sub-element of element IntraConnection is described by the following attributes

- **ISname:** Name of the information system.
- **snode:** Source node.
- **dnode:** Destination node.
- **linktype:** The physical link type of the connection (values can be Ethernet, Token Ring, ISDN, etc.).
- **protocol:** The underlying communication protocol used over the connection.
- **speed:** The maximum speed achievable through the connection.
- **connectivityTypeId**: Unique identifier of the connection.

Each Connection sub-element of element InterConnection is described by the following attributes

- **sISname:** Name of the source information system.
- **snode:** Source node.
- **dISname:** Name of the destination information system.
- **dnode:** Destination node.
- **linktype:** The physical link type of the connection (values can be Ethernet, Token Ring, ISDN, etc.).
- **protocol:** The underlying communication protocol used over the connection.
- **speed:** The maximum speed achievable through the connection.
- **connectivityTypeId:** Unique identifier of the connection.

There can be multiple connections between 2 nodes. Hence, the Connection sub-element can be repeated multiple times.

Figure 3 shows a sample Physical Network Structure of an enterprise.

## Utility of ESRML 2.0

ESRML 2.0 is an XML-based language for specifying information security requirements of an enterprise. The usefulness of this language lies in its structured layout and extensibility. The language has been designed based on the requirements of ISO 27002. An enterprise may capture its security requirements and structure this data according to ESRML 2.0 syntax. Any standard XML-based parser may then be used to automatically parse these security requirements and analyze the same for consistency and completeness. Programs may also be developed to verify the correctness of the physical network structure and access control lists of an enterprise and check for security issues (if any). If a security risk is discovered, it may be plugged by modifying the network structure, access control list, or location of assets within the enterprise. Due to the structured representation provided by ESRML 2.0, it is easy to detect such risks, and remove them.

*Figure 6. Consolidated risk analysis report*

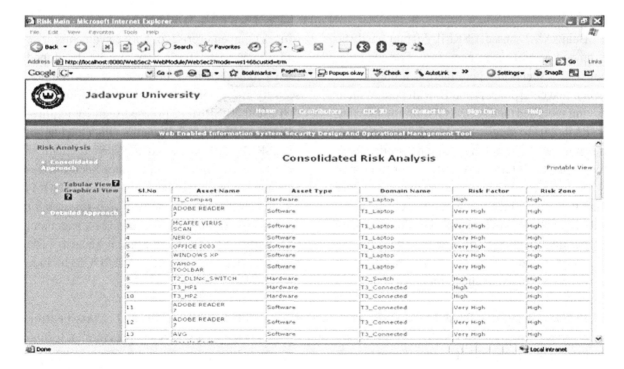

*Figure 7. Detailed risk analysis report*

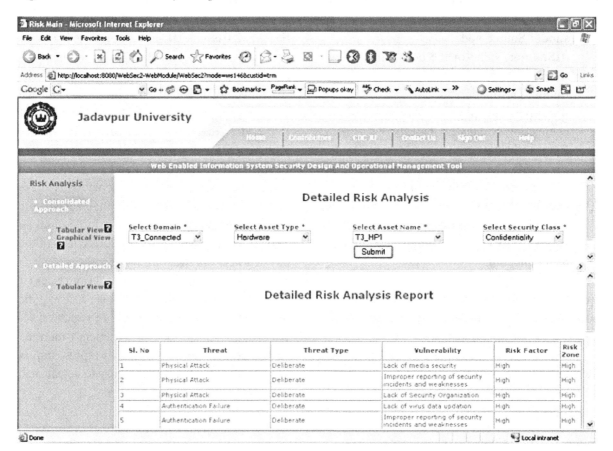

Being XML-based, ESRML 2.0 may easily be extended as and when necessary. For example, consider a scenario where there is a merger between two enterprises A and B, with both of them having specified their security requirements using ESRML 2.0. To specify a combined requirement, it is possible to repeat the element AssetRegister twice, first for enterprise A, and then for enterprise B, or vice-versa. The element NetworkStructure may then be defined to capture the connectivity between the assets of both A and B; this may need proper qualification to differentiate between the assets of A and B. The combined specification may then be parsed to check for consistency and security issues.

Besides, owing to its flexibility and extensibility, it is easy to exchange ESRML 2.0-based security specification data between different branch offices of an enterprise, or between an enterprise and a third party. Tools may also be developed for various security functions, like information security risk analysis, policy formulation, etc., that use the ESRML 2.0-based security requirements specification for seamless data exchange.

ESRML 2.0 has aided the development of Web-Enabled Information System Security Design and Operational Management (WISSDOM) tool, which consists of a suite of web-services for facilitating the analysis, design and management of Enterprise Information System Security. The major services offered under WISSDOM include the following:

- **Asset Identification and Classification Service:** This service provides a forms-based Graphic User Interface (GUI) for specifying the details of security requirements of all enterprise assets, their accessibilities, and also the structure of the existing network, including connectivity between assets. Security requirements include Confidentiality (C), Integrity (I), and Availability (A) needs of assets and also their threat and vulnerability perceptions. The requirements can be entered either online or offline. In the offline version, a user can download a GUI-based application, fill in the security needs, generate a requirement specification file (structured as per ESRML 2.0), and upload the same to the application server for further analysis.

- **Consolidated Risk Analysis:** A risk analysis is performed on the existing assets of an enterprise with consideration to sensitivity levels (C, I, A values) and security concern (threat-vulnerability perception) of the assets. A summary report is generated that displays the existing risk to enterprise assets. A fuzzy-logic based methodology is used to compute risk values.

- **Detailed risk analysis:** A detailed risk analysis is performed to identify all threat-vulnerability pairs that cause risks to the identified enterprise assets. The comprehensive report is used for selecting controls to reduce risks to assets.

- **Control list Generation (compliant with ISO 27002):** Based on the type of business an enterprise conducts, its security needs, and perceived risks, a list of relevant security controls pertaining to ISO 27002:2005 (ISO/IEC, 2005) is generated.

*Figure 8. Asset-based infrastructure advisory*

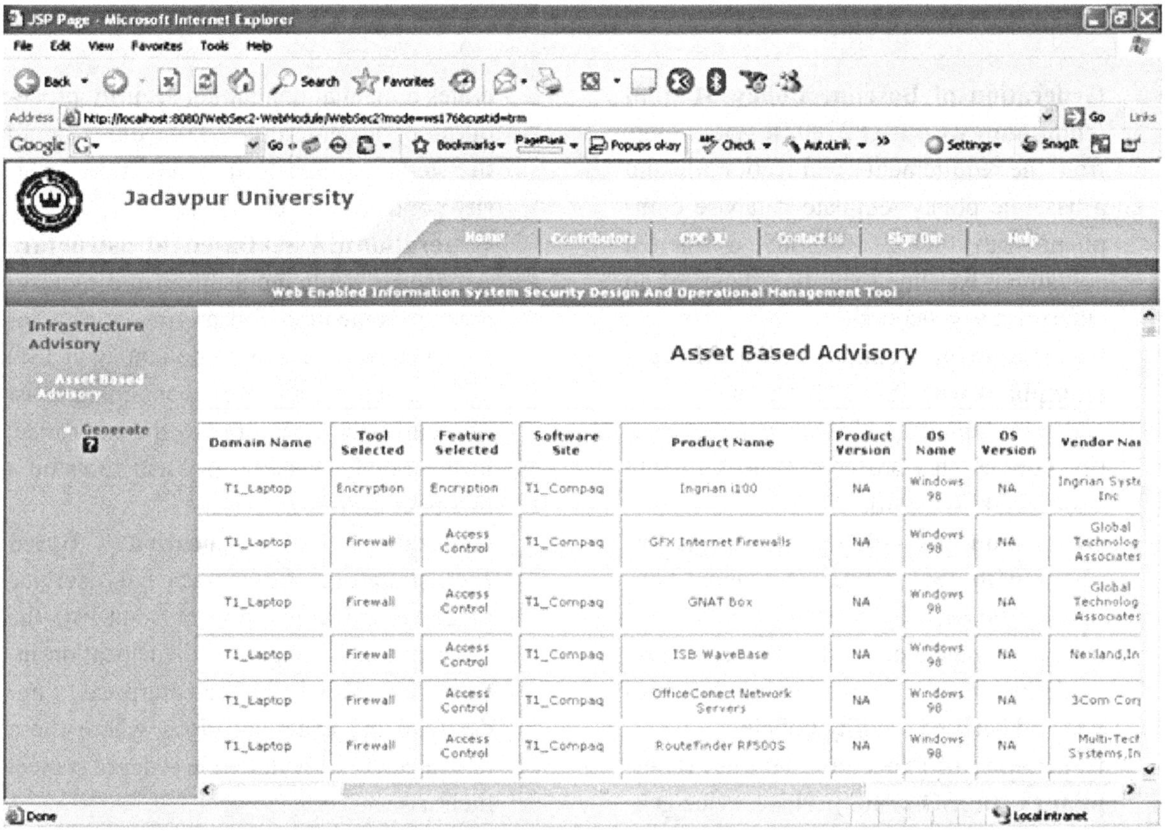

*Figure 9. Location-based infrastructure advisory*

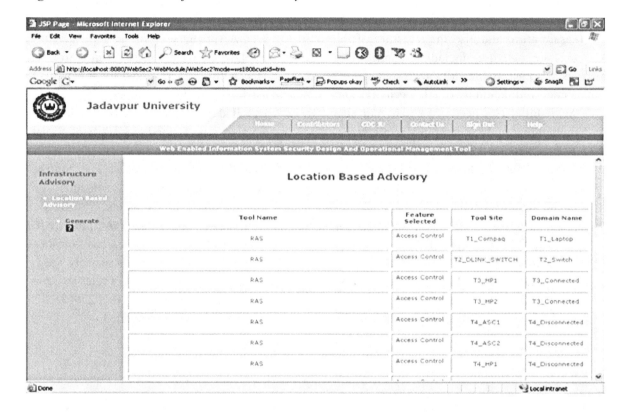

- **Generation of Baseline Policy Manual (compliant with ISO 27002):** With inputs from the requirement specification file and a baseline policy template database compliant with ISO 27002:2005, a manual containing baseline security policies of an enterprise is generated.
- **Generation of Detailed Policy Manual (compliant with ISO 27002):** This service generates detailed and issue-specific security policies that are compliant with ISO 27002:2005 standard.
- **Generation of Guideline Manual (compliant with ISO 27002):** A manual containing the security guidelines of an enterprise is generated by this service. These guidelines help in implementing the baseline and detailed security policies.
- **Generation of Procedure Manual (compliant with ISO 27002):** This service gen-

erates a manual containing security procedures of an enterprise. Procedures detail the steps required to implement the security policies of an enterprise.

- **Generation of Asset Based Infrastructure Advisory:** With inputs from the requirement specification file and a security infrastructure database compliant with ISO 27002:2005, an advisory, containing a list of security tools required by the enterprise, is generated. This advisory lists tools on a per-asset basis.
- **Generation of Location Based Infrastructure Advisory:** This service produces a detailed advisory that lists the security tools along with their location information. This helps the enterprise to understand the exact locations where these tools need to be installed in order to protect their assets.

Thus, Asset Identification and Classification service gathers information regarding the assets (hardware, software, information, and service assets) of an enterprise. This information is assimilated to generate a Security Requirement Specification file, which is a structured xml file based on ESRML 2.0. This file is then analyzed to perform risk analyses, and generate policy manuals and infrastructure advisories. The fact that ESRML 2.0 is structured according to the clauses and controls of ISO 27002, makes the tasks of analyzing enterprise risks and generating manuals and advisories that much easier.

An illustrative example of an actual implementation of WISSDOM services in an enterprise scenario is given in the following sub-section.

### Illustrative Example

Figure 4 shows the Services page of WISSDOM. An enterprise first enters details of assets, including their security needs.

Figure 5 shows the GUI for entering hardware asset information. Similarly, software and information asset information are input. The output of this service is a security requirement specification file as shown in Figure 10 of the Appendix.

Based on these requirements, consolidated risk analysis is performed, followed by a detailed risk analysis. Figure 6 illustrates the result of the former, while the latter is shown in Figure 7.

The list of security controls based on ISO 27002:2005 are generated on clicking Control List Generation service as shown in Figure 4. Based on these controls, security policies, procedures, and guidelines relevant to the enterprise, are generated. Finally, asset-based and location-based infrastructure advisories are generated, as shown in Figure 8 and Figure 9, respectively.

Thus, WISSDOM helps in generating various security advisories based on the security requirements input by an enterprise.

## CONCLUSION AND FUTURE WORK

This paper presents the constructs of ESRML 2.0, an XML-based language that provides an effective way for specifying information security requirements of an enterprise. Security requirements, structured as per ESRML 2.0 syntax, may be parsed automatically using standard XML parsers. This helps in the automatic analysis and verification of enterprise information security requirements. Automation of enterprise information security aspects is of utmost importance in today's dynamic ISG environment, where there is a need to constantly monitor and evaluate perpetually-evolving information security needs.

Future work is geared towards enriching ESRML 2.0 by incorporating the requirements of other ISG standards like CobiT (IT Governance Institute, 2007) and ITBPM (ITBPM, 2007). This will lead to better inter-operability and hence, wider acceptance of the language in diverse business sectors.

## ACKNOWLEDGMENT

This research was partially supported from grants allocated by the Department of Information Technology, Govt. of India.

## REFERENCES

Allen, J. (2005). *Governing for Enterprise Security* (Tech. Rep. No. CMU/SEI-2005-TN-023). Pittsburgh, PA: Carnegie Mellon, Software Engineering Institute.

Brotby, W. K. (2006). *Information Security Governance: Guidance for Boards of Directors and Executive Management* (2nd ed.). Rolling Meadows, IL: IT Governance Institute.

German Federal Office for Information Security. (2007). *IT Baseline Protection Manual*. Bonn, Germany: Author.

Gligor, V. D., Gavrila, S. I., & Ferraiolo, D. (1998, May 3-6). On the Formal Definition of Separation-of-Duty Policies and their Composition. In *Proceedings of the IEEE Symposium on Security and Privacy*, Oakland, CA.

ISO/IEC. (2000). *Information Technology – Code of practice for information security management, ISO/IEC 17799:2000*. Geneva, Switzerland: Author.

ISO/IEC. (2005). *Information Technology – Code of practice for information security management, ISO/IEC 27002:2005*. Geneva, Switzerland: Author.

IT Governance Institute. (2007). *Control Objectives for Information and Related Technology (COBIT) 4.1*. Rolling Meadows, IL: Author.

Moulton, R., & Coles, R. S. (2003). Applying information security governance. *Computers & Security, 22*(7). doi:10.1016/S0167-4048(03)00705-3

OASIS. (2001). *Security Services Markup Language (S2ML)*. Retrieved August 1, 2009, from http://xml.coverpages.org/s2ml.html

OASIS. (2004a). *Application Vulnerability Description Language (AVDL)*. Retrieved August 1, 2009, from http://www.oasis-open.org/committees/avdl/

OASIS. (2004b). *Intrusion Detection Message Exchange Format (IDMEF)*. Retrieved July 20, 2009, from http://xml.coverpages.org/idmef.html

OASIS. (2005). *OASIS eXtensible Access Control Markup Language (XACML)*. Retrieved August 1, 2009, from http://www.oasis-open.org/committees/xacml/

OASIS. (2006). *OASIS Emergency Management*. Retrieved August 1, 2009, from http://www.oasis-open.org/committees/emergency/

OASIS. (2008). *Security Assertion Markup Language (SAML)*. Retrieved August 1, 2009, from http://xml.coverpages.org/saml.html

Roy, J., Barik, M. S., & Mazumdar, C. (2004). ESRML: A Markup Language for Enterprise Security Requirement Specification. In *Proceedings of the IEEE INDICON 2004 Conference*, Kharagpur, India (pp. 509-512).

Sengupta, A., & Mazumdar, C. (2010). ESRML 2.0: A Markup Language for Expressing Requirements for Information Security Governance. In *Proceedings of the 1ˢᵗ International Conference on Management of Technologies and Information Security (ICMIS 2010)*, Allahabad, India.

Solms, S. H. V., & Solms, R. V. (2009). *Information Security Governance*. Berlin, Germany: Springer. doi:10.1007/978-0-387-79984-1

Stoneburner, G. (2001). *Underlying Technical Models for Information Technology Security* (Tech. Rep. No. 800-33). Gaithersburg, MD: National Institute of Standards and Technology.

Williams, P. (2001). Information Security Governance. *Information Security Technical Report, 6*(3), 60–70. doi:10.1016/S1363-4127(01)00309-0

World Wide Web Consortium. (W3C). (2003). *Extensible Markup Language (XML)*. Retrieved July 27, 2009, from http://www.w3.org/xml

# APPENDIX

## Sample Security Requirement Specification Using ESRML 2.0

Figure 10 shows a sample information security requirement specification of an enterprise using ESRML 2.0.

*Figure 10. Sample information security requirement specification of an enterprise using ESRML 2.0*

```
<?xml version="2.0"?>
<Requirement>
  <AssetRegister>
    <ManagerialVulnerability>
      <Vulnerability id="2" name="Lack of Network Access Control" loc="Low" severity="Low"/>
    </ManagerialVulnerability>

    <EnvironmentalThreat>
      <Threat name="Cyclone" loc="Low" severity="Low" id="1"/>
      <Threat name="Earthquake" loc="Low" severity="Low" id="2"/>
    </EnvironmentalThreat>

    <InformationSystem>
      <no_of_IS>2</no_of_IS>

      <ISInformation id="1" name="abc1" no_of_hardwareasset="2">
        <HardwareAsset id="1" ISname="abc1" name="AS" type="Server" owner="SAS" custodian="SAS"
vendor="SS" model="SSS" price="222" typeId="14" mobility="" no_of_s="1" no_of_info="1">

          <SecurityClass cVal="2" iVal="2" aVal="2" auVal="2" liVal="2" lcVal="N"/>

          <User name="admin" r="Y" w="Y" d="Y" e="Y" m="N" a="N" cu="Y" ru="Y" gr="Y" re="Y">
            <User name="107761" w="N" d="N" cu="N" ru="N" gr="N" re="N"/>
          </User>
          <User name="guest" r="Y" w="N" d="N" e="Y" m="N" a="N" cu="N" ru="N" gr="N" re="N"/>

          <HardwareAccessControlList>
            <Subject ISname="abc2" hname="AS3" subname="User" r="Y" w="Y" d="Y" e="Y" m="N"
a="N"/>
          </HardwareAccessControlList>

          <SoftwareAsset id="1" ISname="abc1" hname="AS" name="S1" type="Multimedia" owner="SAS"
custodian="SAS" vendor="as" version="as" price="222" typeId="21" SubTypeId="27" mobility="N"
subtype="Adobe Illustrator 8.0">

            <SecurityClass cVal="2" iVal="2" aVal="2" auVal="2" liVal="2" lcVal="N"/>

            <SoftwareAccessControlList>
              <Subject ISname="abc1" hname="AS" subname="User" r="Y" w="Y" d="Y" e="Y" m="N"
a="N"/>
            </SoftwareAccessControlList>

            <SoftwareThreat>
              <AccidentalThreat name="Denial of Service" loc="Low" id="35"/>
              <AccidentalThreat name="Authentication Failure" loc="Low" id="23"/>
              <AccidentalThreat name="Information Leakage" loc="Low" id="24"/>
            </SoftwareThreat>
            <SoftwareThreat>
              <DeliberateThreat name="Malicious Code" loc="Low" id="41"/>
              <DeliberateThreat name="Denial of Service" loc="Low" id="43"/>
              <DeliberateThreat name="Password Leakage" loc="Low" id="25"/>
              <DeliberateThreat name="Information Leakage" loc="Low" id="26"/>
              <DeliberateThreat name="Physical Attack" loc="Low" id="37"/>
              <DeliberateThreat name="Hacking" loc="Low" id="27"/>
            </SoftwareThreat>
```

*Figure 11.*

```
<SoftwareVulnerability>
  <Vulnerability id="7" name="Bad password handling" severity="Low"/>
  <Vulnerability id="8" name="Uncontrolled copying of proprietary information or software"
severity="Low"/>
  <Vulnerability id="9" name="Bugs in Software" severity="Low"/>
</SoftwareVulnerability>
</SoftwareAsset>

<InformationAsset id="1" ISname="abc1" name="sdf" type="Personnel Files" owner="SAS"
custodian="sad" price="333" typeId="64" mobility="N" hname="AS">

<SecurityClass cVal="2" iVal="3" aVal="2" auVal="2" liVal="2" lcVal="N" nrVal="N"/>

<InformationAccessControlList>
  <Subject ISname="abc1" hname="sdf" subname="User" r="Y" w="Y" d="Y" e="Y" m="N"
a="N"/>
</InformationAccessControlList>

<InformationThreat>
  <AccidentalThreat name="Denial of Service" loc="Low" id="36"/>
  <AccidentalThreat name="Authentication Failure" loc="Low" id="2"/>
  <AccidentalThreat name="Information Leakage" loc="Low" id="3"/>
</InformationThreat>
<InformationThreat>
  <DeliberateThreat name="Malicious Code" loc="VeryLow" id="42"/>
  <DeliberateThreat name="Denial of Service" loc="Medium" id="44"/>
  <DeliberateThreat name="Authentication Failure" loc="Low" id="46"/>
  <DeliberateThreat name="Unauthorized Access" loc="Low" id="18"/>
  <DeliberateThreat name="Password Leakage" loc="VeryLow" id="8"/>
  <DeliberateThreat name="Information Leakage" loc="Low" id="9"/>
  <DeliberateThreat name="Physical Attack" loc="Low" id="38"/>
  <DeliberateThreat name="Hacking" loc="Low" id="11"/>
</InformationThreat>

<InformationVulnerability>
  <Vulnerability id="1" name="Bad password handling" severity="Low"/>
  <Vulnerability id="2" name="Lack of guidelines when to apply cryptographic controls"
severity="Low"/>
  <Vulnerability id="3" name="Uncontrolled copying of proprietary information or software"
severity="Low"/>
  <Vulnerability id="4" name="Lack of policy governing the use of cryptographic controls"
severity="Low"/>
  <Vulnerability id="5" name="Lack of back-up processes" severity="Low"/>
  <Vulnerability id="6" name="Lack of or inappropriate management of cryptographic keys"
severity="Low"/>
</InformationVulnerability>
</InformationAsset>

<HardwareThreat>
  <AccidentalThreat name="Denial of Service" loc="High" id="1"/>
  <AccidentalThreat name="Hardware Failure" loc="High" id="33"/>
</HardwareThreat>
<HardwareThreat>
  <DeliberateThreat name="Malicious Code" loc="Low" id="15"/>
  <DeliberateThreat name="Denial of Service" loc="Medium" id="16"/>
  <DeliberateThreat name="Authentication Failure" loc="Very High" id="17"/>
  <DeliberateThreat name="Unauthorized Access" loc="Low" id="32"/>
```

*Figure 12.*

```
                <DeliberateThreat name="Physical Attack" loc="Low" id="10"/>
            </HardwareThreat>

            <HardwareVulnerability>
                <Vulnerability id="10" name="Lack of equipment security" severity="Low"/>
                <Vulnerability id="11" name="Deterioration of hardware" severity="Low"/>
            </HardwareVulnerability>
        </HardwareAsset>

        <HardwareAsset id="2" ISname="abc1" name="AS1" type="Net PC" owner="WQE"
custodian="WQE" vendor="WEQ" model="WE" price="222" typeId="3" mobility="" no_of_s="0"
no_of_info="0">
            <SecurityClass cVal="2" iVal="2" aVal="2" auVal="2" liVal="2" lcVal="N"/>
            <User name="User" r="Y" w="Y" d="Y" e="Y" m="N" a="N" cu="N" ru="N" gr="N" re="N"/>
            <HardwareAccessControlList>
                <Subject ISname="abc1" hname="AS" subname="admin" r="Y" w="Y" d="Y" e="Y" m="N"
a="N"/>
            </HardwareAccessControlList>
        </HardwareAsset>
    </ISInformation>

    <ISInformation id="2" name="abc2" no_of_hardwareasset="1">
        <HardwareAsset id="1" ISname="abc2" name="AS3" type="PC" owner="dsf" custodian="dsf"
vendor="df" model="df" price="333" typeId="5" mobility="" no_of_s="0" no_of_info="0">
            <SecurityClass cVal="2" iVal="2" aVal="2" auVal="2" liVal="2" lcVal="N"/>
            <User name="admin" r="Y" w="Y" d="Y" e="Y" m="N" a="N" cu="Y" ru="Y" gr="Y" re="Y"/>
            <User name="guest" r="Y" w="N" d="N" e="Y" m="N" a="N" cu="N" ru="N" gr="N" re="N"/>
            <HardwareAccessControlList>
                <Subject ISname="abc1" hname="AS1" subname="User" r="Y" w="Y" d="Y" e="Y" m="N"
a="N"/>
            </HardwareAccessControlList>
        </HardwareAsset>
    </ISInformation>
</InformationSystem>

<ServiceAssets>
    <ServiceAsset id="1" ISnamelist="abc1" hnamelist="AS, AS1" name="SV" type="UPS" owner="SAS"
custodian="SAS" vendor="SS" model="AAA" price="20" typeId="3" mobility="" no_of_IS="1" no_of_h="2">

        <SecurityClass cVal="1" iVal="3" aVal="4" auVal="2" liVal="2" lcVal="N"/>

        <ServiceAccessControlList>
            <Subject ISname="abc2" hname="AS3" subname="User" r="Y" w="Y" d="Y" e="Y" m="N"
a="N"/>
        </ServiceAccessControlList>

        <ServiceThreat>
            <AccidentalThreat name="Denial of Service" loc="High" id="1"/>
        </ServiceThreat>
        <ServiceThreat>
            <DeliberateThreat name="Denial of Service" loc="Medium" id="16"/>
            <DeliberateThreat name="Unauthorized Access" loc="Low" id="32"/>
            <DeliberateThreat name="Physical Attack" loc="Low" id="10"/>
        </ServiceThreat>

        <ServiceVulnerability>
            <Vulnerability id="10" name="Lack of equipment security" severity="Low"/>
        </ServiceVulnerability>

    </ServiceAsset>

</ServiceAssets>

</AssetRegister>

<NetworkStructure>
    <InterConnection>
        <Connection sISname="abc1" snode="AS" dISname="abc2" dnode="AS3" linktype="Ethernet"
protocol="TCP/IP" speed="10MBPS" connectivityTypeId="1"/>
    </InterConnection>
    <IntraConnection>
        <Connection ISname="abc1" snode="AS" dnode="AS1" linktype="Ethernet" protocol="TCP/IP"
speed="10MBPS" connectivityTypeId="1"/>
    </IntraConnection>
</NetworkStructure>

</Requirement>
```

*This work was previously published in the International Journal of Information Security and Privacy, Volume 5, Issue 2, edited by Hamid Nemati, pp. 33-53, copyright 2011 by IGI Publishing (an imprint of IGI Global).*

124

# Chapter 8
# On the Security of Self–Certified Public Keys

**Cheng-Chi Lee**
*Fu Jen Catholic University, Taiwan*

**Min-Shiang Hwang**
*Asia University, Taiwan*

**I-En Liao**
*National Chung Hsing University, Taiwan*

## ABSTRACT

*Many cryptosystems have been developed to solve the problem of information security, and some approaches are based on the self-certified public key proposed by Girault. In Girault's scheme, the public key is computed cooperatively by both the system authority (SA) and the user. One of the advantages is that the public key is able to implicitly authenticate itself without any additional certificates. Another advantage is that the SA is not able to forge a public key without knowing the user's secret key. Despite the advantages of Girault's system, in this paper, the authors demonstrate that the system still suffers from two main weaknesses. As a result, the authors propose a slight improvement on Girault's system.*

## INTRODUCTION

Some well-known public key systems have been developed since 1976 (Diffie & Hellman, 1976; ElGamal, 1985; Hwang, Chang, & Hwang, 2002; Rivest, Shamir, & Adleman, 1978). In those systems, each user has two keys, namely, the private key and the public key. The private key is kept secretly by a user, and it is used to provide the legal signature of a message or to decrypt a message sent by another user. The public key is accessible to public through directory lookup, and it is used to verify the validity of a signature or to encrypt a message. Since the public key is published to the public key directory, an adversary can modify the public key of a target user from the public key directory. A public-key authentication is an important research's issue. The purpose of

DOI: 10.4018/978-1-4666-2050-6.ch008

public-key authentication is to verify the public key of a legal user and to prevent public key from being forged.

Three of the most popular schemes for public-key authentication are ID-based scheme (Shamir, 1984), certificate-based scheme (Kohnfelder, 1978) and self-certified scheme (Girault, 1991). We briefly review each of them in the following.

In ID-based scheme, a user first chooses his/her own secret key, and then the system authority (SA) generates a public key using the user's identity and the secret key. Since the public key is derived from the user's identity, the direct relation between the identity and the public key makes it impossible for an evil user to forge a public key. In addition, there is no need to store the public key in a public directory. However, this scheme has a drawback that the SA can impersonate a user, since SA knows every user's secret key. In general, public keys are derived from user's identities and secret keys. For example, the public key is equal to $s=ID^d \bmod n$, where $ID$ is user's identity and $d$ is user's secret key. This procedure is generated by SA.

In certificate-based scheme, the public key of a user is generated by the SA and is used as the user's certificate. The process of generating a public key is also known to the public. The difference between ID-based scheme and certificate-based scheme is that the certificate-based scheme has a certificate to verify the public key of a user. The procedure of generating public keys is public. For example, the public is $(y, C)$, where $y$ is user's public key and $C$ is the public key's certificate. Therefore, one can recalculate a user's public key and compare it with the one stored in the SA's system to verify the validity of a public key. These schemes suffers from the same drawback as in the ID-based scheme, namely, the SA is able to impersonate a user by generating a false certificate. In addition, the certificates have to be stored in SA's system which may occupy too much storage space.

The self-certified scheme was developed by Girault to overcome the problems of the above two, in which a user first chooses his/her own

secret key, and then the public key is computed using both the user's and SA's secret keys. That is to say, the public key is generated by both of user and SA. If SA doesn't know the user's secret key, SA cannot generate public key. The detail of this procedure can be seen in another section. The main feature of this system is that the SA is a trusted parity. The SA is unable to forge a public key. In other words, it makes the SA more trust worthy. Due to such an advantage, this scheme received a lot more attentions than the other schemes did (Chang, Wu, & Huang, 2000; Saeednia, 1997; Saeednia & Ghodosi, 1999; Tseng & Jan, 1999; Yang, Choi, & Ann, 1996). These schemes also need an SA to help users to sign users' public keys. The public key is computed by using both of the user's and SA's secret keys. Therefore, SA cannot impersonate a user to derive a user's public key. Using the Girault's system, theses schemes can achieve their proposed requirements.

Despite the advantages of Girault's system, Saeednia showed that their system is insecure (Saeednia, 2003). Saeednia pointed out that the authority SA can know the users' secret keys if the authority generates modulo $n$ in a special dishonest way. In this paper, we will propose a different cryptanalysis of the system. We assume that the authority is a trusted parity. This paper will show two weaknesses that an evil user who impersonates the SA and generates a legal public key of a user without knowing the secret key of the SA. Next, we will propose a slight improvement on Girault's system.

The rest of the paper is organized as follows. In the next section, the Girault's self-certified public key is briefly reviewed. The problem of Girault's system is described. Finally, we give a few concluding remarks and a slight improvement.

## GIRAULT'S SELF-CERTIFIED PUBLIC KEY SYSTEM

Girault proposed a self-certified public key system (Girault, 1991) that is based on the RSA cryptosystem (Chang & Hwang, 1996; Rivest, Shamir, & Adleman, 1978) and consists of three phases: the initialization, the registration, and the verification phases.

## INITIALIZATION PHASE

The SA first generates an RSA key pair $(e, d)$ satisfying $e*d \bmod (p-1)(q-1)=1$, where $p$ and $q$ are two large primes. Here, $e$ and $d$ denote a public key and secret key of the SA, respectively. Then the SA calculates two integers $n$ and $g$, where $n=p*q$ and $g$ is a maximal order in the multiplicative group $(Z/nZ)^*$. After that, the parameters $p$, $q$, and $d$ are kept secret by the SA and $n$, $e$, and $g$ are open to the public.

## REGISTRATION PHASE

When a user $U_i$ with identity $ID_i$, wants to join the system, he/she chooses a secret key $s_i$ and calculates an integer $v_i$ in the following:

$$v_i=g^{-si} \bmod n. \tag{1}$$

Next, $U_i$ sends $ID_i$ and $v_i$ to the SA. Upon receiving these messages, the SA calculates a public key $p_i$ for the user by

$$p_i=(v_i\text{-}ID_i)^d \bmod n, \tag{2}$$

and then the SA sends $p_i$ back to $U_i$. Upon receiving $p_i$, $U_i$ checks the validity of $p_i$ by

$$(p_i^e+ID_i) \bmod n=v_i. \tag{3}$$

If the above equation holds, $U_i$ is certain that $p_i$ is indeed generated by the SA. Note that the public key $p_i$ of a user $U_i$ is generated by SA using both the secret key $s_i$ of $U_i$ and $d$ of SA. However, $s_i$ is unknown to the SA. The registration phase is shown in Figure 1.

## VERIFICATION PHASE

When a verifier wants to verify the validity of a user's $p_i$, he/she can follow identity $ID_i$ (Beth, 1988; Schnorr, 1990):

**Step 1:** $U_i$ sends $ID_i$ and $p_i$ to the verifier, who then calculates $v_i=(p_i^e+ID_i) \bmod n$.
**Step 2:** $U_i$ selects a random integer $r_i$, calculates $t_i=g^{ri} \bmod n$, and then sends $t_i$ to the verifier.
**Step 3:** The verifier selects a random integer $r_v$ and sends it to $U_i$.
**Step 4:** $U_i$ calculates $y_i=r_i+s_i*r_v$, and sends it to the verifier.
**Step 5:** Upon receiving $y_i$, the verifier checks the following equation $(g^{yi}*v_i^{rv}) \bmod n=t_i$. If it holds, the verifier proves that $ID_i$ is valid and $p_i$ was generated by the SA. This phase is shown in Figure 2.

*Figure 1. The registration phase of Girault's scheme*

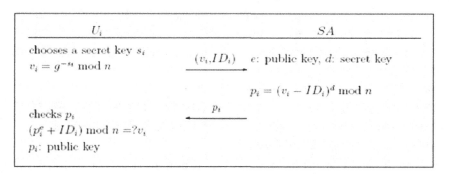

*Figure 2. The verification phase of Girault's scheme*

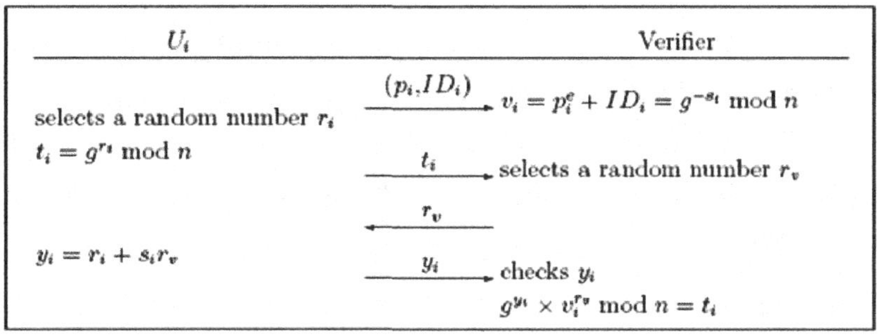

Note the name self-certified comes from the fact that no certificate is necessary when verifying $ID_i$ and $p_i$, as the certificate is embedded in the public key itself. An evil user, who has the knowledge of $p_i$, is highly unlikely to obtain $U_i$'s secret key $s_i$ by solving the discrete logarithm problem (Girault, 1991), although the SA can impersonate $U_i$ by generating a false public key $p_i'$ with the use of an arbitrary secret key $s_i'$. The existence of two or more public keys linked to $U_i$ can prove that the SA has cheated, as the SA can generate only one valid public key for a particular user.

## CRYPTANALYSIS OF GIRAULT'S SYSTEM

Despite the advantages of Girault's self-certified public key system, it is still vulnerable that an evil user who impersonates the SA to sign a legal public key for a user. We propose two weaknesses as follows.

## WEAKNESS ONE

**Step 1:** An evil user $U_i$ arbitrarily chooses a random secret key $s_i'$ and calculates $v_i'=g^{si'} \bmod n$, which satisfies $v_i+ID_i= v_i'-ID_i'$, where $ID_i'$ is $U_i$'s another identity.

**Step 2:** $U_i$ registers his/her another $ID_i'$ to SA, and sends $(ID_i', v_i')$ to SA.

**Step 3:** SA calculates a legal public key $p_i'$ for the user $ID_i'$ by $p_i'=(v_i'-ID_i')^d \bmod n$ and sends it to $U_i$.

**Step 4:** Upon receiving $p_i'$, $U_i$ checks it by Equation (3), who was convinced that $p_i'$ is signed by SA.

**Step 5:** $U_i$ impersonates SA to sign a legal $p_i''$ for $ID_i''$ as follows, where $p_i''= p_i*p_i'$ and $ID_i''= ID_i^2$.

$$p_i''= p_i*p_i' \qquad (4)$$

$$=(v_i-ID_i)^d*(v_i'-ID_i')^d \bmod n$$

$$=[(v_i-ID_i)*(v_i+ID_i)]^d \bmod n$$

$$=(v_i^2-ID_i^2)^d \bmod n$$

The secret key of $ID_i''$ is $2s_i$ which is derived from $v_i''=v_i^2 \bmod n =g^{-2si} \bmod n$. Therefore, $U_i$ can impersonate SA to sign a validity of $p_i''$ and $ID_i''$. But, SA does not know that $ID_i''$ is a forged user.

When a verifier wants to verify the validity of a user's $p_i''$, he/she can identity $ID_i''$ in the following verification phase:

**Step 1:** $U_i$ sends $ID_i''$ and $p_i''$ to the verifier, who then calculates $v_i''=(p_i''^e+ID_i'') \bmod n$.

**Step 2:** $U_i$ selects a random integer $r_i$, calculates $t_i=g^{ri} \bmod n$, and then sends $t_i$ to the verifier.

**Step 3:** The verifier selects a random integer $r_v$ and sends it to $U_i$.

*Figure 3. Our improved registration phase*

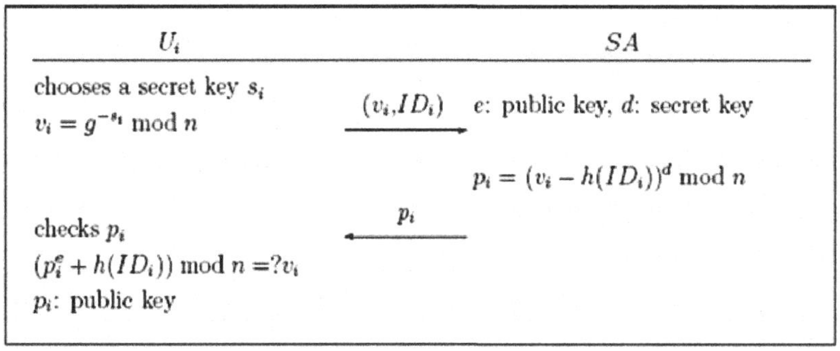

**Step 4:** $U_i$ calculates $y_i=r_i+s_i''*r_v$, where $s_i''=2s_i$, and sends $y_i$ to the verifier.

**Step 5:** Upon receiving $y_i$, the verifier checks the following equation: $(g^{yi}*v_i''^{rv})$ $mod\ n=t_i$. If it holds, the verifier can prove that $ID_i''$ is valid and $p_i''$ was generated by the SA.

It is quite obvious that an evil user $U_i$ can impersonate SA to sign a validity of $p_i''$ and $ID_i''$. It also passes the public-key authentication by the above protocol. That is to say, it is possible that this weakness can be performed if a user can find a correct format $ID_i'$ and $ID_i''$ such that $v_i+ID_i= v_i'-ID_i'$ and $ID_i''=ID_i^2$.

## WEAKNESS TWO

**Step 1:** An evil user $U_i$ arbitrarily chooses a random secret key $s_i'$ and a public key $p_i'$.

**Step 2:** $U_i$ calculates $v_i'=g^{si'}\ mod\ n$.

**Step 3:** $U_i$ derives $ID_i'$ by $(p_i'^e+ID_i')\ mod\ n= v_i'$.

**Step 4:** $U_i$ keeps the triplet $(ID_i', s_i', p_i')$, where the $ID_i'$ is $U_i$'s another identity, and $(s_i', p_i')$ is his/her another key pair. Therefore, $U_i$ can impersonate SA to sign a validity of $p_i'$ and $ID_i'$, SA is unknown to that $ID_i'$ is a forged user.

When a verifier wants to verify the validity of a user's $p_i'$, he/she can identity $ID_i'$ in the following verification phase:

**Step 1:** $U_i$ sends $ID_i'$ and $p_i'$ to the verifier, who then calculates $v_i'=(p_i'^e+ID_i')\ mod\ n$.

**Step 2:** $U_i$ selects a random integer $r_i$, calculates $t_i=g^{ri}\ mod\ n$, and then sends $t_i$ to the verifier.

**Step 3:** The verifier selects a random integer $r_v$ and sends it to $U_i$.

*Figure 4. Our improved verification phase*

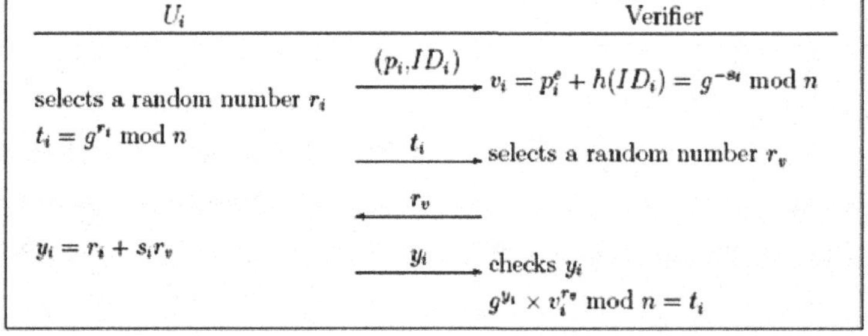

**Step 4:** $U_i$ calculates $y_i=r_i+s_i'*r_v$, and sends $y_i$ to the verifier.

**Step 5:** Upon receiving $y_i$, the verifier checks the following equation: $(g^{yi}*v_i'^{rv})\ mod\ n=t_i$. If it holds, the verifier can prove that $ID_i'$ is valid and $p_i'$ was generated by the SA.

It can prove that an evil user $U_i$ can impersonate SA to sign a validity of $p_i'$ and $ID_i'$. Therefore, the self-certified public key system is vulnerable. That is to say, it is possible that this weakness can be performed if a user $U_i$ can find a correct format $ID_i'$ such that $(p_i'^e+ID_i')\ mod\ n=v_i'$.

## DISCUSSION AND CONCLUSION

We have shown that Girault's self-certified public key system is possible that it has two weaknesses: An evil user can easily impersonate the SA to sign a public key without knowing the secret key of the SA. We can see that an evil user can easily generate the valid pair of $(ID_i, p_i)$ in which they can be only generated by the SA.

To overcome these weaknesses, we proposed a slight improvement on Girault's system. The proposed slight improvement is shown in Figures 3 and 4. Our proposed improvement uses the concept of one-way hash function. This function, $h: x{\rightarrow}y$, has the following properties (Gligoroski, 2009; Hwang & Sung, 2006; Lee, 2001, 2007):

1.  The function $h$ can take a message of arbitrary-length input and produce a message digest of a fixed-length output.
2.  The function $h$ is one-way, given $x$, It is easy to compute $h(x)=y$. However, given $y$, It is hard to compute $h^{-1}(y)=x$.
3.  The function $h$, given $x$, it is computationally infeasible to find $x'{\neq}x$ such that $h(x')=h(x)$.
4.  The function $h$, it is computationally infeasible to find any two pair $x$ and $x'$ such that $x'{\neq}x$ and $h(x')=h(x)$.

The difference between the Girault's system and our improvement is that we only hash the user's identity ($ID_i$). The proposed improvement does not only achieve their advantages but also enhances their security by withstanding the security weaknesses. Of course, our improvement can apply to other self-certified based public key cryptosystems (Li & Wang, 2007; Shao, 2005).

## ACKNOWLEDGMENT

This research was partially supported by the National Science Council, Taiwan, R.O.C., under contract no.: NSC96-2219-E-009-013 and NSC99-2221-E-030-022.

## REFERENCES

Beth, T. (1988). A Fiat-Shamir-like authentication protocol for the ElGamal scheme. In *Advances in Cryptology: Proceedings of EUROCRYPT'88*, Davos, Switzerland (pp. 77-86).

Chang, C. C., & Hwang, M. S. (1996). Parallel computation of the generating keys for RSA cryptosystems. *Electronics Letters*, *32*(15), 1365–1366. doi:10.1049/el:19960886

Chang, Y. S., Wu, T. C., & Huang, S. C. (2000). ElGamal-like digital signature and multisignature schemes using self-certified public keys. *Journal of Systems and Software*, *50*, 99–105. doi:10.1016/S0164-1212(99)00080-1

Diffie, W., & Hellman, M. E. (1976). New directions in cryptography. *IEEE Transactions on Information Theory*, *22*, 644–654. doi:10.1109/TIT.1976.1055638

ElGamal, T. (1985). A public-key cryptosystem and a signature scheme based on discrete logarithms. *IEEE Transactions on Information Theory*, *31*, 469–472. doi:10.1109/TIT.1985.1057074

Girault, M. (1991, April 8-11). Self-certified public keys. In *Advances in Cryptology: Proceedings of EUROCRYPT'91,* Brighton, UK (pp. 491-497).

Gligoroski, D. (2009). On a family of minimal candidate one-way functions and one-way permutations. *International Journal of Network Security, 8*(3), 211–220.

Hwang, M. S., Chang, C. C., & Hwang, K. F. (2002). An ElGamal-like cryptosystem for enciphering large messages. *IEEE Transactions on Knowledge and Data Engineering, 14*(2), 445–446. doi:10.1109/69.991728

Hwang, M. S., & Sung, P. C. (2006). A study of micro-payment based on one-way hash chain. *International Journal of Network Security, 2*(2), 81–90.

Kohnfelder, M. (1978). *A method for certification (Tech. Rep.)*. Cambridge, MA: MIT, Laboratory for Computer Science.

Lee, C. C. (2001). *User authentication schemes for mobile communications.* Unpublished doctoral dissertation, Chaoyang University of Technology, Taiwan.

Lee, C. C. (2007). *Mobile users' privacy and authentication in wireless communication systems.* Unpublished doctoral dissertation, National Chung Hsing University, China.

Li, J., & Wang, S. (2007). New efficient proxy blind signature scheme using verifiable self-certified public key. *International Journal of Network Security, 4*(2), 193–200.

Rivest, R. L., Shamir, A., & Adleman, L. (1978). A method for obtaining digital signatures and public key cryptosystems. *Communications of the ACM, 21*, 120–126. doi:10.1145/359340.359342

Saeednia, S. (1997). Identity-based and self-certified key-exchange protocols. In *Proceedings of the 2nd Australasian Conference on Information Security and Privacy,* Sydney, Australia (pp. 303-313).

Saeednia, S. (2003). A note on Girault's self-certified model. *Information Processing Letters, 86*(6), 323–327. doi:10.1016/S0020-0190(03)00203-5

Saeednia, S., & Ghodosi, H. (1999). A self-certified group-oriented cryptosystem without a combiner. In *Proceedings of the 4th Australasian Conference on Information Security and Privacy,* Sydney, Australia (pp. 192-201).

Schnorr, C. P. (1990, March 14-16). Key distribution system using ID-related information directory suitable for mail systems. In *Proceedings of the SECURICOM'90 Conference,* Paris, France (pp. 115-122).

Shamir, A. (1984). Identity based cryptosystems & signature schemes. In *Advances in Cryptology: Proceedings of CRYPTO'84,* Santa Barbara, CA (pp. 47-53).

Shao, Z. (2005). Improvement of threshold signature using self-certified public keys. *International Journal of Network Security, 1*(1), 24–31.

Tseng, Y. M., & Jan, J. K. (1999). A group signature scheme using self-certified public keys. In *Proceedings of the 9th National Conference Information Security,* Taichung, Taiwan (pp. 165-172).

Yang, H. K., Choi, J. H., & Ann, Y. H. (1996, November 26-29). Self-certified identity information using the minimum knowledge. In *Proceedings of the Digital Signal Processing Applications Conference (IEEE TENCON),* Perth, WA, Australia (pp. 641-647).

*This work was previously published in the International Journal of Information Security and Privacy, Volume 5, Issue 2, edited by Hamid Nemati, pp. 54-60, copyright 2011 by IGI Publishing (an imprint of IGI Global).*

# Chapter 9
# Design and Implementation of a Zero-Knowledge Authentication Framework for Java Card

**Ahmed Patel**
*Universiti Kebangsaan Malaysia, Malaysia & Kingston University, UK*

**Kenan Kalajdzic**
*Center for Computing Education, Bosnia and Herzegovina*

**Laleh Golafshan**
*Department of Computer Engineering and IT, Science and Research Branch, Islamic Azad University, Fars, Iran*

**Mona Taghavi**
*Department of Computer, Science and Research Branch, Islamic Azad University, Tehran, Iran*

## ABSTRACT

*Zero-knowledge authentication protocols are an alternative to authentication protocols based on public key cryptography. Low processing and memory consumption make them especially suitable for implementation in smart card microprocessors, which are severely limited in processing power and memory space. This paper describes a design and implementation of a software library providing smart card application developers with a reliable authentication mechanism based on well-known zero-knowledge authentication schemes. Java Card is used as the target smart card platform implementation based on the evaluation of the Fiat-Shamir (F-S) and Guillou-Quisquater (G-Q) protocols under various performance criteria are presented to show the effectiveness of the implementation and that G-Q is a more efficient protocol.*

## 1. INTRODUCTION

User authentication is essential in many networked and Internet applications. It is a process by which a user proves his/ her identity to the system, thus proving his/ her rights to use particular informa-tion and services. The essence of authentication is the demonstration of either the knowledge of a secret, the possession of a physical object, or the authenticity of a certain human body characteristic.

The most popular mechanism of user authen-tication is the use of passwords. It is cheap to

DOI: 10.4018/978-1-4666-2050-6.ch009

deploy and easy to use. While suitable for many applications, password authentication is lacking many features necessary for security critical applications. Badly chosen passwords are easy to guess, can be intercepted in transmission and re-used later for impersonating legitimate users. Passwords cannot be used directly to sign digital documents.

Cryptography offers better methods of authentication, but their use is connected with manipulating secret cryptographic keys, which are difficult to remember. For sensible use, cryptographic keys need to be stored in some well-protected computing devices. For people on the go, such a device has to be small enough to fit into a pocket. Smart cards are probably the most widespread device of this sort.

A Smart card is a credit card sized plastic card with an embedded single-chip microcomputer. The use of special manufacturing technology makes physical tampering or probing of the microcomputer circuitry difficult, although not completely impossible. Smart card microcomputers are characterized by low clock frequencies (around 1 MHz) and small memory capacity (1-16 KB of ROM and less than 1 KB of RAM). Thus, smart cards are portable and small computers with different types of memory. Java Card technology is used in order to enable smart cards for running small applications in secure mode for a variety of environments, such as telephone networks and banking industry (ORACLE, 2010; Chen, 2000) and mobile agent e-marketplaces (Wei & Patel, 2009; Patel, 2010). Typically, it is touched wherever authentication and security are essential to access valuable data.

The limitations of smartcards severely impact the choice of cryptographic techniques available for use in smartcard applications. Currently, only techniques based on symmetric cryptography are in wide use. Although asymmetric (public key) cryptography offers a richer range of functionality, it requires more memory space and processing

power than is available in the majority of currently available smartcards.

In the domain of authentication protocols, an alternative to both symmetric and asymmetric cryptography is the use of zero-knowledge proof techniques. Zero-knowledge authentication protocols offer same level of convenience as authentication protocols based on asymmetric cryptography, but require less memory space and processing power. Zero-knowledge protocols consist of two essential parts, the prover and verifier (Kapron *et al.*, 2007). For a more detailed account regarding the background and content of zero-knowledge protocol see published paper by Vadhan (2004).

To validate practical applicability of zero-knowledge techniques in smartcard environment, the authors developed a prototype software library that implements a well-known zero-knowledge authentication protocol. Java Card specification was used as the target smartcard platform. The results of this work are discussed in the rest of this paper.

Section 2 gives a brief overview of smartcard technology and related standards. Section 3 gives an introduction into zero-knowledge proofs and zero-knowledge authentication protocols. Thereafter, the design and implementation of a prototype library based on the evaluated zero-knowledge protocols are discussed in Section 4 and the conclusions given in Section 5.

## 2. SMARTCARDS

A smartcard looks like a normal credit card with a chip embedded in it. Smartcards can be divided into three main categories according to the capabilities of the chip:

- Memory cards, which can just store data and have no data processing capabilities.
- Wired Logic Intelligent Memory cards, which contain also some built-in logic,

usually used to control the access to the memory of the card.

- Processor cards, which contain memory and processor and have data processing capabilities.

Smartcards have to communicate with some other devices to gain access to a network. Therefore, they can be plugged into a reader, commonly referred to as a card terminal, or they can operate using Radio Frequencies (RF). In the former type of card, the connection is made when the reader contacts a small golden chip on front of the card whilst the latter (contactless card) can communicate via an antenna, eliminating the need to insert and remove the card by hand. All that is necessary to start the interaction is to get close enough to a receiver. Contactless cards are practical in applications in which speed is important or in which card insertion/removal may be impractical (an example could be the Subscriber Identity Module (SIM) cards in mobile phones). Some manufacturers are making cards that function in both contact and contactless mode.

All smartcards contain three types of memory: persistent non-mutable memory, persistent mutable memory and non-persistent mutable memory. ROM, EEPROM and RAM are the most widely used memories for the three respective types in the current smartcards.

A typical processor card with contacts has 16KB ROM, 512 bytes of RAM and an eight-bit processor, although the technology is moving towards 16 or 32-bit CPU (Oritz, 2003; ORACLE, 2010).

Although smartcards are more expensive than ordinary magnetic stripe cards, their use is increasing because of several reasons. Firstly, smartcards are more secure than magnetic stripe cards. In fact, it is easy today to purchase tools needed to hack into confidential data on a magnetic stripe card whilst smartcards are considered tamper resistant. However, unfortunately smartcards are not as tamper resistant as it is believed. Firstly, the

technology to read protected memory or reverse-engineer smartcards' CPU is relatively easy, and with the present state of the art, they cannot resist well planned invasive tampering like side-channel signal pickup and differential power analysis (Kocher *et al.*, 1999). Secondly, processor cards with their processing capabilities and increased memory capacity can perform more activities than simple magnetic stripe cards that require a host system to store and process all data, which make them open to tampering.

Smartcards are used to cover the personal secure information, and it is significant that they play a critical role in security systems. Smartcards are the authentication devices that are used to store secret keys because of the lack of secure PCs. On the other hand, cryptographic operations are done via secret key (Herbst *et al.*, 2006).

## A. Standards

Several standards for smartcards have been defined by International Standards Organisation (ISO) and the International Electro-technical Commission (IEC). The important ones are shown in Figure 1 based on reading and writing the data from the card, type of chips, and its capacities as well. Here, we restrict our discussion to processor cards with contacts.

## 1. ISO/IEC 7816

This ISO/IEC 7816 standard covers various aspects of integrated circuit cards with electrical contacts. It consists of the following fourteen parts with a fifteen part numbering - minus part 14 - (International Organization for Standardization, 1987):

- **Physical characteristics (Part 1):** Defines the physical dimensions of contact smartcards and their resistance to static electricity, electromagnetic radiation and mechan-

*Figure 1. Smartcards types*

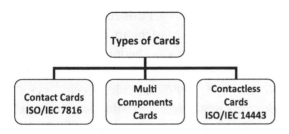

ical stress. It also prescribes the physical location of an embossing area.

- **Dimension and location of the contacts (Part 2):** Defines the location, purpose and electrical characteristics of the card's metallic contacts.
- **Electronic interface signals and transmission protocols (Part 3):** Defines the voltage and current requirements for the electrical contacts defined in Part 2 and asynchronous half-duplex character transmission protocol.
- **Organisation, security and commands for interchange (Part 4):** Establishes a set of commands to provide access, security and transmission of card data. Within the basic kernel, for example, are commands to verify access control, secure messaging, read, write and update records.
- **Registration of application provider's identifiers (Part 5):** Defines how to use an application identifier to ascertain the presence of and/or perform the retrieval of an application in a card through data elements and interchange with the integrated circuit card.
- **Inter-industry data elements interchange (Part 6):** Describes encoding rules for data needed in many applications, e.g. name and photograph of the owner, his/her preference of languages, etc.
- **Inter-industry commands for Structured Query Language (SQL) (Part 7):** Describes how to use the database para-

digm in cards through the concept of views and the standard SQL command.

- **Commands for security operations (Part 8):** To facilitate cryptographic operations, complementing commands given in Part 4.
- **Commands for card management (Part 9):** To facilitate card and file management, e.g. file creation and deletion.
- **Electronic signals and answer to reset for synchronous cards (Part 10):** Specifies the power, signal structures, and the structure for the answer to reset between an integrated circuit card(s) with synchronous transmission and an interface device such as a terminal.
- **Personal verification through biometric methods (Part 11):** Specifies the usage of inter-industry commands and data objects related to personal verification through biometric methods in integrated circuit cards.
- **Cards with contacts — USB electrical interface and operating procedures (Part 12):** Specifies the operating conditions of an integrated circuit card that provides a USB interface.
- **Commands for application management in multi-application environment (Part 13):** Specifies commands for application management in a multi-application environment.
- No Part 14.
- **Cryptographic information application (Part 15):** Specifies a card application which contains information on cryptographic functionality and multiple cryptographic algorithms.

In addition to the above, the ISO/IEC 14443 proximity card standard consists of four parts and related amendments for smart cards on a different physical communication support mechanism (International Organization for Standardization, 2000).

*Figure 2. Physical appearance of smartcards*

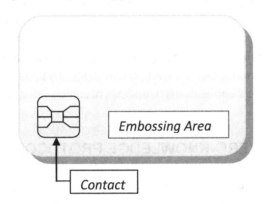

Figures 2 and 3 show the physical appearance of a smartcard as defined in ISO7816 part 1.

Typically smartcard's physical chip appearance in credit card or SIM dimensions has contacts or contactless circuitry as shown in Figure 4.

It houses the computer configuration as shown in Figure 5.

A more comprehensive layout of the computer configuration is shown in Figure 6.

It consists of:

- **Central Processing Unit (CPU):** Which is the heart of the chip?
- **Security logic:** Which detects abnormal conditions such as low voltage levels?
- **Serial I/O interface:** Which allows contact to the "outside" world?
- **Test logic:** Which permits self-test procedures to run?
- ROM consisting of:
  - Card operating system
  - Self-test procedures
  - Typically 16 KBytes
  - Future 32/64 KBytes
- RAM consisting of:
  - "Scratch pad" of the processor
  - Typically 512 bytes (1/2 Kbyte)
  - Future 1 KByte
- EEPROM consisting of:
  - Cryptographic keys
  - PIN code
  - Biometric template
  - Balance
  - Application code
  - Typically 8 or 16 KBytes
  - Future 32 KBytes
- **Databus:** This connects elements of the chip on an 8 or 16 bits wide bus structure.

Normally, a smartcard does not contain a power supply, a display, or a keyboard. It interacts with the outside world using the serial communication interface via its eight contact points.

The embossing area is reserved to personalize the card, for embossing or laser engraving the name of the owner, the card number or other personal details relevant to the application in which the card is involved.

Among other things, ISO7816 (part 4) also defines a standard data format for interaction between the card and the outside world called APDU (Application Protocol Data Unit). If we consider the communication protocol in terms of master/slave paradigm, the card has always a passive role, waiting for a command APDU from the terminal in which it's inserted. In reply to the command, the card sends a response APDU.

## 2. Java Card

There is no standard smartcard programming language today. Smartcard companies use different languages to develop smartcard software; code is

*Figure 3. Chip appearance*

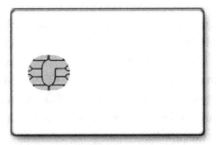

*Figure 4. Chip contact circuitry*

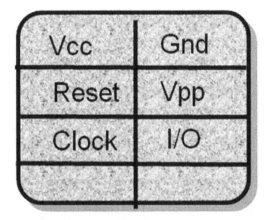

compiled into machine language and embedded into the chip (Sun Microsystems, 1997). The major problem is non-portability of smartcard software and a small universe of knowledgeable programmers (Coleman, 1998; Peyret, 1995).

How to overcome these problems that slow down the adoption of smartcards in many applications? Java programming language offers a possible solution. Java is an object-oriented programming language that compiles into a platform-independent byte code that can be run on any platform providing a Java byte code interpreter. The idea to give smartcards developers the ability to write applications once and have them run on all platforms led, in November 1996, to the release of the Java Card API Specification. One year later, with the release of Java Card API 2.0, every major vendor of smartcards in the world had licensed the technology (Coleman, 1998). For these reasons, Java Card was chosen as the target platform for this project.

The Java Card API is a part of the smallest virtual machine specification for Java. It is designed to allow Java to run on an 8-bit microprocessor, with 8 kilobytes of electrically erasable and programmable read only memory (EEPROM), 16 kilobytes of read only memory (ROM), and 256 bytes of random access memory (RAM) (Chen & Giorgio, 1998).

Java Card programs, called applets, are small enough so that several can fit into the small amounts of memory available on smartcards. Applets can be easily updated, and Java Card functionality can therefore be continually updated as new applications or updates become available.

## 3. ZERO-KNOWLEDGE PROTOCOLS

Zero-knowledge is one of the most popular, useful and powerful protocol in cryptographic design which was introduced by Goldwasser et al. (1985).

Zero-knowledge protocols, as their name suggest, are cryptographic protocols in which one party (the prover) can demonstrate the knowledge of some secret to another party (the verifier) without revealing the secret. This way, an eavesdropper, as well as the verifier, can gain no information about the secret and cannot convince a third party that they know the secret. More precisely, the properties of a zero-knowledge protocol are as follows:

- The prover cannot cheat the verifier unless the prover is extremely lucky; By reiterating the protocol, the odds of an impostor passing as a legitimate user can be made as minimal as necessary.
- The verifier cannot pretend to be the prover to any third party because during the protocol execution the verifier gains no knowledge of the secret.
- The verifier cannot convince a third party of the validity of the authentication proof.

A good introduction into the field of zero-knowledge proof and protocols is given by Quisquater *et al.* (1990).

Zero-knowledge proofs that yield nothing but their validity is a must in the methodology of cryptographic protocol design (Goldreich, 1991). They play an important role in cryptography and it is applicable in solving NP (type

*Figure 5. Chip and computer configuration*

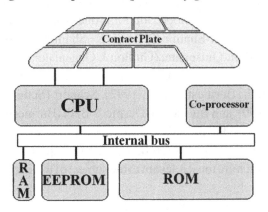

of problems in computational theory defined as nondeterministic polynomial time) issues through interaction and randomness (Kapron *et al.*, 2007). The zero-knowledge protocol has been used to solve different problems. For instance, Kapron *et al.* (2007) presented a new characterization of zero-knowledge protocols as Non-interactive Instance-dependent Commitment schemes (NIC), and by this knowledge they believed that a NIC has a *V-bit* zero-knowledge protocol. Besides, with regards to previous related works (Vadhan, 2004; Nguyen & Vadhan, 2007; Ong & Vadhan, 2007) it is possible to prove unconditional results about zero-knowledge protocols, which has used zero-knowledge protocols as special bit commitment-schemes.

## A. Basic Zero-Knowledge Protocol

Let's consider the basic operation of a zero-knowledge protocol on the following example taken from Schneier (1996).

Assume that the prover knows some information, and furthermore that the information is the solution to a hard problem. The basic protocol consists of several rounds: what is explained below is repeated *n* times.

The prover uses the information he/she knows and a random number to transform the hard problem into another hard problem, one that is

isomorphic to the original one. Not all problems and transformations, of course, are suitable for this purpose; the prover must be sure that the verifier cannot deduce any knowledge from the execution of the protocol, even after many iterations of it.

Then, the prover uses the information he/she knows and the random number to solve the new instance of the hard problem, then commits to the solution, using a bit-commitment scheme. This kind of scheme is used when someone wants to commit to a result but does not want to reveal it until sometime later and, meanwhile; the counterpart wants to make sure that the result is not going to be changed after the commitment.

The prover reveals the new problem instance to the verifier, but the verifier cannot use this problem to get any information about the original instance or its solution. At this stage, the verifier asks the prover either to prove that the old and the new instances are isomorphic (i.e. two different solutions to two related problems) or to open the solution to which the prover committed before and show that it's a solution to the new instance. The prover complies.

In this protocol, the verifier does not get any knowledge of the secret information and the prover cannot cheat. Also, the verifier cannot use a transcription of the exchange to convince a third party that the prover knows the secret, because the verifier cannot demonstrate that she did not

*Figure 6. Chip internal circuitry*

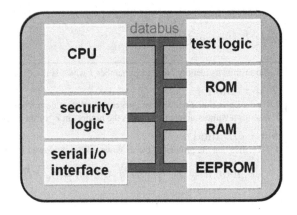

collude with the prover to build a simulator that fakes the prover's knowledge.

## B. Which Problems can be Used in Zero-Knowledge Protocols?

The notion of Zero-Knowledge proof was set forward in 1985 by Goldwasser et al. (1985). One year later Goldwasser (1986) proved that any problem in NP class has a zero-knowledge proof, assuming the existence of one-way functions.

Unfortunately, not all problems in NP class are suitable for a realistic implementation. Like in other cryptographic protocols, the problems most widely used in actual zero-knowledge protocols are the following (Aronsson, 1996):

- The problem of finding discrete logarithms for large natural numbers
- The problem of checking that $y$ is ($x2$ mod $n$) for some natural number $x$, if the factors of n are unknown
- The problem of factoring a large natural number which is a product of two or more large primes

## C. Real Zero-Knowledge Authentication Protocols

Amos Fiat and Adi Shamir (1986) showed how to utilize zero-knowledge proofs for authentication and generating digital signatures. Their protocol, called Fiat-Shamir, was the first realistic zero-

knowledge protocol; a number of other protocols have been developed after this one. This includes Feige-Fiat-Shamir (Micali & Shamir, 1990), Guillou-Quisquater (Guillou & Quisquater, 1988, 1990), Ohta-Okamoto (Ohta & Okamoto, 1990), Beth (Burmester *et al.*, 1992), Schnorr (Schnorr, 1990), and Burmester-Desmedt-Beth (Burmester et al., 1992) protocols. In this paper we review only Fiat-Shamir and Guillou-Quisquater protocols, which are most relevant to the subject of this paper.

### 1. Fiat-Shamir Protocol

A trusted process chooses and makes public a modulus $n$ that is the product of two large prime numbers $p$ and $q$ known only to the process. The process then generates for each user the public key $v_1, v_2, ..., v_k$ and the private key $s_1, s_2, ..., s_k$ such that $s_i = v_i^{-1}$ (mod $n$).

To embed the identity of the user into her or his public key, the trusted process prepares a string $I$ which contains all the relevant information about the user. The process also chooses and makes public a pseudo random function $f$ which maps arbitrary strings to the range $[0,n)$. The function $f$ must be indistinguishable from a truly random function by a polynomially bounded computation. To generate the public key, the process then computes a number of values $v'_j = f(I,j)$, where $j = 1,2,...,N$, and $I,j$ means concatenation of $I$ with a string representing $j$. For the public key, the process selects $k$ values of $v'_j$ for which there

*Table 1. Protocol steps*

| |
|---|
| 1. *P* transmits its identity *I* and a test number *T* which is the $v^{th}$ power in $\mathbf{Z}_n$ of an integer *r* picked at random in $\mathbf{Z}_n{}^*$ : |
| $$T = r^v \bmod n$$ |
| 2. *V* asks a question *d* which is an integer picked at random from *0* to *v-1* |
| 3. *P* sends a witness number *t* which is the product in $\mathbf{Z}_n$ of the integer *r* by the $d^{th}$ power of the authentication number *B*: |
| $$t = r \cdot B^d \bmod n$$ |
| 4. *V* verifies that the product of the $d^{th}$ power of the shadowed identity *J* by the $v^{th}$ power of witness *t*, it's equal to *T*: |
| $$J^d \cdot t^v \bmod n = J^d \cdot \left(r \cdot B^d\right)^v \bmod n = \left(J \cdot B^v\right)^d \cdot r^v \bmod n = T$$ |

*Table 2. Evaluation of F-S and G-Q protocols under performance criteria*

|  | Fiat-Shamir | Guillou-Quisquater |
|---|---|---|
| **No. of bit transmitted** | $t \cdot (2 \cdot |n| + k)$ | $2 \cdot |n| + |v|$ |
| **No. of modular multiplications (prover)** | $t \cdot (k + 2)/2$ | $3 \cdot |v| + 1$ |
| **No. of modular multiplications (verifier)** | $t \cdot (k + 2)/2$ | $3 \cdot |v| + 1$ |
| **Memory requirements** | $k \cdot |n|$ | $|n|$ |
| **Security level** | $2^{-kt}$ | $2^{-|v|}$ |

Notation: $t$ = the number of iterations of the basic protocol

$n$ = the modulus

$|n|$ = the length in bits of $n$ (usually 512)

$k$ = the number of secret keys

$v$ = the public exponent

$|v|$ = the length in bits of $v$

is a square root (modulo $n$). The selected values become $v_1, v_2, \ldots, v_k$.

The proof is based on the following protocol (the prover is identified with $P$, the verifier with $V$):

1. $P$ sends $I$ to $V$
2. $V$ generates $k$ $v_j$ values using same algorithm as the trusted process

The following steps are repeated $t$ times:

3. $P$ selects a random number $r$ from $[0,n)$ and sends $V$ a value of $x = r^2 \pmod n$
4. $V$ sends a random binary vector $(e_1, \ldots, e_k)$ to $P$
5. $P$ sends to $V$: $y = r \cdot \prod_{e_j=1} s_j \bmod n$
6. $V$ checks that $x = y^2 \cdot \prod_{e_j=1} v_j \bmod n$

$V$ accepts $P$'s proof of identity only if all $t$ iterations are successful.

$V$ can get no knowledge of the secret key from the protocol. He cannot recover the secret values $s_j$ from the public values $v_j$, because the calculation of a square root modulus $n$ is considered computationally infeasible for large values of $n$ and $v_j$.

A lucky cheater could guess the correct vector $(e_1, \ldots, e_k)$ sending then to $V$:

$$x = r^2 \prod_{e_j=1} v_j \left( \bmod n \right) \qquad \text{and} \qquad y = r.$$

However, the probability of this event is only $2^{-k}$ per iteration and $2^{-kt}$ for the whole protocol. $k$ and $t$ can be chosen to achieve level of security appropriate for a particular application. A digital signature scheme was constructed on the basis of this protocol.

## 2. Guillou-Quisquater Protocol

$$B^v \cdot J \bmod n = 1$$

where

$$J = \text{Red} \left( I \right)$$

- Red (Redundancy Rule) is a published function, or preferably standardized, that completes $I$, which is half shorter than n, to obtain $J$, the "shadowed identity", that is a number as large as $n$.
- $v$ is an exponent, both published by the authority and known to each verifier. $v$ must be relatively prime to $(p-1)$ and $(q-1)$ to ease the operation of calculating the number $B$ for the user.

*Table 3. F-S and G-Q for a $2^{-20}$ level of security (\*values recommended by Fiat & Shamir, 1986)*

| Parameters & Key factors | t | k | No. of bits transmitted | No. of modular multiplications | Memory requirements |
|---|---|---|---|---|---|
| Fiat-Shamir | 1 | 20 | 1044 | 11 | 10240 |
| Fiat-Shamir | 2 | 10 | 2068 | 12 | 5120 |
| Fiat-Shamir (*) | 4 | 5 | 4116 | 14 | 2560 |
| Fiat-Shamir | 5 | 4 | 5140 | 20 | 2048 |
| Fiat-Shamir | 10 | 2 | 10260 | 20 | 1024 |
| Fiat-Shamir | 20 | 1 | 20500 | 30 | 512 |
| Guillou-Quisquater | |v| = 20 | | 1044 | 61 | 512 |

- $n$ is known by everyone, but only the authority knows its factorization.

The protocol requires only one round and it consists of the steps seen in Table 1.

The strength of the protocol is in the computational complexity of calculating roots of $v^{th}$ power modulo $n$.

Any cheater, having guessed the question $d$, can obviously prepare a pair of $T$ and $t$ by, firstly, picking $t$ at random in $\mathbf{Z}_n$ and, secondly, deducing $T$ by computing exactly as the verifier would do. A cheater, however, has only one chance to guess $d$, which means that the level of security is $2^{-|v|}$, where $|v|$ is the length of $v$ in bits. A digital signature scheme was developed to ascertain and verify this for Guillou-Quisquater protocol as well as for Fiat-Shamir protocol.

## D. The Chess Grandmaster Problem

Although the idea behind zero-knowledge proofs of identity is quite powerful, zero-knowledge protocols are not perfect. The man-in-the-middle attack, for example, cannot be avoided as illustrated by the "Chess Grandmaster Problem" described in Goldwasser *et al.* (1985).

To defeat a world championship level grandmaster, someone (let's call her NICE MONA) could set up a two-room game, inviting two grandmasters to play with her. Neither grandmaster knows about the other.

NICE MONA starts the game with the grandmaster that plays with white pieces (the other one plays with black) so that she can see his first move. Then NICE MONA records the move and walks in the other room. Since NICE MONA plays white, she makes the first move in the game with the second grandmaster. She simply repeats the move of the first grandmaster. This continues, until NICE MONA wins one game and loses the other, or both games end in a draw.

This kind of fraud can be used against zero-knowledge proofs of identity: while the prover is proving her identity to the verifier, the verifier can simultaneously prove to another verifier that she is the prover. The only reasonable counterattack to the man-in-the-middle problem is imposing time limits for the replies.

## 4. DESIGN AND IMPLEMENTATION OF AN AUTHENTICATION LIBRARY FOR JAVA CARD

In this section, we discuss our major design decisions and the architecture of the authentication library for Java Card that implements a zero-knowledge authentication protocol.

## A. Evaluated Choice of the Protocol

All public key protocols and the majority of analysed zero-knowledge protocols suffer from the problem of key integrity. In other words, a key has to be bound to the identity of its owner by means of a key certificate issued by an authorized trusted third party. Unfortunately, key certificates, especially those conforming to ITU-T X.509 Recommendation (ITU-T, 2005), are quite big and can easily take up to 1.5 to 2 Kbytes each (Meckley, 1998). Although storing such certificates inside smartcards makes perfect sense, it is problematic due to the small amount of memory available in modern smartcards. Some zero-knowledge protocols (the identity based ones) seem to solve the problem. In these protocols, the public key is generated from the identity of the user, which eliminates the need for certificates (Schneier, 2007).

Three of the well-known zero-knowledge protocols, Fiat-Shamir, Guillou-Quisquater and Beth, are identity based. The public key is derived from the identity of the user via a publicly known pseudo-random one-way function. The verifier knows the function as well as the prover and can generate the public key of the prover from the identity of the prover.

Only the process issuing secret keys can calculate the prover's secret key (or keys) on the basis of the secret information it has (in Fiat-Shamir and Guillou-Quisquater protocols this information

are the factors of the modulus $n$). The verifier has no access to this information, thus, identity based public key generation does not reduce the security of the protocols, while eliminating the problem of certificates. After secret key generation, no further interaction with the process is required.

No interaction with the prover will enable verifiers to reproduce prover's secret, and even the knowledge of the prover's secret will not enable adversaries to create new identities or to modify existing ones without the help of the key issuing process (Fiat & Shamir, 1986).

Including the serial number of the smartcard as part of the identity ensures that if the user's secret is compromised, new public and secret keys can be generated for the replacement card (Guillou & Quisquater, 1990).

Beth's protocol does not offer a digital signature scheme, so we restricted our choice of protocol to Fiat-Shamir (F-S) and Guillou-Quisquater (G-Q).

An authentication scheme should be both secure and efficient, so that security overhead is minimized. Efficiency is particularly important in the context of smartcards, whose computational power and memory are severely restricted.

As the minimum security level recommended for authentication schemes is $2^{-20}$, the theoretical performances of protocols are compared at this

*Figure 7. Comparison of key factors of protocols*

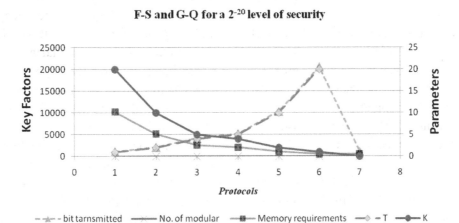

*Figure 8. Presentation of number of bit transmitted*

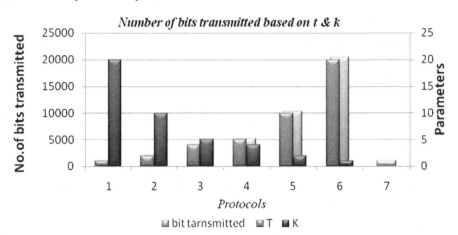

level. The criteria by which we compare these protocols are transmission cost (the amount of transmitted data, without considering the communication overhead), number of modular multiplication, and memory required.

Modular multiplication is one of the slowest operations performed, taking 0.5 sec on average using modern smartcard technology. Thus, we approximate the processing power required for each protocol by the number of modular multiplications required as shown in Table 2.

The number of modular multiplications is calculated on average for Fiat-Shamir (considering that a random vector has on average the same number of '0' and '1'), and in the worst case for Guillou-Quisquater. Exponentiation modulo $n$ is approximated with $3/2 \cdot (\log_2 exponent)$ modular multiplications.

Table 3 shows the respective values for a level of security $2^{-20}$, for $|n| = 512$.

The Guillou-Quisquater protocol minimizes the communication cost and the memory cost at the price of more computations (only 3 times Fiat-Shamir), which will be acceptable assuming the future growth of processing power in the new generation of smartcards.

Based on Table 3, it can be seen that the Guillou-Quisquater protocol has an effective performance in minimizing the memory and communication

cost based on control parameter $V$. Another protocol, Fiat-Shamir, is tested according to two key parameters $t$ and $k$. These two parameters are presented by the number of iterations of the basic protocol and the number of secret keys, respectively. Figure 7 shows the comparison among transmission cost, number of modular multiplications, and memory requirements to measure the performance of these protocols based on control parameters. Regarding these key factors, the suitable protocol is chosen. Although the rate of the bit transmitted of Fait-Shamir is acceptable on average with fewer numbers of iteration ($t = 1$), but the rate of memory requirements is high. In contrast, Guillou-Quisquater provides low memory requirements in terms of length of bits are 20 and consideration to the rate of transmitted data. It can be seen the relation between parameters and key factors for protocols. It is noticeable that the $t$ parameter is consequential in computing cost transmission and processing power required for Fiat-Shamir, whilst the increase of $k$ parameter (the number of secret key) will enhance the rate of memory requirements.

The number of bits transmitted is considered as an important factor to choose a useful protocol for implementation. So, for investigation of this factor, control parameters have been tested with different values to compare two existing protocols.

As the chart shows (Figure8), the number of bits transmitted has a significant increase when the number of iterations of the protocol has changed from low value to high value for Fiat-Shamir protocol. In contrast, the number of bits transmitted of Guillou-Quisquater protocol is computed based on the length in bits of the public exponent.

It is noticeable that Guillou-Quisquater protocol needs less memory in comparison with Fiat-Shamir, basically (Figure 9). Therefore, we chose Guillou-Quisquater protocol for implementation in the authentication library based on the efficiency and security of the protocol. The performance is measured regarding to key factors at $2^{-20}$ minimum security level.

## B. Operational Scenarios

The functionality for the prototype authentication library was specified as two operational scenarios. Given below is a summary of these two scenarios.

### 1. Initialization Scenario

*Actors:* Authentication process, user.

During initialization, the authentication process must generate the exponent $v$, the two prime numbers $p$ and $q$ and their product $n$ according to the desired security level. The process then, on a user request, must perform user initialization. To do so the process calculates the user public key and private key from the user's identity. The process generates a Private Identification Number (PIN) for the user as well. At the end of the initialization, a card is issued.

### 2. User Authentication Scenario

*Actors:* User, user interface, card reader, verifier process, Java Card applet (prover).

The user authentication scenario is shown in Figure 10. The arrows denote the direction of the information flow and the names on the arrows denote the corresponding data elements.

The user enters PIN through the user interface software, which starts the verification process. The reader interface software operates card reader hardware and provides a means for communication between the applet, the user interface and the verifier process. The verification process begins by the reader communicating an authentication request (containing PIN) to the applet. After that, the verifier and the applet perform Guillou-Quisquater protocol as described previously.

*Figure 9. Memory requirements*

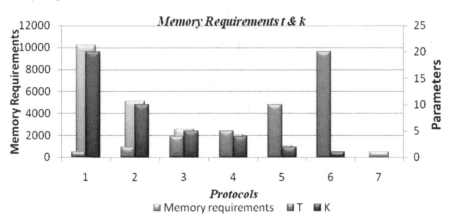

## C. Library Implementation

The implemented prototype library consists of five Java packages:

- Package applets.lib contains BigInt and RandomBigInt classes implementing arbitrary precision integer arithmetic.
- Package applets.Auth contains Auth class, a JavaCard applet that implements the prover functionality of the Guillou-Quisquater protocol.
- Package verifier contains the Verifier class that starts a daemon process servicing authentication requests submitted via custom protocol running on top of TCP/IP.
- Package auth_process contains SystemInitialization class that calculates private and public keys and communicates them to the prover (Auth applet) and the verifier process respectively.
- Package cardReader contains CardReaderInterface class that specifies the interface to the card reader device for Java applications and provides communication between the JavaCard applet and

the verifier process. The implementation of CardReaderInterface is platform dependent. In our case, it was implemented using socket interface to Java Card platform Workstation Development Environment (JCWDE) simulator and to the verifier process.

- Package userInterface contains a set of classes and a standalone Java application providing a window based interface to the user. It allows the user to input the PIN code, after which it then starts the authentication process.

The application based on this authentication library must implement classes derived from (or using) the applet and verifier components. In addition, it may have to provide an implementation for the reader interface component.

## D. Implementation Difficulties

Number of technical problems arose during implementation. These may be of interest to other Java Card developers.

*Figure 10. User authentication scenario*

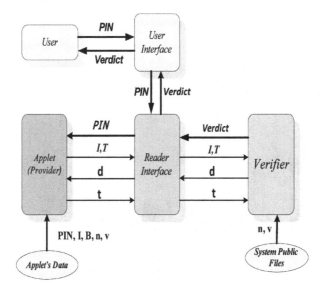

Java Cards support only bytes and shorts (), a 16-bit signed two's complement integer to save memory in large arrays in situations where the memory savings actually matters; while the applets in our application need to handle numbers up to 64 bits long. The solution was to implement a library class, residing on the "card", for arbitrary-precision nonnegative integers. The class provides all necessary integer operations for the implementation of the protocol. Modular arithmetic operations have been provided for computing residues and for exponentiation. All operations implement algorithms described by Knuth (1997) with radix 256.

Due to U.S. export regulations on cryptography, the javacardx.crypto package is not included in the JC2RI (Java Card 2.0 Reference Implementation User's Guide), so the class RandomData for generation of pseudo-random arbitrary-precision integers, necessary for the generation of the random numbers, is not available. A class with the same functionality has been implemented.

The simulation requires a suitable implementation of the verifier process that can generate and pass APDUs to the Java Card simulator. The APDU Generator Window for manual generation of APDUs was insufficient for this purpose. A separate Java application employing socket connection to the simulator was developed for this purpose.

Finally, it transpired that the designed library was too heavy for the modern smartcard devices. The code downloaded into the card is 9303 bytes long and requires 478 bytes of variables (assuming $|n| = 512$ bits), which is too much for devices with 16 KB ROM and less than 1 KB RAM. Despite this result, we believe that if the current trends in the smartcard technology are to continue, the future smartcards will be more resourceful and suitable for the developed authentication library. This is also facilitated by Java Card 3 which is a major evolution and upgrade of the Java Card 2 platform. While Java Card 3 enhances the basic security, interoperability, interworking, and multiple-application support in the platform that exploits new higher capacity smartcards hardware features with more and faster memory, higher processing power and far reaching communication capabilities (Allenbach, 2009).

## 5. CONCLUSION

This paper described the development of a prototype software library providing a zero-knowledge authentication method for smartcards conforming to Java Card specification. In summary, the following goals have been achieved:

- The limitations of smartcards in general and Java Card specification in particular were investigated.
- The problems of zero-knowledge authentication protocols were studied and a comparative analysis of the available protocols was performed, in order to find one most suitable for implementation in a smartcard environment.
- A prototype library implementing the Guillou-Quisquater protocol for use in the Java Card environment was developed, and tested using Java Card simulator provided with the Java Card developer's kit.

The development of the software showed that implementation of zero-knowledge protocols for Java Card programming environment is possible but too unwieldy for existing Java Card devices with limited capacity. Our next big challenge is to experiment zero-knowledge protocols on JAVA Card 3 platform and considering all the issues related to the economics of security and privacy (Katos and Patel, 2008) and how to incorporate evidence-based reputation facilities (Cvrček et al., 2005).

# REFERENCES

Allenbach, P. (2009). *Java Card 3: Classic functionality gets a connectivity boost.* Retrieved from http://java.sun.com/developer/technicalArticles/javacard/javacard3/

Aronsson, H. A. (1995). *Zero knowledge protocols and small systems.* Retrieved from http://www.tml.tkk.fi/Opinnot/Tik-110.501/1995/zeroknowledge.html

Beth, T. (1988). Efficient zero-knowledge identification scheme for smart cards. In D. Barstow, W. Brauer, P. Brinch Hansen, D. Gries, D. Luckham, C. Moler et al. (Eds.), *Proceedings of the Workshop on Advances in Cryptology* (LNCS 330, pp. 77-84).

Burmester, M., Desmedt, Y., & Beth, T. (1992). Efficient zero-knowledge identification schemes for smart cards. *The Computer Journal, 35*(1), 21–29. doi:10.1093/comjnl/35.1.21

Chen, Z. (2000). *Java card technology for smart cards: Architecture and programmer's guide.* Upper Saddle River, NJ: Prentice Hall.

Chen, Z., & Giorgio, R. D. (1998). *Understanding Java Card 2.0-Java World.* Retrieved from http://www.javaworld.com/javaworld/jw-03-1998/jw-03-javadev.html

Coleman, A. (1998). *Giving currency to the Java Card API.* Retrieved from http://www.javaworld.com/javaworld/jw-02-1998/jw-02-javacard.html

Cvrček, D., Matyáš, V., & Patel, A. (2005). Evidence processing and privacy issues in evidence-based reputation systems. *Computer Standards & Interfaces, 27*(5), 533–545. doi:10.1016/j.csi.2005.01.011

Fiat, A., & Shamir, A. (1986). How to prove yourself: Practical solutions to identification and signature problems. In A. M. Odlyzko (Ed.), *Proceedings of the Workshop on Advances in Cryptology* (LNCS 263, pp. 186-194).

Goldreich, O., Micali, S., & Wigderson, A. (1991). Proofs that yield nothing but their validity or all languages in NP have zero-knowledge proof systems. *Journal of the ACM, 38*(3). doi:10.1145/116825.116852

Goldwasser, S., Micali, S., & Rackoff, C. (1985). The knowledge complexity of interactive proof-systems. In *Proceedings of the Seventeenth Annual ACM Symposium on Theory of Computing* (pp. 291-304).

Guillou, L., & Quisquater, J. J. (1988). A practical zero-knowledge protocol fitted to security microprocessor minimizing both transmission and memory. In D. Barstow, W. Brauer, P. Brinch Hansen, D. Gries, D. Luckham, C. Moler et al. (Eds.), *Proceedings of the Workshop on Advances in Cryptology* (LNCS 330, pp. 123-128).

Guillou, L., & Quisquater, J. J. (1990). A "paradoxical" dentity-based signature scheme resulting from zero-knowledge. In S. Goldwasser (Ed.), *Proceedings of the Workshop on Advances in Cryptology* (LNCS 403, pp. 216-231).

Herbst, C., Oswald, E., & Mangard, S. (2006). An AES smart card mplementation resistant to power analysis attacks. In J. Zhou, M. Yung, & F. Bao (Eds.), *Proceedings of the 4th International Conference on Applied Cryptography and Network Security* (LNCS, 3989, pp. 239-252).

http://www.oracle.com/technetwork/java/javacard/javacard1-139251.html

International Organization for Standardization. (1987). *ISO/IEC 7816: Electronic identification cards with contacts, especially smart cards 15 minus 1 Part Series.* Geneva, Switzerland: International Standards Organisation (ISO) and the International Electrotechnical Commission (IEC).

International Organization for Standardization. (2000). *ISO/IEC 14443: Proximity cards (PICCs) 4 Part Series.* Geneva, Switzerland: International Standards Organisation (ISO) and the International Electrotechnical Commission (IEC).

ITU-T. (2005). *ITU-T recommendation X.509/ISO/IEC 9594-8: Information technology. Open systems interconnection - The directory: Public-key and attribute certificate frameworks*. Retrieved from http://www.infosecurity.org.cn/content/pki_pmi/x509v4.pdf

Kapron, B., Malka, L., & Srinivasan, V. (2007). A characterization of non-interactive instance-dependent commitment-schemes (NIC). In *Proceedings of the 34th International EATCS Colloquium on Automata, Languages and Programming* (pp. 328-339).

Katos, V., & Patel, A. (2008). A Partial Equilibrium View on Security and Privacy. *Information Management & Computer Security*, *16*(1), 74–83. doi:10.1108/09685220810862760

Knuth, D. E. (1997). The art of computer programming: *Vol. 2. Seminumerical algorithms* (3rd ed.). Reading, MA: Addison-Wesley.

Kocher, P., Jaffe, J., & Jun, B. (1999). Differential power analysis. In M. J. Wiener (Ed.), *Proceedings of the Workshop on Advances in Cryptology* (LNCS 1666, pp. 388-397).

Meckley, J. (1998). *Definition - Smart card*. Retrieved from http://searchsecurity.techtarget.com/definition/smart-card

Micali, S., & Shamir, A. (1990). An improvement of the Fiat-Shamir identification and signature scheme. In S. Goldwasser (Ed.), *Proceedings of the Workshop on Advances in Cryptology* (LNCS 403, pp. 244-247).

Nguyen, M.-H., & Vadhan, S. (2006, May 21-23). Zero knowledge with efficient provers. In *Proceedings of the Thirty-Eighth Annual ACM Symposium on Theory of Computing*, Seattle, WA (pp. 287-295).

Ohta, K., & Okamoto, T. (1990). A modification of the Fiat-Shamir scheme. In S. Goldwasser (Ed.), *Proceedings of the Workshop on Advances in Cryptology* (LNCS 403, pp. 232-243).

Ong, S., & Vadhan, S. (2007). Zero knowledge and soundness are symmetric. In M. Naor (Ed.), *Proceedings of the 26th Annual International Conference on Advances in Cryptology* (LNCS 4515, pp. 187-209).

Oracle. (2010). *Java Card platform specification 2.2.2*. Retrieved from http://java.sun.com/javacard/specs.html

Oracle. (2010). *Smart Card overview-Chip comparisons*. Retrieved from http://www.oracle.com/technetwork/java/javacard/documentation/smartcards-136372.html#chart

Oritz, C. E. (2003). *An introduction to JAVA Card technology – Part 1*. Retrieved from.

Patel, A. (2010). Concept of mobile agent-based electronic marketplace – Safety measures. In Lee, I. (Ed.), *Encyclopedia of e-business development and management in the digital economy* (*Vol. 1*, pp. 252–264). Hershey, PA: IGI Global.

Peyret, P. (1995). *Which Smart Card technologies will you need to ride the information highway safely?* Retrieved from http://www.gemalto.com/gemplus/index.html

Quisquater, J. J., Quisquater, M., Guillou, L., Guillou, M., Guillou, G., Guillou, A., et al. (1990). How to explain zero-knowledge protocols to your children. In G. Brassard (Ed.), *Proceedings of the Workshop on Advances in Cryptology* (LNCS 435, pp. 628-631).

Schneier, B. (1996). *Applied cryptography: Protocols, algorithms, and source code in C* (2nd ed.). New York, NY: John Wiley & Sons.

Schnorr, C. P. (1990). Efficient identification and signatures for smart cards. In G. Brassard (Ed.), *Proceedings of the Workshop on Advances in Cryptology* (LNCS 435, pp. 239-251).

Sun Microsystems. (1997). *Java Card 2.0 reference implementation user's guide Java Card 2.0 programming concept.* Retrieved from http://www.it.iitb.ac.in/~satish/phd/smartcard/usinix_99/javacardapi21/jc2ri-users-guide.pdf

Vadhan, S. P. (2004). An unconditional study of computational zero knowledge. In *Proceedings of the 45th Annual IEEE Symposium on Foundations of Computer Science* (pp. 176-185).

Wei, Q., & Patel, A. (2009). A secure and trustworthy framework for mobile agent-based e-marketplace with digital forensics and security protocols. *International Journal of Mobile Computing and Multimedia Communications, 1*(3), 8–26. doi:10.4018/jmcmc.2009070102

*This work was previously published in the International Journal of Information Security and Privacy, Volume 5, Issue 3, edited by Hamid Nemati, pp. 1-18, copyright 2011 by IGI Publishing (an imprint of IGI Global).*

# Chapter 10
# E-Voting Risk Assessment:
## A Threat Tree for Direct Recording Electronic Systems

**Harold Pardue**
*University of South Alabama, USA*

**Jeffrey Landry**
*University of South Alabama, USA*

**Alec Yasinsac**
*University of South Alabama, USA*

## ABSTRACT

*Approximately 25% (according to http://verifiedvoting.com/) of voting jurisdictions use direct recording electronic systems to record votes. Accurate tabulation of voter intent is critical to safeguard this fundamental act of democracy: voting. Electronic voting systems are known to be vulnerable to attack. Assessing risk to these systems requires a systematic treatment and cataloging of threats, vulnerabilities, technologies, controls, and operational environments. This paper presents a threat tree for direct recording electronic (DRE) voting systems. The threat tree is organized as a hierarchy of threat actions, the goal of which is to exploit a system vulnerability in the context of specific technologies, controls, and operational environment. As an abstraction, the threat tree allows the analyst to reason comparatively about threats. A panel of elections officials, security experts, academics, election law attorneys, representatives from governmental agencies, voting equipment vendors, and voting equipment testing labs vetted the DRE threat tree. The authors submit that the DRE threat tree supports both individual and group risk assessment processes and techniques.*

## INTRODUCTION

Voting systems function to capture voter intent and anonymously convert that intent into tallied votes. Accuracy and secret ballots are fundamental to democracy. However, ensuring the accuracy of

a tally and the anonymity of a voter is extremely difficult in electronic voting systems because the processes occur through a complex interaction of software, hardware, networks, people, policies and legislation (Jones, 2005; Khono, Stubblefield, Rubin, & Wallach, 2004; Weldemariam, 2009; Yasinsac & Bishop, 2008).

DOI: 10.4018/978-1-4666-2050-6.ch010

The voting system literature is replete with examples of attacks to electronic voting systems (Calindrino et al., 2007; Dill, Mercuri, Neumann, & Wallach, 2008; Epstein, 2007; Feldman, Halderman, & Felten, 2006; Fischer, 2003; Frisina, Herron, Honaker, & Lewis, 2008; Gardner et al., 2007; Hasen, 2000; Hursti, 2006; Kohno, Stubblefield, Rubin, & Wallach, 2004; NIST, 2005; Norden, 2008; Ohio Secretary of State, 2003; Yasinsac et al., 2007).

A pivotal aspect of ensuring integrity of elections conducted on DREs is that, because there is no physical record of each voter's selections, security is dependent on the DRE software. Software is inherently complex. Theory shows that it is impossible to prove non-trivial properties about arbitrary programs (Rice, 1953) and that at best, testing "… can be a very effective way to show the presence of bugs, but is hopelessly inadequate for showing their absence" (Ditkrtra, 1972).

Was that not bad enough, it is also very difficult even to determine if a computer is executing the intended software (Thompson, 1984). Thus, even if a DRE is properly built, configured, and operated, anyone with private access to the device may be able to install malicious software (i.e., malware) that can alter or control election results.

There are many approaches to securing electronic voting systems: due diligence, compliance, and business enablement (Parker, 2006). Another means of securing voting systems is to conduct a risk assessment. Risk assessment involves assigning a quantitative or qualitative value to the risk of a threat in a specific situation. Assigning a value to the risk of a threat allows the analyst to judiciously allocate relatively scarce resources, conduct sensitivity analysis, perform cost-benefit analyses, and compute residual risk. One approach to conducting risk assessment involves threat trees (Schneier, 1999; Pardue, Landry, & Yasinsac, 2009; Yasinsac & Pardue, 2010).

A threat tree is an abstraction that models threat source/vulnerability pairs as a hierarchy of threat actions. Threat actions denote the means by which

a threat source exploits a vulnerability or how a vulnerability is accidently exploited through a sequence of events or failures. A vulnerability can be defined as a "flaw or weakness in system security procedures, design, implementation, or internal controls that could be exploited to accomplish a security breach or a violation of the system's security policy" (Stoneburner, Goguen, & Feringa, 2002).

The purpose of this paper is to describe a threat tree for DRE voting systems. By being an abstraction, a threat tree allows the analyst to reason comparatively about threats to electronic voting systems. That is, the analyst can reason comparatively about different hardware and software configurations, different types and sizes of elections, different controls, and different types of attackers. By organizing a threat as a hierarchy of threat actions, it informs the risk assessment process. That is, the analyst is able to define, in precise terms, the specific threat that is under consideration and can assign metrics that describe the cost and impact of a threat if successfully executed. It should be noted that the DRE threat tree presented in this paper is not presented an exhaustive or definitive catalog of threats to DRE voting systems. The DRE threats cataloged consider computer-based technology used inside of polling places and brought outside for curbside voting. The use of voter verified paper trails are not considered.

A Direct Recording Electronic Voting Machine (DRE) is a VotingMachine that conducts VoterInteraction, VoteCommitment, and VoteCapture; Counts each Vote; and generates a persistent BallotImage based on VoterInteraction. The essence of its name is that a DRE captures and records each voter's selections electronically, with no need for a paper ballot. The most common DRE architecture uses touch screen technology for voter interaction, presenting each contest on the screen and allowing the voter to "touch" their selection. Voting integrity activists decry use of DREs because of the absence of physical records. Conversely, advocacy groups for disabled voters promote the expanded access that DREs can provide.

The remainder of this paper is organized as follows. The next section provides a brief overview of threat trees. The next section describes the process by which the DRE threat tree was constructed and vetted. The next section describes the six high-level threats comprising the DRE threat tree. This is followed by a discussion of the DRE threat tree. The paper finishes with a conclusion section.

## THREAT TREE OVERVIEW

A threat tree organizes threat actions as a hierarchy. Threat actions are nodes connected by directional edges. Each of the six high-level threats described in the DRE threat tree are decomposed hierarchically as sub-actions. Box 1 contains a simplified threat tree in indented, outline numbered list format.

Indentation and the corresponding outline number denote subordination. In the simplified tree in Box 1, there are two high-level threats: threaten voting equipment and perform insider threat. The first high-level threat, threaten voting equipment, is decomposed into three sub-actions: gather knowledge, gain insider access, and subvert component. The "A" to the left of "1 Threaten voting equipment" indicates this is an "AND" node and that all directly subordinate nodes are required. That is, in order to threaten voting equipment, the attacker must "O 1.1 gather knowledge" AND "O 1.2 gain insider access" AND "O 1.3 subvert component". The "O" to the left of the node "1.3 Subvert component" indicates this is an "OR" node. Nodes directly subordinate are optional threat actions. That is, the attacker can subvert the component by either attacking hardware "O 1.3.1 Subvert hardware" OR software "A 1.3.2 subvert software". The "T" to the left of the node "T 1.3.1.1 Swap boot media" indicates this is a "TERMINAL" node or is a primitive threat action requiring no further decomposition. The level to

*Box 1. Simplified threat tree*

| Node type - Outline number - Threat action |
| --- |
| A 1 Threaten voting equipment |
| O 1.1 Gather knowledge |
| O 1.2 Gain insider access |
| T 1.2.1 at voting system vendor |
| O 1.3 Subvert component |
| O 1.3.1 Subvert hardware |
| T 1.3.1.1 Swap boot media |
| T 1.3.1.2 compromise install |
| A 1.3.2 subvert software |
| T 1.3.2.1 develop malware |
| O 1.3.2.2 select targets |
| T 1.3.2.2.1 select locations by expected voting pattern |
| O 1.3.2.3 inject malware |
| A 2 Perform insider threat |

which a node is decomposed is at the discretion of the analyst. By "requiring no further decomposition" it is meant that the node contains sufficient detail for the analyst to assess risk. Decomposition adds complexity. All things being equal, a simpler threat tree will be easier to use than a complex one. Therefore, a threat tree should have only as much decomposition as is necessary to assess risk.

Paragraphs are indented one half inch and the space key should never be used to set the indention. Instead, the Tab key should be used. The paper should be double spaced and everything in the paper, including quotations, should be double spaced. The only exception would be to allow an additional line before a complicated table or figure. Another change is that there is now a double space after each punctuation mark at the end of a sentence. Remember that paragraphs in an actual paper should never be shorter than three sentences.

## THREAT TREE DEVELOPMENT

The DRE threat tree was developed through a two phase process. The first phase resembled the first step (System Characterization) in a 9-step risk assessment process described in the US government guideline for risk assessment NIST 800-30 (Stoneburner, 2002) (National Institute for Standards and Technology).

*Figure 1. Voting machine state transition diagram*

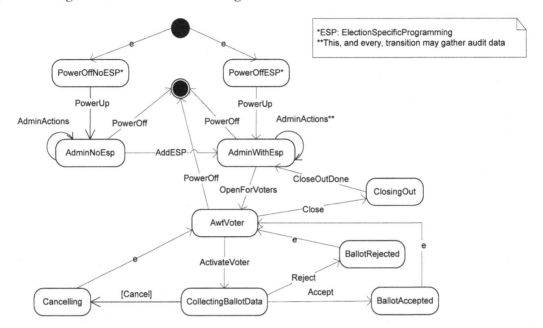

System characterization of DRE voting systems was based on an extensive literature review and the expertise and knowledge of domain experts. The system characterization of DRE voting systems was modeled using UML diagrams. A goal of these models was to identify vulnerable technology, people, and processes. UML diagrams provided a concise and systematic means of identifying and documenting system vulnerabilities. A sample UML diagram of a state transition diagram for a voting machine is depicted in Figure 1.

The UML models of the DRE voting systems and processes were vetted by a face-to-face panel consisting of election officials, a representative from NIST, security experts, voting equipment vendors, voting equipment testing labs, election law attorneys, and academics. Over a two-day session, the panelists validated the models and provided a rich and extensive set of suggestions where were incorporated into the models. By validate we mean the panelists agreed the models accurately represent their understanding of current DRE voting systems and processes.

Phase 2 followed steps 2 through 4 of the NIST 800-30 process: threat identification, vulnerability identification, and control analysis. The resulting threats, vulnerabilities, and controls were cataloged as a threat matrix and organized as the DRE threat tree. The row in the DRE threat matrix for node "O 1.3.2.3 inject malware" in the threat tree (Box 1) is reproduced in Table 1. Each row in the threat matrix corresponds to one node in the threat tree. The threat matrix contains the details associated with each node in the threat tree. The data in a row of the threat matrix comes from a mix of sources: literature review, expert knowledge, and a careful study of the UML models. Key data attributes include the threatening Action, usually formed as a verb phrase (inject malware) and the lengthier accompanying Description; the Source (human-deliberate) of the threat action; the Vulnerability triggered by a threat action against an election asset; potential Controls that may mitigate risks posed by threats; and a descriptive narrative threat Scenario that illustrates and actual or hypothetical example of the threat.

The potential controls identified in Table 1 were selected from the NIST 800-53 guide (Ross, Katzke, Johnson, Swanson, & Stoneburner, 2007). Controls included those of a managerial, techni-

*Table 1. Sample threat matrix entry*

| Matrix Element | Value |
|---|---|
| Threat ID | 1030 |
| Node Type | O |
| Outline No | 1.3.2.3 |
| Action | inject malware |
| Description | Exploit existing vulnerability to inject malware |
| Source | Human-deliberate |
| Vulnerability | Poor physical and network security on voting terminals |
| Potential Controls | System and service acquisition, system and information integrity, access control, audit and accountability, identification and authentication, and system and communications protection(The potential controls identified were selected from the NIST 800-53 guide (Ross et al., 2007). Controls included those of a managerial, technical, and operational nature. The six potential controls in the inject malware threat are each a family of controls that compose a subset of between 5 and 23 specific controls identified in the NIST 800-53.) |
| Scenario | An attacker breaks into a storage warehouse to gain physical access to a machine. In less than five minutes, the attacker installs malicious code on the voting machine. On election day, voters cast their votes normally, but the malicious code inserted will alter the votes undetectably, modifying all the records, logs and counters to be consistent with the fraudulent vote counts it creates. The malicious code spreads automatically and silently from machine to machine during normal election activities - a voting machine virus (Jones, 2005) |

cal, and operational nature. The six potential controls in the inject malware threat are each a family of controls that compose a subset of between 5 and 23 specific controls identified in the NIST 800-53. Most of the families of controls chosen for inject malware, or four of six, are technical controls, as the primary objective is to prevent or detect the unauthorized access leading to malware injection.

The initial threat matrix was constructed through asynchronous contributions by individual researchers. These threats were merged into a master list with duplicates removed. The researchers then convened a face-to-face one-and-a-half day session with security and domain experts to evaluate the existing threat matrix and to brainstorm new threats. The purpose of the brain-storming portion was to identify any threats missed by individual contributors.

There were two major challenges to developing the DRE threat matrix and threat tree: identifying labels and phrases that were accurate yet widely recognizable and organizing a list of threats (threat matrix) into a hierarchical structure. The variety of forms of voting in the U.S. is exceeded only by the variety of vernacular used to describe it. In addition, a term or phrase that appears innocuous to a security expert may be considered inflammatory by an elections official, or biased by a systems vendor. The terms used in the DRE threat tree are the result of lengthy debates and a large collaborative effort among the research team and panel of experts.

Initially, we thought to organize the threat matrix into a tree collaboratively. But it became readily apparent that there were as many ways to organize the DRE threat tree as there were organizers. Instead, we designated one member from the research team to craft an initial "straw man" threat tree and worked collaboratively to refine this initial structure through a lengthy series of face-to-face meetings and email exchanges.

The DRE threat tree was then distributed for review by domain and security experts other than the researchers. Reviewers were asked for open-ended, unstructured feedback. The research team received several hundred detailed suggestions for revisions. These suggestions were reconciled and implemented by the research team. In the main, the reviewers found the DRE threat tree to be accurate and representative. No new threats were identified.

Following the asynchronous review, a panel of domain and security experts was convened to review and validate the threat tree. The composition of the panel was similar to the panel that reviewed the UML diagrams. The panelists were given the threat tree as pre-reading in advance of the meeting. Panelists were guided to give very structured feedback. Emphasis was on a reality check of nomenclature, identification of errors, omissions, and assessing the usefulness of the DRE threat tree for risk assessment.

The general consensus of the panel was that the DRE tree was representative, accurate, and useful. The panel produced an extensive and rich set of recommendations for improving the quality of the DRE threat tree. The threat tree presented in this paper incorporates those recommendations.

## THREAT TREE DEVELOPMENT

The DRE voting threat tree has six high-level threats: threaten voting equipment, perform insider threat, subvert voting process, experience technical failure, subvert audit, and disrupt operations. The critical distinction among the threats is the context of the threat and the threat source. The same threat in a different context or with a different threat source can require a different control and result in a different risk estimate. The following six sections provide a brief synopsis of each threat tree.

## Threaten Voting Equipment

### Synopsis

The threatening actions are carried out intentionally by malicious outsiders who gain insider access and use computer-based technical capabilities to subvert an election contest (Box 2).

### Sample Threat Scenario

An attacker breaks into a storage warehouse to gain physical access to a machine. In less than five minutes, the attacker installs malicious code on the voting machine. On election day, voters cast their vote normally, but the malicious code alters the votes undetectably, modifying all the records, logs and counters to be consistent with the fraudulent vote counts it creates. The malicious code spreads automatically and silently from machine to machine during normal election activities—a voting machine virus.

### Discussion

There is little history of voting systems being compromised by malicious computer experts. However, if and when these threats occur, there is a potential for wholesale, or high, impact on election outcomes.

## Perform Insider Threat

### Synopsis

The threats are carried out by inside threat sources, such as election officials, pollworkers or election observers, who might intentionally or unintentionally commit a threatening action. Threat actions within a polling place environment include discouraging voters or altering the voter's vote. Insider threats also include actions beyond the voting process in the polling places. Insiders may poorly design ballots, misinform voters, add,

## Box 2. Threaten voting equipment

```
Node type - Outline number - Threat action
A 1 Threaten voting equipment
O 1.1 Gather knowledge
T 1.1.1 from insider
O 1.1.2 from examining components
T 1.1.2.1 Infiltrate as insider
T 1.1.2.2 Obtain a machine
T 1.1.2.3 Legally acquire machine
T 1.1.2.4 Study a machine in transit
T 1.1.2.5 Find source code
T 1.1.2.6 Compromise existing source code escrow
T 1.1.3 from published reports
O 1.2 Gain insider access
T 1.2.1 at voting system vendor
T 1.2.2 in supply chain
T 1.2.3 in elections org
T 1.2.4 by illegal insider entry
T 1.2.5 by remote network access
O 1.3 Subvert component
O 1.3.1 Subvert hardware
T 1.3.1.1 Swap boot media
T 1.3.1.2 Compromise install
T 1.3.1.3 Cestroy RemovableMedia
A 1.3.2 Subvert software
T 1.3.2.1 Develop malware
O 1.3.2.2 Select targets
T 1.3.2.2.1 Select locations by expected voting pattern
T 1.3.2.2.2 Select all locations
O 1.3.2.3 Inject malware
T 1.3.2.3.1 by remote bug exploitation
T 1.3.2.3.2 by local bug exploitation
T 1.3.2.3.3 by human interface exploit
O 1.3.2.4 Execute malware
T 1.3.2.4.1 that alters artifact directly
T 1.3.2.4.2 that self-propagates
T 1.3.2.4.3 that remains resident
O 1.3.2.5 Mitigate risk of detection
T 1.3.2.5.1 Coerce testing staff
T 1.3.2.5.2 Subvert after testing
T 1.3.2.5.3 Obtain cooperation of testers
T 1.3.2.5.4 Access testing scripts
O 1.3.2.6 Use infected component
O 1.3.2.6.1 Supply cryptic knock
T 1.3.2.6.1.1 during logic and accuracy testing
T 1.3.2.6.1.2 during machine setup
T 1.3.2.6.1.3 during voting
T 1.3.2.6.1.4 as anti-knock
T 1.3.2.6.1.5 using AC power flicker
T 1.3.2.6.1.6 to detect realistic patterns of voting
T 1.3.2.6.1.7 to employ calendar/clock tricks
T 1.3.2.6.1.8 in ballot definition files
O 1.3.2.6.2 Control/parameterize threat
T 1.3.2.6.2.1 Voter knowingly enables threat
T 1.3.2.6.2.2 Enable by unknowing voter
T 1.3.2.6.2.3 Enable by technical consultant
T 1.3.2.6.2.4 Employ unparameterized threat
T 1.3.2.6.2.5 Add commands to ballot def file
O 1.3.3 Subvert data
O 1.3.3.1 using malware
O 1.3.3.1.1 Select method and alter
T 1.3.3.1.1.1 by malware
T 1.3.3.1.1.2 by infected software
T 1.3.3.1.1.3 by infected config data
T 1.3.3.1.2 Alter ballot definition file
T 1.3.3.1.3 Alter device tallies
T 1.3.3.1.4 Alter tabulation SW
O 1.3.3.2 Modify data on storage medium
T 1.3.3.2.1 Modify tabulation data
O 1.3.3.2.2 Modify data before use
T 1.3.3.2.2.1 pre-load votes
T 1.3.3.2.2.2 flip votes
T 1.3.3.2.2.3 alter config data
T 1.3.3.2.3 Alter electronic ballots using administrator account access
T 1.3.3.3 Alter ballot creation software
O 1.3.4 Subvert comlinks
T 1.3.4.1 Subvert linked tabulator
T 1.3.4.2 Subvert wireless
```

## Box 3. Perform insider threat

```
Node type - Outline number - Threat action
A 2 Perform insider threat
O 2.1 form inside attack team
T 2.1.1 Infiltrate as volunteer pollworker
T 2.1.2 Infiltrate as observer
T 2.1.3 Staff with attackers
T 2.1.4 Collude with other insiders
T 2.1.5 Allow pollworker rotation
O 2.2 Execute insider threat
O 2.2.1 Threaten at polling place
O 2.2.1.1 Discourage voters
O 2.2.1.1.1 Challenge at CheckIn
T 2.2.1.1.1.1 Falsely reject voter registration
T 2.2.1.1.1.2 Falsely reject id check
T 2.2.1.1.1.3 Selectively challenge voters
T 2.2.1.1.1.4 Falsely challenge voters on target list
T 2.2.1.1.1.5 Destroy registered cards
O 2.2.1.1.2 Delay opening or closing
T 2.2.1.1.2.1 Damage / tamper with electronic voting equipment
T 2.2.1.1.2.2 Damage / tamper with artifacts
T 2.2.1.1.2.3 Allocate insufficient resources
O 2.2.1.1.3 Create long lines
T 2.2.1.1.3.1 Work slowly to stymie
T 2.2.1.1.3.2 Program the DRE printer to exhaust the paper supply
T 2.2.1.1.3.3 Damage / tamper with electronic voting equipment
T 2.2.1.1.3.4 Damage / tamper with artifacts
T 2.2.1.1.3.5 Allocate insufficient resources
T 2.2.1.1.4 Delay voters with poor assistance
T 2.2.1.1.5 Stymie voters needing assistance
T 2.2.1.1.6 Issue incorrect ballot style
T 2.2.1.1.7 Mislead w/phony ballot change
T 2.2.1.1.8 Mislead w/one party only ruse
T 2.2.1.1.9 Discourage provisional voting
T 2.2.1.1.10 Impede voter access
T 2.2.1.1.11 Persuade voter selections
T 2.2.1.1.12 Send voter to wrong place
T 2.2.1.1.13 Use faulty headsets
T 2.2.1.1.14 Mispronounce names of candidates on audio ballot
O 2.2.1.1.15 Issue erroneous VotableBallot
T 2.2.1.1.15.1 of the incorrect ballot style
T 2.2.1.1.15.2 with errors in contests or candidates
T 2.2.1.1.15.3 with errors in selection rules
A 2.2.1.2 Alter voter's vote
O 2.2.1.2.1 Access ballots to alter votes
O 2.2.1.2.1.1 Obtain MarkedBallot
T 2.2.1.2.1.1.1 Disable machine
T 2.2.1.2.1.1.2 Mislead about committing ballot
A 2.2.1.2.1.2 Obtain provisional ballot
T 2.2.1.2.1.2.1 Force provisional vote
T 2.2.1.2.1.2.2 Obtain provisional ballot
T 2.2.1.2.1.3 Take control of assisted voter terminals
O 2.2.1.2.2 Tamper with ballots
A 2.2.1.2.2.1 Subvert no-show vote
O 2.2.1.2.2.1.1 Conceal pollbook tampering
T 2.2.1.2.2.1.1.1 Wait until polls close
T 2.2.1.2.2.1.1.2 Target unlikely voters
T 2.2.1.2.2.1.1.3 Make excuses for marked pollbook
T 2.2.1.2.2.1.2 Mark VotableBallot
T 2.2.1.2.2.1.3 Tamper with pollbook
O 2.2.1.2.2.2 Subvert MarkedBallot of voter
T 2.2.1.2.2.2.1 Mark undervote to create vote
T 2.2.1.2.2.2.2 Mark vote to create overvote
T 2.2.1.2.2.2.3 Flip voter's electronic vote
T 2.2.1.2.3 Commit subverted ballot
T 2.2.1.3 Send voter to subverted machine
O 2.2.2 Threaten other than polls
A 2.2.2.1 Threaten ballots
T 2.2.2.1.1 Access ballots
O 2.2.2.1.2 Tamper with ballots
T 2.2.2.1.2.1 by subverting ballot rotation
T 2.2.2.1.2.2 by subverting provisional envelope
T 2.2.2.1.2.3 with physical damage
O 2.2.2.1.3 Replace ballots
T 2.2.2.1.3.1 Record voter's ballot as other than depicted on screen
T 2.2.2.1.3.2 Switch MarkedBallots during transport
O 2.2.2.2 Misinform about overvoting / undervoting
T 2.2.2.2.1 Allow undervotes without warning
T 2.2.2.2.2 Allow overvotes without warning
T 2.2.2.2.3 Encourage voter override
O 2.2.2.3 Confuse voters with poor ballot design
T 2.2.2.3.1 by splitting contests ups
T 2.2.2.3.2 by spreading response options
```

*continued on following page*

*Box 3. Continued*

```
T 2.2.2.3.3 by placing different contests on the same touch screen
T 2.2.2.3.4 because not enough spacing between candidate issues/blocks
T 2.2.2.3.5 by keeping disqualified candidates
T 2.2.2.3.6 with inconsistent formats
T 2.2.2.3.7 by omitting useful shading
T 2.2.2.3.8 by omitting use of bold
T 2.2.2.3.9 with complex instructions
T 2.2.2.3.10 with distant instructions
T 2.2.2.3.11 with no correction guidance
T 2.2.2.4 Force least-objectionable choice
T 2.2.2.5 Publish invalid sample ballots
T 2.2.2.6 Stuff ballots after closing
T 2.2.2.7 Stuff during canvass or recount
O 2.2.2.8 Make mistakes in ballot adjudication
O 2.2.2.8.1 Incorrectly accept provisional ballots
T 2.2.2.8.1.1 due to premature counting
T 2.2.2.8.1.2 due to selective review
T 2.2.2.8.2 Incorrectly reject provisional ballots
T 2.2.2.9 Selectively recount
T 2.2.2.10 Subvert tabulation
O 2.2.2.11 Threaten tabulated results
T 2.2.2.11.1 Subvert reported results
T 2.2.2.11.2 Falsely announce results
T 2.2.2.11.3 Alter results transmission
```

remove, or alter votes, and subvert post-voting operations, such as tabulations, recounts, ballot adjudication, or reporting of results (Box 3).

## Sample Threat Scenario

A particular DRE system has a two-step process for voters to complete the voting process. Voters must press a touch screen "VOTE" button followed by an extra confirmation screen that requires clicking on a "confirm vote" button. Taking advantage of ambiguous printed instructions at the polling place that omit mention of the final confirmation step, conspiring pollworkers mislead voters by instructing them that pressing the "VOTE" button is the final step. After the voters walk away from the machines with the final screen still showing, a pollworker could sneakily change votes on the still-showing screen before finalizing the voter's electronic ballot.

## Discussion

The susceptibility of access by insiders with malicious intent makes election operations vulnerable. Unintentional insider actions are mistakes made that are frequent, but that usually will have a low impact. The intentional actions by insiders may or may not have a high impact on election outcomes, depending on the particular type of threatening action and how likely it is to systematically perform the action without detection.

## Perform Insider Threat

### Synopsis

Subverting the voting process involves the legal voter or someone impersonating a legal voter to subvert that voter's vote. This category includes vote fraud, including voter coercion, and other threatening actions that can be committed by the voter while they are legitimately in the polling place (Box 4).

### Sample Threat Scenario

An incumbent candidate seeking reelection sends a loyal confederate to the polls accompanying the incumbents' employees, who are coerced to vote for the incumbent, once they receive their votable ballots. Using a small recording device, voters manage to capture digital video of their ballot casting, and produce it to the confederate as evidence.

### Discussion

Voters are outsiders but then are given insider access through the voter authentication process at the polls, at which time they have temporary insider access to voting equipment and processes, and their own ballot. They may subvert their own vote or carry out others attacks, such as ballot box stuffing or some other computer-based attack similar to those modeled by *threaten voting equipment*.

*Box 4. Subvert voting process*

```
Node type - Outline number - Threat action
A 3 Subvert voting process
O 3.1 Target polling places
T 3.1.1 by expected voting pattern
T 3.1.2 where PollWorkers not likely to know Voters
T 3.1.3 that exploit electoral college rules
T 3.1.4 where PollWorkers can be co-opted
T 3.1.5 with lax enforcement of procedures
O 3.2 Form attack team
A 3.2.1 Use cell captains to execute deniable impersonation
         threat
T 3.2.1.1 Recruit cell captains
T 3.2.1.2 Motivate cell captains
T 3.2.1.3 Educate cell captains
T 3.2.1.4 Provide rewards for cell captains to distribute
T 3.2.1.5 Recruit attackers
T 3.2.2 Recruit attackers among LegalVoters
T 3.2.3 Recruit brokers
O 3.3 Commit vote fraud
A 3.3.1 Perform voter impersonation threat
O 3.3.1.1 Create target list of voters to impersonate
O 3.3.1.1.1 based on fraudulent registrations
T 3.3.1.1.1.1 Register as an housemate
T 3.3.1.1.1.2 Register as a dead person
T 3.3.1.1.1.3 Register an ineligible person
T 3.3.1.1.1.4 Register as a fictitious person
O 3.3.1.1.2 based on LegalVoter lists
T 3.3.1.1.2.1 unlikely voters
T 3.3.1.1.2.2 voters likely to vote late in the day
A 3.3.1.2 Execute impersonated voting
T 3.3.1.2.1 Assign impersonator to voter
T 3.3.1.2.2 Go to target voter's polling place
T 3.3.1.2.3 Check in as the impersonated voter
T 3.3.1.2.4 Vote in place of voter
T 3.3.1.2.5 Supply rewards
A 3.3.2 Purchase or coerce vote
O 3.3.2.1 Motivate voter
O 3.3.2.1.1 Pay
O 3.3.2.1.1.1 Pay for candidate support
T 3.3.2.1.1.1.1 Pay voters cash
T 3.3.2.1.1.1.2 Make a non-cash payment
T 3.3.2.1.1.2 Promise to pay
O 3.3.2.1.2 Persuade or coerce
T 3.3.2.1.2.1 Promise to punish
T 3.3.2.1.2.2 Punish and promise more
T 3.3.2.1.2.3 Punish and promise repair
O 3.3.2.2 Direct voters
T 3.3.2.2.1 to make specific votes
T 3.3.2.2.2 to not make specific votes
O 3.3.2.3 Verify bought vote
T 3.3.2.3.1 by self-recorded casting
T 3.3.2.3.2 with phony voter assistant
T 3.3.2.3.3 using write-ins as code
T 3.3.2.3.4 by capturing electronic emanations
T 3.3.2.3.5 by headphone eavesdropping
T 3.3.2.4 Supply rewards or punishment
O 3.3.3 Cast multiple votes
T 3.3.3.1 Vote using more than one method
T 3.3.3.2 Vote in more than one place
O 3.3.3.3 Engineer multiple access keys
T 3.3.3.3.1 Create bogus authorization codes
T 3.3.3.3.2 Program the smart card to ignore the deactivation
            command of the system
T 3.3.3.3.3 Stuff ballot box using fraudulent smart cards
```

## Experience Technical Failure

### Synopsis

This threat category is for equipment breakdowns not attributable to causes identified elsewhere. These failures are primarily hardware failures, software errors caused by human programming or data entry errors, or equipment failure caused by external sources, such as water, dust, or improper or excessive use (Box 5).

### Sample Threat Scenario

Election officials in one state's most populous county found that a flaw in ballot programming software caused 67,000 absentee and early-voting ballots to be incorrectly counted during a presidential election (Blaze, 2009).

### Discussion

Some hardware failures are predictable and to be expected, and can be controlled by routine maintenance plans, including replacement and repair of equipment. Undetected software errors pose a bigger problem, because they impact elections on a systematic basis. Good software engineering practices, and detection mechanisms, such as audits, are needed.

## Subvert Audit

### Synopsis

These threats are carried out by malicious insiders or outsiders, either in isolation, to erode voter confidence, or in conjunction with other attacks, in order to circumvent detection. Successful audit attacks require knowledge of how audits are performed and how audit data is used (Box 6).

*Box 5. Experience technical failure*

```
Node type - Outline number - Threat action
O 4 experience technical failure
O 4.1 experience operational error
T 4.1.1 by miscalibrating equipment
T 4.1.2 due to foreign substances
T 4.1.3 through erroneous settings
T 4.1.4 by mismatching precinct and actual
T 4.1.5 in software from bad data
T 4.1.6 causing hardware failure
T 4.1.7 causing device failure
T 4.1.8 due to manufacturer error
O 4.2 experience undetected tabulation errors
T 4.2.1 in straight-party vote tabulation
T 4.2.2 due to improper tabulation technique
T 4.2.3 due to software error
T 4.2.4 from mistakes by ballot designer
T 4.2.5 due to flawed ballot creation software
T 4.2.6 by omitting tallies from totals
T 4.2.7 by adding tallies multiple times
O 4.3 experience errors in ballot preparation
T 4.3.1 encode incorrect contest counting rule
T 4.3.2 supply erroneous ballot definition data
T 4.3.3 supply erroneous voting equipment data
T 4.3.4 misconfigure ballot by operator
T 4.4 failure of batteries
```

## Sample Threat Scenario

An election official, with the help of some auditors, completes their random selection of auditable materials, as should normally be done. Then, they subvert the tabulation server so that their attack is carried out only on unaudited items. They then proceed to publish the election results.

## Discussion

These threats may be difficult to carry out without insider collusion, and are typically combined with other attacks to prevent detection.

## **Disrupt Operations**

## Synopsis

The threats include a variety of human (terrorist threats, voters destroying equipment), and non-human sources, such as natural (weather, earthquakes) and environmental (power outages,

*Box 6. Subvert audit*

```
Node type - Outline number - Threat action
O 5 Subvert audit
O 5.1 Threaten election evidence
T 5.1.1 Destroy ElectionArtifacts
T 5.1.2 Mishandle ElectionArtifacts
T 5.1.3 Add new fraudulent evidence
O 5.1.4 Modify ElectionArtifacts
A 5.1.4.1 Modify deliberately
T 5.1.4.1.1 Replace paper tape with fraud
T 5.1.4.1.2 Rewrite data on RemovableMedia
T 5.1.4.1.3 Modify pollbooks for audit
T 5.1.4.1.4 Modify logbooks and logdata used in audit
T 5.1.4.2 Modify unintentionally
T 5.1.4.3 Modify deliberately by computer
T 5.1.4.4 Modify unintentionally by computer
T 5.1.4.5 Modify via malware threat
T 5.1.4.6 Modify via malware at artifact creation
O 5.2 Improperly select audit samples
T 5.2.1 Select audit units before election
T 5.2.2 Select non-randomly
T 5.2.3 Use subverted selection method
T 5.2.4 Ignore proper selections
O 5.3 Use poor audit process
T 5.3.1 Misguide auditors
T 5.3.2 Audit insufficient sample
T 5.3.3 Exploit variation in batch sizes
T 5.3.4 Establish single contest audit rule
T 5.3.5 Arrange contest audit
T 5.3.6 Select audited items before commit
T 5.3.7 Tamper with audit totals
T 5.3.8 Avoid correction
T 5.3.9 Overwhelm audit observers
T 5.4 Commit auditing error
T 5.5 Compromise auditors
O 5.6 Subvert audit results
T 5.6.1 Mishandle media
T 5.6.2 Add fraudulent result data
O 5.6.3 Subvert audit data
O 5.6.3.1 Modify deliberately
T 5.6.3.1.1 Modify pollbooks for audit
T 5.6.3.1.2 Modify logbooks and logdata used in audit
T 5.6.3.2 Modify unintentionally
T 5.6.3.3 Modify via malware threat
T 5.6.4 Publish bogus audit results
```

chemical leaks) sources, that disrupt election operations though usually not altering results, and then only for extremely close contests (Box 7).

## Sample Threat Scenario

An election eve fire adjacent to a small Pennsylvania town's only polling place caused a power outage and forced election officials to move the polling place in the middle of the night. Makeshift

*Box 7. Disrupt operations*

```
Node type - Outline number - Threat action
O 6 Disrupt operations
O 6.1 Disruption from natural events
T 6.1.1 Natural disaster
T 6.1.2 Severe weather
O 6.2 Disruption from environmental events
O 6.2.1 Environmental failures
T 6.2.1.1 Experience a fire
T 6.2.1.2 Experience power disruptions
T 6.2.2 Hazardous accidents
O 6.3 Disruption from human-created events
O 6.3.1 that damage equipment
T 6.3.1.1 Render e-voting equipment inoperable
T 6.3.1.2 Render removable media not working
T 6.3.2 Deploy faulty equipment
T 6.3.3 with environmental effects
O 6.4 Discourage voter participation
T 6.4.1 Misinform voters
T 6.4.2 Threaten personal violence
T 6.4.3 Threaten mass violence
T 6.4.4 Commit an act of terror
T 6.4.5 Intimidate to suppress turnout
```

signs throughout town redirected voters to a new polling place for the November 4, 2008 election. The effect on voter turnout was unknown (Potts, 2008).

## Discussion

These threats have mostly a low impact on election outcomes. However, they can, at least temporarily, put a halt to elections operations on a local or regional basis, significantly impact voter confidence, and result in damage and destruction of election assets and, in the case of terrorism, threaten human life.

## DISCUSSION

If governing power in a democracy is to be derived from the people, the systems that determine voter intent must result in accurate tallies and maintain the anonymity of the voter. To the degree that electronic voting systems are vulnerable to attack, so also is democracy. One means towards securing electronic voting systems is risk assessment. Risk

assessment facilitates determining where to apply resources to the mitigation of risk. In this paper, we presented a DRE threat tree for informing the risk assessment process. The rich classification and organization of DRE threats is useful for ongoing elections operations risk management. Several suggested uses of the DRE threat tree are discussed briefly.

One application of threat trees to risk assessment is the rank-ordering of threats (Pardue, Landry, & Yasinsac, 2009). By studying the threat trees of the six threats to DRE, an analyst can assign a qualitative value to each threat such as high, medium, or low. This assessment is based on the analyst's knowledge, expertise, and experience. The analyst can assess each threat under a variety of contexts and sets of controls or mitigations. This allows the analyst to reason comparatively about the threats. Because a threat tree is an abstraction, one analyst's assessment can be compared to another analyst's. For example, if analyst A ranked "threaten voting equipment" as a high risk threat while analyst B ranked it as a low risk threat, these two analysts have a common point of reference upon which to base their discussion. Perhaps analyst B considers it very unlikely that an attacker will ever gain sufficient insider access to compromise a system and therefore ranks it as a low risk threat while analyst A considers it very likely. Or perhaps one analyst was assuming a specific mitigation while the other was not.

In addition to qualitative assessment, threat trees lend themselves to quantitative analysis. The analyst can assign metrics to each node of a threat tree and then apply formal methods to arrive a quantitative estimate of risk (Yasinsac & Pardue 2010). Metrics can include such quantitative variables as dollar cost, man-hours of effort, number of attackers, level of expertise, and risk of detection (Jones, 2005; Tipton & Henry, 2007). In addition to the ability to rank-order threats, quantitative metrics allow the analyst to assess relative magnitude with a finer granularity. Analyst can posit statements such as "Experience technical failure" is five times riskier than "threaten voting equipment". Because a threat tree provides a common point of reference, quantitative risk estimates can be compared across contexts, sets of mitigations and analysts.

A major challenge with using threat trees for either qualitative or quantitative risk assessment is state space explosion. For any given threat tree, there is a computationally burdensome number of combinations of threat actions that successfully exploit a system vulnerability. One solution is to define specific threat scenarios. That is, define a collection of subsets of threat actions to assess rather than attempting to assess the entire threat tree. For example, Box 8 contains a sample threat scenario where an attacker exercises a vulnerability associated with the ability to swap a machine's boot media. An analyst is encouraged to document assumptions regarding a scenario and ideally write a brief synopsis of the attack. For example, in the sample threat scenario given in Box 8, the attacker gathers the knowledge necessary to threaten a DRE voting machine by purchasing a used Diebold machine over the Internet. By studying the hardware, the attacker learns how to best swap the machine's boot media so as to minimize detection and maximize impact. The media is physically swapped by an insider conspirator during a "sleepover." The hardware is subverted by swapping the vendor supplied boot media with a compromised media that disables the machine and thereby disenfranchise voters at those polling stations.

The DRE threat tree can be used as the basis for group risk assessment such as in a facilitated risk analysis process (FRAP) (Peltier, 2001). FRAP is a formal process for analyzing risks to systems, applications, or processes. A FRAP involves a facilitator and a team of 5 to 8 domain experts. The team's goal is to prioritize a list of threats. Risk is often defined as the product of likelihood and impact. However, the intent is not to obtain accurate point estimates for probability and impact. Rather, the participant's estimation

*Box 8. Sample threat scenario: hardware-swap boot media*

| Node type - Outline number - Threat action |
| --- |
| A 1 threaten voting equipment |
| O 1.1 gather knowledge |
| O 1.1.2 from examining components |
| T 1.1.2.2 obtain a machine |
| O 1.2 gain insider access |
| T 1.2.4 by illegal insider entry |
| O 1.3 subvert component |
| O 1.3.1 subvert hardware |
| T 1.3.1.1 swap boot media |

of risk and impact are used to assign a priority or rank to a threat.

It is recommended that the FRAP facilitator have the participants define several threat scenarios. Possibly the group could work to identify the top 3 to 4 most likely scenarios. In addition, the FRAP participants should carefully document their assumptions regarding terms, controls, mitigations, and context. Different assumptions can lead to varying risk assessments for the same threat scenario. For example, the risk of the hardware attack illustrated in Box 8 might be considerably higher in a razor close race, in a multi-language, semi-rural precinct than in an urban precinct with a widely popular incumbent.

## CONCLUSION

Direct Recording Electronic voting systems solve many election challenges and risks, such as those that rocketed into national attention in the presidential election of 2000, by eliminating the need for paper ballots. On the other hand, they introduce new risks with fundamentally different properties.

We demonstrated that there are a plethora of specific threats to DRE voting systems. There are threats posed by insiders, such as election officials and pollworkers, malicious outsiders, and by voters and those impersonating voters. Natural and environment threats, and equipment failure, are also of concern, but are less likely to cause major election impacts than threats intended to do so. Made vulnerable to these threats are our key election assets: voting hardware, software, and data; voters; and election operations—not only voting but ballot preparation, tabulation, auditing, recounting and results reporting.

With such a volume and variety of threats, the importance of risk assessment to analyze and prioritize the risk posed by those threats is justified. We proceeded to demonstrate one approach to characterizing the risk of DRE voting systems. This approach utilized a structured framework, threat matrices and threat trees, for categorizing and organizing threats and threat information so as to be useful in risk assessment. We show how mitigations can reduce or eliminate risk in certain areas, but with residual risk and we show how professional elections officials can use this information to make informed decisions with respect to the different DRE risks.

Despite the wide variety of threats and threat sources that target DRE systems, this paper makes no attempt to compare threats to DRE systems to any other voting process technology. Indeed, many of the threats impacting DREs are common to other systems, because they involve the same or similar election operations, equipment, people, and environments. The framework provided is extensible, too, given its hierarchical nature and standard reporting form.

## ACKNOWLEDGMENT

This work was supported in part by the Election Assistance Commission under grant EAC-RDV08-R-001.

## REFERENCES

Blaze, M. (2009). *Is the e-voting honeymoon over? Electronic vote rigging in Kentucky*. Retrieved from http://www.crypto.com/blog/vote_fraud_in_kentucky/

Calandrino, J. A., Feldman, A. J., Halderman, J. A., Wagner, D., Yu, H., & Zeller, W. P. (2007). *Source code review of the Diebold voting system*. Retrieved from http://www.sos.ca.gov/elections/voting_systems/ttbr/diebold-source-public-jul29.pdf

Dijkstra, E. W. (1972). The humble programmer. *Communications of the ACM, 15*(10), 859–866. doi:10.1145/355604.361591

Dill, D. L., Mercuri, R., Neumann, P. G., & Wallach, D. S. (2008). *Frequently asked questions about DRE voting system*. Retrieved from http://www.verifiedvoting.org/article.php?id=5018

Epstein, J. (2007). Electronic voting. *Computer, 40*(8), 92–95. doi:10.1109/MC.2007.271

Feldman, A. J., Halderman, J. A., & Felten, E. W. (2006). *Security analysis of the Diebold AccuVote-TS voting machine*. Princeton, NJ: Princeton University.

Fishcher, E. A. (2003). *Election reform and electronic voting systems (DREs): Analysis of security issues*. Retrieved from http://people.csail.mit.edu/rivest/voting/reports/Fischer-ElectionReformAndElectronicVotingSystemsDREs.pdf

Frisina, L., Herron, M. C., Honaker, J., & Lewis, J. B. (2008). Ballot formats, touchscreens, and undervotes: A study of the 2006 midterm elections in Florida. *Election Law Journal: Rules, Politics, and Policy, 7*(1), 25–47.

Gardner, R., Yasinsac, A., Bishop, M., Kohno, T., Hartley, Z., Kerski, J., et al. (2007). *Software review and security analysis of the Diebold voting machine software*. Retrieved from http://election.dos.state.fl.us/voting-systems/pdf/SAITreport.pdf

Hasen, R. L. (2000). Vote buying. *California Law Review*, 88.

Hursti, H. (2006). *Critical security issues with Diebold TSx*. Retrieved from http://www.blackboxvoting.org/BBVtsxstudy.pdf

Jones, D. W. (2005). *Threats to voting systems.* Paper presented at the NIST Workshop on Threats to Voting Systems, Gaithersburg, MD.

Kohno, T., Stubblefield, A., Rubin, A. D., & Wallach, D. S. (2004). Analysis of an electronic voting system. In *Proceedings of the IEEE Symposium on Security and Privacy* (pp. 27-40.)

NIST. (2005). *Developing an analysis of threats to voting systems: Preliminary workshop summary.* Gaithersburg, MD: NIST.

Norden, L., Kimball, D., Quesenbery, W., & Chen, M. (2008). *Better ballots.* Retrieved from http://www.brennancenter.org/content/resource/better_ballots

Ohio Secretary of State. (2003). *Direct recording electronic (DRE), Technical security assessment report.* Retrieved from http://www.sos.state.oh.us/sos/upload/everest/01-compuware112103.pdf

Pardue, H., Landry, J., & Yasinsac, A. (2009). A risk assessment model for voting systems using threat trees and Monte Carlo simulation. In *Proceedings of the First International Workshop on Requirements Engineering for E-voting Systems*, Atlanta, GA (pp. 55-60).

Parker, D. B. (2006). Making the case for replacing risk-based security. *ISSA Journal*, 6-9.

Peltier, T. R. (2001). *Information security risk analysis* (2nd ed.). Boca Raton, FL: Auerbach.

Potts, T. (2008, November 5). *Fire guts Patton store, forces change of polls.* Retrieved from http://www.tribune-democrat.com/local/local_story_310012455.html

Rice, H. G. (1953). Classes of recursively enumerable sets and their decision problems. *Transactions of the American Mathematical Society*, *74*, 358–366. doi:10.1090/S0002-9947-1953-0053041-6

Ross, R., Katzke, S. W., Johnson, L. A., Swanson, M., Stoneburner, G., & Rogers, G. (2007). *Recommended security controls for federal information systems.* Retrieved from http://csrc.nist.gov/publications/nistpubs/800-53-Rev3/sp800-53-rev3-final.pdf

Schneier, B. (1999). Attack trees. *Dr. Dobb's Journal of Software Tools*, *24*, 21–29.

Stoneburner, G., Goguen, A., & Feringa, A. (2002). *Risk management guide for information technology systems.* Gaithersburg, MD: National Institute of Standards and Technology.

Thompson, K. (1984). Reflections on trusting trust. *Communications of the ACM*, *27*(8), 761–763. doi:10.1145/358198.358210

Tipton, H. F., & Henry, K. (2007). *Official (ISC)2 guide to the CISSP CBK.* Boca Raton, FL: Taylor & Francis.

Weldemariam, K., & Mattioli, A. V. (2009). Experiments and data analysis of electronic voting system. In *Proceedings of the 4th International Conference on Risks and Security of Internet and Systems*, Toulouse, France.

Yasinsac, A., & Bishop, M. (2008). The dynamics of counting and recounting votes. *IEEE SandP Magazine, 6*(3), 22-29.

Yasinsac, A., & Pardue, H. (2010). Voting system risk assessment using threat trees. In *Proceedings of the Conference on Information Systems Applied Research*, Nashville, TN.

Yasinsac, A., Wagner, D., Bishop, M., Baker, T., De Medeiros, B., Tyson, G., et al. (2007). *Software review and security analysis of the ES&S iVotronic 8.0.1.2 voting machine firmware, final report.* Tallahassee, FL: Security and Assurance in Information Technology (SAIT) Laboratory, Florida State University.

*This work was previously published in the International Journal of Information Security and Privacy, Volume 5, Issue 3, edited by Hamid Nemati, pp. 19-35, copyright 2011 by IGI Publishing (an imprint of IGI Global).*

# Chapter 11
# Intrusion Detection Algorithm for MANET

**S. Srinivasan**
*Texas A&M International University, USA*

**S. P. Alampalayam**
*APS Technologies, USA*

## ABSTRACT

*Mobile ad hoc networks (MANET) present the opportunity to connect transient nodes to the internet without having central control. This very design supports new nodes to join and leave the network based on their proximity to the MANET. Concurrently, it creates many security challenges for authenticating nodes that are not present in a traditional wired network. Much of the existing work on MANET security has focused on routing and mobility. In this paper, the authors present an algorithm that considers the neighboring nodes' status to determine if a particular node is malicious or not. The authors used NS2 simulation tool to test the algorithm and present the results in the paper. The major benefits of this research work are in military applications.*

## INTRODUCTION

A Mobile Ad hoc Network (MANET) is a collection of mobile nodes forming an adhoc network without central control of the network. The main benefit of MANET is that the nodes could enter or leave the network based on their proximity to the MANET. Such a network does not require any fixed infrastructure to support the mobile nodes. The major beneficiaries of the use of MANET are the first responders responding to a disaster or soldiers in a battlefield. MANET is one of the well researched areas in the literature. Even though MANETs have been looked at from various angles, much of the work involving MANET have been with regard to routing, performance, and mobility (Hubaux, Buttyan, & Capkun, 2001). These are important aspects to look at but, given the inherent nature of MANET to support many new nodes, authentication is an important aspect. Focusing

DOI: 10.4018/978-1-4666-2050-6.ch011

on security and dependability of the MANET is essential in order to support future applications involving these networks.

Traditional networks have been successful based on their reliability and the security guarantees. In such networks the nodes that enter the network have fixed access points such as a port in a router and stay on the network for an extended period of time. On the other hand, in a mobile ad hoc network there is no central server to authenticate nodes. By design, a MANET supports nodes that enter the network based on their proximity to the MANET and also leave the network after a brief period of time. So, one has to make sure that any node that enters the network has good intentions. This means that the node will have access to the network to reach an access point for the Internet and at the same time should facilitate other nodes that require the necessary forwarding of packets. Studies have shown that when a node is on a MANET, it tries to conserve power and the activity that drains much of the power is routing packets. It is estimated that a node on a MANET would use up 65 percent of its power in facilitating packet forwarding. For this reason, nodes tend to become greedy after a while to conserve power. Thus, algorithms are needed to detect when a node is no longer an active participant in the network. Given the mobile nature of a nodes' participation in MANET this is not a major hurdle to overcome.

The most common method of securing a communication is by using encryption. It works well in wired networks which could support extensive decryption methodologies since electrical power is not a factor to be worried about. However, nodes in a MANET are power constrained and as such cannot support extensive decryption technologies (Zhang, Lee, & Huang, 2003). The alternative then is to monitor every node in a MANET. This would not be a major burden since the number of nodes in MANET at any given time is limited to less than 50 nodes. Another important factor to consider in an ad hoc network is trust between

nodes. Since the nodes enter and leave an ad hoc network periodically there should be some way to build trust. This is one of the reasons why intrusion detection is essential in a MANET.

In the research literature we find a vast amount of material on various approaches to intrusion detection (ID). Zhang et al studied ID in wireless networks in general (Zhang, Lee, & Huang, 2003). Vigna et al. (2004) looked at ID in AODV-based ad hoc networks. AODV (Ad hoc On demand Distance Vector) networks find the shortest path from source to destination among a set of nodes that are neighbors. Bhargava and Agarwal (2001) as well as Klein-Berndt (2001) considered the security aspects of AODV protocols. Puttini et al.'s (2004) study involved a fully integrated approach to detecting intruders in a MANET. In another paper, Puttini et al. (2003) studied a modular architecture for distributed intrusion detection systems. This is an important contribution in that this identifies several new methods of distributed attacks. Alampalayam et al. (2005) viewed intrusion from a security perspective and developed a taxonomy. Sen and Clark (2009) did a similar study on intrusion detection in MANETs. Sterne et al. (2005) took a novel approach and studied a cooperative intrusion detection architecture. Li and Wei (2004) developed guidelines for selecting the appropriate method for intrusion detection. Mandala et al. (2007) did an extensive survey of intrusion detection methods. The results highlighted in this survey were also part of the other works cited in this paper.

Another important contribution in intrusion detection in wireless networks was presented by Nadkarni and Misra (2004). They took a novel approach to detect intrusion in wireless ad hoc networks (Nadkarni & Misra, 2004). The approach Patwardhan et al. (2005) took for considering intrusion detection was widely looked at by several others as well. They looked at ID from a secure routing perspective (Patwardhan et al., 2005). Traditionally the intrusion detection mechanisms are applied both to the AODV and

DSDV (Destination Sequenced Distance Vector) protocols. Morshed et al. (2010) considered the performance aspects both for DSDV and AODV protocols in routing for MANETs. Wan et al. (2004) studied the DSDV routing protocol from a security perspective so that any intrusion perpetrated on such networks could be detected quickly. Raghani et al. (2007) considered an essential aspect of intrusion detection, namely, the ability to validate the certificates presented by the nodes. This study considered evaluating the certificates in a dynamic manner. Our analysis of these important papers showed that there was no response to the intrusion in order to protect the integrity of the ad hoc network. An effective intrusion response should be automated. Unfortunately in many ID architectures the designers take the view that the operator should respond to the intrusion in an effective way rather than find an automated solution. This is one of the motivating factors for us in developing the algorithm to launch an automated intrusion response based on an identification of intrusion into the ad hoc network. Development of this automated response depended on statistical analysis of data gathered. Agresti and Franklin (2006) highlight the effectiveness of data analysis in their book. In the next section, we describe the most common methods available to launch an intrusion response.

## Intrusion Response Approaches

There are several intrusion response approaches that vary depending on the response being passive or active, manual or automated, static or adaptive, proactive or delayed, independent or cooperative. All these aspects were clearly enunciated in the taxonomy paper by Stakhanova, Basu, and Wong (2006). We briefly summarize these different aspects below for easy reference (Stakhanova, Basu, & Wong, 2006).

## Passive vs. Active

In a Passive response system there is no attempt to minimize the damage already caused by the attack or prevent further attacks. The main goal of this approach is to notify the responsible parties with details of the attack. On the other hand, Active responses try to minimize the damage caused and attempt to identify the intruder. We follow the active response approach in our model as we identify and isolate the intruder.

## Manual vs. Automatic

The Manual response approach provides minimal automation of response than automatic response approaches. Even though the speed of response is inhibited by the minimal automation, it still provides a higher degree of automation than the notification-only approach. The Automatic response approach immediately tackles the intrusion through automated decision making processes. In our model we automate the decision making process to isolate the intruder.

## Static vs. Adaptive

Most of the intrusion response approaches since the response selection mechanism remains the same during the attack period rather than adapt based on the state of the network. However, the Adaptive responses adjust dynamically to response selection based on the network environment at the time of attack. Adaptive aspects relate to one of the following:

- Modification of system resources available for intrusion response.
- Take into account the outcome of prior responses made by the system.

We take the static response approach. A more detailed discussion on the adaptive approach can be found in Alampalayam and Kumar (2003).

## Proactive vs. Delayed

In the Proactive response approach one is able to anticipate the intrusion before damage is done to the resource. Anticipating an attack requires extensive data as well as the attacker following a known approach. Both are highly unlikely to happen. Consequently, predicting an attack is very hard and often relies on the likelihood of how the current user/system behavior is similar to a past pattern. Moreover, the necessary action requires that the detection and response be highly correlated. The alternative to this approach is the Delayed response which allows for the action to be delayed until the attack is confirmed. Developing the necessary metrics for this is feasible. In developing our model we follow the delayed response approach since the responses are fired once the attack is confirmed.

## Independent vs. Cooperative

The Independent response approach calls for handling the intrusion at the node where it was detected. The widely deployed intrusion detection systems are host-based and when an intrusion is detected at a node it triggers a local independent response such as terminating the affected process or disabling the host. This appears to be a preferred approach to the Cooperative response approach where multiple systems have to combine their resources to respond to an intrusion. The Cooperative approach is complex since it needs to come up with a global action based on several local information pieces. Such systems already exist in network-based Intrusion Detection. We take into account the state of the neighbors in arriving at an action and as such our model could be characterized as a cooperative response approach.

In the rest of the paper we describe our model. This paper builds on the work of Alampalayam and Kumar (2004b) and Alampalayam and Srinivasan (2009). We present the algorithm for the intruder identification and response framework. We then describe the intrusion response framework using an example. Finally, we describe the results of the simulation experiment. This section represents the main contributions of this paper.

## RELATED WORK

This paper builds on the work of Alampalayam and Kumar (2004b) and Alampalayam and Srinivasan (2009) on Intrusion Recovery in MANETs. We developed a feedback model for intrusion response. The model keeps track of the values of several counters for neighbors of an ad hoc node. These counters are used to detect intrusion based on how their values change. This process involves the use of Threat Index that we introduced in an earlier paper (Alampalayam & Kumar, 2004b). This concept is crucial to our current work in developing the intrusion response. For the sake of completeness we define Threat Index (TI) from Alampalayam and Kumar (2004b).

*Definition:* Let X represent a sample space containing different significant parameters that represent an attack. We denote $X = \{x_i, 1 < i < n\}$. The fuzzy set A in X is a set of ordered pairs defined as:

$$A = \{(x_i, \mu_j(x_i)), x \in X\} \tag{3.11}$$

where $\mu_j$ is the grade of membership of $x_i$. Threat Index (TI) is then defined as:

$$TI = \frac{\sum_{j=1}^{m} w_j y_j}{\sum_{j=1}^{m} w_j} \tag{3.12}$$

Here $y_j$ indicates the output value associated with the consequent of that particular rule j in the fuzzy set and $w_j$ indicates the rule strength for the rule j. The rule strength illustrates how active or

*Figure 1. Feedback control based security model*

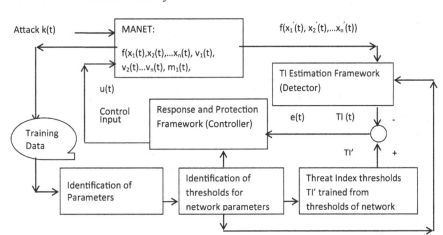

reliable a rule is in the fuzzy set. The rule strength is calculated as:

$$w_j = \min(\mu_j(x_i)), \; i < 1 < n \qquad (3.13)$$

and n is number of input metrics for each rule.

The basic architecture of the security model is shown in Figure 1.

In Figure 1, wireless MANET is represented as a function: $f(x_1(t), x_2(t),...x_n(t), v_1(t), v_2(t)...$ $v_n(t), m_1(t), m_2(t),...m_n(t), k(t), u(t))$, where $x_n(t)$ represents the significant attack sensitive network parameters, $v_n(t)$ represents the network parameters which are not significant in representing the node vulnerability, $m_n(t)$ represents the mobility parameters, $k(t)$ represents the attack and $u(t)$ represents the control input. The value $x_n'(t)$ denotes the modified values of the significant attack sensitive network parameter due to the influence of the attack $k(t)$ and the control input $u(t)$. Threat Index (TI) for a node is calculated by the detection framework from the attack sensitive network parameters, $x_n'(t)$ using fuzzy logic. The computed Threat Index $TI(t)$ is compared with the threshold values of the Threat Index TI'. The Threat Index thresholds TI' are obtained with the help of the training dataset where the state of each record is labeled. Data records collected from simulation environment with and without attack

are used as training dataset for identifying the Threat Index thresholds. As shown in Figure 1, the training data is derived from the MANET and is used in the identification of significant parameters and the thresholds of these parameters and the threat index. If the computed TI(t) of a node is greater than or equal to vulnerable state threshold reference TI', the node is identified to be under threat. Upon detecting that a node is under threat, the neighboring nodes are subjected to the response and protection algorithm in the response framework. This response algorithm identifies the intruder and sends the control signal u(t) to isolate the intruder from the MANET. The control signal u(t) varies depending upon the type of the intrusion. The different types of control actions are explained in the following sections. This control signal reconfigures the MANET and modifies $f(x_1'(t+1), x_2'(t+1),...x_n'(t+1))$ such that TI(t+1) reaches the steady normal state. It should however be noted that $f(x_1'(t+1), x_2'(t+1),...$ $x_n'(t+1))$ also depends on any new attack k(t+1). The following experiments describe in detail the intruder identification and response framework of the model. The significant parameter identification, threat index calculation and intrusion detection aspect of the model were described in detail in Alampalayam and Kumar (2004a, 2004b) and Alampalayam and Srinivasan (2009).

## INTRUDER IDENTIFICATION AND RESPONSE ALGORITHM FOR THE MODEL

In this section we describe the main algorithm developed for identification of malicious nodes and the actions planned based on the identification (see Box 1 for the algorithm).

## EXAMPLE ILLUSTRATING THE INTRUSION RESPONSE FRAMEWORK

Let us consider the MANET where the detection mechanism identified node $N_1$ to be under attack at 200 ms. Since the MANET is detected to be under attack, the intrusion response framework gets invoked. Here the threshold values $UCL_{vs}$ and $UCL_{us}$ are included for reference and the parameter values on each link is classified into normal state (NS), uncertain state (US) and vulnerable state (VS) by comparing against the threshold references.

We describe in Table 1 the various threshold values and significant parameter values for the nodes in Figure 2. In Table 2 we show the counter values and the response plan.

From Table 1, we find that on the link where the neighboring source node is $M_{11}$ and the destination is $N_1$, QL and EC are in normal state and PD is in uncertain state. So the normal counter is incremented twice and takes a value of 2. Uncertain counter is incremented once and takes a value of 1. Since none of the significant parameters is in vulnerable state, the abnormal counter value is not incremented and remains 0. Since the value of the normal counter is greater than the sum of uncertain and abnormal counters, the "normal" flag is asserted for the link's source $M_{11}$.

On the link where the source is $M_{12}$ and destination is $N_1$, PD, QL and EC are in vulnerable state. So the abnormal counter is incremented thrice and takes a value of 3. The normal and uncertain counters are not incremented and they remain at 0. Since the value of the abnormal counter is greater than the sum of uncertain and normal counters, the "malicious" flag is asserted for this link's source $M_{12}$.

On the link where the source is $M_{13}$ and destination is $N_1$, PD and QL are in normal state, and so the normal counter is incremented twice and takes a value of 2. Since EC is in vulnerable state, abnormal counter is incremented once and hence take a value of 1. Since none of the significant parameters is in uncertain state, the uncertain counter value is not incremented and remains 0. Since the value of the normal counter is greater than the sum of uncertain and abnormal counters, the "normal" flag is asserted for this link's source $M_{13}$.

On the link where the source is $M_{14}$ and destination is $N_1$, PD and QL are in normal state, and so the normal counter is incremented twice and takes a value of 2. Since EC is in vulnerable state, the abnormal counter is incremented once and results in a value of 1. None of the significant parameters is in uncertain state and so the uncertain counter is not incremented and it remains at 0. Since the value of the normal counter is greater than the sum of abnormal and uncertain counters, the "normal" flag is asserted for this link's source $M_{14}$.

On the link where the source is $M_{15}$ and destination is $N_1$, PD and QL are in normal state, and so the normal counter is incremented twice and takes a value of 2. As EC is in vulnerable state the abnormal counter is incremented once and hence results in a value of 1. None of the significant parameters is in uncertain state and so the uncertain counter is not incremented and it remains 0. Since the value of the normal counter is greater than the sum of abnormal and uncertain counters, the "normal" flag is asserted for this link's source $M_{15}$. Using this information, Table 2 is populated.

Each row in Table 2 represents the counter values and the flag of the neighboring source node for the node under threat and the type of the action plan that needs to be taken against the neighboring node. The agent implementation of

*Box 1.*

1. Let $N_1$, $N_2$,…$N_k$ be the nodes which are detected to be under threat based on Intrusion Detection Algorithm.
2. Let $x_1$, $x_2$,…$x_n$ be the significant metric parameters which have been identified using data mining.
3. For each node under threat ($N_i$), where $1< i<k$ and 'k' being the number of nodes under threat
    3.1. For each adjacent source node, ($M_{i,z}$), where $1<z<m$ and 'm' being the number of adjacent source nodes to the node under threat
        3.1.1 Initialize its {abnormal, uncertain, normal} $counter_{iz}$
        3.1.2 For each significant parameter ($x_j$), where $1<j<n$ and 'n' being the number of significant parameters
            i. Identify the parameter value ($Val(x_{izj})$) for the node ($M_{i,z}$).
            ii. If $Val(x_{izj})$ is in {abnormal state, uncertain state, normal state} increment the {abnormal, uncertain, normal} $counter_{iz}$ of source node ($M_{i,z}$)
respectively. Abnormal state can have very high values or very low values
depending on the nature of the parameter.
    3.2. For each adjacent source node ($M_{i,z}$),
        3.2.1. if (its $abnormalcounter_{iz}$ is greater than sum of $normalcounter_{iz}$ and
$uncertaincounter_{iz}$)
            {set the flag for node ($M_{i,z}$) to malicious}
            else
                if (its $uncertaincounter_{iz}$ is > sum of $abnormalcounter_{iz}$ and
$normalcounter_{iz}$)
                    {set the flag for node ($M_{i,z}$) to uncertain}
                else
                    {set the flag for node ($M_{i,z}$) to normal}
                end-if
            end-if
        3.2.2. if (flag of node $M_{i,z}$ is malicious)
            {Execute Action Plan 3: this plan executes drastic action like cutting
off the node and restoration of the links.}
            else
                if(flag of node $M_{i,z}$ is uncertain)
                    {Execute Action plan 2: this plan executes moderate response action
like automatic re-authentication of the node.}
                else
                    {Execute Action Plan 1: No action is needed since the node is
neither malicious nor selfish. In order to avoid unnecessary overhead, apply time period check before further collaborative
monitoring, whenever the action plan is Action Plan 1}
                end-if
            end-if

*Table 1. Threshold values and values of significant parameters during attack*

| Parameter | $UCL_{vs}$ | $UCL_{us}$ | $M_{11}$ to $N_1$ | $M_{12}$ to $N_1$ | $M_{13}$ to $N_1$ | $M_{14}$ to $N_1$ | $M_{15}$ to $N_1$ |
|---|---|---|---|---|---|---|---|
| (PD) | 208.6336 | 119.081 | 155 / US | 2000 /VS | 20/NS | 20/NS | 20/NS |
| (QL) | 1157.721 | 656.014 | 120 / NS | 12000/ VS | 120/NS | 120/NS | 120 / NS |
| (EC) Joules | 1.9941 | 1.3397 | 1.30 /NS | 3.92/VS | 2.33/VS | 2.36/VS | 2.61/ VS |

*Figure 2. Illustration of node under threat with malicious neighboring nodes*

UCL = Uncertainty Level    VS = Vulnerable State    US = Uncertain State
PD = Packet Drop    QL = Queue Length    EC = Energy Consumption

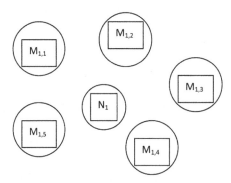

*Table 2. Illustration of response framework*

| Node Under Threat | Neighboring Nodes | Normal Counter | Uncertain Counter | Abnormal Counter | Flag | Action Plan |
|---|---|---|---|---|---|---|
| $N_1$ | $M_{1,1}$ | 2 | 1 | 0 | Normal | Action Plan 1 |
| | $M_{1,2}$ | 0 | 0 | 3 | Malicious | Action Plan 3 |
| | $M_{1,3}$ | 2 | 0 | 1 | Normal | Action Plan 1 |
| | $M_{1,4}$ | 2 | 0 | 1 | Normal | Action Plan 1 |
| | $M_{1,5}$ | 2 | 0 | 1 | Normal | Action Plan 1 |

the routing protocol in mobile ad hoc network has the view of the Table 2 and takes appropriate response action based on the counters and the flag value. In Table 2, sum of abnormal, uncertain and normal counters for every neighboring node to a node under threat will be equal to the number of significant parameters. This is due to the reason that for every neighboring node to a node under threat, the effect of each significant parameter is analyzed and categorized into three possible states, and the normal, uncertain or abnormal and counters are incremented based on these states.

## SIMULATION RESULTS

The MANET simulation was done using NS2 (2011). In this experiment we varied the number of mobile nodes in the range 6 to 100. We used both Ad hoc On Demand Distance Vector (AODV) routing protocol and Destination Sequenced Distance Vector (DSDV) routing protocol in the simulation experiments. The results for AODV simulation are described in Alampalayam and Srinivasan (2009). In this paper we present only the DSDV simulation results. The main network parameters used in the simulation were: packet drop rate, energy consumption and queue length. The threshold values needed for the simulation was obtained using the training data set. Additional relevant factors used in the simulation are as follows:

1. **Channel type:** Wireless
2. **Propagation model:** Two Ray Ground
3. **Node mobility model:** Random Waypoint
4. **MAC layer protocol:** Distribution Coordination Function
5. **Packet transmission model:** CSMA/CA
6. **Channel capacity:** 2 Mbps
7. **Signal range:** 250 m
8. **Focus area:** 1000 m x 500 m
9. **Duration:** 1000 seconds
10. **Bit Rate:** Constant Bit Rate
11. **Operating System:** Red Hat 9.0 – Linux Kernel 2.6

The main focus of our simulation was identification of intrusion. For this part we looked at the Denial of Service (DoS) attack on a host node by one of the mobile agents. It appears that many of the intrusions occur using the Denial of Service attacks as the starting point. Karig and Lee (2001) studied both DoS attacks and countermeasures against them from a remote node. We took this aspect into account in our simulation. In this simulation node $M_1$ is neighbor for node $N_1$. Because a mobile node could reach additional nodes as well, we assume that all nodes $M_i$, i = 0 to 6, are all neighbor to $N_1$. In our scenario we designated $M_2$ to be the malicious node. Since $M_2$ launched a DoS attack on $N_1$, the host $N_1$ was unable to provide service to its other neighbors $M_0$, $M_1$, $M_3$, $M_4$ and $M_5$. Our algorithm identified that $N_1$

was under attack by $M_2$. As part of the response the node $N_2$ was isolated from the network as it dispatched $M_2$. The results of this simulation are described below using several figures generated from NS2 for the DSDV protocol.

Table 3 shows the values of the normal, uncertain and abnormal counters for each node that is neighbor to node under threat ($N_1$). The agent implementation for the DSDV routing protocol in mobile ad hoc network is shown in Table 3. The values are recorded every 100 ms of the simulation. As explained earlier, if the value of the parameter exceeds the vulnerable threshold level, the abnormal counter is incremented. If the parameter exceeds the uncertain threshold level, the uncertain counter is incremented. Otherwise, the normal counter is incremented. For malicious node $N_2$, at around 100 to 200 ms, the abnormal counter reaches the value of 3, thus resulting in the response plan 3 to be executed, to isolate the node. For every other neighboring node at all the time during the simulation, the normal counter is higher than the sum of vulnerable and uncertain counter, thus resulting in their flag to be normal. The values for the parameters shown in Figures 3 through 8 validate the value of the counters and the flag in Table 3 for each node that is a neighbor to the node under threat ($N_1$).

Figures 3 through 8 give the plot of values of the significant attack sensitive network parameters without the response and with the response applied, for each neighboring node to the node under threat $N_1$. Figures 3 and 4 represent control chart for the queue length metric during the DoS attack and after application of response respectively. As shown in Figure 3, queue length metric for the link between source node $N_2$ and host is significantly above the vulnerable state threshold (2800) when no response is applied during the attack. After response is applied, the queue length metric for the link between node $N_2$ and host $N_1$ is within the normal state threshold control limit as seen in Figure 4, since it is cut off from the network.

*Table 3. Values of counters used for response action in DSDV experimentation*

| Node Under Threat | Neighboring Nodes | Time (ms) | Normal Counter | Uncertain Counter | Abnormal Counter | Flag | Action Plan |
|---|---|---|---|---|---|---|---|
| $N_1$ | $N_0$ | 100 | 2 | 1 | 0 | Normal | Resp Plan 1 |
| | | 200 | 2 | 1 | 0 | Normal | Resp Plan 1 |
| | | 300 | 2 | 1 | 0 | Normal | Resp Plan 1 |
| | | 400 | 2 | 1 | 0 | Normal | Resp Plan 1 |
| | | 500 | 2 | 1 | 0 | Normal | Resp Plan 1 |
| | | 600 | 2 | 1 | 0 | Normal | Resp Plan 1 |
| | $N_2$ | 100 | 2 | 0 | 1 | Normal | Resp Plan 1 |
| | | 200 | 0 | 0 | 3 | Malicious | Resp Plan 3 |
| | $N_3$ | 100 | 2 | 1 | 0 | Normal | Resp Plan 1 |
| | | 200 | 2 | 1 | 0 | Normal | Resp Plan 1 |
| | | 300 | 2 | 1 | 0 | Normal | Resp Plan 1 |
| | | 400 | 2 | 1 | 0 | Normal | Resp Plan 1 |
| | | 500 | 2 | 1 | 0 | Normal | Resp Plan 1 |
| | | 600 | 2 | 1 | 0 | Normal | Resp Plan 1 |
| | $N_4$ | 100 | 2 | 1 | 0 | Normal | Resp Plan 1 |
| | | 200 | 2 | 1 | 0 | Normal | Resp Plan 1 |
| | | 300 | 2 | 1 | 0 | Normal | Resp Plan 1 |
| | | 400 | 2 | 1 | 0 | Normal | Resp Plan 1 |
| | | 500 | 2 | 1 | 0 | Normal | Resp Plan 1 |
| | | 600 | 2 | 1 | 0 | Normal | Resp Plan 1 |
| | $N_5$ | 100 | 2 | 1 | 0 | Normal | Resp Plan 1 |
| | | 200 | 2 | 1 | 0 | Normal | Resp Plan 1 |
| | | 300 | 2 | 1 | 0 | Normal | Resp Plan 1 |
| | | 400 | 2 | 1 | 0 | Normal | Resp Plan 1 |
| | | 500 | 2 | 1 | 0 | Normal | Resp Plan 1 |
| | | 600 | 2 | 1 | 0 | Normal | Resp Plan 1 |

*Figure 3. Control chart of queue length metric without response for DSDV*

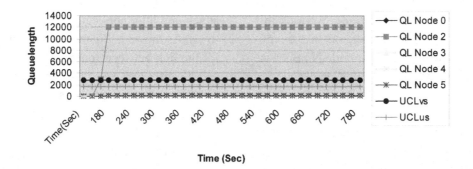

*Figure 4. Control chart of queue length metric with response for DSDV*

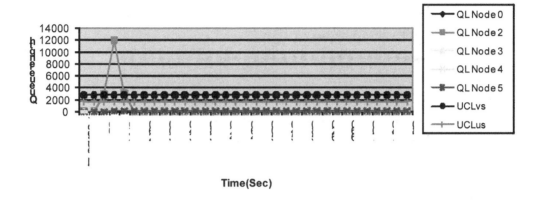

*Figure 5. Control chart of packet drop metric without response for DSDV*

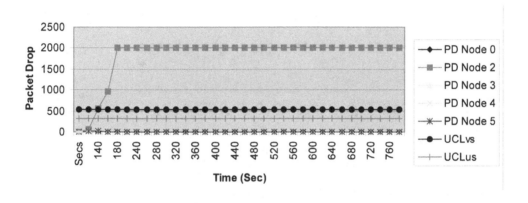

*Figure 6. Control chart of packet drop metric with response for DSDV*

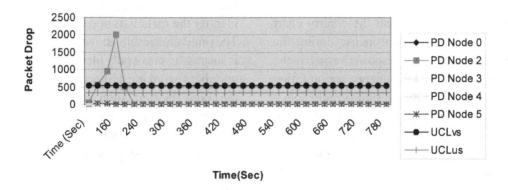

Figures 5 and 6 represent the control chart for the packet drop metric during the DoS attack and after the application of response respectively. As shown in Figure 5, the packet drop metric for the link between source node $N_2$ and host $N_1$ is significantly above the vulnerable state threshold (537) when no response is applied during the attack. As shown in Figure 6, once the malicious node $N_2$

*Figure 7. Control chart of energy consumption metric without response for DSDV*

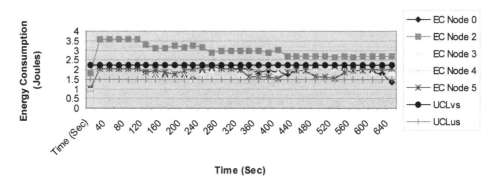

*Figure 8. Control chart of energy consumption metric with response for DSDV*

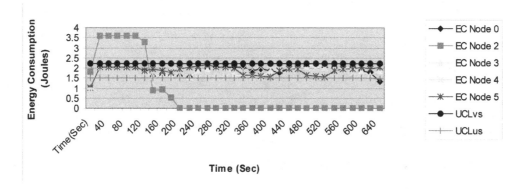

is identified and isolated from the network, there are no packet drops associated with the malicious node $N_2$ and the host $N_1$.

Figures 7 and 8 represent the control chart for the energy consumption metric during the DoS attack and after the response respectively. As shown in Figure 7, the energy consumption metric for source node $N_2$ is significantly above the vulnerable state threshold (2 joules) when no response is applied during the attack. After response is applied, the energy consumption metric for the source node $N_2$ is within the normal state threshold control limit as seen in Figure 8.

## CONCLUSION

We analyzed the MANET scenario where we identify the malicious node using our algorithm. The simulation results above show that this method is successful in not only identifying the malicious node but also taking the necessary action to isolate the node. The simulation shows that the MANET performs properly after the node causing the Denial of Service attack is removed. We studied the DSDV routing protocol in this simulation. The three parameters that we considered in this simulation are packet drop rate, queue length for packet transmission and energy consumption of the device. A similar approach applies to the AODV routing protocol as well and the related work is cited in the reference.

# REFERENCES

Agresti, A., & Franklin, C. A. (2006). *Statistics: The art and science of learning from data*. Upper Saddle River, NJ: Prentice Hall.

Alampalayam, S., & Srinivasan, S. (2009). Intrusion recovery framework for tactical mobile ad hoc networks. *International Journal of Computer Science and Network Security, 9*, 1–10.

Alampalayam, S. P., & Kumar, A. (2003). Adaptive security model for mobile agents in wireless networks. In *Proceedings of the IEEE Global Communications Conference* (pp. 1516-1521).

Alampalayam, S. P., & Kumar, A. (2004a). Predictive security model using data mining. In *Proceedings of the IEEE Global Communications Conference* (pp. 2208-2212).

Alampalayam, S. P., & Kumar, A. (2004b). An adaptive and predictive security model for mobile ad hoc networks. *Kluwer Personal Communications Journal, 29*(6), 263–281.

Alampalayam, S. P., Kumar, A., & Srinivasan, S. (2005). Mobile ad hoc networks security – A taxonomy. In *Proceedings of the International Conference on Adaptive Science and Technology* (pp. 839-844).

Bhargava, S., & Agrawal, D. P. (2001). Security enhancements in AODV protocol for wireless ad hoc networks. In *Proceedings of the IEEE Vehicular Technology Conference* (pp. 2143-2147).

Hubaux, J., Buttyan, L., & Capkun, S. (2001). The quest for security in mobile ad hoc networks. In *Proceedings of the Conference on Mobile Ad Hoc Networking and Computing* (pp. 146-155).

Karig, D., & Lee, R. (2001). *Remote denial of service attacks and countermeasures* (Tech. Rep. No. CE-L2001-002). Princeton, NJ: Princeton University.

Klein-Berndt, L. (2001). *A quick guide to AODV routing*. Retrieved from http://www.antd.nist.gov/wctg/aodv_kernel/aodv_guide.pdf

Li, Y., & Wei, J. (2004). Guidelines on selecting intrusion detection methods in MANET. In *Proceedings of the Information Systems Education Conference, 21*, 1–17.

Mandala, S., Ngadi, M. A., & Abdullah, A. H. (2007). A survey on MANET intrusion detection. *International Journal of Computer Science and Security, 2*(1), 1–11.

Morshed, M. M., Ko, F. I. S., Lim, D., Rahman, M. H., Mazumder, M. R. R., & Ghosh, J. (2010). Performance evaluation of DSDV and AODV routing protocols in mobile ad hoc networks. In *Proceedings of the IEEE Conference on New Trends in Information Science and Service Science*, Dongguk, South Korea (pp. 399-403).

NS2. (2011). *The network simulator*. Retrieved from http://www.isi.edu/nsnam/ns

Nadkarni, K., & Misra, A. (2004). A novel intrusion detection approach for wireless ad hoc networks. In *Proceedings of the IEEE Wireless Communications and Networking Conference* (pp. 831-836).

Patwardhan, A., Parker, J., Joshi, A., Iorga, M., & Karygiannis, T. (2005). Secure routing and intrusion detection in ad hoc networks. In *Proceedings of the 3rd International Conference on Pervasive Computing and Communications* (pp. 191-199).

Puttini, R., Percher, J., Me, L., Camp, O., & De Souza, R. (2003). A modular architecture for distributed IDS. In V. Kumar, M. L. Gavrilova, C. J. Tan, & P. L'Ecuyer (Eds.), *Proceedings of the International Conference on Computational Science and its Applications* (LNCS 2669, pp. 91-113)

Puttini, R., Percher, J., Me, L., & Sousa, R. (2004). A fully distributed IDS for MANET. In *Proceedings of the IEEE Symposium on Computers and Communications* (pp. 331-338).

Raghani, S., Toshniwal, D., & Joshi, R. C. (2007). Distributed certification authority for mobile ad hoc networks – A dynamic approach. *Journal of Convergence Information Technology*, *2*(2), 10–20.

Sen, S., & Clark, J. A. (2009). Intrusion detection in mobile ad hoc networks. In Misra, S., Woungang, I., & Misra, S. C. (Eds.), *Guide to wireless ad hoc networks* (pp. 427–454). London, UK: Springer. doi:10.1007/978-1-84800-328-6_17

Stakhanova, N., Basu, S., & Wong, J. (2006). *Taxonomy of intrusion response systems* (Tech. Rep. No. 06-05). Ames, IA: Iowa State University.

Sterne, D., Balasubramanyam, P., Carman, D., Wilson, B., Talpade, R., Ko, C., et al. (2005). A general cooperative intrusion detection architecture for MANETs. In *Proceedings of the 3rd IEEE International Workshop on Information Assurance* (pp. 57-70).

Vigna, G., Gwalani, S., Srinivasan, K., Belding-Royer, K. E., & Kemmerer, R. (2004). An intrusion detection tool for AODV-based ad hoc wireless networks. In *Proceedings of the 20th Annual Computer Security Applications Conference* (pp. 16-27).

Wan, T., Kranakis, E., & van Oorschot, P. C. (2004). Securing the destination-sequenced distance vector routing protocol (S-DSDV). In *Proceedings of the 6th International Conference on Information and Communications Security* (pp. 358-374).

Zhang, Y., Lee, W., & Huang, Y. (2003). Intrusion detection techniques for mobile wireless networks. *Wireless Networks*, *9*(5), 545–556. doi:10.1023/A:1024600519144

*This work was previously published in the International Journal of Information Security and Privacy, Volume 5, Issue 3, edited by Hamid Nemati, pp. 36-49, copyright 2011 by IGI Publishing (an imprint of IGI Global).*

# Chapter 12
# An Integrated Security Governance Framework for Effective PCI DSS Implementation

**Mathew Nicho**
*University of Dubai, UAE*

**Hussein Fakhry**
*University of Dubai, UAE*

## ABSTRACT

*This paper analyses relevant IT governance and security frameworks/standards used in IT assurance and security to propose an integrated framework for ensuring effective PCI DSS implementation. Merchants dealing with credit cards have to comply with the Payment Card Industry Data Security Standards (PCI DSS) or face penalties for non-compliance. With more transactions based on credit cards, merchants are finding it costly and increasingly difficult to implement and interpret the PCI standard. One of the top reasons cited for merchants to fail PCI audit, and a leading factor in data theft, is the failure to ad-equately protect stored cardholder data. Although implementation of the PCI DSS is not a guarantee for perfect protection, effective implementation of the PCI standards can be ensured through the divergence of the PCI standard into wider information security governance to provide a comprehensive overview of information security based not only on security but also security audit and control. The contribution of this paper is the development of an integrated comprehensive security governance framework for 'information security' (rather than data protection) incorporating Control Objectives for Information and related Technology (COBIT), Information Technology Infrastructure Library (ITIL) and ISO 27002.*

DOI: 10.4018/978-1-4666-2050-6.ch012

## 1. INTRODUCTION

Compliance is one of the major issues in information security management (Al-Hamdani, 2009), but due to time deadline, lack of expertise in this area, multitude of regulations, lack of experienced staff, and cost factor they generally adopt a highly fragmented and siloed approach to governance, compliance and security. It has been stated that in order for information security measures to become effective, security should not only be built like a staircase of combined measures (Hagen, Albrechtsen, & Howden, 2008) but the range of security policies and support activities needs to be broadened (Sundt, 2006). While it is a widely accepted fact that information security has currently moved away from its technical focus, it still needs to be addressed from a multidimensional, holistic and comprehensive view for ensuring a secure information systems environment (von Solms, 2001). Implementing information security is thus not only a time consuming and complex process, but also a multidisciplinary concept cutting across several related disciplines (Elof & Elof, 2005). IS security viewed from this holistic perspective considers strategic, tactical, and operational issues surrounding the planning, analysis, design, implementation, and maintenance of an organization's information security (Choobineh, Dhillon, Grimaila, & Rees, 2007). This perspective requires the PCI DSS version 2.0 not only to diverge from its focused technical domain and expand to its outer concentric rings of the greater IS domain, but also forces it to link to the organizational strategic goals which is a major concern for IS managers. This strategic alignment of IS with business is the main focus of IT governance. In a survey conducted by PWC and IT Governance Institute in 2005 and 2008 (ITGI, 2006, 2008b) the importance of strategic alignment of organisational goals with the IT goals was cited by 90% of the respondents as being vital to the organisation. Hence, strategic alignment can come about (result) if the PCI DSS goal of securing cardholder data is

aligned with the IS goals and finally to the higher level organisational goals. Thus, an information security governance approach of PCI DSS can ensure greater security than an isolated siloed approach of PCI DSS standards implementation.

Since the purpose of this paper is to ensure the effectiveness of the PCI DSS implementation through an integrated approach of linking it with the wider relevant IT governance and security frameworks, the result is an integrated security governance framework. With this objective in mind the paper is divided into the following three sections. The first section provides an overview of the PCI DSS and its relevance followed by cases of security breaches. Section 2 takes a multidimensional view of information security by analysing relevant IT governance models that are relevant for ensuring a comprehensive but optimally integrated IS security. Section 3 proposes the final conceptual model incorporating PCI DSS along with the selected governance models.

## 2. PCI DSS

The Payment Card Industry Data Security Standards is an open global forum launched in 2006 by the five global payment brands namely American Express, Discover Financial Services, JCB International, MasterCard Worldwide, and Visa Inc. It was created for developing, managing, educating, and communicating the PCI Security Standards, including the Data Security Standard (PCI DSS), Payment Application Data Security Standard (PA-DSS), and PIN Transaction Security (PTS). It is the very first industry-wide standard which focuses on the credit card industry that aims at achieving a strong protection of sensitive consumer and cardholder data, and preventing major security issues (Liu, Xiao, Chen, Ozdemir, Dodle, & Singh, 2010). The objective of the standard was to enhance the security of the cardholder through protection of cardholder data and thus help facilitate global adoption of consistent data security measures

*Table 1. Merchant levels defined by MasterCard for PCI DSS compliance (adapted from MasterCard, 2011)*

| Merchant Definition | Criteria | Onsite Assessment | Self Assessment | Network Security Scan | Deadline |
|---|---|---|---|---|---|
| Level 1 | • Any merchant that has suffered a hack or an attack that resulted in an account data compromise<br>• Any merchant having greater than six million total combined MasterCard and Maestro transactions annually<br>• Any merchant meeting the Level 1 criteria of Visa<br>• Any merchant that MasterCard, in its sole discretion, determines should meet the Level 1 merchant requirements to minimize risk to the system | Required Annually | Not Required | Required Quarterly | 30 June 2011 |
| Level 2 | • Any merchant with greater than one million but less than or equal to six million total combined MasterCard and Maestro transactions annually<br>• Any merchant meeting the Level 2 criteria of Visa | At Merchant Discretion | Required Annually | Required Quarterly | 30 June 2011 |
| Level 3 | • Any merchant with greater than 20,000 combined MasterCard and Maestro e-commerce transactions annually but less than or equal to one million total combined MasterCard and Maestro ecommerce transactions annually<br>• Any merchant meeting the Level 3 criteria of Visa | Not Required[3] | Required Annually | Required Quarterly | 30 June 2005 |
| Level 4 | • All other merchants | Not Required | Required Annually | Required Quarterly | Consult Acquirer |

created to mitigate data breaches and prevent cardholder data fraud. Compliance is enforced on those dealing with credit cards and there are penalties for non-conformance of the PCI DSS standard by PCI Security Standards Council. The PCI DSS 2.0 version (released on October 2010) comprises of 6 principles, 12 major requirements, 45 sub requirements, 75 detailed requirements with corresponding testing procedures for the requirements and sub requirements. For the basis of evaluation by PCI, the merchants are divided into four levels with various requirements. Table 1 provides the matrix that is valid for merchants dealing with MasterCard.

Merchants dealing with credit cards are faced with two extremes. On one side is the risk of credit card transaction breaches and fraud along with penalties for not complying with the PCI standards; and on the other hand merchants face huge cost in complying with the PCI standards. For example in 2008 level-1 merchants (those dealing with more than 6 million transactions per year) spend an average of US $ 3.38 million to become PCI compliant including the cost of PCI assessment services (Amanto-McCoy, 2009). Since 2006, merchants have collectively spent in excess of $1 billion on compliance with the PCI DSS as part of their security programs (First Data, 2009). Based on VeriSign Global Security Consulting Services' PCI assessments of merchant companies it was found out that 79 percent of the implementations were cited for failure to protect stored data and thus fail their assessments (First Data, 2009). Moreover the UK Corporate IT Forum (CIF) in a 2009 survey estimated that only 1% of the surveyed companies are fully PCI compliant, 9% has failed their audit while the rest were trying to achieve conformance. In fact, a study on 500 U.S. and multinational organisations found out that on an average it was necessary to dedicate 35% of the IS security budget to any compliance effort (Everett, 2009).

## 2.1 Data Breaches

According to Verizon 2010 study (Baker et al., 2010) PCI compliant organizations were 50% less likely to be attacked than the non-compliant ones. While compliance to PCI DSS is a mandatory requirement and an appropriate way to protect cardholder data, full compliance with the PCI DSS does not ensure adequate protection as there are factors beyond the control of PCI DSS that can affect a breach like insider threat or failing to follow non PCI DSS process and outsourcing. A sensational case of breach of a company that is PCI complaint occurred in Hannaford in the year 2008. It is a supermarket chain with reported thefts of 4.2 million customer credit and debit card numbers with 1,800 cases of fraud. The data breach began on Dec. 7, unusual credit card activity became known on Feb. 27 and the breach was not contained until March 10 and reported only on March 17. The company stated that unauthorized software that was secretly installed on servers in nearly all of Hannaford Bros. Co.'s supermarkets enabled the massive data breach that compromised up to 4.2 million credit and debit cards (Harkavy, 2008). It has been argued by experts that this is the work of an insider which PCI DSS compliance alone might not have been able to prevent.

One of the most serious data breach in recent history occurred in 2006 at TJX Company Inc (non PCI complaint at the time of fraud) which was classified as the largest off-price apparel and home fashions retailer in both the United States and the world. Prior to the breach it ranked 133rd on the Fortune 500 list with an annual revenues of $17 billion, 125,000 employees with over 2400 stores worldwide. But in one of the largest security breach ever reported, in late 2006, hackers broke into the systems of TJX and stole vital customer information. It was estimated that the full financial impact of this incident might amount up to one billion dollars (Xu, Grant, Nguyen, & Dai, 2008). The hackers gained entry by exploiting the poor network security on a wireless network at a particular store. This allowed them to sit outside the store and intercept customers' credit card numbers as they made transactions. Then they used their open access point to track back to the company's central database. Since the company was storing customers' personal data and complete credit card numbers in an unencrypted format it allowed the thieves to simply download them. It was estimated that at least 94 million Visa and MasterCard accounts might have been exposed to the potential fraud (Jewell, 2007).

Even highly secured environments like the U.S. Department of Defense was not spared and most of it occurred due to non-technical aspects that are beyond the scope of the PCI DSS. In a breach involving the U.S. Department of Defense in 2007, the U.S. Department of Veterans Affairs caught a former employee who has stolen 1.8 million Social Security Numbers from the office. He quit when he discovered that they were about to do a background check on him (ITRC, 2008). A simple overlook from the side of employees can also result in breach, as in the following case where 76 million records of U.S. military veterans, including millions of Social Security numbers dating to 1972 were stolen when a defective hard drive was sent back to its vendor for repair and recycling without first destroying the data in the year 2009 (ITRC, 2010). The magnitude of data breaches are enormous as according to *Washington Post* at least 8.3 million personal and financial records of consumers were compromised by data spills or breaches at businesses, universities and government agencies in the first quarter of 2008 alone. According to the ITRC in 2008, 641 breaches were reported resulting in 35,597,210 records being exposed. One such incident happened at the University of Miami where 2.1 million records were exposed when the confidential information of tens of thousands of University of Miami patients was stolen when thieves took a case out of a vehicle used by a private off-site storage

*Figure 1. Sources of data breaches 2009 & 2010 (compiled from Verizon 2010 data breach investigation report)*

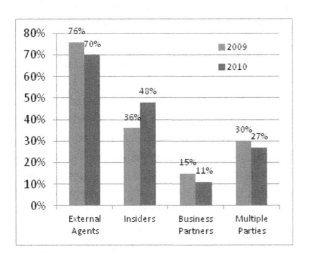

*Figure 2. Types of data breaches (compiled from Verizon 2010 data breach investigation report)*

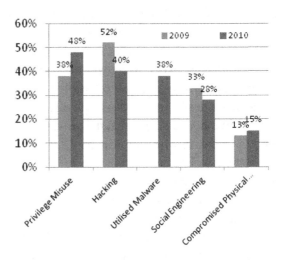

company. The data included names, addresses, Social Security numbers or health information (ITRC, 2009).

If the latest statistics is taken, then as of June 30, 2010, the ITRC recorded 341 individual breaches for the first 6 months of 2010 and this does not include the breaches not reported, veiled from public and unknown. The 2010 Verizon data breach investigation report conducted by the Verizon Risk team and the U.S. Secret Service revealed the source and nature of these breaches as is given in Figures 1 and 2 (Baker et al., 2010). In most of these cases it was revealed that non-technical and human factors were observed as reasons for these breaches which PCI DSS standards might not have been able to prevent. While compliance to PCI DSS is not a guarantee for full protection against data breaches, it considerably reduces the risk and the liability to the company. This certainly supports the argument that for PCI DSS to be effective it has to be viewed from a wider information security governance perspective.

From Figure 1 it is evident that having a strong defense in depth is not a complete guarantee for security. Here while the insider source of threat

has grown substantially (26% growth rate), the threat from hackers has been reduced to a great extent (9% decline). This fact is emphasised in Figure 2 where the insider threat (privilege misuse risen by about 26%) is repeated and is growing at an alarming rate.

The major focus of the PCI DSS is to protect cardholder data. This has been emphasised in all the 12 high level requirements under six categories and the corresponding testing procedure to fulfill these requirements. The failure to adequately protect stored data by companies is the leading factor in data theft and is also a main reason for merchants to fail a PCI audit. VeriSign Global Security Consulting Services, a division of security services vendor VeriSign, has conducted hundreds of PCI assessments in recent years. Of the merchant companies assessed by VeriSign Global Security Consulting Services, (a division of security services vendor VeriSign) it was found that 79 percent of those assessed were cited for the failure in their PCI audit due to their failure to protect stored data (First Data, 2009). The inability of organisations to adequately focus on non-technical issues namely the basic IT policies, procedures, practices, and strategies in organizations could attribute to the high incidence of data breach (Ifendo, 2009). Research on standards setting has found that proper governance is a key to success and success is more likely if the governance structure includes all of the various interests in the network. Moreover the standards themselves need to be effective yet flexible enough to satisfy competitive interests (Sullivan, 2010).

It should not be denied that the provisions of the PCI standard when implemented for online transaction would undoubtedly provide secure protection for some aspects of the retailer's interests that fall outside the narrow definition of credit card transaction management (protection of cardholder data). But still the retailer may need to take a broader view of security requirements by adopting the hybrid approach of PCI baseline implementation supplemented by risk assessment to address those matters outside PCI scope (Rowlingson & Winsborrow, 2006). Even though (as on 2009) 77 percent of the merchants have complied with PCI rules, this does not mean that their networks are totally secure (Ngugi, Vega, & Dardick, 2009).

## 3. COMPLIANCE FRAMEWORKS FOR INFORMATION SECURITY

Considering the fact that effective and efficient utilization of information technology requires the alignment of the IT strategies with the business strategies (Luftman, Lewis, & Oldach, 1993; Luftman & Brier, 1999) it is worthwhile to look at security from a wider perspective covering both the internal and external issues that can impact on IS security. Thus, information security should not be regarded as a technical issue, but as a business and governance challenge that involves adequate risk management, reporting, and accountability. Therefore, information security must be addressed at the highest levels of the organization and not regarded as a technical specialty relegated to the information technology (IT) department (Musa,

2010). Although compliance standards such as Sarbanes Oxley, Basel II and PCI DSS have been around for the last few years, now that organisations run the risk of the Information Commissioners' Office (ICO) fining them £500,000 for a data breach, there has never been a more pressing time to implement a holistic approach to compliance (Coburn, 2010).

An internal control provides reasonable assurance regarding the achievement of objectives in the area of effectiveness and efficiency of operations, reliability of financial reporting and compliance with regulations (Pathak, 2003). As far as implementing the PCI DSS standard is concerned, the requirements set by PCI DSS are in line with the IT security best practices required by widely recognised standards such as ISO 27002, 'Code of Best Practices for Information Security Management' or COBIT (Laredo, 2009). Moreover IT control implementers have been encouraged to use ITIL to define strategies, plans and processes, use COBIT for metrics, benchmarks and audits and use ISO/IEC 27002 to address security issues to mitigate the risks (Sahibudin, Sharifi, & Ayat, 2008).

In a survey of security professionals, the Enterprise Strategy Group (ESG) discovered that 72 percent of North American organizations with 1,000 or more employees have implemented one or more formal IT best-practice control and process models and among these the most widely used commercial IT control frameworks are ITIL, ISO 27002 and COBIT which provide optimal security management (Turner, Oltsik, & McKnigh, 2009). Furthermore ISO/IEC 27002, COBIT, ISO 20000, and ITIL are the most applicable and widely used standards to manage and maintain IT services (Sahibudin, Sharifi, & Ayat, 2009). Between these standards, in a comparative study of ISO 27000 with PCI DSS, by Gikas (2010) he listed 70 similar technical features between the two. Thus, the above review of literature made us to focus on COBIT, ITIL, ISO 27002 and PCI DSS for the purpose of this study. To make sure that the above selected models/ frameworks/

*Table 2. IS security governance framework (mapped with the relevant frameworks) (adapted from Posthumus & von Solms, 2004)*

| | Domains | Relevant Frameworks |
|---|---|---|
| **External** | Legal/ regulatory | PCI DSS |
| | Standards/ best practices | ISO 27002<br>ISO 20000 |
| **Internal** | Business issues | COBIT |
| | IT infrastructure | ITIL |

standards (hereinafter referred to as frameworks) are suitable for the governance of information security, the internal and external component of the information security governance framework proposed by Posthumus and von Solms (2004) was analysed to see if the different dimensions of security governance are represented by the frameworks. Table 2 presents a mapping of these frameworks with that of Posthumous and von Solms' internal and external criteria.

Legal and regulatory requirements stimulate and develop corporate information security efforts and include country specific statutes and laws while standards and best practices are used to inspire global information security principles. Likewise internal requirements that includes business issues translates requirements into organizational needs for IS security while IT infrastructure help to define relevant requirement that protect assets (Posthumus & von Solms, 2004). As stated in Section 2 PCI DSS is a regulatory requirements that is mandatory for those dealing with credit cards to ensure the protection of cardholder data while the standard (best practice) ISO 27002 is a code of practice for information security (International Organization for Standardization, 2011). ISO/IEC 20000 which is the first international standard for IT Service Management is implemented through ITIL which is an internal requirement. On the other hand COBIT address the business issues namely company-wide principles, goals and needs in terms of information processing (Humphreys et al., as cited in Posthumus &

von Solms, 2004) through its various controls in the four domains of IS. These five frameworks are thus reviewed to evaluate the relevance of these in a comprehensive security governance framework to enhance PCI DSS. Since ISO 20000 is based on ITIL V3 (Iden & Langeland, 2010), it will not be discussed in this section.

## 3.1 COBIT

COBIT published by the IT Governance Institute is a comprehensive framework of control objectives based on 41 international source documents, providing a global perspective and a best practice point of view (Lainhart, 2001). It is a set of guidelines for IT auditing consisting of processes, practices and controls (Anthes, 2004). It has divided the IT activities into four domains namely (i) plan and organize, (ii) acquire and implement, (iii) deliver and support, and (iv) monitor and evaluate, comprises around 34 high level control objectives (HLCO, also termed as control process) and 318 detailed control objectives (DCO). Since its introduction in 1996, COBIT had been revised thrice and currently 10% of the IT population worldwide use COBIT (ITGI, 2006). COBIT provides IT controls and IT metrics (Wallhoff, 2004) and is used as a high level governance and control framework (Gaynor, 2002; Hardy, 2006) with growing acceptance worldwide (Guildentops & Haes, 2002; Hussain & Siddiqui, 2005; Lainhart, 2000; Oliver, 2003; Ridley, Young, & Carroll, 2004; Singleton, 2006). It is exhaustive

(Edelstein, 2004) and encompasses the complete lifecycle of IT investment (Debreceny, 2006). COBIT comes up with 34 high level processes and 318 detailed processes touching all aspects of information systems.

## 3.2 ITIL

The Information Technology Infrastructure Library (ITIL) is a framework of best practices intended to facilitate the delivery of high quality IT services (Conger, 2009). It was developed by the CCTA (Central Communication and Telecom Agency, now subsumed under the Office of Government Commerce, UK (OGC) in 1980s through research into successful organizations and interviews with experts. The latest version released in June 2007 (ITIL Version 3) provides a well matured framework for the governance of IT by covering all requirement of IT Governance (Sahibuddin et al., 2008). It consists of a set of books that contain proper procedures to handle situations that any IT organization would come into contact with in IT service. Thus it is regarded as a process focused tool sharing common themes with process improvement, project management and IT governance and other supporting frameworks like COBIT (Polard & Cater-Steel, 2009). Many organisations have adopted ITIL to provide effective management and control of IT service delivery and support as it enables managers to document, audit, and improve their IT service management processes (Cater-Steel & Tan, 2005). ITIL offers more than just guidance and is aligned with ISO/IEC 20000 (Service Management Standard, previously BS 15000). ITIL show the goals, general activities, inputs and outputs of the various processes, which can be incorporated within IT organisations. Organisations that implement ITIL can use a series of templates (check lists, tasks) and procedures, to implement it to their enterprise. ITIL is broken up into a series of processes. Each of the processes defined in ITIL is designed to drive a specific IT business function or discipline

(Latif, Din, & Ismael, 2010). The ITIL service management practices are comprised of three main sets of products and services namely ITIL service management practices – core guidance, ITIL service management practices (complementary guidance) and ITIL web support services. The core set consists of six publications:

- Introduction to ITIL Service Management Practices
- Service Strategy (SS)
- Service Design (SD)
- Service Transition (ST)
- Service Operation (SO)
- Continual Service Improvement (CSI)

Each of these core set comes with support processes (Table 3)

## 3.3 ISO 27002

The ISO 27002 standards establish guidelines and general principles for initiating, implementing, maintaining, and improving information security management within an organization. The actual controls listed in the standard are intended to address the specific requirements identified via a formal risk assessment. The standard is also intended to provide a guide for the development of "organizational security standards and effective security management practices and to help build confidence in inter-organizational activities" (International Organization for Standardization, 2008). It focuses on operational security, application security, computing platform security, network security and physical security. From an ISO 27002 perspective, the term 'information' includes all forms of data, documents, communications, conversations, messages, recordings, photographs, digital data, email, and fax communications (International Organization for Standardization, 2010). Since cardholder information can be transmitted in any of these forms, implementation of ISO 27002 along with PCI DSS enhances the security

*Table 3. COBIT mapped with ITIL and ISO 27002 (adapted from ITGI, 2008a)*

| COBIT 4.1 Domain: Plan and Organise (PO) | | | |
|---|---|---|---|
| PO4 Define the IT Processes, Organisation and Relationships | | | |
| CobiT 4.1 Control Objective | Key Areas | ITIL V3 Supporting Information | ISO/IEC 27002:2005 Supporting Information |
| PO4.6 Establishment of roles and responsibilities | • Explicit roles and responsibilities<br>• Clear accountabilities and end-user authorities | • SS 2.6 Functions and processes across the life cycle<br>• SD 6.2 Activity analysis<br>• SD 6.4 Roles and responsibilities<br>• ST 6.3 Organisation models to support service transition<br>• SO 6.6 Service operation roles and responsibilities<br>• CSI 6 Organising for continual service improvement | • 6.1.2 Information security co-ordination<br>• 6.1.3 Allocation of information security responsibilities<br>• 6.1.5 Confidentiality agreements<br>• 8.1.1 Roles and responsibilities<br>• 8.1.2 Screening<br>• 8.1.3 Terms and conditions of employment<br>• 8.2.2 Information security awareness, education and training<br>• 15.1.4 Data protection and privacy of personal information |
| PO4.7 Responsibility for IT quality assurance (QA) | • Responsibility, expertise and placement of QA according to organisational requirements | • CSI 6 Organising for continual service improvement | N/A |
| PO4.8 Responsibility for risk, security and compliance | • Ownership of IT risks in the business<br>• Roles for managing critical risks<br>• Enterprise wide risk and security management<br>• System-specific security<br>• Direction on risk appetite and acceptance of residual risks | • SD 6.4 Roles and responsibilities | • 6.1.1 Management commitment to information security<br>• 6.1.2 Information security co-ordination<br>• 6.1.3 Allocation of information security responsibilities<br>• 8.1.1 Roles and responsibilities<br>• 8.2.1 Management responsibilities<br>• 8.2.3 Disciplinary process<br>• 15.1.1 Identification of applicable legislation<br>• 15.1.2 Intellectual property rights (IPR)<br>• 15.1.3 Protection of organisational records<br>• 15.1.4 Data protection and privacy of personal information<br>• 15.1.6 Regulation of cryptographic controls<br>• 15.2.1 Compliance with security policies and standards |

*Box 1. An ISO 2007 standard that closely relate to PCI DSS*

| |
|---|
| 10.Communication and operations management<br>10.4 Protect against malicious and mobile code<br>10.4.1 Establish controls to handle malicious code |

of cardholder data. Quite similar to COBIT and PCI DSS, ISO 27002 has identified 11 control areas, 39 control objectives, and 133 controls. For example the ISO 27002 is demonstrated by taking a control that closely correlates with COBIT, and PCI DSS controls (Box 1).

## 4. COMPARING COBIT, ITIL, ISO 27002, AND PCI DSS

While PCI DSS comes with 6 major 'principles', 12 major requirements that follows the principles, 45 sub requirements, 75 detailed requirements, and testing procedures for the corresponding sub requirements and detailed sub requirements, COBIT comes up with 34 high level processes (corresponding to the 6 major principles of PCI DSS), and 318 detailed processes (corresponding to the 12 major requirements of PCI DSS). But on a detailed analysis of the 318 detailed processes

*Table 4. General comparison of COBIT 4.1 and PCI DSS 2.0 frameworks*

| Evaluative Criteria | COBIT 4.1 | PCI DSS 2.0 |
|---|---|---|
| Major goal/objective | Align business goals with IT goals | To encourage and enhance cardholder data security and facilitate the broad adoption of consistent data security measures globally |
| Technical focus | Less technically reliant on compliance | Very much reliant on technology for compliance |
| Process orientation | Subdivides IT into four domains and 34 processes in line with the responsibility areas of plan, build, run and monitor, providing an end-to-end view of IT | Provides a baseline of technical and operational requirements designed to protect cardholder data based on 6 principles, 12 requirements, numerous sub requirements that are further sub divided and corresponding testing procedures. |
| Implementation guidance | Generic and need to be customized | Specific, focused, in depth and detailed |
| Focus on | Organisational wide information security and control assurance | Protection of Cardholder data only |
| Domain of application | Includes all IS domain | Includes only those networks, locations and flows of cardholder data |
| Target audience | Organisations who need to comply with global and country wise regulations/ requirements like SOX and who need to implement best practices in ITG | All merchants who accept credit and debit cards; credit card processors, issuers and acquirers, third party processors and gateways; developers and software providers |
| Implementation | Voluntary in most countries and organisations | Mandatory |
| Personnel allocation | RACI | No evidence |
| Information criteria | Effectiveness, efficiency, confidentiality, integrity, availability, compliance, reliability and integrated into the control processes. | Not evident and not integrated into the requirements but can be based on the extended CIA triangle – confidentiality, integrity, availability, possession, utility, accuracy, authenticity. |
| Identified IT resources/ scope/ Target domain | Applications, information, infrastructure, people | System components (linked to cardholder data environment), people, process, technology |
| Role/ responsibility charting | RACI chart for all activities | Not defined |
| Measurement done by: | Benchmarking; goals and metrics; compliance – 'complaint' and 'not complaint' | Compliance – 'in place' and 'not in place' |
| Measures | Various measures used like 'degree of ..', 'percent of..', level of.', delay between..'. 'no. of …', 'frequency..', 'elapsed time..', 'unit cost per service…', 'average of…' 'standard deviation..'. | Not defined |
| Goals and metrics | Defined | Not defined |
| Maturity model | Defined | Not defined |

it can be seen that these can be segmented further to correspond to the 45 sub requirements, and 75 detailed requirements of the PCI DSS. COBIT further elaborates the detailed processes with 'activities' that can be equated with the 'testing procedures' of the PCI DSS. Here the missing links in PCI DSS from a COBIT perspective are the 'information criteria', the 'RACI chart', 'IT goals', and 'measures' (Table 4). For example the control DS5.9 Malicious Software Prevention, Detection and Correction is given as (Box 2).

An example of the Requirement 5: Use and regularly update anti-virus software or programs is given in Box 3.

*Box 2. A sample control taken from PCI DSS*

III. DS Delivery and Support
DS 5 Ensure Systems Security
DS5.9 Malicious Software Prevention, Detection and Correction
[Put preventive, detective and corrective measures in place (especially up-to-date security patches and virus control) across the organisation to protect information systems and technology from malware (e.g., viruses, worms, spyware, spam).]

*Box 3. A sample control taken from PCI DSS*

Principle 3. Maintain a Vulnerability Management Program
  Requirement **5**: Use and regularly update anti-virus software or programs
Sub requirement **5.1** Deploy anti-virus software on all systems commonly affected by malicious software (particularly personal computers and servers).
  *[Testing procedure: **5.1** For a sample of system components including all operating system types commonly affected by malicious software, verify that anti-virus software is deployed if applicable anti-virus technology exists]*
  **5.1.1** Ensure that all anti-virus programs are capable of detecting, removing, and protecting against all known types of malicious software.
    *[Testing procedure:**5.1.1** For a sample of system components, verify that all anti-virus programs detect, remove, and protect against all known types of malicious software (for example, viruses, Trojans, worms, spyware, adware, and rootkits).*

COBIT has been considered as high level IT governance framework combining in itself IT security, IT audit and IT assurance. Being very comprehensive covering the entire life cycle of information systems, the processes of ITIL, ISO 27002 and PCI DSS are stated as broad controls in COBIT. According to Conradie and Hoekstra (2002) of PWC, ITIL is strong in IT processes, but limited in security and system development; COBIT is strong in IT controls and IT metrics, but does not say how and does not have a security focus; and ISO 17799 is strong in security controls (Since ISO 17799 which is a code of practice of practice for information security has been renamed as ISO 27002 the statement can be true of ISO 27002 also) but does not say how the process flows. Thus COBIT, ITIL and ISO 27002 can be aligned for mutual benefit and this has been demonstrated by the IT Governance Institute (ITGI) and the Office of Government Commerce (OGC) in 2008 when they mapped each of the processes of the three frameworks in a single document as guidance for practitioners to combine the two frameworks with the ISO standard (Table 3).

When ITIL is benchmarked with COBIT, it has been found that they correspond with each other to a high degree, especially, when the processes of COBIT are ITIL based as in its latest version (Sahibuddin et al., 2008). Since COBIT encompasses the controls, and processes of ITIL, ISO 27002 and PCI DSS, integration of these into COBIT provides a governance view of security. Moreover a comparison is made between COBIT and PCI DSS (Table 4) that provide rationale for integrating PCI DSS into COBIT for comprehensive IS security. From the comparison it is evident that COBIT that is more generic and less technical, focus on the security and assurance aspects of the entire IS domain in an organisation, while PCI DSS is technical and focus on the specific domain of protecting cardholder data. Hence PCI DSS functionalities can either be subsumed under COBIT or can be complemented with COBIT through its added functionalities like the RACI chart, information criteria, and measurement frameworks.

## 5. INTEGRATED IS SECURITY GOVERNANCE MODEL

From the evaluation of the four frameworks COBIT has emerged as the most comprehensive of all IT governance models incorporating in it aspects of PCI DSS, ITIL and ISO 27002. But due to organisational differences and priorities, different frameworks have been implemented as the major one with others providing a support role. Hence it is not uncommon to find organisations implementing ITIL as the major framework with relevant COBIT controls attached to it. The same is the case with the other two frameworks. Likewise for consistency in the terminology the controls, processes, principles and requirements of COBIT, PCI DSS, ITIL will be referred to as 'controls'.

From Table 4 it is evident that while process wise COBIT and PCI DSS are similar, PCI DSS is lacking the wider business perspective of information system. Moreover there are no evidence of any information criteria, responsibility allocations (as per the RACI chart of COBIT), nor a maturity model or metrics/measurement tools. Thus the advantage of incorporating COBIT comes from its detailed guidance on various aspects of control, audit, measurement and assessment of maturity. For each control of COBIT there are the RACI (Responsible, accountable, consulted and informed) chart which specifies who is responsible for each control, the person who is accountable, to be consulted and informed which is linked to each control activity derived from the COBIT control. The RACI chart can either be applied at the higher level of COBIT control or at the level of PCI DSS principles or requirement. This is again linked to the goals and metrics and aligned to the maturity model. COBIT also specifies and defines the COBIT maturity model for each high level control. Regarding the balance score card (BSC) even though it is not defined in the COBIT controls, guidance has been given by ITGI on

*Figure 3. Integrated IS security governance model: option 1*

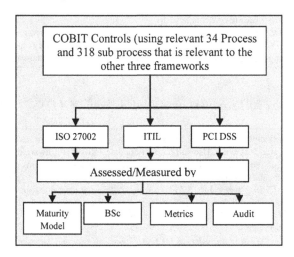

how to attach the BSC. Considering all of these functionalities in COBIT there are three options for integrating PCI DSS with COBIT. The resulting integrated audit security management models are given in Figures 3 through 5.

## Option 1 (COBIT Umbrella in Figure 3)

COBIT as an umbrella control with the PCI DSS principles attached under relevant COBIT controls along with ITIL and ISO 27002: The PCI DSS requirements can be linked to a related control of COBIT (like DS 5) to generate a list of sub controls corresponding to the requirements/sub requirements of PCI DSS. In this manner the COBIT control is modified to suit the terminology of the PCI DSS. Hence all those controls of COBIT that map to PCI DSS are selected as the basis for implementing PCI DSS. In this way those relevant controls of COBIT that are representative of PCI DSS can be decomposed further down using the PCI DSS requirements, sub requirements and testing procedures of PCI DSS and then measured using an optimal mix of measurement, performance indicators and assessments. This also

*Figure 4. Integrated IS security governance model: option 2*

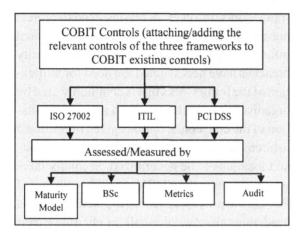

*Figure 5. Integrated IS security governance model: option 3*

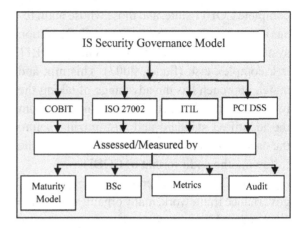

assumes that ITIL and ISO 27002 are integrated into COBIT in the same manner. Option 1 is thus suitable for those organisations that have a well established COBIT framework in place since PCI DSS principles can be attached seamlessly onto the relevant controls of COBIT. In this manner PCI DSS can also avail of the information criteria, the RACI chart, maturity model and metrics.

The first step in this direction is to go through and evaluate each of the 34 high level controls of COBIT to decide on the PCI DSS requirements that can be incorporated into it followed by mapping PCI DSS to COBIT (as was done in Table 2 where COBIT controls was mapped with ITIL practices by ITGI). But this requires involving IT security and audit experts (through empirical research) and is a separate research project in itself.

## Option 2 (PCI DSS based COBIT in Figure 4)

In this scenario COBIT is considered as a method where COBIT controls are replaced with PCI DSS principles or added along with. Here the PCI DSS principles take the role of the COBIT along with ITIL and ISO 27002. Hence rather than looking at COBIT controls to fit PCI principles into, this

necessities the addition of PCI DSS principles/ requirements into the overall COBIT framework in addition to the existing COBIT controls being used in the organisation. This option suits those organisations that primarily focus on PCI DSS rather than COBIT and also for those organisations that are using only a few controls of COBIT as they don't need to modify COBIT to suit PCI DSS. It would be easier for them to modify the PCI DSS to suit into the COBIT template. More-over if they already have COBIT running they can make a comparative evaluation of the attached PCI DSS controls with those COBIT controls already running that is related to PCI DSS.

## Option 3 (IS Security Governance Approach in Figure 5)

This option presents a comprehensive IS security framework incorporating only the relevant aspects of PCI DSS, COBIT, ITIL and ISO 27002. This scenario does not provide for any one framework to act as an umbrella for the others, rather relevant controls suitable for the organisational goals are chosen from each of these frameworks and then integrated into a tight framework incorporating only the best practices of COBIT to suit organisational needs. This approach may suit those organisations that do not want to implement the complete COBIT suite, and those whose main focus is security governance rather than information systems governance, since implementing COBIT is a complex task (Etzler, 2007). This mix and match approach has the advantage of taking the relevant controls, practices and principles from the identified standard and customizing it into the organisational requirements at the same time following the audit format of COBIT.

While COBIT is regarded as a preferred IT governance framework, many organisations have implemented their own proprietary governance and security frameworks since a common weakness attributed to COBIT is that it is not always very detailed in terms of 'how' to do certain things and the DCOs are more addressed to the 'what' must be done (von Solms, 2005). This very generic nature of COBIT is its strength as the organisations have the flexibility and freedom to adapt, customize or borrow the best practices of COBIT to suit individual organisational needs.

Evaluating the best option out the three approach by an organisation thus depends on the maturity level of the organisation's IS governance and security structure, the organisational focus (security or governance or both), the relative size of the organisation, the industry sector, the regulatory environment in the region and the relevant industry standard.

## 6. CONCLUSION

The objective of this paper was to propose a comprehensive integrated framework for information security governance to enhance the security of the PCI DSS standard. This was done by searching, evaluating, analyzing and selecting relevant information technology governance and security frameworks used widely in organisations that best complement and integrate with each other seamlessly and at the same time avoid duplication of internal control. The convergence and overlap of the various information systems governance frameworks, the ever increasing need to protect not only customer data but also the organisational information, and the increasing threat of security breaches have necessitated the need for unification of the frameworks that is commonly used by organisations. Further research involves validation of the conceptual options given in Section 5 to be empirically tested in different environments and locations to be generalized. Secondly there is a need to map the COBIT controls with that of PCI DSS to provide guidance to practitioners and academics alike and this call for eliciting expert advice through Delphi method. Finally other than COBIT, the three frameworks does not come with detailed guidance on the 'information criteria', the responsibility chart – 'RACI', or any sort of measures/assessments like maturity models/ balance score cards/ metrics. Thus research is called for in this domain on the methodology to customise and attach these into either the PCI DSS or to the integrated IS security governance model (for example the COBIT maturity model, the information criteria and the RACI chart are specific to the IT Governance concept rather than IT security governance). Information security being a multidimensional discipline understanding it in a wider context will ensure that the organisational information assets are well protected through a well-structured and effective security layer.

Becoming PCI complaint doesn't mean that the company is insulated from all sorts of cyber fraud but effective implementation by integrating with relevant security and governance frameworks can mitigate the risk to a great extent. This proposed model in this research provide the PCI DSS not only with added functionality, but also the presence of other frameworks and standards like ITIL and ISO 27002 provides an added IS security layer to the company's information system that is not only comprehensive but also with a defense-in-depth approach.

# REFERENCES

Al-Hamdani, W. A. (2009). Three models to measure information security compliance. *International Journal of Information Security and Privacy, 3*(4), 43–64. doi:10.4018/jisp.2009100104

Amato-McCoy, D. M. (2009). The next phase of PCI security. *Chain Store Age*, 48-49.

Anthes, G. H. (2004). Quality model mania. *Computerworld, 38*, 41–44.

Baker, W., Dahn, M., Greiner, T., Hutton, A., Hylender, C. D., Lindstrom, P., et al. (2010). *Verizon 2010 payment card industry compliance report*. Retrieved from http://www.verizonbusiness.com/resources/reports/rp_2010-payment-card-industry-compliance-report_en_xg.pdf

Cater-Steel, A., & Tan, W.-G. (2005). *Implementation of IT infrastructure library (ITIL) in Australia: Progress and success factors*. Paper presented at the International IT Governance Conference, Auckland, New Zealand.

Choobineh, J., Dhillon, G., Grimaila, M. R., & Rees, J. (2007). Management of information security: Challenges and research directions. *Communications of the Association for Information Systems, 20*(57), 958–971.

Coburn, A. (2010). Fitting PCI DSS within a wider governance framework. *Computer Fraud & Security*, 11–13. doi:10.1016/S1361-3723(10)70121-4

Conger, S. (2009). Information technology service management and opportunities for information systems curricula. *International Journal of Information Systems in the Service Sector, 1*(2), 58–68. doi:10.4018/jisss.2009040104

Conradie, N., & Hoekstra, A. (2002). *CobiT, ITIL and ISO17799: How to use them in conjunction*. Retrieved from http://www.cccure.org/Documents/COBIT/COBIT_ITIL_and_BS7799.pdf

Debreceny, R. S. (2006). Re-engineering IT internal controls: Applying capability maturity models to the evaluation of IT controls. In *Proceedings of the 39th Hawaii International Conference on Systems Sciences*.

Edelstein, S. M. (2004). Sarbanes-Oxley compliance for non-accelerated filers: Solving the internal control puzzle. *The CPA Journal, 74*(12), 52–58.

Eloff, J. H. P., & Eloff, M. M. (2005). Information security architecture. *Computer Fraud & Security*, 10–16. doi:10.1016/S1361-3723(05)70275-X

Etzler, J. (2007). *IT governance according to COBIT*. Stockholm, Sweden: Royal Institute of Technology.

Everett, C. (2009). PCI DSS: Lack of direction or lack of commitment? *Computer Fraud & Security, 12*, 18–20. doi:10.1016/S1361-3723(09)70155-1

First Data. (2009). *PCI DSS and handling sensitive cardholder data*. Retrieved from http://www.firstdata.com

Gaynor, D. (2002). IT governance. *Accountancy Ireland, 34*(4), 28.

Gikas, C. (2010). A general comparison of FISMA, HIPAA, ISO 27000 and PCI-DSS standards. *Information Security Journal: A Global Perspective, 19*, 132-141.

Guildentops, E., & Haes, S. D. (2002). COBIT 3rd edition usage survey: Growing acceptance of COBIT. *Information Systems Control Journal, 6*, 25-27.

Hagen, J. M., Albrechtsen, E., & Hovden, J. (2008). Implementation and effectiveness of organizational information security measures. *Information Management & Computer Security, 16*(4), 377–397. doi:10.1108/09685220810908796

Hardy, G. (2006b). Guidance on aligning COBIT, ITIL and ISO 17799. *Information Systems Control Journal, 1*.

Harkavy, J. (2008). *Secret software blamed for Hannaford Breach*. Retrieved from http://www.msnbc.msn.com/id/23846014/ns/technology_and_science-security/

Hussain, S. J., & Siddiqui, M. S. (2005). Quantified model of COBIT for corporate IT governance. In *Proceedings of the 1st International Conference on Information and Communication Technologies*.

Iden, J., & Langeland, L. (2010). Setting the stage for a successful ITIL adoption: A Delphi study of IT experts in the Norwegian Armed Forces. *Information Systems Management, 27*(2), 103–112. doi:10.1080/10580531003708378

Identity Theft Resource Centre (ITRC). (2008). *2009 Data Breach Statistics*. San Diego, CA: Author.

Identity Theft Resource Centre (ITRC). (2009). *2009 Data Breach Statistics*. San Diego, CA: Author.

Identity Theft Resource Centre (ITRC). (2010). *2010 Data Breach Statistics*. San Diego, CA: Author.

Ifinedo, P. (2009). Information technology security management concerns in global financial services institutions is national culture a differentiator? *Information Management & Computer Security, 17*(5), 372–387. doi:10.1108/09685220911006678

International Organization for Standardization (ISO). (2005). *ISO/IEC 27002:2005: Information technology -- Security techniques -- Code of practice for information security management*. Retrieved from http://www.iso.org/iso/catalogue_detail?csnumber=50297

International Organization for Standardization (ISO). (2008). *Introduction to ISO 27002*. Retrieved from http://www.27000.org/iso-27002.htm

IT Governance Institute (ITGI). (2006). *IT Governance Global Status Report - 2006*. Rolling Meadows, IL: Author.

IT Governance Institute (ITGI). (2008a). *Aligning COBIT 4.1, ITIL V3 and ISO/IEC 27002 for Business Benefit*. Rolling Meadows, IL: Author.

IT Governance Institute (ITGI). (2008b). *IT Governance Global Status Report*. Rolling Meadows, IL: Author.

Jewell, M. (2007). *TJX breach could top 94 million accounts*. Retrieved from http://www.msnbc.msn.com/id/21454847/ns/technology_and_science-security/

Lainhart, J. W. (2000). COBIT: A methodology for managing and controlling information and information technology risks and vulnerabilities. *Journal of Information Systems, 14*, 21–25. doi:10.2308/jis.2000.14.s-1.21

Lainhart, J. W. (2001). COBIT: An IT assurance framework for the future. *The Ohio CPA Journal, 60*(1), 19–23.

Laredo, V. G. (2009). PCI DSS compliance: A matter of strategy. *Card Technology Today, 20*(4), 9. doi:10.1016/S0965-2590(08)70094-X

Latif, A. A., Din, M. M., & Ismail, R. (2010). *Challenges in adopting and integrating ITIL and CMMi in ICT division of a public utility company*. Paper presented at the 2nd International Conference on Computer Engineering and Applications, Bali, Indonesia.

Liu, J., Xiao, Y., Chen, H., Ozdemir, S., Dodle, S., & Singh, V. (2010). A survey of payment card industry data security standard. *IEEE Communications Surveys & Tutorials, 12*(3), 287–303. doi:10.1109/SURV.2010.031810.00083

Luftman, J. N., & Brier, T. (1999). Achieving and sustaining business-IT alignment. *California Management Review, 1*, 109–122. doi:10.2307/41166021

Luftman, J. N., Lewis, P. R., & Oldach, S. H. (1993). Transforming the enterprise: The alignment of business and information technology strategies. *IBM Systems Journal, 32*(1). doi:10.1147/sj.321.0198

MasterCard. (2011). *Merchant levels defined.* Retrieved from http://www.mastercard.com/us/sdp/merchants/merchant_levels.html

Musa, A. (2010). Information security governance in Saudi organizations: An empirical study. *Information Management & Computer Security, 18*(4), 226–276. doi:10.1108/09685221011079180

Ngugi, B., Vega, G., & Dardick, G. (2009). PCI compliance: Overcoming the challenges. *International Journal of Information Security and Privacy, 3*(2), 54–67. doi:10.4018/jisp.2009040104

Oliver, D. J. (2003). A Selective Approach to COBIT. *Information Systems Control Journal, 3.*

Pathak, J. (2003). Internal audit and e-commerce controls. *Internal Auditing, 18*(2), 30–34.

Pollard, C., & Cater-Steel, A. (2009). Justifications, strategies, and critical success factors in successful ITIL implementations in US and Australian companies: An exploratory study. *Information Systems Management, 26*, 164–175. doi:10.1080/10580530902797540

Posthumus, S., & von Solms, R. (2004). A framework for the governance of information security. *Computers & Security, 23*, 638–646. doi:10.1016/j.cose.2004.10.006

Ridley, G., Young, J., & Carroll, P. (2004). COBIT and its utilization: A framework from the literature. In *Proceedings of the 37th Hawaii International Conference on System Sciences.*

Rowlingson, R., & Winsborrow, R. (2006). A comparison of the payment card industry data security standard with ISO17799. *Computer Fraud & Security*, 16–19. doi:10.1016/S1361-3723(06)70323-2

Sahibudin, S., Sharifi, M., & Ayat, M. (2008). Combining ITIL, COBIT and ISO/IEC 27002 in order to design a comprehensive IT framework in organizations. In *Proceedings of the 2nd Asia International Conference on Modelling & Simulation* (pp. 749-753).

Singleton, T. W. (2006). COBIT- A key to success as an IT auditor. *Information Systems Control Journal, 1.*

Sullivan, R. J. (2010). The changing nature of U.S. card payment fraud: Issues For industry and public policy. In *Proceedings of the Workshop on the Economics of Information Security.*

Sundt, C. (2006). Information security and the law. *Information Security Technical Report, 11*, 2–9. doi:10.1016/j.istr.2005.11.003

Turner, M. J., Oltsik, J., & McKnight, J. (2009). *ISO, ITIL, & COBIT together foster optimal security investment.* Retrieved from http://www.thecomplianceauthority.com/iso-itil-a-cobit.php

Von Solms, B. (2001). Information security – A multidimensional discipline. *Computers & Security, 20*, 504–508. doi:10.1016/S0167-4048(01)00608-3

Von Solms, S. H. B. (2005). Information security governance- Compliance management vs. Operational management. *Computers & Security, 24*, 443–447. doi:10.1016/j.cose.2005.07.003

Wallhoff, J. (2004). *Combining ITIL with COBIT and 17799.* Retrieved from http://www.scillani.se/assets/pdf/Scillani%20Article%20Combining%20ITIL%20with%20Cobit%20and%2017799.pdf

Xu, W., Grant, G., Nguyen, H., & Dai, X. (2008). Security breach: The case of TJX Companies, Inc. *Communications of the Association for Information Systems, 23*(1).

# Chapter 13
# A Privacy Agreement Negotiation Model in B2C E-Commerce Transactions

**Murthy V. Rallapalli**
*IBM and Stevens Institute of Technology, USA*

## ABSTRACT

*This article presents an alternate approach to effectively address the way privacy agreements are initiated through web services. In this new framework, the consumer and the service provider can mutually negotiate on the privacy terms. It contains a privacy model in which the transaction takes place after a negotiation between the service provider and the web user is completed. In addition, this framework would support various negotiation levels of the agreement lifecycle which is an important aspect of the dynamic environment of a B2C e-commerce scenario. A third party trusted agency and a privacy filter are included to handle privacy information of the web user. The author seeks to raise awareness of the issues surrounding privacy transactions and the potential ongoing impact to both service providers and clients as the use of web services accelerates.*

## INTRODUCTION

Privacy agreements are invariably a one-sided agreement with the service provider asking the web user, "Unless you accept it, you can go no further with this transaction". In this scenario as shown in Figure 1, the customer has no choice but to click on 'I agree' to proceed further with the transaction. If the web user chooses not to agree to the terms, the application will not allow the web user to go any further. The agreement is just a good gesture on the part of the service providers. However, lately, it has become a privacy weapon where service providers impose their version of the privacy policies with no room for any type of negotiation. Today, every individual who conducts e-commerce transactions on the web is guaranteed to part with certain private information in order to complete the transaction. This leads to concerns that privacy information being collected may be misused by the collecting organizations or businesses. For a secure e-commerce transaction

DOI: 10.4018/978-1-4666-2050-6.ch013

experience with minimal risk, it is important to build customer confidence with service providers, particularly, when these service providers collect privacy data. Figure 1 is an example of a typical privacy agreement. Service providers leverage web services to present such privacy policies of the service provider's organization.

Privacy agreements (similar to Figure 1) presented to the customer state what the organization would do with the personal information. However, simply presenting a privacy policy to the web user does not guarantee the protection of personal information of the customer. A verbal promise through this type of agreement has very little legal ground to hold the service provider responsible for any privacy data misuse (Powers, 2002). There is a need for something more secure; a more formal (legally binding) than what is currently provided in a privacy agreement today.

Today's privacy agreements are notorious for being a one-sided agreement presented by the service provider to the service consumer. The service providers dynamically revise their privacy policies as well to accommodate new business strategies, changes to laws and regulations. Another concern is what happens to this collected data. In many situations it is being bought back by various industries and corporate information systems. Consider institutions such as banking, insurance, telecom and how they are leveraging this personal data to customize products and minimize fraud, which may lead to discriminatory trends. Worse is that these trends may even be automated (Davis, 2000). For example tracking people through mobile phone roaming may indicate that they drive frequently through low income neighborhoods and thus may be categorized as high risk for car insurance. People purchasing cigarettes online could be categorized as higher risk for health problems by insurance companies which result in increases in health premiums. This type of data mining is often used to create separate "categories" of people. As organizations collect more and more personal information, everyday behavior will be aggregated by corporations and governments to augment social control (Newman, 2009). The fundamental point of entry into the collector's archives is through web transactions. It is when a web user logs on, and if the privacy data is being controlled, then data aggregation will also be controlled.

In this paper, I propose a framework where the consumer and service provider interactively decide on privacy terms. The framework develops

*Figure 1. A privacy agreement presented to the customer*

an agreement between the web user and the service provider interactively until the privacy terms are agreed upon, taking into account elements such as the flow of data and expiration of the data use as part of the agreement. The features of the framework are:

- Types of privacy elements pertaining to the web user and the privacy principles of the service provider. These elements are defined together as one element called Privacy Agreement, which represents a contractual agreement between the consumer and the provider.
- The framework supports a lifecycle management of the privacy data that the web user has agreed to share under agreed upon time guidelines. The agreement clearly articulates the consumer's concurrence on how long he/she would like the privacy data to be kept in a data store.
- A negotiation protocol allows the web user and the service provider to negotiate the privacy terms until a satisfactory agreement is reached. For example, a consumer can specify that his/her telephone number should be removed from the data store 25 days after the transaction is successfully concluded.

## PRIVACY FRAMEWORK

### Privacy Framework Structure

Conceptually this can be expanded into multiple actors including a SOA appliance providing the appropriate filtering of the privacy data. For this paper, privacy framework structure consists of three actors. The web user is a primary actor of the framework. The web user is defined as the actor whose privacy information is being collected to execute a B2C e-commerce transaction. In other words, web user is the person trying to purchase a book or a product online. As part of the purchas-

ing process, he/she will need to provide certain privacy information such as Credit card details, telephone number, address etc as required by the service provider. In today's world, once privacy information is provide online, the web user has very little control over how the information is being used.

The second actor in the scenario is service provider, like any online books or product seller online for a price. In return, the service providers like to collect some information, for specific reasons. The service provider needs to collect the credit card information, validate it and charge the expense using the card number. The service provider, for valid reasons, collects a lot of personal/private information, sometimes more than what the immediate sale requires. For example, many times a survey is provided asking for the household income. The web user and the service provider are the primary participants in any typical e-commerce transaction (Figure 2).

The proposed Privacy model introduces a new actor called a Third Party Trusted Agency (TTPA); it is this element which makes the model unique and different from the current models.

In this new model all the e-commerce transactions are first filtered by a third party trusted agency (Figure 3). The third party trusted agency is, as the name suggests, is a neutral agency trusted by the users and the service providers equally. More detailed discussion of the third party agency is covered later in the paper. There are several models available that were reviewed as part of this research including Corba (2002) and Chiu (2002). However, this paper attempts to come up with an implement able framework which differs from other work.

### Privacy Agreement Structure

As part of this model, a privacy agreement structure is defined:

- **Default policy agreement:** This specifies the default terms of a service provider in-

*Figure 2. A web user connecting to a website for an e-commerce transaction*

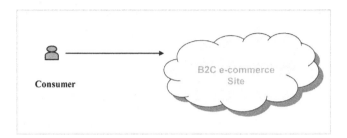

cluding a guarantee dealing with the specific privacy data items of the consumer. For example, in this scenario, the service provider agrees to collect the privacy data of the consumer and in addition, purge it within x number of days after successful conclusion of the e-commerce transaction. For example, credit card information collected from the web user, according to this policy agreement, will be deleted within 20 days (for example) after the e-commerce transaction is successfully concluded. This has two distinct advantages:

- The service provider does not have to worry about guarding the ever increasing privacy data of their consumers.
- Web user gets an assurance and a digital proof of transaction purge to show his/her private data has been removed from the service provider's database.

## Privacy Scenario Using Framework

As shown in Figure 4, the service provider, as a default, is agreeing to retain the first name of the consumer at least for a period of 30 days. After 30 days from the date the e-commerce transaction is concluded, the service provider will ensure that the First name will be permanently purged from its databases.

In this structure the negotiation level specifies all possible privacy data terms and the purge intervals by the web user. This allows the web user to negotiate the terms for each of the privacy items that are being provided as part of the transaction. For example, the service provider may be committing to purging of credit card data within 30 days (refer to Figure 4) of the transaction conclusion. However, the consumer would like to negotiate this to 15 days after the transaction conclusion. This model provides a method for this negotiation to take place between the web user and the service provider until a mutually agreed upon terms are reached.

As shown in Figure 5, the service provider is committing to purging the customer's private data (e.g., credit card) in 30 days. This time, the web user is counter proposing or negotiating with the service provider to purge his/her data within 20 days. This process of mutual negotiation allows the service provider and web user to reach an amicable agreement on timing of privacy data purge from the service provider's database, after the e-commerce transaction is successfully concluded.

## Third Party Trusted Agency (TPTA)

Once the service provider and the web user reach an agreement on the privacy terms, the next step is to ensure that the service provider is living up to purging the data at the end of the expiration term. This is where the third party trusted agency plays a primary role. It takes the burden out of the service provider having to keep track of the privacy terms and conditions. Instead, it is the TPTA that would actually purge the data and sends confirmation via a digital certificate. In other words, the TPTA is owner of the private data. This accomplishes two goals:

1.  The Service provider no longer has to deal with data protection and instead can focus more on its core business functionality.
2.  The web user receives certain levels of assurance that his/her privacy data is indeed not used beyond the terms agreed upon during the transaction.

The TPTA is a Privacy server that delineates the data into two data streams:

1.  Shopping cart data containing the order details of the consumer.
2.  Privacy data & Terms of expiration.

The only information that the service provider needs to know to complete the transaction is in the shopping cart details. Information required for tasks including credit checking, mailing, business analytics etc. is held by the TPTA and provides some exposed web services for the service provider to query as needed. This does put the burden of protecting the privacy data solely on TPTA. The

TPTA is master protector of privacy data of all the transactions between the consumer and the service provider(s). In addition, since the TPTA has the terms of expiration data, it could execute the purging of privacy data upon expiration of data. The following scenario explains a simple e-commerce transaction example:

**Step 1:** Joe places an order for a book on a book website.

**Step 2:** Joe and book web site agree upon the following terms: Name, Address, Telephone number will be deleted within 20 days of e-commerce transaction; Credit card data and expiration data will be purged within 15 days of e-commerce transaction.

**Step 3:** Joe places the order.

**Step 4:** The privacy data is sent to the TPTA.

**Step 5:** The shopping cart data is sent to the book web site provider.

**Step 6:** The provider looks at the shopping cart details, and executes exposed web services of the TPTA to obtain required privacy information (address, telephone etc.).

**Step 7:** TPTA, after 15 days, purges the credit card and expiration date data. After 20 days, it will purge the Name, Address and telephone # data will be purged.

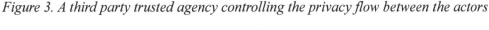

*Figure 3. A third party trusted agency controlling the privacy flow between the actors*

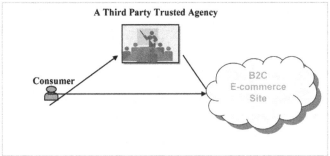

*Figure 4. Service providers default agreement on purging privacy data*

| Attributes | Retention Period | | Agreement |
|---|---|---|---|
| *First Name | 30 days | | |
| *Last Name | 30 days | | |
| Company | 30 days | | Accept  Decline  Negotiate |
| *Address | 30 days | | |
| Address | 30 days | | |
| *City, *State | 30 days | | |
| *Zip | 30 days | | |
| *Billing Phone | 30 days | | |
| FAX | 30 days | | |
| *Email Address | 30 days | | |
| *Credit Card Number | 30 days | | |
| *Credit Card Expiration | 30 days | | |

The TPTA at the end of the expiration date sends out a confirmation to the consumer on the successful purging of his/her data. This would be retained as a digital proof by the consumer that his/her privacy data is indeed purged.

## CONCLUSION AND FUTURE WORK

Over the past few years, web services related privacy issues are attracting significant attention from the industry and research community. While the numbers of web services being used are increasing exponentially in the business applications, there is a corresponding increase in demand for privacy-enhancing technologies for web services (Carminati, 2003). This paper proposes a Privacy framework strategy to tackle the complex negotiation of privacy terms between the service provider and the web user. This is a realistic approach without any significant overhead, to implement a framework, where harmonious negotiations can take place between the various parties in an e-commerce environment. The very concept that a B2C provider's main focus should be on selling products, not spending time and money on protecting privacy is at the core of this paper. The introduction of a trusted third party seeks to addresses this in a way that is beneficial to the service provider. The web user, at the same time,

*Figure 5. Web user entering negotiating terms*

| Privacy Information Terms | | |
|---|---|---|
| **Attributes** | | |
| *First Name | 30 days | 20 |
| *Last Name | 30 days | 30 |
| Company | 30 days | 30 |
| *Address | 30 days | 20 |
| Address | 30 days | 30 |
| *City, *State | 30 days | 30 |
| *Zip | 30 days | 30 |
| *Billing Phone | 30 days | 20 |
| FAX | 30 days | |
| *Email Address | 30 days | 20 |
| *Credit Card Number | 30 days | 20 |
| *Credit Card Expiration | 30 days | 20 |

next

should be able to control on his/her personal data. It is the responsibility of the third party trusted agency to manage the privacy data which provides a more trusted environment for the consumer. The model presented here is just one of many that can be used to implement this approach.

# REFERENCES

Bertino, E., Carminati, B., & Ferrari, E. (2003, June). A flexible authentication method for UDDI registries. In *Proceedings of the International Conference on Web Services*, Las Vegas, NV.

Bertino, E., Carminati, B., Ferrari, E., Thuraisingham, B., & Gupta, A. (2003). Selective and authentic third-party distribution of XML documents. *IEEE Transactions on Knowledge and Data Engineering*, *16*(10), 1263–1278. doi:10.1109/TKDE.2004.63

Chiu, D. K. W., Chiung, S. C., & Till, S. (2002). A three-layer architecture for e-contract enforcement in an e-service environment. In *Proceedings of the 36th Hawaii International Conference on System Science*.

Davis, J. C. (2000). Protecting privacy in the cyber era. *IEEE Technology and Society Magazine*, 10–22. doi:10.1109/44.846270

Hinde, S. (2002). In Audit, I. S. (Ed.), *The perils of privacy* (pp. 424–432). Amsterdam, The Netherlands: Elsevier Science.

Industry Canada. (2003). *Privacy and the information highway, regulatory options for Canada* (Ch. 6). Retrieved September 5, 2003, from http://strategis.ic.gc.ca/SSG/ca00257e.html#6

Jones, V. E., Ching, N., & Winslett, M. (1995, August 22-25). Credentials for privacy and interoperation. In *Proceedings of the New Security Paradigms Workshop* (pp. 92-100).

Kenny, S., & Korba, L. (2002). Adapting digital rights management to privacy rights management. *Computers & Security*, *21*(7), 648–664. doi:10.1016/S0167-4048(02)01117-3

Newman, A. (2009). *Regulating personal data in the global economy*. Ithaca, NY: Cornell University.

Powers, C. S., Ashley, P., & Schunter, M. (2002). Privacy promises, access control, and privacy management - Enforcing privacy throughout an enterprise by extending access control. In *Proceedings of the 3rd International Symposium on Electronic Commerce* (pp. 13-21).

*This work was previously published in the International Journal of Information Security and Privacy, Volume 5, Issue 4, edited by Hamid Nemati, pp. 1-7, copyright 2011 by IGI Publishing (an imprint of IGI Global).*

# Chapter 14
# A Unified Use–Misuse Case Model for Capturing and Analysing Safety and Security Requirements

**O. T. Arogundade**
*Chinese Academy of Sciences, China*

**Z. Jin**
*Peking University, China*

**A. T. Akinwale**
*University of Agriculture, Abeokuta, Nigeria*

**X. G. Yang**
*Chinese Academy of Sciences, China*

## ABSTRACT

*This paper proposes an enhanced use-misuse case model that allows both safety and security requirements to be captured during requirements elicitation. The proposed model extends the concept of misuse case by incorporating vulnerable use case and abuse case notations and relations that allows understanding and modeling different attackers and abusers behaviors during early stage of system development life cycle and finishes with a practical consistent combined model for engineering safety and security requirements.*

*The model was successfully applied using health care information system gathered through the university of Kansas HISPC project. The authors were able to capture both security and safety requirements necessary for effective functioning of the system. In order to enhance the integration of the proposed model into risk analysis, the authors give both textual and detailed description of the model. The authors compare the proposed approach with other existing methods that identify and analyze safety and security requirements and discovered that it captures more security and safety threats.*

DOI: 10.4018/978-1-4666-2050-6.ch014

## INTRODUCTION

Use case method is a research tool in Requirement Engineering (RE) field where the concept of use case is used to model functional requirements and misuse case is used to model non-functional requirements for a system. The use of use case is becoming popular for determining, communicating, specifying and documenting requirements (Constantine & Lockwood, 1999; Cockburn, 2001; Jacobson et al., 1992; Kulak & Guiney, 2000; Rumbaugh, 1994). Misuse case, the extension of use case by Sindre and Opdahl (2005), allows the concept of use case to be useful in eliciting non-functional requirements. Safety and security requirements are often developed independently of the rest of the requirements engineering activity and hence are not integrated into the mainstream of the requirements activities. As a result, safety and security requirements that are specific to the system and that provide for protection of essential services, features and assets are often neglected (Mead, 2007).

The ad hoc integration of safety and security mechanisms into a software system which has already been developed has a negative impact on the maintainability and security of the system (Eduardo, Jurjens, Trujillo, & Sushil, 2009)

With the ever increasing exploitation of networking technologies, it is now imperative that both safety and security will be taken into account during the early stage of system development life cycle (Harrison & Sujan, 2008).

In our initial work (Arogundade et al., in press) we have introduced vulnerable use case including inside abuser in order to address the issue of deliberate act for safety concerns. This paper refines this initial work by proposing an enhanced use-misuse case model for eliciting and analyzing safety and security requirements in a unified framework. The ideas in this paper have been applied to one realistic case study, the e-health care system. The e-health care information used in this paper is retrieved from Health Information

Technology Resource Toolkit developed through the university of Kansas HISPC project (http://ehealth.kansashealthonline.org).

## Safety vs. Security

In some stream of research the differences they claim between safety and security are often very narrow to be comprehended. Some authors, e.g., Firesmith (2003), use the term security for what concerns malicious (or deliberate) harm on the IS, and they use the term safety for what concerns accidental harm on the IS. This author used the broader notion of survivability to cover both security (in the above sense) and safety. The same notion was adopted by Sindre (2007). The notion of security and safety that we adopt in this work, and that defines our scope, is broader. We are looking at both deliberate and accidental safety and security incidents distinctly. We therefore refer to both safety and security as safeguard (Figure 1).

We define safety as 'avoidance of accidents and mishaps (unplanned events) that result in death, injury, illness, damage to or loss of property or environmental harm'. These unplanned events are caused by either planned actions (deliberate) or unplanned actions. The unplanned actions are the accidental incidents (mistakes or faults) while the planned actions are the deliberate incidents. In IS safety the purpose of deliberate incidents is not directly related to the incident and consequences. The deliberate incident within IS safety do not want incidents to happen, the deliberate acts are made in order to do work more efficiently and less effortful (the abuse case in the use-misuse case model). The deliberate acts can be characterized as cynical, calculating and ignorant. The intention behind both the planned and unplanned actions in IS safety is not malicious but the consequences can be grave.

We defined security as 'protection against planned and unplanned events in order to attain fundamental objectives of preserving the confidentiality, integrity and availability of information system resources which includes hardware, software, firmware, information or data and telecommunication. Similarly these planned and unplanned events are caused by either unplanned actions (unintended, e.g., loss of access device or password) or planned actions (deliberate). These unplanned actions can be utilized by potential attackers to maliciously harm the system. In contrast to IS safety, the purpose of deliberate incidents in IS security is mainly to get a benefit from the incidents regardless of the consequences of the incident. Deliberate acts within IS security are malicious acts forcing the incident to happen by the desire of beneficial consequences for the attackers.

In this sense misuse case is a set of actions that are not to be supported by the system under development either intentionally malicious or unintentionally non-malicious.

All events (planned or unplanned) have negative impacts on the information system.

The rest of this paper is organized as follows. We discuss previous work and current state of the art in security and safety requirements engineering. The next section describes the proposed model in details including the concepts, concepts hierarchy, relations and notations. Then, we present the modeling process and demonstrate with a case study and present a discussion and comparison of the proposed model. Finally the last part provides conclusion and further research work.

## RELATED WORK

To our knowledge, there are few existing proposals that has explore misuse cases with the purpose of identifying safety and security threats and capturing safety and security requirements in a single framework. Therefore we aim to enhance and explore misuse cases (both textual and diagram) for eliciting both safety and security requirements in a unified framework.

Alexander explained in a series of paper (Alexander, 2002, 2003) the concept of misuse cases and their use in eliciting non-functional requirements and modeling of conflicting goals. He defined misuse case as the inverse of a use case i.e., a function that the system should not allow. A misactor is an actor who initiates misuse cases.

Misuse cases being an extension of use case allows each attack to be attached to a use case. Various relations were defined between use case and misuse cases. There can be 'includes' or 'extends' relation from a misuse case to another misuse case. Alexander introduced 'threatens', 'mitigates', 'conflicts with' and 'aggravates'. By his definition a use case mitigates misuse case and misuse case threatens use case.

The Common Criteria (CC) is a comprehensive, standardized method for security requirements elicitation, specification, and analysis developed by the National Institute for Standards and Technology (CCIMB-2007-09-002). It is intended to be a repeatable method for documenting Information Technology (IT) security requirements and has been adopted by seven governmental organizations worldwide, including the United States.

Tropos (Castro, Kolp, & Mylopoulos, 2002) is an information systems development method that relies heavily on i* models. Secure Tropos (Giorgini, Massacci, Mylopoulos, & Zannone, 2005) is an extension of Tropos that addresses security-related concerns through the concepts of ownership, permission and delegation. Lamsweerde et al. (2003) extend the goal oriented KAOS language with anti-goals, which can be used to express the goals of an intruder who aims to exploit or otherwise harm the system. Lin et al. (2004) similarly discuss abuse frames, extending problem frames (Jackson, 2001) with anti-requirements that would be held by potential attackers and whose satisfaction would make the resulting system insecure. Formal specification languages like Z (Spivey, 1992) have also been suggested for specifying security-critical systems.

*Figure 1. Safeguard taxonomy*

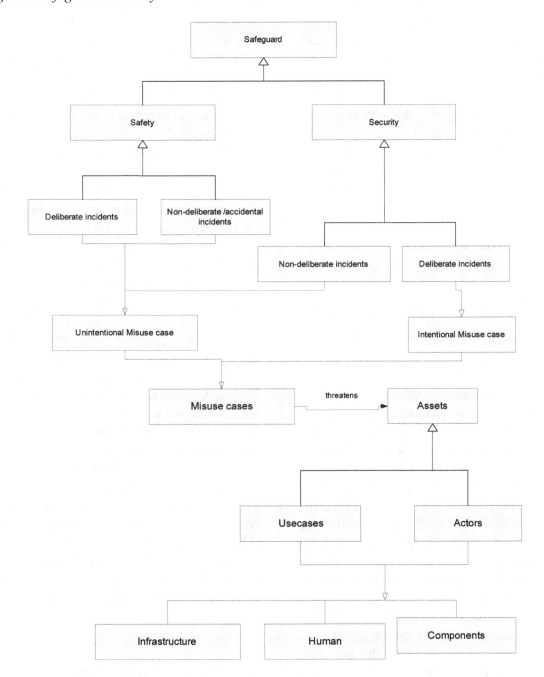

McDermott and Fox (1999) proposed 'abuse case'. Abuse cases are complementary to misuse cases. They focused specifically on security requirements and their relation to design. The authors do not show 'use' and 'abuse case' in the same diagram so no relationships between use case and abuse case can be depicted either. McDermott (2001) defines abuse in terms of interactions that result in actual harm by an abusing actor. He also commented that the actors in an abuse case model are the same kinds of agents that participate in use cases but they should not be the same actors. He viewed abuse case from malicious point of view only.

The conceptual modeling frameworks that focus on security requirements engineering, model vulnerabilities in various ways. Liu et al. (2003) propose a vulnerability analysis method for eliciting security requirements, where vulnerabilities are the weak dependencies that may jeopardize the goals of depender actors in the network of social and organizational dependencies. Matulevicius et al. (2008) treat vulnerabilities as beliefs in the knowledge base of attackers which may contribute to the success of an attack. In (Mayer, Rifaut, & Dubois, 2005), the i* framework is extended to represent vulnerabilities and their relation with threats and other elements of the i* models.

Rostad in her paper extended misuse case notation in eliciting security requirements by including vulnerabilities and insider threat (Rostad, 2006). The author defined vulnerabilities as weak points in the system that may be exploited to affect the system in a negative way. CORAS (den Braber et al., 2003) provides modeling constructs to express threats, vulnerabilities, threats scenarios, unwanted incidents, risks, assets and treatment scenarios. CORAS models do not show what actions or scenario in the system introduce vulnerabilities. The exploit relationship is not explicitly expressed, and the models do not express the effect of vulnerabilities exploitation explicitly.

Sindre and Opdahl (2001) discussed extension of use cases namely misuse cases and give a full description of templates for their textual description. But a detail discussion of how to go about misuse case modeling was missing. Sindre (2007) investigated misuse case for accidental acts of safety concerns. He did not consider deliberate acts of safety concern and neither did he use vulnerability analysis approach and the scope of the work is only on safety issues.

Many authors have adapted UML to address safety issues but then more on the design level. In Jurjens (2003) UML was specifically extended for safety. This was primarily achieved by profiles of packages, class and components diagrams. There have been some researches on safety techniques among software security issues. Safety and security are counted as quality parameters as subsets of defensibility quality parameters (Brostoff & Sasse, 2001; Firesmith, 2003). The main difference between security and safety is that safety addresses accidental loss whereas security deals with maliciously incurred loss (Firesmith, 2005). The deliberate acts for safety concerns are neglected. Many of the existing proposals has addressed security vulnerability problem in addition to direct attacks but we discovered that safety vulnerability problem has not attracted so much attention from RE research world. This is because safety threats are often tagged with accidental incidents. This work is different from the above mentioned in that the focus is engineering safety and security requirements at the early stage of system development using use-misuse cases.

Conclusively, the missing ingredient in all the reviewed approaches is that none of them can extensively elicit both safety and security requirements for a single system in a single model. Besides this there is lack of modeling constructs that express how vulnerable use case enters into the system and how they aggravate attacks and hazards within the system.

In this paper we propose an enhanced use-misuse case model to capture and analyze functional and nonfunctional requirements of an information system. The basic idea of the proposed model is to integrate and enhance the concept of use cases and misuse cases to allow for the elicitation of both safety and security of a single system together, hence the model could take care of some of the weaknesses and lacks in some of the related works.

## USE-MISUSE CASE MODEL

## Description of the Use-Misuse Case Concepts

This section explains the basic concepts, concepts hierarchy and notations of the proposed model. The proposed use-misuse case based model consists of essentially seven elements which are: actors (include inside abuser, inside attackers and unlucky actor), use cases, abuse cases, misuse cases, misactors (include outside attackers and natural agents), vulnerable use case and safeguard use case. The conceptual model is shown in Figure 2.

Misactor is an actor that initiates misuse cases and abuse cases. It includes the inside attacker, inside abuser, unlucky actor, natural agents and the outside attacker. The inside attackers and outside attackers initiate misuse cases intentionally that is with malicious intentions to harm the system. The inside attacker can be a legal user of the system. Such a user can be referred to as a rogue. The outside attacker is not a legal user of the system. The attacks principally imply deliberate incidents.

Abuse case is a kind of actions that result from abuse of right by the actors in the system. This action is not always with the intention to harm the system but they are actions that the system should not support. The conception of abuse case here is a bit different from that of McDermott (1999). His notion of abuse case was from malicious point of view.

The inside abuser is an actor that initiates abuse cases. The aim of inside abuser actions is not for incidents to happen, the deliberate acts are made in order to do work more efficiently

*Figure 2. Use-misuse case conceptual model*

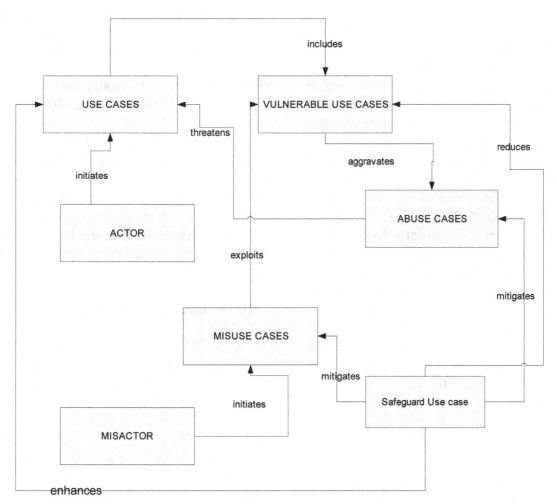

and less effortful. Those acts can be classified as cynical and ignorant.

Unlucky actor is an actor that initiates misuse cases inadvertently by committing some mistakes. He does not have a malicious intention. This may be due to over work, fault or failures, incompetence or is just being unlucky. The unlucky actors, inside abusers and inside attackers are legal actors in the system but their behaviors are different.

Vulnerable use case can be defined as use case whose initiation can lead to some abuse cases by inside abuser or/ and exploited by inside attackers and outside attackers to harm the system. The inside and outside attackers are said to be exploiting the vulnerable use case because they are not the legal actor of the vulnerable use case but they are also stakeholders in the system. The inside abuser is the legal actor of the vulnerable use case so in the process of carrying out his legal actions he can inadvertently initiate abuse cases. In this wise he is not exploiting vulnerable use case. Vulnerable use cases introduce vulnerabilities into the system.

Misuse case is a set of actions that are not to be supported by the system under development. Misuse cases can stem from hostile actors to the system with malicious intention or from user's errors and omissions (mistakes), accidental or careless without malicious intention within the normal use cases. In this paper we categorize misuse cases into two, intentional and unintentional. Abuse case can be seen as a kind of unintentional misuse case but there is need to separate it from misuse case since it is a special unwanted action that can only be prompted by vulnerable use case that is initiated by the inside abuser.

Use case is the specification of a set of actions performed by an actor. This yields an observable result that is of value for one or more actors or stakeholders Use cases are the wanted actions and the actors are legal actors interacting with the system (Rumbaugh, 1994). An actor initiates use cases.

The safeguard use cases for the system are the protective, detective and corrective actions mitigating the misuse cases and abuse cases, reducing the exploitation and abuse of vulnerable use cases in order to aid effective and efficient functioning of the system.

In order to have a better understanding, we categorized misuse cases and Misactor based on intention, and status. These are shown in Figures 3, 4 and 5. The intentional misuse case implies that the actors involved had malicious intention to harm the system while the unintentional misuse case implies that the actors involved do not have malicious intention to harm the system.

In the proposed model we represent five different misactors. They are: natural agents, outside attackers, unlucky actors, inside attackers and inside abusers. We categorized these misactors as shown in Figure 5. The inside misactors implies that these misactors are part of the system stakeholders while the outside misactor implies that they are not part of the system stakeholders.

## Rules Governing Creation of Relations in the Proposed Model

Alexander (2003) proposes rule-based linking. Rules govern creation of relationships between use and misuse case. In this article we are extending the rule based linking to include safeguard use case and vulnerable use case as shown in Table 1.

In accordance with the rules in Table 1 we present the concepts and their relations in Table 2.

## Use-Misuse Case Notations

By addressing both safety and security issues in the same diagram, we distinguish between the two as it might be of importance to know whether something happens as a result of deliberate malicious intention, accidental or as a result of deliberate non- malicious actions. In this paper we use red color for illustration of unintentional misuse cases, abuse cases and the misactors and black color for intentional misuse cases and the

*Figure 3. Misuse cases concepts based on motive and types of misuse*

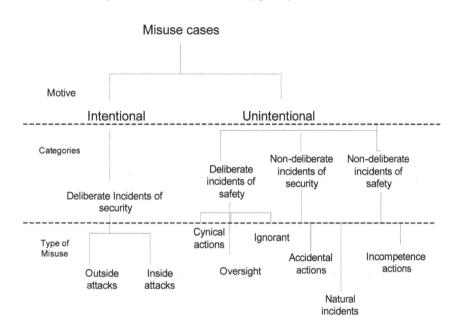

misactors. Following the recommendation of Zhou and Stgtlhane (2004) we represent automated and natural actors with square heads so as to distinguish them from human actors. These automated and natural actors may be a computer system, an application, sensors, flood, earthquake and so on. The concepts and the corresponding notations are shown in Table 3.

The elements of the model and the relationship between them are further illustrated using Figures 6 and 7 and conforming to use-misuse case concept notation. In Figures 6 and 7, the left column stick man denote any of the stakeholders (actor) in the system and the left oval denote use cases, and they represent the functional features of the system. The black oval denotes the intentional misuse cases and the red oval denote unintentional misuse cases and abuse cases. The black stick man denotes the intentional misactors and the red stick man denote unintentional misactors and inside abusers. Vulnerable use cases are depicted in grey colors on the left column of the diagram. The middle column and bottom left and bottom right symbols denote 'safeguard use

cases'. This symbol is proposed for safeguard use case to distinguish it from the normal use cases. These safeguard use cases resembles the security use cases by Firesmiths (2003) but the safeguard use cases encompasses both safety and security. The arrows between the notations indicate the relationships that exist between them.

For a better understanding of the different misactors and their behaviors we present the kind of misuse cases identified with each of them in Table 4.

## USE-MISUSE CASE MODELING PROCESS

In this section the modeling processes of use-misuse case model for capturing safety and security requirements is presented. The modeling process is use-case driven, iterative and incremental in nature. The use-misuse case model is aimed to be used in a well defined application area. The modeling process is iterative because each activity is cyclically repeated to cover every parts of the

*Figure 4. Misactor specializations based on intention*

```
                          ┌──────────────┐
                          │   Misactor   │
                          └──────┬───────┘
        ┌────────────┬───────────┼───────────┬────────────┐
    malicious    malicious    Non-        Non-         Non-
                              malicious   malicious    malicious
    ┌────────┐  ┌────────┐  ┌────────┐  ┌──────────┐  ┌────────┐
    │ Inside │  │Outside │  │Natural │  │ Unlucky  │  │ Inside │
    │attackers│ │attackers│ │ agents │  │  actor   │  │ abuser │
    └────────┘  └────────┘  └────────┘  └──────────┘  └────────┘
```

information system that is to be developed. At the end of every stage the result is more detailed than the previous stage this make it to be incremental in nature.

The modeling process consists of three basic phases.

1. Identifying use cases and Actors
2. Identifying Safety and security threats
3. Defining Safeguard requirements

Each of these phases involves some sub steps within it to achieve the purpose of each phase. Each of the phases and the steps that composed them will be more elaborated in the next section. The sequencing of the activities involved in the modeling process is shown in Figure 8.

## Identifying Use Cases and Actors

The functional requirements (business and system) of the intended information system are capture at this stage. The functional requirements have corresponding actors that initiate them. Both the use cases and the actors are things of great value to the organization. Also safety and security goals or objectives are specified for the use cases and the actors. Specifying these objectives will unfold more valuable ingredients in the system that needed to be protected. It involves identifying the stakeholders/actors with the key roles and interactions between them. Every interaction must be started by one agent and must involve another agent. This layer involves the human actors (Users), components actors (e.g., the hardware, software) and infra-

*Figure 5. Misactor specializations based on status (inside or outside)*

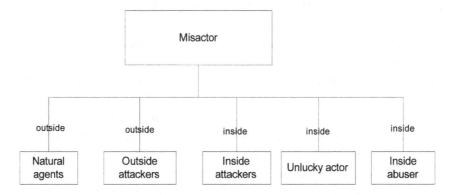

*Table 1. Rule based linking for the use case, abuse case and misuse case of the proposed model*

| | USE CASE | MISUSE CASE | SAFEGUARD USE CASE | VULNERABLE USE CASE | Abuse case |
|---|---|---|---|---|---|
| USE CASE | includes | threatens | Enhances | N/A | Threatens |
| MISUSE CASE | N/A | includes | Mitigates | N/A | N/A |
| SAFEGUARD USE CASE | N/A | N/A | N/A | N/A | N/A |
| VULNERABLE USE CASE | includes | exploits | Reduces | N/A | N/A |
| Abuse case | N/A | N/A | Mitigates | aggravates | Includes |

structure actors (e.g., fire extinguishers) and the interactions between them. Each of the key roles of these actors or interactions is referred to as the use cases. In order to achieve these objectives there may be need to employ one or two of the methods for gathering requirements. It may be by interview with the stakeholders and the domain experts. One or more story boards and scenarios may have to be written in order to have a right understanding of the system in question.

## Identifying Safety and Security Threats

Identifying the safety and security threats concerns vulnerable use cases and misuse cases. These entail examining the system functional requirements (use cases) and consider each one carefully to decide if it may be exploited for malicious or harmful purposes. Investigate each of the human actors to know which of them can abuse his privilege to

*Table 2. Use-misuse case concepts and relations*

| Concepts I | Relations | Concepts II |
|---|---|---|
| Misuse cases | threatens | Use cases |
| Misuse cases | Exploits | Vulnerable use cases |
| Misuse cases | includes | Misuse cases |
| Abuse cases | threatens | Use cases |
| Vulnerable use cases | aggravates | Abuse cases |
| Use cases | includes | Vulnerable use cases, Use cases |
| Natural Agents (Misactor) | initiate | Unintentional Misuse cases |
| Outside attackers (Misactor) | initiate | Intentional Misuse cases |
| Unlucky Actor (Misactor) | initiate | Unintentional Misuse cases |
| Inside attackers (Misactor) | initiate | Intentional Misuse case |
| Inside abuser (Misactor | initiate | Abuse cases (unintentional misuse cases) |
| Actor | initiates | Use cases |
| Safeguard Use cases | mitigate | Misuse cases |
| Safeguard Use cases | enhances | Use cases |
| Safeguard Use cases | reduce | Vulnerable use cases |

*Table 3. Concepts and their notations*

| Concepts | Notations |
|---|---|
| Use cases | In white color |
| Misuse cases | Same as use case but in black color |
| Actor | Same as outside attackers but in white color |
| Unlucky actor | Same as outside attackers but in red color |
| Outside attackers | |
| Inside attackers | Same as outside attackers |
| Safeguard use cases | |
| Natural agents | Same as inhuman agents |
| Inhuman agents | |
| Inside abusers | Same as outside attackers but in red color |
| Vulnerable Use cases | In grey color |
| Abuse cases | In red color |

do what can eventually harm the system. This is when initiation of vulnerable use case by inside abusers can also lead to abuse cases.

Investigating and identifying how 'negative' agents would attempt to defeat the information system purpose or thwart some of the steps in the use case description; this leads to major misuse cases. During these sessions the focus should be to identify as many ways an attacker and natural factors could cause harm in the service provided by the use case in focus. Each of these modes of disruption becomes a candidate misuse case. The

goal is to identify security threats (misuse cases) against each of the functions, areas, processes, data and transactions involved in the use case from different potential risks such as unauthorized access from within and without, denial of service attacks, privacy violations, confidentiality, availability and integrity violations and malicious hacking attacks.

In addition to modes of attacks, the processes should also try to uncover possible users' mistakes in the course of interaction with the system and the system responses to them. Often these mistakes

*Figure 6. A representation of the notations of the original misuse case model (Sindre & Opdahl, 2001)*

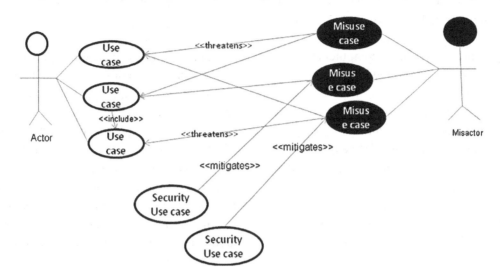

could cause serious issues in the functioning, safety and security of the system.

By identifying all inappropriate actors and actions that could be taken, we would capture all actions of abnormal system use – by genuine users in terms of accidental or careless mistakes and abuse of legitimate right and by attackers trying to break the system function and natural disaster that may harm or disrupt the normal functioning of the system.

Investigate the potential relations between misuse cases, use cases, mistakes and vulnerable use case. This is very important since many threats to a system can largely be achieved by using that system's normal functionality as for instance "harmful self treatment" abuse case of our example.

## Identifying Safety and Security Requirements

The safety and security requirements are referred to as safeguard use cases. After all forms of misuse cases and misactors have been constructed, then there is need to identify safeguards use cases to counter or thwart the intended purpose of each misuse case, abuse case and to achieve the security objectives of the use cases and the actors. This

can be achieved by carefully examining each of the misuse cases and the misactors and suggest actions that can counteract them in form of protection, detection and correction.

## Case Study

As anticipated in this work the case study addressed is the Health care system. The goal of the case study was to evaluate effectiveness and efforts involved in using the conceptual model in accordance with the modeling process. In this section, we go through the modeling process using the case study. This case study is part of a real-life system, called Electronic Health Record (EHR), developed at the University of Kansas HISPC project (http://ehealth.kansashealthonline.org). The electronic health record might include:

- Basic information, such as name, address, phone number and who to call in an emergency
- Medical history
- List of medications, allergies and shots you have had
- Laboratory test results, such as blood work
- Radiology images, such as X-rays, CAT scans and MRIs

- Advanced directives, living wills, and health powers of attorney

Patients can readily use the computers in some specific places to do the following:

- View their medical record online.
- Get their lab results online.
- Schedule or change appointments online.
- Receive reminders for regular tests and checkups online.
- Print a copy of their medical record and medicines to take to another doctor.
- E-mail their doctor to ask a question.

- Get their medications renewed online.

To make this example simpler and more understandable, we consider a substantial part of the EHR system. In the considered Health care system a patient need to create an online account, use the online account to interact with other related stakeholders in the system. A story board can look like this: "a patient uses the log-in account to access the medical record, schedule appointment, and renew medication. The physician sends the next appointment to the patient and sends the list of the new medication to the pharmacist. The pharmacist supplies the drugs to the patient". Following the

*Figure 7. Notations representing the core elements of the proposed use-misuse case model*

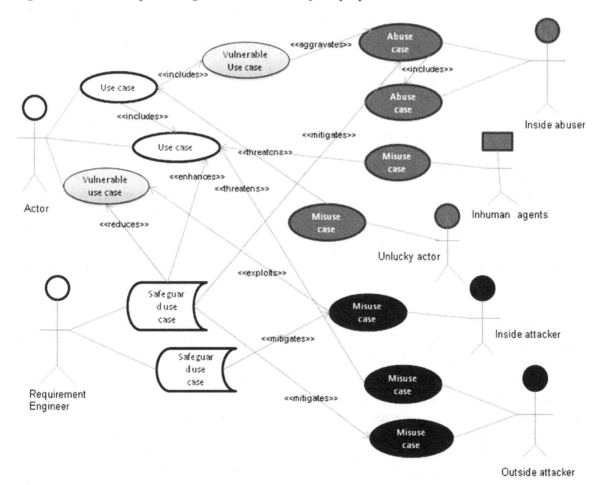

*Table 4. Different categories of misactors and misuse cases identified with them*

| Misactors | Type of misuse cases |
|---|---|
| Outside attackers | Deliberate acts of security misuse cases (intentional misuse cases) |
| Inside Attackers | Deliberate acts of security misuse cases by exploiting vulnerable use cases (intentional misuse cases) |
| Unlucky Actor and natural agents | Accidental acts of safety misuse cases and security misuse cases (unintentional misuse cases) |
| Inside Abuser | Deliberate acts of safety misuse cases by initiating vulnerable use case which aggravates abuse cases (unintentional misuse cases) |

steps involved in the first phase of the modeling process we have the following:

1. The purpose of the health care system is to provide quality safe and timely health care.
2. The system boundaries are the patient, physician and HIS.
3. The stakeholders are patients, physicians and pharmacist.
4. Patient interaction with the Health care system is: access medical record.
5. Patient interactions with the physician through the Health care system are: schedule appointment and renew medication.
6. Physician interaction with the patient is: send next appointment to the patient.
7. Physician interaction with the pharmacist is: send list of new medication.
8. Pharmacist interaction with the patient is: supply drug.

The outputs of this layer are:

- The actors which are: EHR system, Physician, Patients, and Pharmacists.
- The use cases for each of the actors are as shown in Table 5.
- The security and safety objectives for the use cases and the actors are:
  - UC1, UC2, UC3, UC5, UC7 and UC10 ----------------- Sec: Availability; Safety: Ensure patients do not go into self medication, Ensure Doctor visit their patient regularly,
  - UC1, UC7, UC8, UC9 and UC10 --------------------------- Sec: Confidentiality,
  - UC1, UC5, UC7, UC8, UC9 and UC10 --------------------- Sec: Integrity.

In accordance to the modeling process we shall present a use case diagram to represent one of the actors including the use cases because of lack of space (Figure 9).

The actor is the patient and the use cases are shown in the white oval shapes taken the physician and the EHR as the system boundary.

The output of this phase will act as input for the next stage.

Considering our case study we shall follow the modeling process to build the safety and security threats using the scenario in the previous section. We represent each of the elements using the notations shown in Figure 7.

Taking the first actor (patient) and the use cases, we identify use case 'view personal and medical record' as a vulnerable use case. We recognize a negative agent outside attacker who can exploit the vulnerable use case to cause harm for the system and also an inside abuser who can initiate abuse case in the process of initiating the vulnerable use case. Some of the actions of the negative agents are: corrupt info in transit, Denial of service and get user privilege. The abuse cases

*Figure 8. Use-misuse case modeling process*

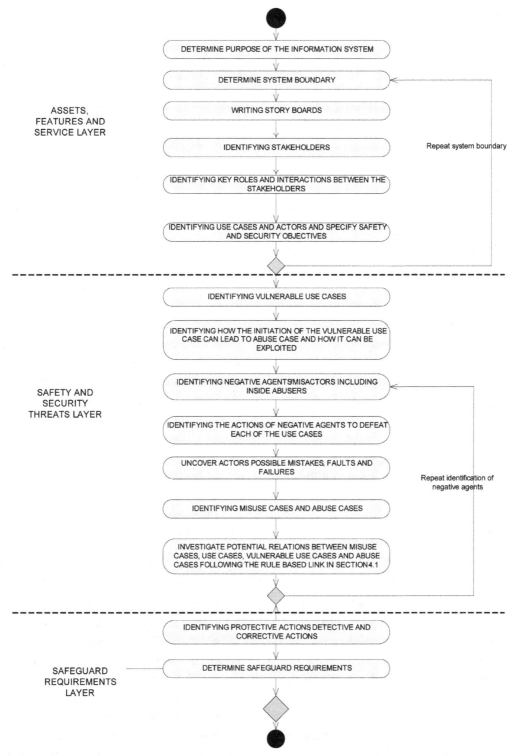

*Table 5. Actors and their use cases*

| Actors | Use cases (UC) |
|---|---|
| Patients | Access medical records (UC1), Schedule appointment (UC2), renew medication (UC3) |
| Physician | Send next appointment (UC4), send list of medication (UC5), provide quality medical services (UC6), Access patients record (UC10) |
| EHR system | Provides required information to the users (UC7) |
| Pharmacist | Receives list of drugs (UC8), supply drugs (UC9) |

that can result from the vulnerable use case are: harmful self diagnostic and self treatment.

Some of the mistake that can occur is 'loss of passwords'. From the information we can gather three constructs they are; misuse cases, the abuse cases and the vulnerable use cases. Following the rule based link, we have the following relations existing between the instances of these constructs as shown in Table 6.

These are illustrated in the use-misuse case diagram in Figure 10.

The unlucky actor and the inside abuser are legal stakeholders in the system. The outside attacker is not part of the system. All the three are misactors but their behaviors are different. The actions of the inside abuser and the unlucky actor are not with malicious intention but the actions of the outside attackers are malicious. They are to harm the system. In Figure 11, loss of password is a kind of accidental incidents of security misuse cases, harmful self diagnostic and self treatment of patients are deliberate incidents of safety misuse cases, corrupt info in transit, get user privilege and denial of service are direct and deliberate incidents of security misuse cases.

The safety and security requirements (security and safety awareness, block unauthorized users, make info unreadable and ethical training) identified to mitigate the misuse cases and achieve the safety and security goals as a result of our analysis are shown and illustrated with the use-misuse case diagram.

## An Excerpt of Textual Detailed Description of Some of the Use Cases and Misuse Cases

In this section a set of textual description will be presented using the light weight approach that is, describing misuse within the textual description of a use case. The light weight option gives a significant gain in customer and analyst awareness of security threats, with very little extra cost beyond normal use case specification. Indeed for applications where security is important it would make sense to include the threat slot as standard in the normal use case template (Sindre & Opdahl, 2005). This is an extension of Constantine and Lockwood's (Constantine & Lockwood, 1999) work about user, threat, stakeholders and risks columns. The textual description for some of

*Table 6. Instances of misuse cases, abuse cases and vulnerable use cases*

| Actor Involved | Instance I | Relations | Instance II |
|---|---|---|---|
| Patients | Loss of Password | threatens | Schedule Appointment |
| Patients | Self treatment | threatens | Receive quality medical treatment |
| Patients<br>Crook | View personal and Medical record<br>Corrupt info in transit | aggravates<br>threatens | Harmful diagnostics and self treatment<br>View medical record |

*Figure 9. Use case diagram for the actor patient*

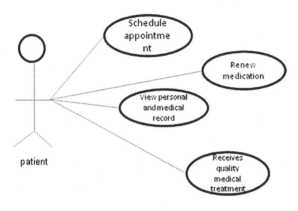

the use cases and misuse cases are displayed in Tables 7 and 8.

## DISCUSSIONS AND COMPARISON OF THE PROPOSED MODEL WITH EXISTING PROPOSALS

The techniques for capturing and analyzing safety and security requirements should offer both a structured and detailed descriptions of how important safety and security requirements can be identified. This will enable creativity among participants on identifying as many of these requirements as possible. Since misuse cases are known for eliciting non-functional requirements we compare our proposal with existing proposals that explored misuse cases for capturing non-functional requirements. The aim of this comparison is to evaluate the approaches for their capability of identifying security and safety misuse cases which are prerequisite to eliciting and analyzing safety and security requirements. The comparison is based on some parameters discussed in paper and also some guide attributes expected of techniques for capturing and analyzing safety and security requirements. The threats are categorized as shown in Table 4. In addition to the categorized threats, there may be natural disasters or threats.

In this paper we have basically examined further, the possibility of enhancing and applying misuse cases (both diagram and textual description) for identifying security and safety threats in a unified framework. These in turn help to elicit safety and security requirements. Several examples of security and safety related misuse case diagrams and textual descriptions have been shown.

Table 9 compares the capabilities of existing misuse case based modeling approaches with respect to threats identification and capturing of subsequent safety and security requirements. None of these approaches provide explicit constructs for modeling vulnerable use cases for safety problem. In Alexander (2003) and Sindre (2007) safety issues are being considered from accidental point of view alone. They do not investigate the possibility of initiating any of the vulnerable use cases by the actors which may lead to some actions that may have grave consequences which are related to safety specifically. Rostad (2006) actually investigated vulnerabilities exploitations but only for security issues. Her definition of vulnerability is satisfactory with engineering security requirements only. The detailed and structured modeling process for better participation of stakeholders in requirement engineering is lacking in Alexander (2003) and Sindre (2007).

The proposed use-misuse case based model shows the actions in the system that introduces vulnerable use case. The exploit and aggravate relationships are explicitly expressed with the consequences. This can be seen in Figure 10 where a patient (actor) abuse his action of having access to the result of medical test by going into self treatment which in turn threatens his receiving quality medical services. These features were lacking in the work done in Sindre and Opdahl (2005).

The model does not only design the diagrammatic notation for each instance of use-misuse case but also presents the textual description of

*Figure 10. Use-misuse case diagram for the actor patient illustrating the safety and security threats (misuse cases)*

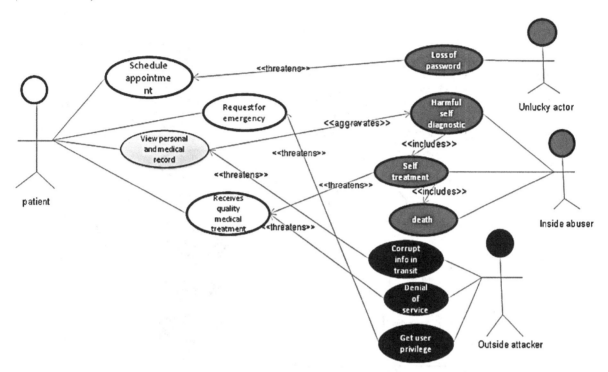

both use-misuse cases. This complements the work done in Alexander (2003).

Our model also gives a detail discussion of how to go about misuse case model for eliciting both safety and security requirements which is missing in Alexander (2003) and Sindre (2007).

In addition to the results of the comparative study the proposed model does exhibit some improved attributes which could not be included in the comparative table. This proposed model incorporates the new identified threat 'abuse case' by introducing vulnerable use case. This is a kind of action carried out by the same actor in the system and not just any of the stakeholders. Though the intention is not to harm the system but it can pose a kind of risk to any of the stakeholders. This is illustrated in Figure 9 and 10.

This contradicts the proposal of McDermott (2001) that abuser cannot be the same actor but any of the stakeholders. The model represents use-misuse cases at a generic level so that they

can be easily reused to give new development projects a flying start in identifying safety and security threats and corresponding safety and security requirements.

Misuse cases are not equally suitable for all kinds of threats, focusing mainly on misuse where an identifiable attacker performs a harmful sequence of actions supported by the system, hence the need for an integrated approach that incorporate vulnerable use case, abuse case notations and relations that allows understanding and modeling different attackers and abusers behaviors in order to capture safety and security requirements..

The Use-misuse cases model provide a framework for more detailed threat modeling and architectural risk analysis. It provides a highly organized way of thinking about safety and security requirements early in the system life cycle. The importance of integrated approach that allows developers to elicit and specify safety and security threats cannot be over emphasized. It

*Figure 11. Use-misuse case diagram for HIS safety and security requirements using physician and HIS as the system boundary*

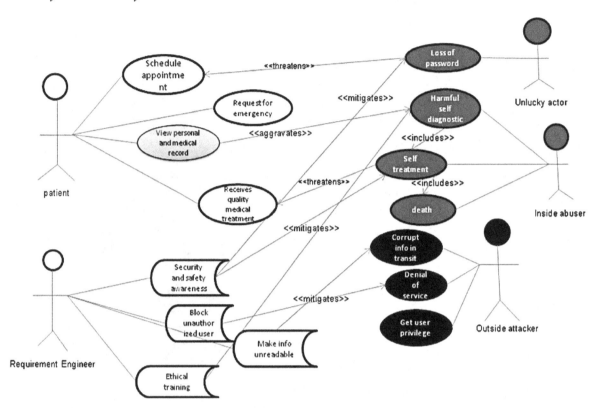

has been argued that treating safety and security requirement engineering in isolation may lead to a number of problems (Sommerville, 2003). These problems include inadequate understanding of safety and security semantics (Burns, McDermid, & Dobson, 1992), lack of common terminology and disparate processes, which makes it difficult to take advantage of commonality between the two disciplines (Rushby,1994). Furthermore, the separation of safety and security requirements engineering may also lead to incompleteness in requirements, incompleteness in essential require-

*Table 7. A light weight vulnerable use case description embedded in the regular use case, view personal and medical record in patient interactions with the e-health information system. Use case: view personal and medical record.*

| USER | USER INTENTION | SYSTEM RESPONSE | THREATS | STAKEHOLDERS AND RISKS |
|------|----------------|-----------------|---------|------------------------|
| Patient | Identify self | Verify identity | Identity spoofed | Stakeholder frustration |
| | Access medical and personal record | Offer options | Identification spied on | |
| | Make choice | Display required info/ form | Info corrupted in transit | Stakeholder misconceived |
| | View record | | Harmful self diagnostic, self treatment | Stakeholder may die |

*Table 8. A light weight misuse case description embedded in the regular use case, schedule appointment in patient interactions through e-health information system. Use case: schedule appointment.*

| USER | USER INTENTION | SYSTEM RESPONSE | THREATS | STAKEHOLDERS AND RISK |
|------|----------------|-----------------|---------|------------------------|
| Patient | Identify self | Verify identity | Identity spoofed | Stakeholder frustration |
| | Schedule appointment | Offer options | Get user privilege | Not able to access the system for some time |
| | Make choice | Display prescription list | Denial of service | |
| | Fill form for new appointment | | Info corrupted | Stakeholder misconceived |

ments characteristics like verifiability and ambiguity in requirements (Firesmith, 2003, 2007).

## CONCLUSION AND FUTURE WORK

This paper proposes a requirement engineering framework that supports the elicitation of both safety and security requirements based on direct attacks and vulnerabilities that requirements bring to the system. The proposed model offers a uniform way of handling both functional and non-functional requirements of information system. This has a plausible significant because a major obstacle to dealing with non-functional requirements is their inherent diversity which

*Table 9. Comparison of misuse case based modeling approaches with the current proposal. The first row shows the parameters on which we base our comparison and the subsequent rows indicate the extent to which each of the proposals was able to take care of the parameters.*

| Authors | Conceptual Frameworks | Diagrammatic Description of Misuse cases | Textual Description of misuse cases | Vulnerability analysis Approach to Security | Vulnerability analysis Approach to Safety | Accidental incidents of Safety and Security | Malicious direct Attacks | Detailed Modeling Process | Other Exceptions and test cases |
|---------|----------------------|------------------------------------------|-------------------------------------|---------------------------------------------|-------------------------------------------|---------------------------------------------|--------------------------|---------------------------|---------------------------------|
| Alexander [11] 2003 | Misuse cases: Use cases with hostile intention | Explicitly expressed | Not expressed | Not expressed | Not expressed | explicitly expressed | Explicitly expressed | Partially expressed | Explicitly expressed |
| Sindre [7] 2005 | Eliciting security requirements with misuse cases | Explicitly expressed | Explicitly expressed | Not expressed | Not expressed | Not expressed | Explicitly expressed | Explicitly expressed | Not expressed |
| Rostad [13] 2006 | An extended misuse case notation: including vulnerabilities and the insider threats | Explicitly expressed | Not expressed | Explicitly expressed | Not expressed | Not expressed | Explicitly expressed | Explicitly expressed | Not expressed |
| Sindre [23] 2007 | A look at misuse case for safety concerns | Explicitly expressed | Explicitly expressed | Partially expressed | Not expressed | Explicitly expressed | Partially expressed | Not expressed | Not expressed |
| Current proposal | | Explicitly expressed | Explicitly expressed | Explicitly expressed | Explicitly expressed | Explicitly expressed | Explicitly expressed | Explicitly expressed | Not expressed |

calls for a broad array of techniques to be used in requirements work but which make the resulting requirements document difficult to organize and comprehend. This work is an on-going project that will aid the system designers in modeling and analyzing safety and security requirements. It will also help them to take care of some other non-functional requirements like survivability requirements and robustness requirements.

In order to realize a secured or trustworthy system, an important part of the foundation is security awareness and education in related areas for all employees. This is a very important area and can be said to be the very basis of everything that has to do with security. Education is the key to a secure system and environment.

In our future work, further investigation is needed to suggest how other requirement engineering techniques can be enhanced to take care of safety and security requirements together in the same framework. We aim to perform empirical evaluation in order to evaluate the expressiveness, ease of use and completeness of the proposed model. Apart from the authors' evaluation done in this paper modelers will be given the framework to be used in modeling a number of case studies so that we can draw conclusions on industrial usefulness of the model. We also aim to integrate the conceptual model with risk analysis.

## AKNOWLEDGMENT

This work is supported by the Key Project of National Natural Science Foundation of China under Grant No.90818026, Swedish International Development Cooperation Agency (SIDA), Organization for Women in Science for the developing World (OWSDW) and International Federation of University Women (IFUW) under Ida Smedley MacLean Fellowship.

## REFERENCES

Alexander, I. F. (2002). Modeling the interplay of conflicting goals with use and misuse cases. In *Proceedings of the 8th International Workshop on Requirements Engineering: Foundation for Software Quality*, Essen, Germany.

Alexander, I. F. (2003). Misuse case help to elicit non-functional requirements. *Computing and Control Engineering Journal*, *14*(1), 40–45. doi:10.1049/cce:20030108

Alexander, I. F. (2003). Misuse cases, use cases with hostile intent. *IEEE Software*, *20*(1), 58–66. doi:10.1109/MS.2003.1159030

Arogundade, O. T., Akinwale, A. T., Jin, Z., & Yang, X. G. (in press). Vulnerability analysis approach to capturing information system safety threats and requirements. *International Journal of Software Engineering and its Applications.*

Brostoff, S., & Sasse, M. (2001). Safe and sound: a safety critical approach to security. In *Proceedings of the 10th ACM/SIGSAC New Security Paradigms Workshop*, Cloudcroft, NM (pp. 41-50).

Burns, A., McDermid, J., & Dobson, V. (1992). On the meaning of safety and security. *The Computer Journal*, *35*(1), 3–15. doi:10.1093/comjnl/35.1.3

Castro, J., Kolp, M., & Mylopoulos, J. (2002). Towards requirements-driven information systems engineering: the Tropos project. *Information Systems*, *27*(6), 356–389. doi:10.1016/S0306-4379(02)00012-1

Cockburn, A. (2001). *Writing effective use cases*. Reading, MA: Addison-Wesley.

Common Criteria Implementation Board. (2007). *Common criteria for information technology security evaluation, version 2.1* (Technical Report CCIMB-2007-09-002). Australia: Author.

Constantine, L. L., & Lockwood, L. A. D. (1999). *Software for use: a practical guide to the models and methods of usage-centered design.* New York, NY: ACM.

den Braber, F., Dimitrakos, T., Gran, B. A., Lund, M. S., Stolen, K., & Aagedal, J. O. (2003). The CORAS methodology: model-based risk assessment using UML and UP. In Favre, L. (Ed.), *UML and the unified process* (pp. 332–357). Hershey, PA: IGI Global.

Elahi, G., & Yu, E. (2007). A goal oriented approach for modeling and analyzing security trade-offs. In C. Parent, K.-D. Schewe, V. C. Storey, & B. Thalheim (Eds.), *Proceedings of the 26th International Conference on Conceptual Modeling* (LNCS 4801, pp. 375-390).

Fernandez-Medina, E., Jurjens, J., Trujillo, J., & Jajodia, S. (Eds.). (2009). Model-driven development for secure information systems. *Information and Software Technology, 51*(5), 809–814. doi:10.1016/j.infsof.2008.05.010

Firesmith, D. G. (2003). *Common concepts underlying safety, security and survivability engineering* (Tech. Rep. No. CMU/SEI2003 TN 033), Pittsburgh, PA: Software Engineering Institute.

Firesmith, D. G. (2003). Security use cases. *Journal of Object Technology, 2*(3), 53–64. doi:10.5381/jot.2003.2.3.c6

Firesmith, D. G. (2005). Analyzing the security significance of system requirements. In *Proceedings of the Symposium on Requirements Engineering for Information Security in conjunction with the 13th IEEE International Requirements Engineering Conference*, Paris, France.

Firesmith, D. G. (2007). Engineering safety and security related requirements for software intensive systems. In *Proceedings of the International Conference on Software Engineering*, Minneapolis, MN (p. 169).

Giorgini, P., Massacci, F., Mylopoulos, J., & Zannone, N. (2005). Modeling security requirements through ownership, permission, and delegation. In *Proceedings of the 13th International Requirements Engineering Conference*, Paris, France (pp. 167-176).

Harrison, M. D., & Sujan, M. A. (Eds.). (2008). *Proceedings of the 27th International Conference on Computer Safety, Reliability and Security*, New Castle upon Tyne, UK (LNCS 4680). Berlin, Germany: Springer-Verlag.

Jackson, M. (2001). *Problem frames.* London, UK: Addison-Wesley.

Jacobson, I. (1992). *Object-oriented software engineering: a use case driven approach.* Reading, MA: Addison-Wesley.

Jurjens, J. (2003). Developing safety-critical systems with UML. In P. Stevens, J. Whittle, & G. Booch (Eds.), *Proceedings of the Sixth International Conference on the Unified Modeling Language*, San Francisco, CA (LNCS 2863, pp. 144-159).

Kulak, D., & Guiney, E. (2000). *Use cases: requirements in context.* New York, NY: ACM.

Lamsweerde, V., Brohez, S., De Landtsheer, R., & Janssens, D. (2003). From system goals to intruder anti-goals: attack generation and resolution for security requirements engineering. In *Proceedings of the 2nd International Workshop on Requirements Engineering for High Assurance Systems*, Pittsburgh, PA (pp.49-56).

Lin, L., Nuseibeh, B., Ince, D., & Jackson, M. (2004). Using abuse frames to bound the scope of security problems. In *Proceedings of the 12th IEEE International Requirements Engineering Conference*, Kyoto, Japan (pp. 354-355).

Liu, L., Yu, E., & Mylopoulos, J. (2003). Security and privacy requirements analysis within a social setting. In *Proceedings of the 11th IEEE International Conference on Requirements Engineering* (pp. 151-161).

Matulevicius, R., Mayer, N., Mouratidis, H., Dubois, E., Heymans, P., & Genon, N. (2008). Adapting secure tropos for security risk management in the early phases of information systems development. In E. Dubois & K. Pohl (Eds.), *Proceedings of the 20th International Conference on Advanced Information Systems Engineering*, Montpellier, France (LNCS 5074, pp 541-555).

Mayer, N., Rifaut, A., & Dubois, E. (2005). Towards a risk-based security requirements engineering framework. In *Proceedings of the International Workshop on Requirements Engineering for Software Quality, Foundations of Software Quality* (pp. 89-104).

McDermott, J. (2001). Abuse-case-based assurance argument. In *Proceedings of the 17th Annual Computer Security Applications Conference*, New Orleans, LA (p. 0366).

McDermott, J., & Fox, C. (1999). Using abuse case model for security requirements analysis. In *Proceedings of the 15th Annual Computer Security Applications Conference*, Phoenix, AZ (p. 55).

McGraw, G. (2006). *Software security: Building security*. Upper Saddle River, NJ: Pearson Education.

Mead, N. R. (2007). *How to compare the security quality requirements engineering (SQUARE) method with other method* (Tech. Rep. No. CMU/SEI2007-TN-021). Pittsburgh, PA: Software Engineering Institute, Carnegie, Mellon University.

Mølmann, R. A. (2003). The Human Factor – Taxonomy for classifying human challenges to information security. In Kufås, I., & Mølmann, R. A. (Eds.), *Informasjonssikkerhet og innsideproblematikk. Institutt for produksjons- og kvalitetsteknikk*. Trondheim, Norway: NTNU.

Rostad, L. (2006). An extended misuse case notation: including vulnerabilities and the insider threats. In *Proceedings of the Conference on Requirements Engineering: Foundation for Software Quality*, Luxembourg (pp 33-43).

Rumbaugh, J. (1994). Getting started: using use cases to capture requirements. *Journal of Object Oriented Programming*, *7*(5), 8–23.

Rushby, J. (1994). Critical system properties: Survey and taxonomy. *Reliability Engineering & System Safety*, *43*(2), 180–219. doi:10.1016/0951-8320(94)90065-5

Sindre, G. (2007). A look at misuse case for safety concerns. In *Proceedings of the IFIP International Federation for Information Processing, Situational Method Engineering: Fundamentals and Experiences* (Vol. 244, pp. 252-266).

Sindre, G., & Opdahl, A. L. (2001). Capturing security requirements through misuse cases. In *Norsk Informatik Konferanse*, Tromso, Norway.

Sindre, G., & Opdahl, A. L. (2005). Eliciting security requirements with misuse cases. *Requirements Engineering*, *10*(1), 34–44. doi:10.1007/s00766-004-0194-4

Sommerville, I. (2003). *An integrated approach to dependability requirements engineering*. Paper presented at the 11th Safety-Critical Systems Symposium, Bristol, UK.

Spivey, J. M. (1992). *The Z Notation: A reference manual*. Upper Saddle River, NJ: Prentice Hall.

Zhou, J., & Stgtlhane, T. (2004). A framework for early robustness assessment. In *Proceedings of the 8th IASTED Conference on Software Engineering and Application*.

*This work was previously published in the International Journal of Information Security and Privacy, Volume 5, Issue 4, edited by Hamid Nemati, pp. 8-30, copyright 2011 by IGI Publishing (an imprint of IGI Global).*

# Chapter 15
# Evaluating the Quality and Usefulness of Data Breach Information Systems

**Benjamin Ngugi**
*Suffolk University, USA*

**Jafar Mana**
*Suffolk University, USA*

**Lydia Segal**
*Suffolk University, USA*

## ABSTRACT

*As the nation confronts a growing tide of security breaches, the importance of having quality data breach information systems becomes paramount. Yet too little attention is paid to evaluating these systems. This article draws on data quality scholarship to develop a yardstick that assesses the quality of data breach notification systems in the U.S. at both the state and national levels from the perspective of key stakeholders, who include law enforcement agencies, consumers, shareholders, investors, researchers, and businesses that sell security products. Findings reveal major shortcomings that reduce the value of data breach information to these stakeholders. The study concludes with detailed recommendations for reform.*

## INTRODUCTION

Data breaches can jeopardize the livelihoods of hundreds of thousands of people (Javelin Strategy and Research, 2010a). Each breach can expose large numbers of customer records. A singular computer intrusion at TJX Companies Inc. in

2007, for instance, resulted in the loss of over 45 million customer records (Privacy Commissioner -Canada & Information & Privacy Commissioner-Alberta, 2007). If a fraction of these records had fallen into the wrong hands, a major identity theft crisis would have been underway. Indeed, security breaches are a leading cause of identity theft, the

DOI: 10.4018/978-1-4666-2050-6.ch015

number one consumer complaint from 2000 to 2010, consisting of 19% of the overall complaints (Federal Trade Commission, 2010, 2011). Data breaches, moreover, are increasing. Between 2005 and 2009, the number of data breaches in the U.S. rose from 157 to 498 (Identity Theft Resource Center, 2010c). Total annual identity fraud has been rising from $45 in 2007 to $54 billion in 2009 (Javelin Strategy and Research, 2010b). Despite this, however, there is no common yardstick by which to evaluate data breach systems.

The goal of this study is to develop a yardstick and evaluate how well current data breach notification systems are meeting stakeholder needs.

The remainder of this article is organized as follows: Part II reviews the relevant literature. Part III sets forth the methodology. Part IV creates a yardstick by which to evaluate data breach notification systems. Part V applies that yardstick to evaluate data breach information systems. Part VI offers recommendations for reform, while Part VII summarizes the contributions and offers suggestions for future research.

## LITERATURE REVIEW

The data quality literature has long discussed the importance of quality (Juran & Godfrey, 1999; Wand & Wang, 1996; Wang, Storey, & Firth, 1995). Decisions made on the basis of corrupt or inferior data will be skewed, with potentially costly consequences (Baltzan & Phillips, 2009; Fisher, Chengalur-Smith, & Ballou, 2003). As Baltzan and Phillips (2009) observe, "decisions are only as good as the quality of data breach information used to make the decisions."

Researchers have devoted much energy to investigating how to evaluate information for quality. One of the most prominent such scholars, professor and Director of the MIT Information Quality Program Richard Wang, has written several seminal papers on the subject. In one such paper, Wang and Strong (1996) develop

a conceptual framework designed to capture "the aspects of data quality that are important to consumers" (Wang & Strong, 1996, p. 5). The framework conceives of data quality as comprising four dimensions. One dimension refers to the intrinsic factors of the data itself. Examples are the data's accuracy, objectivity, believability, and reputation – all of which go to the data's quality in their own right. The second dimension refers to contextual factors. Data quality "must be considered within the context of the task at hand" (Wang & Strong, 1996, p. 6). Contextual factors include value-added, relevance, timeliness, completeness, and appropriate amount of data. Third, the data's representational dimension includes aspects related to its format (e.g., whether it offers a concise and consistent representation) and meaning (e.g., its interpretability and the ease with which it can be understood). The last dimension is its accessibility. Data needs to be secure, while being accessible. This four-dimensional model is widely accepted by other scholars in the data quality field (Bovee, Srivastava, & Mak, 2003; Strong, Lee, & Wang, 1997).

Underlying the four dimensions of Wang and Strong's (1996) model is the concept of usefulness, a notion captured by the "fit to use" principle in the data quality literature. The importance of usefulness stems from the realization that the quality of data "depends on the actual use of data and what may be considered good data in one case (for a specific application or user) may not be sufficient in another case" (Wand & Wang, 1996). The idea is that it is critical to adopt the user's perspective on the data's fitness for whatever use the user requires the data for (Juran & Godfrey, 1999).

The concept of usefulness is built into the very definition of data quality in Wang and Strong's (1996, p. 6) model: they define data quality as data that is fit for use by data consumers. The idea of usefulness has been adopted in a number of fields, such as health surveillance (Buehler, Hopkins, Overhage, Sosin, & Tong, 2004), as part of an effort to assess data quality. Scholars have not, however, applied it yet to data breach notification systems.

Applying a generic model such as Wang and Strong's to the data breach notification area requires the use of metrics appropriate to that area. A metric is a "verifiable measure, stated in quantitative or qualitative terms and defined with respect to a reference point" (Melnyk, Stewart, & Swink, 2004 ; Payne, 2006). Metrics provide a scientific yardstick by which other similar systems can be objectively evaluated and enable a system or data set to be assessed in a way that can be defined, standardized, and systematically processed (Palmer, 2002). As Melnyk et al. (2004) and Payne (2006) note, metrics help provide control by enabling managers and workers to evaluate and control different resources, provide a means of communicating performance both internally and externally, and help identify gaps between actual and targeted performance as a basis for improvement. They enable a generic model to be applied to a specific field or situation. As explained next, we thus culled metrics from the literature that were appropriate to data breach systems.

## METHODOLOGY

Our methodology can be divided into two parts: developing a yardstick by which to assess data breach systems and applying that yardstick to the task. Informing both parts of our methodology was the all-important notion of usefulness. We drew on this concept to identify the main stakeholders of data breach notification systems, as well as to select metrics to evaluate such systems. Our assessment thus implicitly reflects the concept of usefulness.

Following Wang and Strong's (1996) model, we assessed data breach notification systems from the perspective of their users. Our first step was to identify these stakeholders, which we did using popular definitions in the literature. As discussed below, we concluded that the key stakeholders were consumers, shareholders, investors, law enforcement, researchers, information security businesses, and the general public, because each would reasonably rely on and use data breach information.

Our second step, designed to enable us to build a yardstick to evaluate data breach notification systems, was to research what each of these stakeholders would want from a data breach system and how they would use the information. To do this we examined the literature and government reports. For example, we consulted the International Association of Chiefs of Police report (International Association of Chiefs of Police, 2005) the Identity Theft Resource Center (Identity Theft Resource Center, 2010a, 2010b), and the Identity Theft Reporting Information System (Office of the Attorney General- State of UTAH, 2011), which discuss what state law enforcement officials say they need in terms of data breach information. We consulted the President's Identity Theft Task Force Report (The President's Identity Theft Task Force- United States, 2008), which includes input from financial institutions, the consumer data industry, and consumer advocacy groups among others regarding what each wants from data breach information systems to protect against identity theft.

We then selected nine metrics from the 15 that Wang and Strong (1996) offer as part of their model. We selected those metrics that were most likely to be useful to stakeholders, as suggested by our research.

We then applied the nine metrics to data breach notification systems in the U.S. This involved a content analysis, a "technique for making inferences by objectively and systematically identifying specified characteristics of messages" (Holsti, 1969) and classifying communications to "some conceptual framework" (Babbie, 2009), of state laws since the state data breach notification systems are largely the creation of such laws (There are no federal data breach notification laws).

Our analysis was led by the following two research questions that encapsulate the focus of our study:

**RQ1:** What is the quality of the information from the data breach systems?
**RQ2:** What is the usefulness of the information from the data breach systems?

Our analysis of state breach notification laws identified six variables. A results table (Table 2) was created indicating the presence or absence of each variable. The variables were an extension of previous research (Open Security Foundation, 2010b; Scott & Scott, 2010). The following were the coding variables:

1. **Variable 1:** A data breach notification law. While most states have these, some do not. The remaining variables apply only to states that have such laws.
2. **Variable 2:** A requirement that breach data be centralized at state level.
3. **Variable 3:** A provision imposing a civil or criminal penalty on companies that fail to promptly report and notify customers of data breaches. Such a provision may affect the timeliness of information.
4. **Variable 4:** A private right of action provision. This right allows private citizens to sue an organization that violates the law (1A C.J.S. Actions § 56, 2010).
5. **Variable 5:** A reporting exception if the breached documents were encrypted.
6. **Variable 6:** A reporting exception if there is an ongoing criminal investigation.
7. **Variable 7:** A reporting exception for immaterial breaches, or breaches that did not seem to result in the disclosure of critical personal information.

We analyzed the effects of these variables on the quality of data breach information as measured by data quality metrics below.

## CREATING THE YARDSTICK BY WHICH TO EVALUATE DATA BREACH NOTIFICATION SYSTEMS

### Identifying the Key Stakeholders

To identify stakeholders of data breach notification systems, we referred to the definition in the literature of stakeholders as groups who have an interest in and benefit from a system (Freeman, 1984; Phillips, Freeman, & Wicks, 2003). Phillips et al. (2003) specifically explain that, when an institution expressly or implicitly encourages another to rely on its continuing to do certain things, -- to expect that it will continue to do them and to make decisions in part based on that supposition, -- the institution owes a moral obligation to that person, who is, on that basis, deemed a stakeholder. So this definition of a stakeholder inherently reflects something of the notion of usefulness – as someone who would reasonably rely on and use a system. Under this definition, key stakeholders of data breach notification systems would include consumers, shareholders and investors, law enforcement, researchers, information security businesses, and the general public.

Consumers, for instance, as the victims of breaches, would need data breach information for self-protection. Being told that someone may have hacked into their personal data would enable them to take voluntary protective steps (Cavoukian, 2009) such as placing identity locks on their credit records with credit reporting agencies. Shareholders and investors would rely on data breach information to evaluate the investment risks that companies pose. Knowing that a company is or has been subject to a breach would let investors and shareholders gauge its value, for breaches can hurt a company's share price, reputation, and market appeal (Javelin Strategy and Research, 2008).

Law enforcement officials are another major stakeholder. They have repeatedly said that they need better breach data to fight cybercrime (Gross, 2009).

Researchers have an interest in data breach information to explain the incidence, patterns, trends, and root causes of cyber crime.

The general public would have a reasonable expectation and interest that breach data be available to those who could use it to build trust in society's economic and social institutions. Making data available would also give businesses stronger incentives to improve security (Cavoukian, 2009), which benefits the public.

## Determining what the Stakeholders Would Need from Data Breach Systems

To examine what would make a data breach information system useful to stakeholders, we studied documents and reports that offered feedback from various stakeholders.

To be useful to law enforcement agencies, reports suggest that data breach information should enable them to monitor data breach trends, take immediate action where there have been significant breaches, and implement anti-cyber crime strategies (International Association of Chiefs of Police, 2005). The Justice Department said that it needs comprehensive statistics on data breaches and resulting identity theft to understand and properly respond to the menace (The President's Identity Theft Task Force- United States, 2008). The U.S. Department of Homeland Security said that one of its key strategic cyber-crime objectives is prevention (U.S. Department of Homeland Security, 2008). All this requires data that is timely and accurate. Data should also be presented in a way that enables investigators to count the total number of security data breaches and the number of records per breach, as this would let them gauge the frequency and severity of data breach occurrences, which is important for fighting hacking (Identity Theft Resource Center, 2008, 2010c; Open Security Foundation, 2010a).

To be useful to consumers, shareholders, and investors, breach information should enable them to determine which organizations can be trusted and to evaluate a company's financial risk profile (The President's Identity Theft Task Force- United States, 2008). An analysis of 22 data breach events shows that the average stock price loss after a data breach was nearly 5.6% over a three-day period after the news of the event (Garg, Curtis, & Halper, 2003). Seventeen of the 22 events studied resulted in an average loss of $918 million per event. To estimate the cost of a breach to the firm, investors and shareholders would also want to know its severity and the number of people affected, as this would give insight into the expenses that the company will incur to implement preventive controls and inform affected consumers.

To be useful to security businesses, breach information should additionally be timely and detailed enough so that they can decide how to direct research and development expenditures to best anticipate market needs (Cavoukian, 2009).

To be useful to researchers, the data should offer a basis for trend analysis as well as for future research (Romanosky, Telang, & Acquisti, in press).

To be useful to the public, the information should add social value to society in general (Wilson, 1887) and promote the efficiency of the free market system in particular. With access to accurate, timely, and clear information, consumers, investors, and others could direct capital to those companies that put a premium on data safety over those that do not (Stiglitz, 2003), benefiting the public welfare.

## Selecting Nine Data Quality Evaluation Metrics

Wang and Strong (1996) offer 15 metrics for evaluating data quality. Of these, we culled the following nine as most applicable to the needs of stakeholders.

The first metric, "completeness," refers to the "extent to which data is of sufficient breadth, depth and scope for the task at hand" (Wang & Strong, 1996). Applied to a data breach system, completeness would assess the extent to which the system offered breach information from every affected organization as well as the extent to which all compromised records in each organization were reported. Completeness would be useful to all the major stakeholders that we identified.

Wang and Strong (1996) define the second metric, "consistent representation," as the extent to which information is presented in the same format. Applied to the data breach information area this would measure the degree to which information is provided in a uniform format, regardless of the state from which it originates. Consistent representation would be crucial stakeholders such as law enforcement agencies, as it would facilitate communication and data sharing between breach notification systems and the development of nation-wide anti-cyber fraud initiatives.

The third metric, "ease of manipulation," refers to the extent to which information is easy to manipulate and apply to different tasks (Wang & Strong, 1996). This would matter to stakeholders who need to sort the data in multiple ways. Thus while researchers would probably want to be able to sort data on the basis of the total number of breached records across the nation, state law enforcement officers might need to examine only breaches affecting their state. Further, the more manipulable or easy to use the data is, the more likely the system is to gain acceptance by a broad range of users. Studies show that the behavioral intention to accept a new system is proportional to its perceived ease of use (Davis, 1989).

The metric, "accuracy," would measure the degree to which data is correct, reliable, and free from error. Errors in the data breach area can crop up in the data breach information at any stage of reporting input and processing due to the involvement of various parties. Human error is a significant but often ignored cause of common data inaccuracies (Wood & Banks, 1993). All the stakeholders would likely care about accuracy. Take consumers. A data entry error when capturing the address of an affected consumer would mean that the notification letter may not reach them, increasing their exposure to risk.

*"Interpretability," or the extent to which information is in appropriate languages, symbols, and units and the definitions are clear (Wang & Strong, 1996), would be relevant to many stakeholders' needs. If each state defines what qualifies as a reportable data breach differently, or each law's definitions are internally ambiguous, it would be virtually impossible for, say, researchers or law enforcement officers to run comparisons and trend analyses on the data. The former would result in inconsistent application of data breach laws across the U.S.; the latter, in misinterpretations and uncertainty (White & Fisher, 2008).*

The sixth relevant metric is "objectivity," the extent to which information is unbiased, unprejudiced and impartial (Wang & Strong, 1996). In the data breach area, objectivity could mean the degree to which what constitutes a data breach is defined and the information is reported without a vested interest in the outcome. It could also mean the degree to which data breach definitions are standardized across states. The degree to which these are objective would reflect the essential quality of the information, going to its fitness for a variety of stakeholder use from researchers and investors to consumers and law enforcement.

The seventh metric, "reputation," is the extent to which information is highly regarded in terms of its source and content. Reputation is essential to the perception of data accuracy and objectivity. Data breach information collection is a tedious and expensive process. The less credible the information source, the less value it will have for all the stakeholders we identified (Strong et al., 1997).

"Security," another applicable metric, refers to the extent to which access to data is restricted to maintain its security (Wang & Strong, 1996). The three key pillars of information security demand that the "confidentiality, integrity and availability" of information must at all times be protected (Whitman & Mattord, 2005). The importance of security as a key measure of the quality of data is evidenced by the fact that businesses require information that is "reliable, of high integrity and that guards privacy" (Schweitzer, 1987). Security in the data breach area would thus measure the extent to which data on public websites is protected from hacking and from modification or deletion by non-authorized personnel. This metric would provide information useful to all identified stakeholders, ranging from consumers because they may be directly affected, to shareholders and analysts, because the lower firms are on security, the more vulnerable they may be to lawsuits.

Lastly, the metric "timeliness" measures the extent to which the information is sufficiently up-to-date for the task at hand. In the data breach context, timeliness would measure how quickly the breach information was captured and made available in the notification system (Buehler et al., 2004). The timeliness of leads makes all the difference to whether law enforcement officials can use it to apprehend cyber criminals. It also matters to shareholders and analysts who need to make quick decisions.

## FINDINGS: EVALUATING DATA BREACH NOTIFICATION SYSTEMS

### Applying the Metrics to State Data Breach Information Systems: A Content Analysis

Data breach information systems in the U.S. are primarily a state affair. Many states have laws requiring data breach information collection. There is, however, no federal law that requires the collection of such data – though there are some nonprofit organizations that aggregate data from across the country. This Part evaluates the quality of data collected through these two systems: state laws and national nonprofits.

State data breach notification laws are recent and evolving. The first state to pass such a law, California, did so in 2002 (Cal. Civ. Code § 1798.29 (2009)). The most recent state to do so is Mississippi, which enacted its law in April 2010. (H.B. 583, 2010 Leg., Reg. Sess. (MS 2010)). Today, forty-seven states have data breach reporting laws (Table 2).

A typical breach notification law is California's. Enacted in September 2002, the law requires any person, business, or state agency in California to disclose security breaches to those whose unencrypted personal information has been, or is reasonably believed to have been, accessed by an unauthorized person (Cal. Civ. Code § 1798.29 (2009)). Disclosure is to be made expeditiously. However, an exception is provided if a law enforcement agency determines that notification may impede a criminal investigation (Cal. Civ. Code § 1798.29 (2009)). Over 46 states adopted data breach laws, most modeled after California's.

Application of our selected metrics to state data breach information suggests that the data, as a whole, scores mostly poorly on metrics such as consistency, ease of manipulation, and interpretability. The data is not concise, but fragmented and decentralized among the different databases across the forty-seven states that have data breach notification laws. Some of the information is relatively accessible; other is not. Of the forty-seven states that have data breach laws, only 12 require that breach information be reported to a central database (generally in a state law enforcement agency). The data, moreover, is reported in different formats, making integration difficult. There is no standardized reporting structure to control and validate what is being reported. Data in the other 35 states where no central reporting is required is relatively inaccessible. Further, some states task a variety of offices with data security breach notification. For example, in the event that any "New York residents are to be notified, the person or business shall notify the state attorney general, the consumer protection board, and the state office of cyber security" (N.Y. Gen. Bus. Law §899-aa (8)(a) (2005)). The data could be in any one of three offices, heightening the likelihood of data inconsistency, particularly when one office updates material, but the others do not.

State data also scores low on manipulability. Most data reported to states is on paper forms. The best electronic version that the states can offer is a PDF paper scan, which is difficult to manipulate, as the data may not be machine-readable.

The data scores poorly on the interpretability metric. There is no standardized data breach definition among the states (White & Fisher, 2008). Indeed, there are almost as many definitions as there are states (White & Fisher, 2008).

Data breach systems score poorly on the security metric. Those states that post data breach documents on central websites make all of the source documents publicly accessible. This means that contact information that should be private is public. It means that letters detailing the methods used to penetrate the company may be read and serve as a blueprint for aspiring hackers anywhere.

The data also fares poorly on the bias and data completeness metrics. Consider: 45 states have criminal investigation exceptions. This means that the police in these states, may withhold breach information from being reported publicly pending their investigations.

Thirty-seven states have exemptions for data breach incidents involving data that was encrypted, as if consumers' personal information were out of danger and therefore not in need of reporting just because it was encrypted. However, while some encryption systems may be effective, any are less so. Princeton University researchers recently demonstrated a flaw that renders most disk encryption algorithms useless if the intruder obtains physical access to the device, which is common in cases of stolen laptops, computer desktops left unattended in sleep mode, or when displaying the password prompt screen (Halderman et al., 2009). More evidence that encryption is not a failsafe is the computer intrusion at TJX incorporation. Over 45 million customer records were lost because the firm was using a weak encryption protocol (WEP) (Ngugi, Dardick, & Vega, 2009).

Twenty-six states have "immaterial breach" exemptions. California's law, for instance, considers any breach that is not "reasonably likely to subject the customer to unauthorized disclosure of personal information" (Cal. Civ. Code § 1798.29 (2009)) to be immaterial and thus exempt from its notification requirements. The business decides what material is and what isn't.

This last point raises questions about how the data scores on the objectivity metric. State breach notification laws generally allow breached companies to determine whether the relevant breach is too immaterial to be reported. Considering the often brutal pressures that companies face to safeguard their reputations and profits, it is not hard to imagine which way most of them would decide. Indeed, in almost any other arena, giving this decision to firms would be considered a conflict of interest (Carson, 1994), casting doubt on the decisions' objectivity.

Even when companies report a breach, they often fail to report crucial information about the extent and severity of the breach (Identity Theft Resource Center, 2010b). In about 46% of the cases where companies report a breach, they indicate that the number of breached records is not known (Identity Theft Resource Center, 2010b). While firms may only learn the precise number of breached records after a detailed forensic analysis, intelligent estimates are possible and would help stakeholders such as law enforcement agencies prioritize resources in responding to breach cases.

The data also fares poorly on the timeliness metric. Given that criminal investigations can take months, if not years, and that 45 states allow companies to withhold reporting data until such investigations are complete, data is often stale by the time it is released.

As a whole, therefore, state data breach notification systems do not yield quality data according to the nine metrics that we determined would be most useful to stakeholders.

## Evaluating Nation-Wide Data Breach Information Systems

There is no federal law requiring the reporting of data breaches. However, a number non-profit organizations supply breach information on a country-wide basis. The oldest, the Open Security Foundation, operating under the name "Data-LossDB," regularly scouts news feeds, blogs and other websites for data breaches and enters them into its database (DataLossDB, 2010). In operation for 21 years, it collects the latest data breach notification information under each state law through Freedom of Information Law requests.

The Identity Theft Resource Center (ITRC), another leading nonprofit dedicated "to the understanding and prevention of identity theft" (Identity Theft Resource Center, 2010d), has been maintaining a security breach database on its website, which it updates daily, since 2005. It publishes annual synopses and summaries of data breaches, exploring patterns and trends (Identity Theft Resource Center, 2010a).

The Office of Inadequate Security (http://www.databreaches.net/) and the Privacy Rights Clearing House (http://www.privacyrights.org/) also collect breach information. However, as they report information in a raw, unedited, incident-by-incident format that is difficult to analyze, we do not include them in our assessment.

Since the nonprofits that aggregate data on a country-wide basis draw their information from the states, their data reflects the shortcomings of state data. Additionally, since only 47 states have data breach laws, nation-wide data is not complete or fully representative. The data that these nonprofits supply also is even less timely than state data, for it must be obtained through cumbersome Freedom of Information Law (FOIL) requests. These re-quests must often wade their way through a maze of different state offices and departments, some of which are affected by considerable backlogs, before information is released.

To further illuminate the degree to which distortions affect data collected by the nonprofits, we compared data breach incidents and breached records reported by the ITRC and the Open Security Foundation from January 2005, when ITRC began to collect data, to December 2009 (Table 1).

The last column shows the ratios of the Open Security Foundation data compared to those of the ITRC. The number of reported breach incidents and resulting records breaches vary considerably between the two sources, suggesting that either or both lack accuracy. In 2006 and 2008 the number of record breaches reported by Open Security Foundation is more than double those reported by ITRC.

## RECOMMENDATIONS

This article has argued that current data breach information is seriously flawed. Data breach notification systems must be reformed at state and national levels.

### Previous Reform Attempts

Several legislative reform attempts have been made at the federal level. Two bills are pending in Congress regarding data breach notification: the Data Breach Notification Act ("DBNA") (S 139, 2009) ("Data Breach Notification Act," 2009) introduced in 2005 by Senator Dianne Feinstein (D-Ca), and the Personal Data Privacy and Security Act ("PDPSA") (S 1490, 2009) ("Personal Data Privacy and Security Act of 2009," 2009), introduced by Senator Patrick Leahy (D-Vt) in 2009. Both bills would require businesses to inform consumers "without unreasonable delay" if their personal identity information has been breached (S 129 §2(b)(1)(B); S 1490 §311(c)(1)). The bills empower the Attorney General to fine companies that fail to do so up to $1,000 a day per affected person up to a maximum of $1 million per violation (S 139 §8(a); S 1490 §317(a)).

Neither the DBNA nor PDPSA would, however, create a database that could be a repository for comprehensive data breach information that would be as useful as it could be for stakeholders. Although both bills require businesses to notify the Secret Service of security breaches (S 139 §7(b); S 1490 §316(b)), Secret Service notification applies only if over 10,000 people are affected, the breach involves a database that contained personal information on over one million people nationwide, the database is owned by the US government, or the business knows that the affected people are employees and contractors of the US government involved in national security or law enforcement (S 139, §7(a) 2009; S 1490, §316(a), 2009). Barring these conditions, businesses have no obligation to report breaches to the Secret Service.

The upshot would be to leave major gaps in breach reporting since most breaches do not meet the bills' criteria, thus scoring poorly on the completeness metric. For example, out of 3064 data breaches recorded by the Open Security Foundation as of January 3rd, 2011, only 691 breaches had more than 10,000 records breached (Open Security Foundation, 2011). This would mean that only 22.6% of the breaches would have been reported as per the above bills criteria. The bulk

of data security breaches in the U.S. are relatively small breaches that afflict small businesses. However, the aggregate number of victims and total amount of money lost can be substantial. Indeed, the DBNA's and PDPSA's provision that a breach must affect at least 10,000 before it needs to be reported to the Secret Service may push hackers even more to smaller, more frequent attacks, as these would more likely evade the Secret Service.

Nor do the DBNA's and PDPSA's requirement that businesses alert the major media in a state of security breaches that affect its residents (S 139 §4; S 1490 §313) offer an adequate alternative avenue for stakeholders to gather such information. First, the bills' media notification requirements are only triggered if over 5,000 state residents are affected (S 139 §4(2); S 1490 §313(2)). Second, there is no requirement that, even if information is reported, that the media publish it.

The bills also fare poorly on the objectivity metric. Consumer notification requirements are central to both bills. However, the DBNA and PDPSA provide for major loopholes -- "safe harbor" exemptions -- that allow businesses to get out of notifying consumers (1490 §312(b); S 139 §2(b)). Thus the bills allow firms to not inform affected consumers when a risk assessment shows that the security breach posed no significant risk of harm to those individuals (S 1490 §312(b)(1) (A); S 139 §2(b)(1)(A)). Although companies must first notify the Secret Service about the results of their risk assessment and give it ten days to review

*Table 1. Comparison of the number of data breach and data records between 2005 to 2009*

| Year | Identity Theft Resource Center | | Open Security Foundation | | Comparison Ratio (OpenSec/ITRC) | |
|------|------|------|------|------|------|------|
| | Breaches | Records | Breaches | Records | Breaches Ratio | Records Ratio |
| 2009 | 498 | 223,146,989 | 549 | 220,616,421 | 1.10 | 0.99 |
| 2008 | 656 | 35,691,25 | 759 | 86,924,766 | 1.16 | 2.44 |
| 2007 | 446 | 127,717,23 | 499 | 165,210,682 | 1.12 | 1.29 |
| 2006 | 321 | 19,137,84 | 536 | 51,246,706 | 1.67 | 2.68 |
| 2005 | 157 | 66,853,20 | 141 | 55,988,256 | 0.90 | 0.84 |

*Table 2. Results of the content analysis of the 51 states data breach law variables- adapts and extends earlier work (Open Security Foundation, 2010b; Scott & Scott, 2010)*

| Name of State | DB Law | Central DB | Delay Penalty | PrivR Action | Encr Exept | Investig Exept | ImmatBr Except |
|---|---|---|---|---|---|---|---|
| | Variable1 | Variable 2 | Variable 3 | Variable 4 | Variable 5 | Variable 6 | Variable 7 |
| | Does the state have a data base law? | Does the state have a central database to keeps information about security breaches? | Is there any mechanism to deter or punish companies that delay notifying the relevant authorities of a security breach? | Private Right of Action? Some state laws allow for customers to sue the relevant business or agency. In other states there is no private right of action – only the AG can sue. | Some state laws say that, if the data is encrypted, then even if there is a security breach, the business is not liable and therefore has no duty to report or notify. | Some state laws provide that, if the breach or company is under investigation, it does not need to pass along the information to the central authorities. | In some states, if there is no reasonable belief that data is in danger, there is no need to notify. -But who makes this call? |
| Alabama | 0 | 0 | 0 | 0 | 0 | 0 | 0 |
| Alaska | 1 | 0 | 1 | 1 * | 0 | 1 | 1 |
| Arizona | 1 | 0 | 1 | 0 | 1 | 1 | 0 |
| Arkansas | 1 | 0 | 1 | 0 | 1 | 1 | 1 |
| California | 1 | 0 | 0 | 1 | 1 | 1 | 0 |
| Colorado | 1 | 0 | 1 | 0 | 1 | 1 | 1 |
| Connecticut | 1 | 0 | 0 | 0 | 1 | 1 | 1 |
| Delaware | 1 | 0 | 1 | 1 | 1 | 1 | 0 |
| D.of Columbia | 1 | 0 | 1 | 1 | 0 | 1 | 0 |
| Florida | 1 | 0 | 1 | 0 | 1 | 1 | 0 |
| Georgia | 1 | 0 | 0 | 0 | 1 | 1 | 0 |
| Hawaii | 1 | 1 | 1 | 1 | 1 | 1 | 0 |
| Idaho | 1 | 0 | 1 | 0 | 1 | 1 | 1 |
| Illinois | 1 | 0 | 0 | 1 | 1 | 1 | 0 |
| Indiana | 1 | 0 | 0 | 0 | 1 | 1 | 0 |
| Iowa | 1 | 0 | 0 | 0 | 1 | 1 | 1 |
| Kansas | 1 | 0 | 1 | 0 | 1 | 1 | 1 |
| Kentucky | 0 | 0 | 0 | 0 | 0 | 0 | 0 |
| Louisiana | 1 | 0 | 0 | 1 | 0 | 1 | 1 |
| Maine | 1 | 1 | 1 | 0 | 1 | 1 | 0 |
| Maryland | 1 | 1 | 1 | 1 | 1 | 1 | 1 |
| Massachusetts | 1 | 1 | 1 | 0 | 1 | 1 | 1 |
| Michigan | 1 | 0 | 1 | 0 | 1 | 1 | 1 |
| Minnesota | 1 | 0 | 1 | 0 | 1 | 1 | 0 |
| Mississippi | 1 | 0 | 0 | 0 | 1 | 1 | 1 |
| Missouri | 1 | 1 | 1 | 0 | 1 | 1 | 1 |

*continued on following page*

*Table 2. Continued*

| Name of State | DB Law | Central DB | Delay Penalty | PrivR Action | Encr Exept | Investig Exept | ImmatBr Except |
|---|---|---|---|---|---|---|---|
| | Variable1 | Variable 2 | Variable 3 | Variable 4 | Variable 5 | Variable 6 | Variable 7 |
| | Does the state have a data base law? | Does the state have a central database to keeps information about security breaches? | Is there any mechanism to deter or punish companies that delay notifying the relevant authorities of a security breach? | Private Right of Action? Some state laws allow for customers to sue the relevant business or agency. In other states there is no private right of action – only the AG can sue. | Some state laws say that, if the data is encrypted, then even if there is a security breach, the business is not liable and therefore has no duty to report or notify. | Some state laws provide that, if the breach or company is under investigation, it does not need to pass along the information to the central authorities. | In some states, if there is no reasonable belief that data is in danger, there is no need to notify. -But who makes this call? |
| Montana | 1 | 0 | 1 | 0 | 1 | 1 | 0 |
| Nebraska | 1 | 0 | 1 | 1 | 1 | 1 | 1 |
| Nevada | 1 | 0 | 1 | 1 | 1 | 1 | 0 |
| New Hampshire | 1 | 1 | 1 | 0 | 0 | 0 | 0 |
| New Jersey | 1 | 1 | 0 | 0 | 1 | 1 | 1 |
| New Mexico | 0 | 0 | 0 | 0 | 0 | 0 | 0 |
| New York | 1 | 1 | 1 | 0 | 0 | 0 | 0 |
| North Carolina | 1 | 1 | 1 | 1 | 0 | 1 | 1 |
| North Dakota | 1 | 0 | 0 | 0 | 1 | 1 | 0 |
| Ohio | 1 | 0 | 1 | 0 | 0 | 1 | 1 |
| Oklahoma | 1 | 0 | 0 | 0 | 1 | 1 | 0 |
| Oregon | 1 | 0 | 1 | 0 | 1 | 1 | 1 |
| Pennsylvania | 1 | 0 | 1 | 0 | 1 | 1 | 0 |
| Rhode Island | 1 | 0 | 1 | 1 | 1 | 1 | 1 |
| South Carolina | 1 | 1 | 1 | 1 | 1 | 1 | 1 |
| South Dakota | 0 | 0 | 0 | 0 | 0 | 0 | 0 |
| Tennessee | 1 | 0 | 0 | 1 | 1 | 1 | 0 |
| Texas | 1 | 0 | 1 | 0 | 0 | 1 | 0 |
| Utah | 1 | 0 | 1 | 0 | 1 | 1 | 1 |
| Vermont | 1 | 1 | 1 | 0 | 1 | 1 | 1 |
| Virginia | 1 | 1 | 0 | 1 | 1 | 1 | 1 |
| Washington | 1 | 0 | 0 | 1 | 1 | 1 | 1 |
| West Virginia | 1 | 0 | 1 | 0 | 1 | 1 | 1 |
| Wisconsin | 1 | 0 | 0 | 0 | 0 | 1 | 0 |
| Wyoming | 1 | 0 | 1 | 0 | 0 | 1 | 1 |
| Sum | 31 | 11 | 22 | 10 | 23 | 29 | 19 |

those results (S 1490, §312(b)(2)); S 139 §2(b)(1) (B) and (C)), the bills stack the deck in favor of firms that use "best practices" methods such as redaction and access controls (S 1490, §312(b)(1) (B); S 139 §2(b)(2)(A) and (B)). The DBNA and PDPSA provide that there is a presumption that "no significant harm exists" to consumers if the business in question followed such best practices methods (S 1490, §312(b)(1)(B); S 139 §2(b) (2)(A) and (B)). The PDPSA further provides that a firm's use of encryption may also create a presumption that no significant risk exists to consumers (S 1490, §312(b)(1)(A1)).

The problem with all this is that security breaches do occur in companies that are following best practices methods such as redaction, access controls, and encryption. Thus the bills set up a hollow presumption of no-harm that would reduce the likelihood of consumer notification when it may well be needed.

Lastly, the bills weaken consumers' rights to be informed by expressing granting consumers no private cause of action, meaning that they cannot sue businesses for failing to comply with the bills (S 139 §(9)(f); S 1490 §318(f)).

## Our Recommendations

The bills do have some benefits, however. First, the fact that they would be federal laws suggests that they would enhance data quality under the consistent representation metric. Presumably information collected under any federally mandated reporting system would be centralized and hence consistent in format. We would thus urge the passage of either of these federal legislative proposals with, however, certain key modifications and additions. Our modifications flow from stakeholders' need for the database to be comprehensive, representative, and unbiased. The DBNA and PDPSA require notification only if the number of affected individuals exceed certain thresholds. They also exempt firms from having

to report breaches if the firms determine that the breach poses no significant risk of harm and give firms that use best practices methods the benefit of the doubt. We would require all breaches, no matter how small and no matter whether the firm uses best practices or believes the breach to be immaterial, to be reported. As discussed earlier, information must be as complete as possible to be most useful to stakeholders.

The DBNA and PDPSA also gloss over many other measures of data quality that stakeholders care about such as manipulability, interpretability, accuracy, security, and timeliness. We would add requirements to the bills to specifically ensure that each of these metrics above is addressed.

For example, to enhance the clarity and consistency of the data, we suggest that the law require a uniform reporting form, such as the one used by the FBI (The President's Identity Theft Task Force- United States, 2008). To facilitate the integration of new data into the main database system, the law should require organizations to report breaches electronically. This is doable. Most data breaches involve electronic records. So the organization would simply be submitting an electronic file in a format similar to what has been breached. Reported information should also be sufficiently detailed so as to enable law enforcement agencies to conduct investigations.

We further urge that the resulting integrated database be managed by an appropriate national agency, such as the Department of Justice, or an existing unit, such as the FBI's Center on Cyber Security. The purpose of placing the database in one of these agencies' control would be to make some high-profile body responsible for ensuring the information's timeliness, accuracy, and security.

Regarding security and when to withhold data, the agency managing the database should draw on investigative guidelines that promote judicious consideration and due process in such conduct.

## CONTRIBUTIONS, LIMITATIONS AND FUTURE WORK

This study fills a gap in the data breach scholarship by developing an evaluation yardstick for data breach notification systems from the point of view of their stakeholders. The analysis exposes critical flaws and offers recommendations for reform.

This study is limited in that it relies mostly on a content analysis of documentary data, using interviews minimally. Ideally, data would be collected by triangulating several research methods (Cohen & Manion, 2000). Future studies might thus include a greater use of interviews and surveys. Also, some of the information required to assess the usefulness of current data breach information to security agencies was privileged and hence inaccessible. Future work could remedy this by increased collaboration with law enforcement agencies.

## REFERENCES

Babbie, E. (2009). *The practice of social research* (10th ed.). Wadsworth, UK: Thomson Learning.

Baltzan, P., & Phillips, A. (2009). *Essentials of business driven information systems*. New York, NY: McGraw-Hill/Irwin.

Bovee, M., Srivastava, R. P., & Mak, B. (2003). A conceptual framework and belief-function approach to assessing overall information quality. *International Journal of Intelligent Systems, 18*(1), 51–74. doi:10.1002/int.10074

Breach Notification Act, D. 11th Congress, S.139 Cong. Rec. § 2 (2009).

Buehler, J. W., Hopkins, R. S., Overhage, J. M., Sosin, D. M., & Tong, V. (2004). *Framework for evaluating public health surveillance systems for early detection of outbreaks: Recommendations from the CDC Working Group*. Retrieved from http://www.cdc.gov/mmwr/preview/mmwrhtml/rr5305a1.htm

Carson, T. (1994). Conflicts of interest. *Journal of Business Ethics, 13*(5), 387–404. doi:10.1007/BF00871766

Cavoukian, A. (2009). *A discussion paper on privacy externalities, security breach notification and the role of independent oversight*. Retrieved from http://www.ipc.on.ca/images/Resources/privacy_externalities.pdf

Cohen, L., & Manion, L. (2000). *Research methods in education* (5th ed.). London, UK: Routledge. doi:10.4324/9780203224342

DataLossDB. (2010). *About DataLossDB*. Retrieved June, 15, 2010, from http://datalossdb.org/about

Davis, F. D. (1989). Perceived usefulness, perceived ease of use, and user acceptance of information technology. *Management Information Systems Quarterly, 13*(3), 319–340. doi:10.2307/249008

Federal Trade Commission. (2010). *Consumer Sentinel Network Data Book for January- December 2009*. Retrieved from http://www.ftc.gov/sentinel/reports/sentinel-annual-reports/sentinel-cy2009.pdf

Federal Trade Commission. (2011). *Consumer Sentinel Network Data Book for January -December 2010*. Retrieved from http://www.ftc.gov/sentinel/reports/sentinel-annual-reports/sentinel-cy2010.pdf

Fisher, C. W., Chengalur-Smith, I., & Ballou, D. P. (2003). The impact of experience and time on the use of data quality information in decision making. *Information Systems Research, 14*(2), 170–188. doi:10.1287/isre.14.2.170.16017

Freeman, E. (1984). *Strategic management: A stakeholder approach*. Boston, MA: Pitman.

Garg, A., Curtis, J., & Halper, H. (2003). Quantifying the financial impact of IT security breaches. *Information Management & Computer Security, 11*(2). doi:10.1108/09685220310468646

Gross, G. (2009, October 28). FBI: National data-breach law would help fight cybercrime. *PCWorld*.

Halderman, J. A., Seth, D. S., Nadia, H., William, C., William, P., & Joseph, A. C. (2009). Lest we remember: Cold-boot attacks on encryption keys. *Communications of the ACM, 52*(5), 91–98. doi:10.1145/1506409.1506429

Holsti, O. R. (1969). *Content analysis for the social sciences and humanities*. Reading, MA: Addison-Wesley.

Identity Theft Resource Center. (2008). *2007 ITRC Breach Report*. Retrieved August, 26, 2009, from http://idtheftmostwanted.org/ITRC%20 Breach%20Report%202007.pdf

Identity Theft Resource Center. (2010a). *Data Breaches*. Retrieved June 15, 2010, from http:// www.idtheftcenter.org/artman2/publish/lib_survey/ITRC_2008_Breach_List.shtml

Identity Theft Resource Center. (2010b). *Data Breaches: A Black Hole*. Retrieved July 14, 2010, from http://www.idtheftcenter.org/artman2/publish/headlines/Data_Breaches_1H_2010.shtml

Identity Theft Resource Center. (2010c). *Identity Theft Resource Center: 2009 Breach List*. Retrieved March 4, 2010, from http://www.idtheftcenter.org/artman2/uploads/1/ITRC_Breach_Report_20100106.pdf

Identity Theft Resource Center. (2010d). *Identity Theft Resource Center®, Nonprofit Organization*. Retrieved July 7, 2010, from http://www.idtheftcenter.org/

International Association of Chiefs of Police. (2005). *Local Law Enforcement's Response to Identity Theft Crimes*. Retrieved May, 4, 2011, from http://www.theiacp.org/Portals/0/pdfs/ WhatsNew/IdentityTheft.pdf

Javelin Strategy and Research. (2008). *Consumer Survey in Data Breach Notification*. Retrieved July 25, 2010, from http://www.tawpi.org/uploadDocs/ Data_Breach_survey.pdf

Javelin Strategy and Research. (2010a). *2010 Data Breach Prevention and Response: Causes, Consumer Consequences, and Tools for Layered Defense*. Retrieved July 20, 2010, from https://www. javelinstrategy.com/uploads/1016.R_2010%20 Data%20Breach%20Prevention%20and%20 Response%20Sample%20Report.pdf

Javelin Strategy and Research. (2010b). *2010 Identity Fraud Survey Report*. Retrieved July 10, 2010, from https://www.javelinstrategy.com/ research/Brochure-170

Juran, J., & Godfrey, B. (1999). *Juran's quality handbook* (5th ed.). New York, NY: McGraw-Hill.

Melnyk, S. A., Stewart, D. M., & Swink, M. (2004). Metrics and performance measurement in operations management: Dealing with the metrics maze. *Journal of Operations Management, 22*(3), 209–218. doi:10.1016/j.jom.2004.01.004

Ngugi, B., Dardick, G., & Vega, G. (2009). Lessons from computer intrusion at TJX. *The CASE Journal, 3*(2).

Office of the Attorney General- State of UTAH. (2011). *Identity Theft Reporting Information System (IRIS)*. Retrieved from http://www.idtheft. utah.gov/iris.html

Open Security Foundation. (2010a). *Data Loss Statistics*. Retrieved July 20, 2010, from http:// datalossdb.org/statistics

Open Security Foundation. (2010b). *State-by-State Listing of Data Loss and Freedom of Information Legislation*. Retrieved July 10, 2010, from http://datalossdb.org/us_states

Open Security Foundation. (2011). *DataLoss Database*. Retrieved January 3, 2011, from http:// datalossdb.org/download

Palmer, J. W. (2002). Website usability, design and performance metrics. *Information Systems Research, 13*(2), 151–162. doi:10.1287/ isre.13.2.151.88

Payne, S. (2006). *A Guide to Security Metrics-SANS Security Essential GSEC Practical Assignment Version 1.2e*. Retrieved November 5, 2010, from http://www.sans.org/reading_room/whitepapers/auditing/guide-security-metrics_55

Personal Data Privacy and Security Act of 2009, 111th Congress, S.1490 Cong. Rec. (2009).

Phillips, R., Freeman, E., & Wicks, A. (2003). What stakeholder theory is not. *Business Ethics Quarterly*, *13*(4), 479–502.

Privacy Commissioner -Canada, & Information & Privacy Commissioner-Alberta. (2007). *Report of an Investigation into the Security, Collection and Retention of Personal Information at TJX*. Retrieved from http://www.scribd.com/doc/47024592/TJX-Investigation-Report-P2007-IR-0061

Romanosky, S., Telang, R., & Acquisti, A. (in press). Do data breach disclosure laws reduce identity theft? *Journal of Policy Analysis and Management*.

Schweitzer, J. (1987). How security fits in — A management view: Security is essential for quality information. *Computers & Security*, *6*(2), 129–132. doi:10.1016/0167-4048(87)90083-6

Scott & Scott. (2010). *State Data Breach Notification Laws*. Retrieved June 20, 2010, from http://www.scottandscottllp.com/resources/state_data_breach_notification_law.pdf

Stiglitz, J. E. (2003). *Globalization and its discontents*. New York, NY: W. W. Norton.

Strong, D., & Lee, Y., W., & Wang, R., Y. (1997). Data quality in context. *Communications of the ACM*, *40*(5), 103–110. doi:10.1145/253769.253804

The President's Identity Theft Task Force- United States. (2008). *President's Identity Theft Task Force Report*. Retrieved from http://www.idtheft.gov/reports/IDTReport2008.pdf

U.S. Department of Homeland Security. (2008). *One Team, One Mission, Securing Our Homeland: U.S. Department of Homeland Security Strategic Plan Fiscal Years 2008-2013*. Retrieved from http://www.dhs.gov/xlibrary/assets/DHS_Strat-Plan_FINAL_spread.pdf

Wand, Y., & Wang, R. (1996). Anchoring data quality dimensions in ontological foundations. *Communications of the ACM*, *39*(11), 86–95. doi:10.1145/240455.240479

Wang, R. Y., Storey, V. C., & Firth, C. P. (1995). A framework for analysis of data quality research. *IEEE Transactions on Knowledge and Data Engineering*, *7*(4), 623–640. doi:10.1109/69.404034

Wang, R. Y., & Strong, D. M. (1996). Beyond accuracy: What data quality means to data consumers. *Journal of Management Information Systems*, *12*(4), 5–33.

White, M. D., & Fisher, C. (2008). Assessing our knowledge of identity theft: The challenges to effective prevention and control efforts. *Criminal Justice Policy Review*, *19*(1), 3–24. doi:10.1177/0887403407306297

Whitman, M., & Mattord, H. (2005). *Principles of Information Security* (2nd ed.). Boston, MA: Course Technology.

Wilson, W. (1887). The study of administration. *Political Science Quarterly*, *2*(2), 197–222. doi:10.2307/2139277

Wood, C. C., & Banks, W. W. (1993). Human Error: An overlooked but significant information security problem. *Computers & Security*, *12*(1), 51–60. doi:10.1016/0167-4048(93)90012-T

*This work was previously published in the International Journal of Information Security and Privacy, Volume 5, Issue 4, edited by Hamid Nemati, pp. 31-46, copyright 2011 by IGI Publishing (an imprint of IGI Global).*

# Chapter 16
# Wild–Inspired Intrusion Detection System Framework for High Speed Networks (φ|π) IDS Framework

**Hassen Sallay**
*Imam Muhamad Ibn Saud Islamic University,*
*Saudi Arabia*

**Ouissem Ben Fredj**
*Imam Muhamad Ibn Saud Islamic University,*
*Saudi Arabia*

**Mohsen Rouached**
*Imam Muhamad Ibn Saud Islamic University,*
*Saudi Arabia*

**Khalid Al-Shalfan**
*Imam Muhamad Ibn Saud Islamic University,*
*Saudi Arabia*

**Adel Ammar**
*Imam Muhamad Ibn Saud Islamic University,*
*Saudi Arabia*

**Majdi Ben Saad**
*Imam Muhamad Ibn Saud Islamic University,*
*Saudi Arabia*

## ABSTRACT

*While the rise of the Internet and the high speed networks made information easier to acquire, faster to exchange and more flexible to share, it also made the cybernetic attacks and crimes easier to perform, more accurate to hit the target victim and more flexible to conceal the crime evidences. Although people are in an unsafe digital environment, they often feel safe. Being aware of this fact and this fiction, the authors draw in this paper a security framework aiming to build real-time security solutions in the very narrow context of high speed networks. This framework is called (φ|π) since it is inspired by the eleφant self-defense behavior which yields π (22 security tasks for 7 security targets).*

DOI: 10.4018/978-1-4666-2050-6.ch016

# INTRODUCTION

Our digital environment has a fact and a fiction. The fact is that virtual mice, snakes, bats, camels, foxes and wolfs are there. Mice have no aim except the corruption, snakes spout venom everywhere, bats love to work in the dark, hateful camels look for revenge, foxes and wolf use cunning and Rogan to hit victims and conceal the crime. The fiction is that we often feel safe. Some behave as a peacock, proud of its security arsenal and infrastructure even if the attacks rain cats and dogs. Some others behave as an ostrich, only burying the head in the sand. Some others behave as a spider, protecting themselves by a security infrastructure as weak as a spider web. Being aware of this fact and this fiction, several efforts have been conducted in the literature. We survey briefly in the following some of these efforts from both industrial and academic sides.

From the industrial side, several real security platforms provide integral security solutions. They are known as hybrid IDS (Intrusion Detection System), since they are based on a merging between different techniques. We cite here CheckPoint IPS based mainly on Confidence indexing, Cisco IPS and BreachGate WebDefend based on behavior and statistical analysis, DeepNines BBX IPS, AirDefense Guard and BarbedWire IDS based on protocol analysis and data correlation (García-Teodoro et al., 2009). From academia, we cite the misuse based IDS Snort Inline and Snort with SPADE anomaly plug-in. Snort is largely considered as the de facto IDS (Roesch, 1999). BRO, from Lawrence Berkeley National Laboratory, is compatible with snort and includes semantic analysis at the application layer (Dreger et al., 2006), while EMERALD, from SRI laboratory, considers rule-based discovery and Bayesian networks (http://www.sdl.sri.com/projects/emerald/). Some others are based only on anomaly based techniques such that SPADE, Prelude, nPatrol and Mazu profiler (http://www.prelude-technologies.com/). Other research projects from the academic side yielded

several interesting IDS frameworks and systems such as MINDS IDS from University of Minnesota (Ertoz et al, 2004), Orchids from ENS de Cachan (http://www.lsv.ens-cachan.fr/Software/orchids/), Intelligent IDS from Mississippi State University, GIDRE from University of Granada, Genetic Art- IDS from Northwestern University (García-Teodoro et al., 2009) and anagram form Columbia University. We note that the commercial systems basically tend to use well mature known techniques by enhancing their implementation issues while the research systems tend to use much more innovative techniques. Both sides use a large spectrum of techniques such as statistical methods, clustering techniques, diversification, Bayesian inference, genetic algorithms, payload modeling through n-grams, stochastic modeling, fuzzy logic, data mining and neural networks.

While the aforementioned systems provide interesting functionalities, they only partially satisfy the narrow constraints raised by the high speed network context, mainly the real-time criterion. Recently, new approaches and solutions addressing the huge amounts of transferred network data and increasing speeds of today's networks were proposed. Guinde et al. (2010), Kang et al. (2006), Katashita et al. (2007), Kim et al. (2006), Clark et al. (2006), and Lin et al. (2006) aim to accelerate the speed of detection process by using specialized hardware mainly based on FPGA (Field-Programmable Gate Array) technology. Liberouter project (http://www.liberouter.org/projects.php) introduces the COMBO platform with the FlowMon probe and the IDS probe implemented by FPGA. Akhlaq et al. (2010) and Wenbao et al. (2006) proposed a solution based on traffic load balancing between different IDS sensors. In Akhlaq et al. (2010), the clustering technique was used. The load balancer distributes the traffic among cluster nodes on a predefined policy. The authors proposed a logic-ensured maximum utilization of cluster resources by exchanging state information, load sharing, reducing data loss and performing recovery evaluation procedure to maximize the overall efficiency. Wenbao et al. (2006) presented the design and implementation of a new approach for anomaly detection and classification over high speed networks. Mainly, the proposed approach is based on two phases. The first one is a data reduction phase through flow sampling by focusing mainly on short lived flows. The second step is then a random aggregation of some descriptors such as the number of SYN packets per flow in two different data structures. Salem et al. (2010), Foschini et al. (2008), Schuff et al. (2007), and Vallentin et al. (2007) consider the problem of real-time and scalable stateful intrusion detection for high-speed networks. Basically, the authors state that this problem cannot easily be solved by optimizing the packet matching algorithm utilized by a centralized process or by using custom-developed hardware. Instead, there is a need for a parallel approach that is able to decompose the problem into sub-problems of manageable size to master the complexity and improve the scalability. In this context, Salem, Vaton, and Gravey (2010) presented a novel parallel matching algorithm for the signature-based detection of network attacks. The algorithm is able to perform stateful signature matching and has been implemented only using off-the-shelf components. Foshini, Thapliyal, Cavallaro, Kuregel, and Vigna (2008) proposed novel agent-based distributed IDS which integrates the desirable features provided by the distributed agent-based design methodology with the high accuracy and speed response of the Principal Component Classifier. According to the authors, the simulation results show a satisfactory linear relationship between the degradation of response performance and the scalability of the system. Xie et al. (2006) and Yu et al. (2005) deal with the real-time detection and alert management efficiency. Xie, Quirino, Shyu, Chen, and Chang (2006) provided the design of an intrusion detection system architecture and improved pattern matching arithmetic based on protocol analysis and theorization machine on Frete. The proposed architecture can use a network processor to collect and analyze data in network, which enhances the speed and efficiency in intrusion detection systems. Yu, Dai, Shen, Huang, and Zhu (2005) proposed a distributed intrusion alert fusion scheme based on multiple keywords and routing infrastructure. The experimental results show that their scheme has well scalable qualities, and can achieve significant improvement in load balancing.

We observe that even if some interesting generic standard management frameworks and technologies have been proposed, they need an adaptation and an instantiation for the IDS process in high speed networks. We believe that improving efficiency, real-time and scalability of DIDS (Distributed Intrusion Detection System) in HSN (High-Speed Networks) passes through specifying a dedicated integrated security management framework. Such a framework makes it easier to work with complex technologies and it ensures its good and flexible implementation. The intended framework should couple both technical and management plans. The goal of the work undertaken in our group is to build such a framework to manage DIDS entities. Mainly, our target is to reach a security infrastructure that exhibits an elephant behavior i.e., a security solution that is robust, stable and flexible as an elephant is. Moreover, the elephant is distinguished by its high level of intelligence, an interesting security behavior (i.e., it does not attack others and at the same time it does not permit to be attacked), methods of communication and a complex social structure (Xu et al., 2008; MacDonald, 1999).

The paper is organized as follow. We specify the intended framework and it discusses the framework implementation issues. We present our work in progress and it gives some conclusions together with an outlook for future work. An example of the (φ|π) framework is shown in Figure 1.

## (φ|π) FRAMEWORK SPECIFICATION

Following, we enlighten some similarities of our environment with the elephant one:

### Environment Characteristics

- Elephant inhabits a diverse array of habitats including tropical forests, savannas, grasslands, and woodlands. Vs. Our environment contains a variety of network topologies, technologies and services.
- An elephant's day is nearly spent in feeding. It consumes grasses, small plants, bushes, fruits, twigs, tree bark, and roots. Vs. A network day is nearly spent in feeding (incoming and outgoing traffic). It provides several services such that FTP, HTTP, etc.
- An elephant can drink up to 212 L (55 gal.) of water in less than five minutes. Vs. With High Speed Network we can reach a throughput of 40 gigabits/s.
- In contrast to most mammals, elephant lungs are directly attached to the chest wall and therefore rely on direct muscular action to expand the lungs. Vs. In contrast to most networks, HSN has a DMA (Direct Memory Access) and programmable network cards and we write directly into the memory skipping out the NIC (Network Interface Card) and operating systems latencies.

### Security Threats

- An elephant calf's first year of life is its most vulnerable time with mortality rates exceeding 30%. Vs. A network service's first days of deployment constitute its most vulnerable time with the highest rate of hacking.

- African elephants are threatened by poaching for ivory largely more than Asian ones due to their overall smaller tusk size. Vs. More crucial services and sites are more susceptible to attacks than less crucial ones.
- Anthrax is one of the most fatal diseases impacting elephants. It is a bacterium that causes high fever, shivering, ulcers, and swellings. Vs. Malicious attacks are the most fatal diseases impacting network and computers. They cause high troubling of the network, make the service unstable and provoke congestion in the network links.
- This disease may be spread through contaminated water or soil. Vs. This disease is spread through contaminated packet in the network traffic.

### Identification of Security Design Requirements

- Although, elephants are the largest of all land animals, they are very tactile in nature. They use all parts of their body to interact with one another in all forms of behavior. Behaviors include defensive, exploratory, and anti-predator.
  - **Yields. Scalability, Flexibility & Versatility:** The ability to remain efficient when the traffic and security operations increase, and the ability to add, remove, update and cooperate the different security components inside the network and perform a variety of functions according to different security goals.
- Elephants survived the Asian tsunami in 2004. The complete lack of vision did not hinder the blind elephant's ability to fulfill its leadership role.
  - **Yields. Survivability & fault tolerance:** The ability to resist and survive

in the crisis situations and critical constraints, and the ability to continue functioning even if some security components were defected.

- Moreover, the elephant's feet allow secure movement over uneven terrain and swampy ground.
  - **Yields. Adaptability, accuracy & stability:** The ability to adjust and tune the security system in order to cope with a variety of situations and contexts in real-time.
- Elephants are very autonomous and may live in small group with hierarchal ranking social structure. Their trunks are very powerful, capable of uprooting an entire tree trunk, tearing down heavy branches, and lifting weights in excess of 250 kg.
  - **Yields. Autonomy & robustness:** The ability to self protection without complete relying on third party.
- Leaders protect the front and rear of the herd. More docile bulls serve as stabilizing members within the group. Hierarchical roles are reestablished and readjusted whenever a male leaves or enters the group.
  - **Yields. Specialization & Self organization:** The ability of specification of security roles, their distribution and their readjustment through automatic and self-configuration processes.
- Although primarily solitary in nature, bulls (??) will associate with non natal family units (family units to which they are not related). Bulls do not have preferences for specific family units and will randomly move to different groupings daily and even hourly looking for reproductively receptive females.
  - **Yields. Integration with the legacy & Productivity:** The ability to be open and interact with heterogeneous environments to maximize the pro-

duction through searching for more fertile techniques and technologies.

- Elephants have benefic impact by creating trails that other animals and humans use to travel. The tusks are used to dig wells, generating multiple water sources throughout the habitat. As elephants have large size, this helps bring down vegetation, which then become accessible to smaller species.
  - **Yields. Accessibility and sharing:** The ability to have benefic impact on computer security society by opening new research tracks for the security community. By opening the code and sharing the product for free, security solutions become accessible for individual people and small institutions.

## Identification of Security Tasks and Components

Elephants have the biggest brain of any land mammal, highly developed cerebrums involved in movement and muscle coordination, and large temporal lobes which facilitate memory. Elephants have excellent long-term memory (for decades) and are capable of remembering experiences for long periods of time. The elephant's trunk is an extension of the upper lip and nose. It functions for grasping, breathing, feeding, dusting, smelling, drinking, lifting, sound production/communication, defense/protection, and sensing. Elephants' trunks and their keen sense of smell are used to survey the environment. Through this process, elephants are capable of locating water sources up to 19.2 km (12 mi.) away and can even determine the reproductive status of distant elephants. The eyes of an elephant are located on the sides of the head and therefore provide better peripheral vision (angle of vision extending from the sides to the rear), rather than binocular vision (eyes located on the front of the face, in which fields of vision overlap, creating depth perception). The

*Figure 1. (φ|π) Framework (22 tasks, 7 targets)*

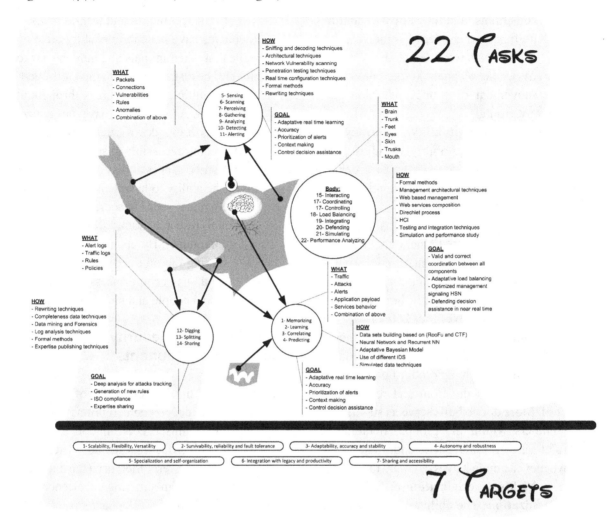

tsunami's approaching vibrations are detected by the elephant's feet and alerts for the approaching storm. The soles of elephant feet assist in the detection of seismic vibrations. Elephant's skin is sensitive to touch, detects insects and changes in its environment. To supplement the diet, elephants dig up earth to obtain salt and minerals. The tusks are used to churn the ground. The elephant then places dislodged pieces of soil into its mouth, to obtain nutrients. By digging, vital minerals are made accessible to other animals and provide valuable food and shelter resources for a diverse array of native wildlife. Finally, the elephant uses all parts of their body to interact with one another in all forms of behavior. Moreover, the elephant's body is very powerful and capable of delivering a forceful blow in self-defense [24,25].

## Brain-Trunk Feet (B-T-F) Component

The B-T-F component should improve the accuracy of detection, permit a prioritization of packet per severity and correlation of alerts, make application context detection and assist to the Control decision. The main idea is to integrate the probabilistic models, feed-forward neural networks (NN), and recurrent neural networks (RNN) to provide an efficient adaptive real-time learning. Basically, the main tasks of this component are:

1. Memorizing all IDS related data and prepare them to the learning process. We complete incomplete data (dataset or logs etc) by using simulated data techniques.
2. Correlating between the different IDS data types (alerts, attacks, etc). Basically we should correlate alerts generated by several IDS types (anomaly-based, misuse-based and specification-based IDS).
3. Learning inclemently about different security aspects. Basically, we should identify the main important features by using NN, reduce the number of features without losing their meanings and impacts by using Principal Component Analysis and integrate the probabilistic models, NN, and RNN to provide an efficient adaptive real-time learning.
4. Predicting different security related behaviors. Mainly, we should predict (1) Traffic behavior (2) Attack behavior (3) Flow behavior (connections) (3) Packets/flow containing attacks per service (4) Packets/flow containing specific attack or class of attack (5) Specific Service behavior and (6) Packet/flow containing tunneled attacks. The prediction model should improve the real-time and the accuracy of the IDS detection process by deeply scanning the predicted suspected malicious packets.
5. Assisting the administrator decision by providing attack classes, alert priorities (security severity level) and service behavior status. Integrating in real-time the manager decision, his new policies, service and traffic behavior to update the learning and decision process in real-time.

The BTF data input is a set of datasets describing (1) the Traffic (2) the Attacks (3) the Alerts (4) the Application payload (5) the Services behavior or a combination of the 5 previous inputs. The input can be obtained from KDD data set, IDSheild data set or through building new data sets based on RootFu and CTF traces.

## Trunk-Eyes-Mouth (T-E-M) Component

The T-E-M component should implement an efficient sniffing and adaptive load balancing strategies to provide a real-time and accurate detection process through a deep analyzing of packets at network and host sides. It should insure a near real-time scanning of the entire environment (network and hosts), perform some penetration testing for the detected vulnerabilities, update the detection rules based on an accurate vulnerabilities scanning report. Finally, it should provide a real-time alerting in case of attacks detection. Basically, the main tasks of this component are:

1. Feeding from the network through an efficient data sniffing by optimizing sniffing and preprocessing by several techniques such as optimization for a specific network service (i.e., HTTP), using a filtered input network data-flow and opt to a real-time configuration in order to get an optimization for a specific HW/SW configuration.
2. Splitting the sniffed data to make an efficient adaptive real-time load balancing between the different IDS sensors. Architectural techniques implementing load balancing based on new approaches such as choquet integration and dirichlet process to improve real-time and efficiency of detection process.
3. Scanning hosts and network to assess the security vulnerabilities. Specializing the detection process to our specific platform through a network and host vulnerability

scanning process using scanning tools such as Nessus and OpenVAS etc.

4. Perceiving the network security status by performing penetration testing scenarios to improve the accuracy of the vulnerability report. Penetration testing techniques can be made using some well known tools such as metasploit, etc.

5. Detecting the malicious attacks in the packet and connection on both incoming and outgoing traffic. The detection algorithm and strategies should be assisted by BTF component. Mainly, we can improve real-time and accuracy of IDS sensor detection by giving more care to the predicted suspected malicious packets

6. Inspecting the tunneled and/or encrypted packet at the host end to improve the accuracy of the detection process. We should also make a context aware (i.e., application layer) detection in the network side for the tunneled and encrypted traffic.

7. Alerting the security administrator, in real-time, of all detected attacks. Specifying alerts' format and alerting strategies to notify the administrator of a detected attack.

The TEM data input is a set of (1) network traffic sniffed packets (2) network traffic sniffed connections (3) the vulnerabilities report (4) the misuse IDS detection rules (5) the network anomaly behavior specification or a combination of the 5 previous inputs. The input can be gotten from a specific network card interface sniffing software traces such as wireshark traces, vulnerability scanning reports, Snort and Bro rules, and anomalies files.

## Tusks-Skin (T-S) Component

The T-S component should improve the efficiency of the detection process by including the specification based detection ingredient in the framework. Through formal methods techniques, we can detect the deviation against a correct behavior of network services specification. Once detected, a security rule should be generated and published. Basically, the main tasks of this component are:

1. Specifying different service policies which describe the normal behavior that should be admitted in the network. For such purpose we should cope with the standard service protocols specification, compliantly with the ISO security guidelines and recommendations. The specification will be translated to event calculus by a specific generator. The main idea is to use the formal methods to discover new attacks.

2. Preprocessing the data of different logs (traffic, alert etc.) to translate them to event calculus data logs. We use some special techniques to solve the problem of data log incompleteness. We use also some rewriting techniques to reduce the size of the logs to improve the efficiency of time analyzing in the next step.

3. Sensing new discovered attacks by deeply analyzing investigating of the mismatching with the preprocessed logs against the policy specification. Mainly, we use the Spike theorem prover which has the ability to trace the mismatches accurately. A Data mining based approach could be also investigated.

4. Generating new security policies remedying these discovered attacks. This task should be performed through an automatic or in worst case semi automatic (i.e., assisted by administrator) process.

5. Sharing the learnt expertise with other parties by publishing the discovered attacks with their security patches through the different publishing techniques and channels.

The TS data input is a set of (1) Security requirements (2) Security assumptions (3) Network specification/ model abstract (4) IDS rules files (5) Event logs.

## Body (B) Component

The B component deals with the overall management aspects in order to satisfy the real-time and scalability issues. Mainly, it should collect management data, analyze it and perform some control measures to implement the self defense process. Basically, the main tasks of this component are:

1. Collecting different data management and integrate them in a unified information model. An optimized management signaling protocol dedicated for HSN should be defined. Basically, we should opt for a web-based management platform.
2. Storing efficiently the gathered data by using the HSN capabilities and putting it in an easy to use format in order to improve its real-time processing.
3. Self-Controlling through an adaptative autonomous self organization along with predefined strategies. The control signaling protocol should be lightweight and real-time oriented. Defending measures should be triggered automatically in near real-time. These measures and strategies will be improved incrementally by learning from Dirichlet process which describes the overall management plan status.
4. Assisted-Controlling the different system component to perform defense by coordinating the different security system through an administrator's assistance. Some architectural management techniques should be investigated to satisfy the near real-time defending constraint. This collaboration and coordination between all components should be valid and correct. For that purpose, some formal methods checking for the correctness and validity will be used. The administrator should be equipped by a friendly GUI compliant with the HCI (Human computer Interaction) rules and techniques to perform his assisted control tasks.

5. Self-Evaluating through simulation techniques, testing and integration techniques and continuous performance analysis process of the overall integrated platform implementing the (φ|π) framework.

The B data input is a set of (1) Management requirements (2) Security policies (3) Management algorithms and strategies (4) Benchmarks.

## WORK IN PROGRESS AND FUTURE WORK

In Ben Fredj et al. (2010), we exposed the different architectures used in High Performance Computing (HPC), the common high-speed networks, the programming models, the communications models, and the communication libraries. In Ben Fredj et al. (2010, pp. 115-121), we stated the need of HPC for Distributed IDS and we discussed the design requirements of the system. We studied the mapping of the different requirements over the software and hardware features of HSN. We proposed several recommendations for the design of IDS over HSN, starting from the communication protocol and the programming model that should be adapted, to the way the system should handle the communication flow, the memory management and the data transfer between IDS sensors. In Rouached et al. (2010, pp. 109-115), we presented a formal based approach to intrusion detection in the context of high speed networks. We proposed the global architecture of our approach and detailed its components. We also showed how the proposed formalism can be used. Sallay and Al-Shalfan (2010) proposed a security model as well as an architecture able to perform automated and procedural security safeguards. Sallay et al. (2009) presented an optimized scalable distributed architecture which is about 10 times quicker than the centralized architecture. The solution is based on switch-based splitting approach that supports intrusion detection on high-speed links by balancing the traffic load among different sensors running Snort placed in each point of access to the internet. Sallay (2009) designed and implemented a P2P platform dedicated to share different types of files such as vulnerability report files, security policy rules, intrusion detection rules, attack alerts files and security reports about the network security status, in a decentralized manner making easy the exchange of these files and the sharing of the security information involved by the DIDS process. Sallay (2011, February) presented some benchmarking of the well known intrusion detection system Snort as well as an integrated monitoring platform dedicated to manage the different components of our architecture developed in Sallay et al. (2009). Ammar et al. (2011) presented the application of an original feature selection method based on neural networks to the problem of intrusion detection. We apply this method to a case study. We show its advantages compared to some existing feature selection approaches, and we measure its dependence to the network architecture and the learning database. Rouached et al. (in press) presented the ingredients to propose a real-time IDS management framework for high speed networks; REST technology and JSON data exchange format. After enumerating the requirements to be taken into account, we have reviewed the existing exchange protocols and their data formats. Then, we have focused on the REST and JSON. Motivations of our choice and illustrations are also exposed.

Ongoing work consists of refining the proposal, developing an automatic parser from IDEMF to JSON, defining the REST-based exchange protocol, and considering a concrete application to show the feasibility of the whole framework. In Faires et al. (2011), we assumed that our internet flood is influenced by several criteria. The goal was to find the continuous time function for aggregation to calculate a total average score in real-time to help the administrator to scan the suspected packets. We proposed a new hierarchical model with a Dirichlet process adapted to the analysis of temporal trajectories analysis which are governed by a stochastic differential equation in random environment and fuzzy integrals based on the Choquet integral which is an extension of the Lebesgue integral and of the balanced sum.

As future work, we plan to more investigate the framework themes which are modeling the brain theme (BTF component), the architectural theme (TEM), the mind theme (TS component) and the management theme (B component) in order to develop an efficient real-time distributed intrusion detection system for high speed networks.

## ACKNOWLEDGMENT

This paper is a partial result of a research project granted by King Abdul Aziz City for Sciences and Technology (KACST), Riyadh, Kingdom of Saudi Arabia, under grant number INF 36-8-08.

## REFERENCES

Akhlaq, M., Alserhani, F., Subhan, A., Awan, I. U., Mellor, J., & Mirchandani, P. (2010). High speed NIDS using dynamic cluster and comparator logic. In *Proceedings of the IEEE 10th International Conference on Computer and Information Technology* (pp. 575-81).

Ammar, A., & Sallay, H. (2011). Measuring connection features' relevance to attack detection using neural networks. In *Proceedings of the 7th International Conference in Computing in Arabic*.

Ben Fredj, O., Sallay, H., Ammar, A., Rouached, M., Al-Shalfan, K., & Ben Saad, M. (2010). A survey on architectures and communication libraries dedicated for high speed networks. In *Proceedings of the 3rd International Conference on Emerging Ubiquitous Systems and Pervasive Network*.

Ben Fredj, O., Sallay, H., Ammar, A., Rouached, M., Al-Shalfan, K., & Ben Saad, M. (2010). On distributed intrusion detection systems design for high speed networks. In *Proceedings of the 9th Conference in Advances in E-Activities, Information Security and Privacy* (pp. 115-121).

CESNET. (n. d.). *Projects*. Retrieved from http://www.liberouter.org/projects.php

Clark, C. R., Ulmer, C. D., & Schimmel, D. E. (2006). An FPGA-based network intrusion detection system with on-chip network interfaces. *International Journal of Electronics*, *93*(18), 403–420. doi:10.1080/00207210600566083

Dreger, H., Feldmann, A., Mai, M., Paxson, V., & Sommer, R. (2006, August). Dynamic Application-Layer Protocol Analysis for Network Intrusion Detection. In *Proceedings of the USENIX Security Symposium*.

Ertoz, L., Eilertson, E., Lazarevic, A., Tan, P.-N., Kumar, V., Srivastava, J., & Dokas, P. (2004). MINDS - Minnesota Intrusion Detection System. In *Next Generation Data Mining*. Cambridge, MA: MIT Press.

Faires, H., Sallay, H., Ammar, A., Ben Fredj, O., Rouached, M., Al-Shalfan, K., & Ben Saad, M. (2011). *On the modeling of the traffic and security attack behaviors*. Riyadh, Saudi Arabia: Unit of Sciences and Technology, Imam Muhamad bin Saud University.

Foschini, L., Thapliyal, A. V., Cavallaro, L., Kruegel, C., & Vigna, G. (2008). A parallel architecture for stateful, high-speed intrusion detection. In *Proceedings of the 4th International Conference on Information Systems Security* (pp. 203-220).

García-Teodoro, P., Díaz-Verdejo, J., Maciá-Fernández, G., & Vázquez, E. (2009). Anomaly-based network intrusion detection: Techniques, systems and challenges. *Computers & Security*, *28*, 18–28. doi:10.1016/j.cose.2008.08.003

Guinde, N. B., & Ziavras, S. G. (2010). Efficient hardware support for pattern matching in network intrusion detection. *Computers & Security*, *29*, 756–769. doi:10.1016/j.cose.2010.05.001

International, S. R. I. (n. d.). *Event Monitoring Enabling Responses to Anomalous Live Disturbances (EMERALD)*. Retrieved from http://www.sdl.sri.com/projects/emerald/

Kang, D.-H., Kim, B.-K., Oh, J.-T., Nam, T.-Y., & Jang, J.-S. (2006). FPGA based intrusion detection system against unknown and known attacks. In Z.-Z. Shi & R. Sadananda (Eds.), *Proceedings of the 9th Pacific Rim International Workshop on Agent Computing and Multi-Agent Systems* (LNCS 4088, pp. 801-806).

Katashita, T., Yamaguchi, Y., Maeda, A., & Toda, K. (2007). FPGA-based intrusion detection system for 10 gigabit ethernet. *IEICE Transactions on Information and Systems*, *90*(12), 1923–1931. doi:10.1093/ietisy/e90-d.12.1923

Kim, B.-K., Heo, Y.-J., & Oh, J.-T. (2006). Design and implementation of FPGA based high-performance intrusion detection system. In S. Mehrotra, D. D. Zeng, H. Chen, B. M. Thuraisingham, & F.-Y. Wang (Eds.), *Proceedings of the IEEE International Conference on Intelligence and Security Informatics* (LNCS 3975, pp. 724-725).

Laboratoire Spécification et Vérification. (n. d.). *Orchids Real-Time Intrusion Detection System (IDS)*. Retrieved from http://www.lsv.ens-cachan.fr/Software/orchids/

Lin, C.-H., Huang, C.-T., Jiang, C.-P., & Chang, S.-C. (2006). Optimization of regular expression pattern matching circuits on FPGA. In *Proceedings of the Conference on Design, Automation and Test in Europe*, Leuven, Belgium (pp. 12-17).

MacDonald, D. (1999). Elephants. In MacDonald, D. (Ed.), *The encyclopedia of mammals*. Oxford, UK: Oxford University Press.

Nowak, R. M. (1991). Elephants. In Nowak, R. M. (Ed.), *Walker's mammals of the world* (5th ed.). Baltimore, MD: The Johns Hopkins University.

Roesch, M. (1999). Snort: Lightweight intrusion detection for networks. In *Proceedings of the 13th USENIX Conference on System Administration* (pp. 229-238).

Rouached, M., Ben Fredj, O., Sallay, H., Ammar, A., Al-Shalfan, K., & Ben Saad, M. (in press). Lightweight RESTful IDS communication model for high speed networks. *Journal of Computer Science and Technology.*

Rouached, M., Sallay, H., Ben Fredj, O., Ammar, A., Al-Shalfan, K., & Ben Saad, M. (2010). Formal analysis of intrusion detection systems for high speed networks. In *Proceedings of the 9th Conference in Advances in E-Activities, Information Security and Privacy* (pp. 109-115).

Salem, O., Vaton, S., & Gravey, A. (2010). A scalable, efficient and informative approach for anomaly-based intrusion detection systems. *International Journal of Network Management, 20*(5), 271–293. doi:10.1002/nem.748

Sallay, H. (2009). An efficient secure manageable P2P Framework. In *Proceedings of the 5th International Computer Engineering Conference*, Cairo, Egypt.

Sallay, H. (2011). Towards an integrated intrusion detection monitoring in high speed networks. *Journal of Computer Science, 7*, 1094–1104. doi:10.3844/jcssp.2011.1094.1104

Sallay, H., & Al-Shalfan, K. (2010). A standard-compliant integrated security framework. *Saudi Computer Journal, Applied Computing & Informatics, 8*(1).

Sallay, H., Al-Shalfan, K., & Ben Fredj, O. (2009). A scalable distributed IDS architecture for high speed networks. *International Journal of Computer Science and Network Security, 9*(8), 9–16.

Schuff, D. L., Choe, Y. R., & Pai, V. S. (2007). Conservative vs. optimistic parallelization of stateful network intrusion detection. In *Proceedings of the 12th ACM SIGPLAN Symposium on Principles and Practice of Parallel Programming* (pp. 138-139).

Vallentin, M., Sommer, R., Lee, J., Leres, C., Paxson, V., & Tierney, B. (2007). The NIDS Cluster: Scalable, stateful network intrusion detection on commodity hardware. In C. Kruegel, R. Lippmann, & A. Clark (Eds.), *Proceedings of the 10th International Symposium on Recent Advances in Intrusion Detection* (LNCS 4637, pp. 107-126).

Wang, K., Parekh, J. J., & Stolfo, S. J. (2006). Anagram: a content anomaly detector resistant to mimicry attack. In D. Zamboni & C. Kruegel (Eds.), *Proceedings of the 9th International Symposium Recent Advances in Intrusion Detection* (LNCS 4219, pp. 226-248).

Wenbao, J., Shuang, H., Yiqi, D., & Tinghua, L. (2006). Load balancing algorithm for high-speed network intrusion detection systems. *Journal of Tsinghua University, 46*(1), 106–110.

Xie, Z. X., Quirino, T., Shyu, M. L., Chen, S. C., & Chang, L. W. (2006). A distributed agent-based approach to intrusion detection using the lightweight PCC anomaly detection classifier. In *Proceedings of the IEEE International Conference on Sensor Networks, Ubiquitous, and Trustworthy Computing* (Vol. 1, pp. 446-453).

Xu, M., Lin, C., & Chen, Q. (2008). A multiple keyword fusion scheme for P2P IDS alert. In *Proceedings of the First International Conference on Intelligent Networks and Intelligent Systems* (pp. 317-320).

Yu, F., Dai, X., Shen, Y., Huang, H., & Zhu, M. (2005). Intrusion detection and simulation for high-speed networks. In *Proceedings of the International Conference on Services Systems and Services Management* (Vol. 2, pp. 835-840).

*This work was previously published in the International Journal of Information Security and Privacy, Volume 5, Issue 4, edited by Hamid Nemati, pp. 47-58, copyright 2011 by IGI Publishing (an imprint of IGI Global).*

# Compilation of References

Ackerman, M. S., Cranor, L. F., & Reagle, J. (1999). Privacy in e-commerce: examining user scenarios and privacy preferences. In *Proceedings of the 1st ACM Conference on Electronic commerce (EC '99)* (pp. 1-8). New York, NY: ACM.

Adams, A., & Sasse, M. A. (1999). Users are Not the Enemy: Why users compromise computer security mechanisms and how to take remedial measures. *Communications of the ACM, 42*(12), 41–46.

Agrawal, R., & Srikant, R. (1994, September). Fast algorithms for mining association rules. In *Proceedings of the 20th International Conference on Very Large Data Bases,* Santiago, Chile (pp. 487-499).

Agresti, A., & Franklin, C. A. (2006). *Statistics: The art and science of learning from data.* Upper Saddle River, NJ: Prentice Hall.

Akhlaq, M., Alserhani, F., Subhan, A., Awan, I. U., Mellor, J., & Mirchandani, P. (2010). High speed NIDS using dynamic cluster and comparator logic. In *Proceedings of the IEEE 10th International Conference on Computer and Information Technology* (pp. 575-81).

Akismet. (n.d.). *Home.* Retrieved from http://akismet.com/

Alampalayam, S. P., & Kumar, A. (2003). Adaptive security model for mobile agents in wireless networks. In *Proceedings of the IEEE Global Communications Conference* (pp. 1516-1521).

Alampalayam, S. P., & Kumar, A. (2004). Predictive security model using data mining. In *Proceedings of the IEEE Global Communications Conference* (pp. 2208-2212).

Alampalayam, S. P., Kumar, A., & Srinivasan, S. (2005). Mobile ad hoc networks security – A taxonomy. In *Proceedings of the International Conference on Adaptive Science and Technology* (pp. 839-844).

Alampalayam, S. P., & Kumar, A. (2004). An adaptive and predictive security model for mobile ad hoc networks. *Kluwer Personal Communications Journal, 29*(6), 263–281.

Alampalayam, S., & Srinivasan, S. (2009). Intrusion recovery framework for tactical mobile ad hoc networks. *International Journal of Computer Science and Network Security, 9,* 1–10.

Alexander, I. F. (2002). Modeling the interplay of conflicting goals with use and misuse cases. In *Proceedings of the 8th International Workshop on Requirements Engineering: Foundation for Software Quality,* Essen, Germany.

Alexander, I. F. (2003). Misuse case help to elicit non-functional requirements. *Computing and Control Engineering Journal, 14*(1), 40–45. doi:10.1049/cce:20030108

Alexander, I. F. (2003). Misuse cases, use cases with hostile intent. *IEEE Software, 20*(1), 58–66. doi:10.1109/MS.2003.1159030

Al-Hamdani, W. A. (2009). Three models to measure information security compliance. *International Journal of Information Security and Privacy, 3*(4), 43–64. doi:10.4018/jisp.2009100104

Allen, J. (2005). *Governing for Enterprise Security* (Tech. Rep. No. CMU/SEI-2005-TN-023). Pittsburgh, PA: Carnegie Mellon, Software Engineering Institute.

Allenbach, P. (2009). *Java Card 3: Classic functionality gets a connectivity boost.* Retrieved from http://java.sun.com/developer/technicalArticles/javacard/javacard3/

Amato-McCoy, D. M. (2009). The next phase of PCI security. *Chain Store Age*, 48-49.

Ammar, A., & Sallay, H. (2011). Measuring connection features' relevance to attack detection using neural networks. In *Proceedings of the 7th International Conference in Computing in Arabic*.

Anthes, G. H. (2004). Quality model mania. *Computerworld*, *38*, 41–44.

Arogundade, O. T., Akinwale, A. T., Jin, Z., & Yang, X. G. (in press). Vulnerability analysis approach to capturing information system safety threats and requirements. *International Journal of Software Engineering and its Applications*.

Aronsson, H. A. (1995). *Zero knowledge protocols and small systems.* Retrieved from http://www.tml.tkk.fi/Opinnot/Tik-110.501/1995/zeroknowledge.html

Assis, F. (2006). A text classification module for Lua – the importance of the training method. In *Proceedings of the 15th Text Retrieval Conference,* Gaithersburg, MD.

Atallah, M., Elmagarmid, A., Ibrahim, M., Bertino, E., & Verykios, V. (1999). Disclosure imitation of sensitive rules. In *Proceedings of the 1999 Workshop on Knowledge and Data Engineering Exchange (KDEX '99)* (p. 45). Washington, DC: IEEE Computer Society.

Babbie, E. (2009). *The practice of social research* (10th ed.). Wadsworth, UK: Thomson Learning.

Baker, W., Dahn, M., Greiner, T., Hutton, A., Hylender, C. D., Lindstrom, P., et al. (2010). *Verizon 2010 payment card industry compliance report.* Retrieved from http://www.verizonbusiness.com/resources/reports/rp_2010-payment-card-industry-compliance-report_en_xg.pdf

Baltzan, P., & Phillips, A. (2009). *Essentials of business driven information systems.* New York, NY: McGraw-Hill/Irwin.

Bargh, M. S., Hulsebosch, R. J., Eertink, E. H., Prasad, A., Wang, H., & Schoo, P. (2004). Fast authentication methods for handovers between IEEE 802.11 wireless LANs. In *Proceedings of the 2nd ACM International Workshop on Wireless Mobile Applications and Services on WLAN Hotspots* (pp. 52-60).

Barnett, J. (2008). The Impact of Privacy Legislation on Patient Care. *International Journal of Information Security and Privacy*, *2*(3), 1–17. doi:10.4018/jisp.2008070101

Becchetti, L., Castillo, C., Donato, D., Leonardi, S., & Baeza-Yates, R. (2005). Link-based Characterization and Detection of Web Spam. In *Proceedings of the 2nd International Workshop on Adversarial Information Retrieval on the Web (AIRWeb),* Seattle, WA.

Ben Fredj, O., Sallay, H., Ammar, A., Rouached, M., Al-Shalfan, K., & Ben Saad, M. (2010). A survey on architectures and communication libraries dedicated for high speed networks. In *Proceedings of the 3rd International Conference on Emerging Ubiquitous Systems and Pervasive Network.*

Ben Fredj, O., Sallay, H., Ammar, A., Rouached, M., Al-Shalfan, K., & Ben Saad, M. (2010). On distributed intrusion detection systems design for high speed networks. In *Proceedings of the 9th Conference in Advances in E-Activities, Information Security and Privacy* (pp. 115-121).

Bertino, E., Carminati, B., & Ferrari, E. (2003, June). A flexible authentication method for UDDI registries. In *Proceedings of the International Conference on Web Services*, Las Vegas, NV.

Bertino, E., Carminati, B., Ferrari, E., Thuraisingham, B., & Gupta, A. (2003). Selective and authentic third-party distribution of XML documents. *IEEE Transactions on Knowledge and Data Engineering*, *16*(10), 1263–1278. doi:10.1109/TKDE.2004.63

Beth, T. (1988). A Fiat-Shamir-like authentication protocol for the ElGamal scheme. In *Advances in Cryptology: Proceedings of EUROCRYPT'88,* Davos, Switzerland (pp. 77-86).

Beth, T. (1988). Efficient zero-knowledge identification scheme for smart cards. In D. Barstow, W. Brauer, P. Brinch Hansen, D. Gries, D. Luckham, C. Moler et al. (Eds.), *Proceedings of the Workshop on Advances in Cryptology* (LNCS 330, pp. 77-84).

Bhagyavati, S. W., & DeJoie, A. (2004, September 17-18). Wireless Security Techniques: An Overview. In *Proceedings of the InfoSecCD Conference 2004,* Kennessaw, GA.

Bhargava, S., & Agrawal, D. P. (2001). Security enhancements in AODV protocol for wireless ad hoc networks. In *Proceedings of the IEEE Vehicular Technology Conference* (pp. 2143-2147).

Bhattarai, A., Rus, V., & Dasgupta, D. (2009, March). Characterizing Comment Spam in the Blogosphere through Content Analysis. In *Proceedings of the Symposium on Computational Intelligence in Cyber Security (CICS), IEEE Symposium Series on Computational Intelligence (SSCI 2009).*

Blaze, M. (2009). *Is the e-voting honeymoon over? Electronic vote rigging in Kentucky.* Retrieved from http://www.crypto.com/blog/vote_fraud_in_kentucky/

Blum, A., & Mitchell, T. (1998). Combining Labeled and Unlabeled Data with Co-Training. In *Proceedings of the 11th Annual Conference on Computational Learning Theory.*

Boorstin, J. (2009). *Facebook sued on privacy concerns.* Retrieved from http://www.cnbc.com/id/32458206/

Bovee, M., Srivastava, R. P., & Mak, B. (2003). A conceptual framework and belief-function approach to assessing overall information quality. *International Journal of Intelligent Systems, 18*(1), 51–74. doi:10.1002/int.10074

Bratko, A., Cormack, G. V., Filipič, B., Lynam, T. R., & Zupan, B. (2006). Spam filtering using statistical data compression models. *Journal of Machine Learning Research, 7,* 2673–2698.

Breach Notification Act, D. 11th Congress, S.139 Cong. Rec. § 2 (2009).

Brodie, C., Karat, C., Karat, J., & Feng, J. (2005, July 6-8). Usable Security and Privacy: A Case Study of Developing Privacy Management Tools. In *Proceedings of the Symposium on Usable Security and Security (SOUPS),* Pittsburgh, PA (pp. 35-43).

Brodsky, J., & McConnell, A. (2009, January 21-22). Jamming and interference induced Denial of Service attacks on IEEE 802.15.4 based wireless networks. In *Proceedings of the SCADA Security Scientific Symposium,* Miami Beach, FL.

Brookshear, J. G. (2005). *Computer Science: An Overview.* Reading, MA: Addison Wesley.

Brostoff, S., & Sasse, M. (2001). Safe and sound: a safety critical approach to security. In *Proceedings of the 10th ACM/SIGSAC New Security Paradigms Workshop,* Cloudcroft, NM (pp. 41-50).

Brotby, W. K. (2006). *Information Security Governance: Guidance for Boards of Directors and Executive Management* (2nd ed.). Rolling Meadows, IL: IT Governance Institute.

Buehler, J. W., Hopkins, R. S., Overhage, J. M., Sosin, D. M., & Tong, V. (2004). *Framework for evaluating public health surveillance systems for early detection of outbreaks: Recommendations from the CDC Working Group.* Retrieved from http://www.cdc.gov/mmwr/preview/mmwrhtml/rr5305a1.htm

Burmester, M., Desmedt, Y., & Beth, T. (1992). Efficient zero-knowledge identification schemes for smart cards. *The Computer Journal, 35*(1), 21–29. doi:10.1093/comjnl/35.1.21

Burns, A., McDermid, J., & Dobson, V. (1992). On the meaning of safety and security. *The Computer Journal, 35*(1), 3–15. doi:10.1093/comjnl/35.1.3

Cable & Wireless Worldwide. (2004). *O2 Airwave appoints Cable & Wireless for bandwidth provision.* Retrieved from http://www.cw.com/media_events/media_centre/releases/2004/06_01_2004_59.html

Calandrino, J. A., Feldman, A. J., Halderman, J. A., Wagner, D., Yu, H., & Zeller, W. P. (2007). *Source code review of the Diebold voting system.* Retrieved from http://www.sos.ca.gov/elections/voting_systems/ttbr/diebold-source-public-jul29.pdf

Camp, L. (1999). Web security and privacy: An American perspective. *The Information Society, 15*(4), 249–256. doi:10.1080/019722499128411

Carreras, X., & Marquez, L. (2001). Boosting trees for anti-spam email filtering. In *Proceedings of RANLP01: 4th International Conference on Recent Advances in Natural Language Processing.*

Carson, T. (1994). Conflicts of interest. *Journal of Business Ethics, 13*(5), 387–404. doi:10.1007/BF00871766

Cassini, J., Medlin, D., & Romaniello, A. (2008). Laws and Regulations Dealing with Information Security and Privacy: An Investigative Study. *International Journal of Information Security and Privacy, 2*(2), 70–82. doi:10.4018/jisp.2008040105

Castillo, C., Donato, D., Becchetti, L., Boldi, P., Leonardi, S., Santini, M., & Vigna, S. (2006). A reference collection for web spam. *ACM SIGIR Forum, 40*(2). comScore. (2009). *The Comscore Data Passport - first half 2009.* Retrieved from http://www.comscore.com/press_events/presentations_whitepapers/2009/comscore_data_passport_-_first_half_2009

Castro, J., Kolp, M., & Mylopoulos, J. (2002). Towards requirements-driven information systems engineering: the Tropos project. *Information Systems, 27*(6), 356–389. doi:10.1016/S0306-4379(02)00012-1

Cater-Steel, A., & Tan, W.-G. (2005). *Implementation of IT infrastructure library (ITIL) in Australia: Progress and success factors.* Paper presented at the International IT Governance Conference, Auckland, New Zealand.

Cavoukian, A. (2009). *A discussion paper on privacy externalities, security breach notification and the role of independent oversight.* Retrieved from http://www.ipc.on.ca/images/Resources/privacy_externalities.pdf

CESNET. (n. d.). *Projects.* Retrieved from http://www.liberouter.org/projects.php

Chandran, R., Phatak, A., & Sambharya, R. (1987). Transborder Data Flows: Implications for Multinational Corporations. *Business Horizons, 30*(6), 74–83. doi:10.1016/0007-6813(87)90055-3

Chang, C. C., & Hwang, M. S. (1996). Parallel computation of the generating keys for RSA cryptosystems. *Electronics Letters, 32*(15), 1365–1366. doi:10.1049/el:19960886

Chang, Y. F., & Chang, C. C. (2005). An efficient authentication protocol for mobile satellite communication systems. *ACM SIGOPS Operating Systems Review, 39,* 70–84. doi:10.1145/1044552.1044560

Chang, Y. S., Wu, T. C., & Huang, S. C. (2000). ElGamal-like digital signature and multisignature schemes using self-certified public keys. *Journal of Systems and Software, 50,* 99–105. doi:10.1016/S0164-1212(99)00080-1

Chen, Z., & Giorgio, R. D. (1998). *Understanding Java Card 2.0-Java World.* Retrieved from http://www.java-world.com/javaworld/jw-03-1998/jw-03-javadev.html

Chen, T. H., Lee, W. B., & Chen, H. B. (2009). A self-verification authentication mechanism for mobile satellite communication systems. *Computers & Electrical Engineering, 35*(1), 41–48. doi:10.1016/j.compeleceng.2008.05.003

Chen, Z. (2000). *Java card technology for smart cards: Architecture and programmer's guide.* Upper Saddle River, NJ: Prentice Hall.

Chini, P., Giambene, G., & Kota, S. (2010). A survey on mobile satellite systems. *International Journal of Satellite Communications and Networking, 28*(1), 29–57.

Chiu, D. K. W., Chiung, S. C., & Till, S. (2002). A three-layer architecture for e-contract enforcement in an e-service environment. In *Proceedings of the 36th Hawaii International Conference on System Science.*

Choobineh, J., Dhillon, G., Grimaila, M. R., & Rees, J. (2007). Management of information security: Challenges and research directions. *Communications of the Association for Information Systems, 20*(57), 958–971.

Clark, C. R., Ulmer, C. D., & Schimmel, D. E. (2006). An FPGA-based network intrusion detection system with on-chip network interfaces. *International Journal of Electronics, 93*(18), 403–420. doi:10.1080/00207210600566083

Clarkson, J. B. (1994). Dense probabilistic encryption. In *Proceedings of the Workshop on Selected Areas of Cryptography* (pp. 120-128).

Coburn, A. (2010). Fitting PCI DSS within a wider governance framework. *Computer Fraud & Security*, 11–13. doi:10.1016/S1361-3723(10)70121-4

Cockburn, A. (2001). *Writing effective use cases.* Reading, MA: Addison-Wesley.

Cockcroft, S., & Clutterbuck, P. (2001). Attitudes towards information privacy. In *Proceedings of the 12ᵗʰ Australasian Conference on Information Systems.*

Cohen, L., & Manion, L. (2000). *Research methods in education* (5th ed.). London, UK: Routledge. doi:10.4324/9780203224342

Coleman, A. (1998). *Giving currency to the Java Card API.* Retrieved from http://www.javaworld.com/javaworld/jw-02-1998/jw-02-javacard.html

Common Criteria Implementation Board. (2007). *Common criteria for information technology security evaluation, version 2.1* (Technical Report CCIMB-2007-09-002). Australia: Author.

Comparetto, G., & Ramirez, R. (1997). Trends in mobile satellite technology. *IEEE Computer*, *30*(2), 44–52.

Conger, S. (2009). Information technology service management and opportunities for information systems curricula. *International Journal of Information Systems in the Service Sector*, *1*(2), 58–68. doi:10.4018/jisss.2009040104

Conradie, N., & Hoekstra, A. (2002). *CobiT, ITIL and ISO17799: How to use them in conjunction.* Retrieved from http://www.cccure.org/Documents/COBIT/COBIT_ITIL_and_BS7799.pdf

Constabulary, F. (n.d.). *Home.* Retrieved from http://www.fife.police.uk

Constantine, L. L., & Lockwood, L. A. D. (1999). *Software for use: a practical guide to the models and methods of usage-centered design.* New York, NY: ACM.

Consulting, B. W. C. S. (2002). *UK Emergency Services Voice Concerns Over Radio Systems in Face of September 11th Scale Disaster.* Retrieved from http://www.bwcs.com/news_detail.cfm

Conti, G., & Sobiesk, E. (2007, July 18-20). An Honest Man Has Nothing to Fear: User Perceptions on Web-based Information Disclosure. In *Proceedings of the Symposium on Usable Privacy and Security (SOUPS),* Pittsburgh, PA (pp. 112-121).

Cormack, G. V., Gomez, J. M., & Sanz, E. P. (2007). Spam Filtering for short messages. In *Proceedings of the 16th ACM Conference on Information and Knowledge Management (CIKM 2007).*

Corson, M. S., & Ephremides, A. (1995). A Distributed Routing Algorithm for Mobile Wireless Networks. *Wireless Networks*, *1*(1), 61–81. doi:10.1007/BF01196259

Cvrček, D., Matyáš, V., & Patel, A. (2005). Evidence processing and privacy issues in evidence-based reputation systems. *Computer Standards & Interfaces*, *27*(5), 533–545. doi:10.1016/j.csi.2005.01.011

Danchev, D. (2009). *Massive comment spam attack on Digg.com leads to malware.* Retrieved from http://blogs.zdnet.com/security/?p=2544

Dasseni, E., Verykios, V. S., Elmagarmid, A. K., & Bertino, E. (2001). Hiding association rules by using confidence and support. In *Proceedings of the 4th International Workshop on Information Hiding (IHW '01),* Pittsburgh, PA (LNCS 2137, pp. 369-383).

DataLossDB. (2010). *About DataLossDB.* Retrieved June, 15, 2010, from http://datalossdb.org/about

Davis, F. D. (1989). Perceived usefulness, perceived ease of use, and user acceptance of information technology. *Management Information Systems Quarterly*, *13*(3), 319–340. doi:10.2307/249008

Davis, J. C. (2000). Protecting privacy in the cyber era. *IEEE Technology and Society Magazine*, 10–22. doi:10.1109/44.846270

Davison, B. D. (2000). Recognizing Nepotistic Links on the Web. In *Proceedings of the AAAI 2000 Workshop on Artificial Intelligence for Web Search,* Austin, TX.

Davison, B. D., & Wu, B. (2005). Identifying link farm pages. In *Proceedings of the 14th International World Wide Web Conference (WWW),* Chiba, Japan.

De Paula, R., Ding, X., Dourish, P., Nies, K., Pillet, B., Redmiles, D., et al. (2005, July 6-8). Two Experiences Designing for Effective Security. In *Proceedings of the Symposium on Usable Privacy and Security (SOUPS)*, Pittsburgh, PA (pp. 25-34).

Debreceny, R. S. (2006). Re-engineering IT internal controls: Applying capability maturity models to the evaluation of IT controls. In *Proceedings of the 39th Hawaii International Conference on Systems Sciences*.

den Braber, F., Dimitrakos, T., Gran, B. A., Lund, M. S., Stolen, K., & Aagedal, J. O. (2003). The CORAS methodology: model-based risk assessment using UML and UP. In Favre, L. (Ed.), *UML and the unified process* (pp. 332–357). Hershey, PA: IGI Global.

DeWitt, A., & Kuljis, J. (2006). Is Usable Security an Oxymoron? *Interaction*, *13*(3), 41–44.

Dhillon, G., & Moores, T. (2001). Internet Privacy: Interpreting Key Issues. *Information Resources Management Journal*, *14*(4), 33–37. doi:10.4018/irmj.2001100104

Diffie, W., & Hellman, M. E. (1976). New directions in cryptography. *IEEE Transactions on Information Theory*, *22*, 644–654. doi:10.1109/TIT.1976.1055638

Dijk, M. V., Gentry, C., Halevi, S., & Vaikuntanathan, V. (2010). Fully homomorphic encryption over the integers. In *Proceedings of the Eurocrypt 2010 Conference* (pp. 24-43).

Dijkstra, E. W. (1972). The humble programmer. *Communications of the ACM*, *15*(10), 859–866. doi:10.1145/355604.361591

Dill, D. L., Mercuri, R., Neumann, P. G., & Wallach, D. S. (2008). *Frequently asked questions about DRE voting system*. Retrieved from http://www.verifiedvoting.org/article.php?id=5018

Dojen, R., Lasc, I., & Coffey, T. (2008, August 28-30). Establishing and Fixing a Freshness Flaw in a Key-Distribution and Authentication Protocol. In *Proceedings of the IEEE 4th International Conference on Intelligent Computer Communication and Processing*, Cluj-Napoca, Romania.

Dourish, P., Grinter, R. E., Delgado de la Flor, J., & Joseph, M. (2003). Security in the Wild: User Strategies for Managing Security as an Everyday, Practical Problem. *Personal and Ubiquitous Computing*, *8*, 391–401.

Dreger, H., Feldmann, A., Mai, M., Paxson, V., & Sommer, R. (2006, August). Dynamic Application-Layer Protocol Analysis for Network Intrusion Detection. In *Proceedings of the USENIX Security Symposium*.

Drost, I., & Scheffer, T. (2005). Thwarting the nigritude ultramarine: Learning to identify link spam. In *Proceedings of the ECML 2005 Conference*.

Drucker, H., Wu, D., & Vapnik, V. (1999). Support vector machines for spam categorization. *IEEE Transactions on Neural Networks*, *10*(5), 1048–1054. doi:10.1109/72.788645

Edelstein, S. M. (2004). Sarbanes-Oxley compliance for non-accelerated filers: Solving the internal control puzzle. *The CPA Journal*, *74*(12), 52–58.

Efron, B., & Tibshirani, R. (1993). *An Introduction to the Bootstrap*. Boca Raton, FL: Chapman & Hall/CRC.

El Gamal, T. (1985). A public key cryptosystem and a signature scheme based on discrete logarithms. In *Proceedings of the Advances in Cryptology Conference (CRYPTO 84)* (LNCS 196, pp. 10-18).

Elahi, G., & Yu, E. (2007). A goal oriented approach for modeling and analyzing security trade-offs. In C. Parent, K.-D. Schewe, V. C. Storey, & B. Thalheim (Eds.), *Proceedings of the 26th International Conference on Conceptual Modeling* (LNCS 4801, pp. 375-390).

ElGamal, T. (1985). A public-key cryptosystem and a signature scheme based on discrete logarithms. *IEEE Transactions on Information Theory*, *31*, 469–472. doi:10.1109/TIT.1985.1057074

Eloff, J. H. P., & Eloff, M. M. (2005). Information security architecture. *Computer Fraud & Security*, 10–16. doi:10.1016/S1361-3723(05)70275-X

Epstein, J. (2007). Electronic voting. *Computer*, *40*(8), 92–95. doi:10.1109/MC.2007.271

Ertoz, L., Eilertson, E., Lazarevic, A., Tan, P.-N., Kumar, V., Srivastava, J., & Dokas, P. (2004). MINDS - Minnesota Intrusion Detection System. In *Next Generation Data Mining*. Cambridge, MA: MIT Press.

ESTI. (1995). *Terrestrial Trunked Radio (TETRA).* Retrieved from http://www.etsi.org/WebSite/Technologies/TETRA

ESTI. (2002). *User Requirement Specification TETRA Release 2*. Retrieved from http://www.etsi.org/WebSite/Technologies/TETRA

ESTI. (2007). *ETSI TETRA (Terrestrial Trunked Radio) technology*. Retrieved from http://www.etsi.org/WebSite/Technologies/TETRA

Etzler, J. (2007). *IT governance according to COBIT*. Stockholm, Sweden: Royal Institute of Technology.

Everett, C. (2009). PCI DSS: Lack of direction or lack of commitment? *Computer Fraud & Security*, *12*, 18–20. doi:10.1016/S1361-3723(09)70155-1

Evmievski, A., Gehrke, J., & Srikant, R. (2003). Limiting privacy breaches in privacy preserving data mining. In *Proceedings of the 22nd ACM SIGMOD-SIGACT-SIGART Symposium on Principles of Database Systems*, San Diego, CA (pp. 211-222). New York, NY: ACM.

Evmievski, A., Srikant, R., Agrawal, R., & Gehrke, J. (2002). Privacy preserving mining of association rules. In *Proceedings of the 8th ACM SIGKDD International Conference on Knowledge Discovery and Data Mining*, Edmonton, AB, Canada (pp. 217-228). New York, NY: ACM.

Faires, H., Sallay, H., Ammar, A., Ben Fredj, O., Rouached, M., Al-Shalfan, K., & Ben Saad, M. (2011). *On the modeling of the traffic and security attack behaviors*. Riyadh, Saudi Arabia: Unit of Sciences and Technology, Imam Muhamad bin Saud University.

Federal Trade Commission. (2010). *Consumer Sentinel Network Data Book for January- December 2009*. Retrieved from http://www.ftc.gov/sentinel/reports/sentinel-annual-reports/sentinel-cy2009.pdf

Federal Trade Commission. (2011). *Consumer Sentinel Network Data Book for January -December 2010*. Retrieved from http://www.ftc.gov/sentinel/reports/sentinel-annual-reports/sentinel-cy2010.pdf

Feldman, A. J., Halderman, J. A., & Felten, E. W. (2006). *Security analysis of the Diebold AccuVote-TS voting machine*. Princeton, NJ: Princeton University.

Felstead, E. B., & Keightley, R. J. (1995, November 7). Robustness capabilities of transponded commercial satellite communications. In *Proceedings of the IEEE Military Communications Conference (MILCOM 95)*, San Diego, CA (Vol. 2, pp. 783-787).

Fernandez-Medina, E., Jurjens, J., Trujillo, J., & Jajodia, S. (Eds.). (2009). Model-driven development for secure information systems. *Information and Software Technology*, *51*(5), 809–814. doi:10.1016/j.infsof.2008.05.010

Fiat, A., & Shamir, A. (1986). How to prove yourself: Practical solutions to identification and signature problems. In A. M. Odlyzko (Ed.), *Proceedings of the Workshop on Advances in Cryptology* (LNCS 263, pp. 186-194).

Firesmith, D. G. (2003). *Common concepts underlying safety, security and survivability engineering* (Tech. Rep. No. CMU/SEI2003 TN 033), Pittsburgh, PA: Software Engineering Institute.

Firesmith, D. G. (2005). Analyzing the security significance of system requirements. In *Proceedings of the Symposium on Requirements Engineering for Information Security in conjunction with the 13th IEEE International Requirements Engineering Conference*, Paris, France.

Firesmith, D. G. (2007). Engineering safety and security related requirements for software intensive systems. In *Proceedings of the International Conference on Software Engineering*, Minneapolis, MN (p. 169).

Firesmith, D. G. (2003). Security use cases. *Journal of Object Technology*, *2*(3), 53–64. doi:10.5381/jot.2003.2.3.c6

First Data. (2009). *PCI DSS and handling sensitive cardholder data*. Retrieved from http://www.firstdata.com

Fishcher, E. A. (2003). *Election reform and electronic voting systems (DREs): Analysis of security issues.* Retrieved from http://people.csail.mit.edu/rivest/voting/reports/Fischer-ElectionReformAndElectronicVoting-SystemsDREs.pdf

Fisher, C. W., Chengalur-Smith, I., & Ballou, D. P. (2003). The impact of experience and time on the use of data quality information in decision making. *Information Systems Research, 14*(2), 170–188. doi:10.1287/isre.14.2.170.16017

Fitzgerald, M. (2009). The privacy paradox. *CIO,* 26-33.

Fogg, B. J., Soohoo, C., Danielson, D., Marable, L., Stanford, J., & Tauber, E. R. (2002). *How Do People Evaluate a Web Site's Credibility? Results from a large study.* Retrieved from http://www.consumerwebwatch.org/pdfs/stanfordPTL.pdf

Foschini, L., Thapliyal, A. V., Cavallaro, L., Kruegel, C., & Vigna, G. (2008). A parallel architecture for stateful, high-speed intrusion detection. In *Proceedings of the 4th International Conference on Information Systems Security* (pp. 203-220).

Frauenheim, E. (2006). Many U.S. multinationals doing little to meet overseas employee data privacy rules. *Workforce Management, 85*(9), 48–51.

Freeman, E. (1984). *Strategic management: A stakeholder approach.* Boston, MA: Pitman.

Friedman, B., Hurley, D., Howe, D., Felten, E., & Nissenbaum, H. (2002, April 20-25). Users' conceptions of risks and harms on the web: a comparative study. In *Proceedings of CHI 2002,* Minneapolis, MN (pp. 746-747).

Frisina, L., Herron, M. C., Honaker, J., & Lewis, J. B. (2008). Ballot formats, touchscreens, and undervotes: A study of the 2006 midterm elections in Florida. *Election Law Journal: Rules, Politics, and Policy, 7*(1), 25–47.

Gafni, E., & Bertsekas, D. (1981). Distributed Algorithms for Generating Loop-free Routes in Networks with Frequently Changing Topology. *IEEE Transactions on Communications, 29*(1), 11–15. doi:10.1109/TCOM.1981.1094876

Gansler, J. S., & Binnendijk, H. (Eds.). (2005). *Information assurance: Trends in vulnerabilities, threats and technologies.* Washington, DC: National Defense University, Center for Technology and National Security Policy.

García-Teodoro, P., Díaz-Verdejo, J., Maciá-Fernández, G., & Vázquez, E. (2009). Anomaly-based network intrusion detection:Techniques, systems and challenges. *Computers & Security, 28,* 18–28. doi:10.1016/j.cose.2008.08.003

Gardner, R., Yasinsac, A., Bishop, M., Kohno, T., Hartley, Z., Kerski, J., et al. (2007). *Software review and security analysis of the Diebold voting machine software.* Retrieved from http://election.dos.state.fl.us/voting-systems/pdf/SAITreport.pdf

Garg, A., Curtis, J., & Halper, H. (2003). Quantifying the financial impact of IT security breaches. *Information Management & Computer Security, 11*(2). doi:10.1108/09685220310468646

Gaynor, D. (2002). IT governance. *Accountancy Ireland, 34*(4), 28.

Geier, J. (1999). *Wireless LANs: Implementing Interoperable Networks.* New York, NY: Macmillan Technical Publishing.

Gentry, C. (2009). Fully homomorphic encryption using ideal lattices, In *Proceedings of the 41st Annual ACM Symposium on Theory of Computing,* Bethesda, MD (pp. 169-178). New York, NY: ACM.

George, J. F. (2004). *Computers in Society: Privacy, Ethics, and the Internet.* Upper Saddle River, NJ: Pearson-Prentice Hall.

German Federal Office for Information Security. (2007). *IT Baseline Protection Manual.* Bonn, Germany: Author.

Gibbons, J. D. (1993). *Nonparametric statistics: an introduction.* Newbury Park, CA: Sage Publications.

Gikas, C. (2010). A general comparison of FISMA, HIPAA, ISO 27000 and PCI-DSS standards. *Information Security Journal: A Global Perspective, 19,* 132-141.

Gilbert, F. (2008). Is your due diligence checklist obsolete? Understanding how information privacy and security affects corporate and commercial transactions. *The Computer & Internet Lawyer, 25*(10), 13–18.

Giorgini, P., Massacci, F., Mylopoulos, J., & Zannone, N. (2005). Modeling security requirements through ownership, permission, and delegation. In *Proceedings of the 13th International Requirements Engineering Conference,* Paris, France (pp. 167-176).

Girault, M. (1991, April 8-11). Self-certified public keys. In *Advances in Cryptology: Proceedings of EUROCRYPT'91*, Brighton, UK (pp. 491-497).

Gligor, V. D., Gavrila, S. I., & Ferraiolo, D. (1998, May 3-6). On the Formal Definition of Separation-of-Duty Policies and their Composition. In *Proceedings of the IEEE Symposium on Security and Privacy*, Oakland, CA.

Gligoroski, D. (2009). On a family of minimal candidate one-way functions and one-way permutations. *International Journal of Network Security, 8*(3), 211–220.

Goldreich, O., Micali, S., & Wigderson, A. (1991). Proofs that yield nothing but their validity or all languages in NP have zero-knowledge proof systems. *Journal of the ACM, 38*(3). doi:10.1145/116825.116852

Goldwasser, S., Micali, S., & Rackoff, C. (1985). The knowledge complexity of interactive proof-systems. In *Proceedings of the Seventeenth Annual ACM Symposium on Theory of Computing* (pp. 291-304).

Google Enterprise. (2009). *Spam Data and Trends.* Retrieved from http://googleenterprise.blogspot.com/2009/03/spam-data-and-trends-q1-2009.html

Google. (2005). *Nofollow*. Retrieved from http://googleblog.blogspot.com/2005/01/preventingcomment-spam.html

Grandinetti, M. (1996). Establishing and maintaining security on the Internet. *Sacramento Business Journal, 13*(25), 22.

Greenwald, S. J., Olthoff, K. G., Raskin, V., & Ruch, W. (2004). The User Non-Acceptance Paradigm: INFOSEC's Dirty Little Secret. In *Proceedings of the 2004 Workshop on New Security Paradigms*, Hunts Point, NS, Canada (pp. 35-43).

Gross, G. (2009, October 28). FBI: National data-breach law would help fight cybercrime. *PCWorld.*

Gross, J. B., & Rosson, M. B. (2007, July 18-20). End User Concern about Security and Privacy Threats. In *Proceedings of the Symposium on Usable Privacy and Security (SOUPS)*, Pittsburgh, PA (pp. 167-168).

Gross, J. B., & Rosson, M. B. (2007, March 30-31). Looking for Trouble: End-User Security Management. In *Proceedings of the 2007 Symposium on Computer Human Interaction for the Management of Information Technology*, Cambridge, MA (Vol. 10).

Guildentops, E., & Haes, S. D. (2002). COBIT 3rd edition usage survey: Growing acceptance of COBIT. *Information Systems Control Journal, 6*, 25-27.

Guillou, L., & Quisquater, J. J. (1988). A practical zero-knowledge protocol fitted to security microprocessor minimizing both transmission and memory. In D. Barstow, W. Brauer, P. Brinch Hansen, D. Gries, D. Luckham, C. Moler et al. (Eds.), *Proceedings of the Workshop on Advances in Cryptology* (LNCS 330, pp. 123-128).

Guillou, L., & Quisquater, J. J. (1990). A "paradoxical" dentity-based signature scheme resulting from zero-knowledge. In S. Goldwasser (Ed.), *Proceedings of the Workshop on Advances in Cryptology* (LNCS 403, pp. 216-231).

Guinde, N. B., & Ziavras, S. G. (2010). Efficient hardware support for pattern matching in network intrusion detection. *Computers & Security, 29*, 756–769. doi:10.1016/j.cose.2010.05.001

Gyongyi, Z., & Hector, G. (2005). Web Spam Taxonomy. In *Proceedings of the Adversarial Information Retrieval on the web (AIRWeb) Conference* (pp. 39-47).

Haas, Z. J., Deng, J., Liang, B., Papadimitratos, P., & Sajama, S. (2001). *Wireless Ad-Hoc Networking*. Retrieved from http://www.ece.cornell.edu/~haas/wnl/html

Haas, Z. J. (2001). *The Interzone Routing Protocol (IERP) for Ad Hoc Networks. Internet Engineering Task Force (IETF)*. MANET Working Group.

Hagen, J. M., Albrechtsen, E., & Hovden, J. (2008). Implementation and effectiveness of organizational information security measures. *Information Management & Computer Security, 16*(4), 377–397. doi:10.1108/09685220810908796

Hajek, P., Havel, I., & Chytil, M. (1966). The GUHA method of automatic hypotheses determination. *Computing, 1*, 293–308. doi:10.1007/BF02345483

Halderman, J. A., Seth, D. S., Nadia, H., William, C., William, P., & Joseph, A. C. (2009). Lest we remember: Cold-boot attacks on encryption keys. *Communications of the ACM, 52*(5), 91–98. doi:10.1145/1506409.1506429

Han, J., Pei, J., & Yin, Y. (2000). Mining frequent patterns without candidate generation. In *Proceedings of the 2000 ACM SIGMOD International Conference on Management of Data*, Dallas, TX (pp. 1-12). New York, NY: ACM.

Han, S., Ahn, Y. Y., Moon, S., & Jeong, H. (2006). Collaborative Blog Spam Filtering Using Adaptive Percolation Search. In *Proceedings of the WWW2006 Conference,* Edinburgh, UK.

Han, J., & Kamber, M. (2006). *Data Mining Concepts and Techniques* (2nd ed.). Amsterdam, The Netherlands: Elsevier.

Han, J., Pei, J., Yin, Y., & Mao, R. (2004). Mining frequent patterns without candidate generation: A frequent-pattern tree approach. *Data Mining and Knowledge Discovery, 8*(1). doi:10.1023/B:DAMI.0000005258.31418.83

Hansen, J. (2002). *802.11a/b A Physical Medium Comparison.* Retrieved from http://mobiledevdesign.com/hardware_news/radio_ba_physical_medium/

Hardee, J. B., West, R., & Mayhorn, C. B. (2006). To Download or Not to Download: An Examination of Computer Security Decision Making. *Interaction, 13*(3), 32–37.

Hardy, G. (2006). Guidance on aligning COBIT, ITIL and ISO 17799. *Information Systems Control Journal, 1.*

Harkavy, J. (2008). *Secret software blamed for Hannaford Breach.* Retrieved from http://www.msnbc.msn.com/id/23846014/ns/technology_and_science-security/

Harris, D., & Harris, S. (2007). *Digital Design and Computer Architecture: From Gates to Processors.* San Francisco, CA: Morgan Kaufmann.

Harrison, M. D., & Sujan, M. A. (Eds.). (2008). *Proceedings of the 27ᵗʰ International Conference on Computer Safety, Reliability and Security,* New Castle upon Tyne, UK (LNCS 4680). Berlin, Germany: Springer-Verlag.

Hartigan, J. A. (1975). *Clustering Algorithms.* New York, NY: Wiley.

Hartleid, J. E., & Casey, L. (1993, June). The Iridium system personal communications anytime, anyplace. In *Proceedings of the 3rd International Mobile Satellite Conference,* Pasadena, CA (pp. 285-290).

Hasen, R. L. (2000). Vote buying. *California Law Review, 88.*

Hassell, L., & Wiedenbeck, S. (2004). *Human Factors and Information Security* (Tech. Rep.). Philadelphia, PA: Drexel University. Retrieved from http://clam.rutgers.edu/~birget/grPssw/hasselSue.pdf

Hearst, M. A., Hurst, M., & Dumais, S. T. (2008). What Should Blog Search Look Like. In *Proceedings of the 2008 ACM Workshop on Search in Social Media,* Napa Valley, CA.

Herbst, C., Oswald, E., & Mangard, S. (2006). An AES smart card mplementation resistant to power analysis attacks. In J. Zhou, M. Yung, & F. Bao (Eds.), *Proceedings of the 4ᵗʰ International Conference on Applied Cryptography and Network Security* (LNCS, 3989, pp. 239-252).

Higgins, J. J. (2004). *An introduction to modern nonparametric statistics.* Pacific Grove, CA: Thomson/Brooks/Cole.

Hinde, S. (2002). In Audit, I. S. (Ed.), *The perils of privacy* (pp. 424–432). Amsterdam, The Netherlands: Elsevier Science.

Hollerung, T. D. (2004). *The Cluster-Based Routing Protocol.* Paderborn, Germany: University of Paderborn.

Holsti, O. R. (1969). *Content analysis for the social sciences and humanities.* Reading, MA: Addison-Wesley.

http://www.oracle.com/technetwork/java/javacard/javacard1-139251.html

Huang, C., Jiang, Q., & Zhang, Y. (2010). Detecting comment spam through content analysis. In *Proceedings of the 2010 International Conference on Web-age Information Management.*

Hubaux, J., Buttyan, L., & Capkun, S. (2001). The quest for security in mobile ad hoc networks. In *Proceedings of the Conference on Mobile Ad Hoc Networking and Computing* (pp. 146-155).

Hursti, H. (2006). *Critical security issues with Diebold TSx.* Retrieved from http://www.blackboxvoting.org/BBVtsxstudy.pdf

Hussain, S. J., & Siddiqui, M. S. (2005). Quantified model of COBIT for corporate IT governance. In *Proceedings of the 1st International Conference on Information and Communication Technologies.*

Hwang, M. S., Chang, C. C., & Hwang, K. F. (2002). An ElGamal-like cryptosystem for enciphering large messages. *IEEE Transactions on Knowledge and Data Engineering, 14*(2), 445–446. doi:10.1109/69.991728

Hwang, M. S., & Sung, P. C. (2006). A study of micropayment based on one-way hash chain. *International Journal of Network Security, 2*(2), 81–90.

Iden, J., & Langeland, L. (2010). Setting the stage for a successful ITIL adoption: A Delphi study of IT experts in the Norwegian Armed Forces. *Information Systems Management, 27*(2), 103–112. doi:10.1080/10580531003708378

Identity Theft Resource Center. (2008). *2007 ITRC Breach Report.* Retrieved August, 26, 2009, from http://idtheftmostwanted.org/ITRC%20Breach%20Report%20 2007.pdf

Identity Theft Resource Center. (2010). *Data Breaches.* Retrieved June 15, 2010, from http://www.idtheftcenter. org/artman2/publish/lib_survey/ITRC_2008_Breach_ List.shtml

Identity Theft Resource Center. (2010). *Data Breaches: A Black Hole.* Retrieved July 14, 2010, from http:// www.idtheftcenter.org/artman2/publish/headlines/ Data_Breaches_1H_2010.shtml

Identity Theft Resource Center. (2010). *Identity Theft Resource Center: 2009 Breach List.* Retrieved March 4, 2010, from http://www.idtheftcenter.org/artman2/ uploads/1/ITRC_Breach_Report_20100106.pdf

Identity Theft Resource Center. (2010). *Identity Theft Resource Center®, Nonprofit Organization.* Retrieved July 7, 2010, from http://www.idtheftcenter.org/

Identity Theft Resource Centre (ITRC). (2008). *2009 Data Breach Statistics.* San Diego, CA: Author.

Identity Theft Resource Centre (ITRC). (2009). *2009 Data Breach Statistics.* San Diego, CA: Author.

Identity Theft Resource Centre (ITRC). (2010). *2010 Data Breach Statistics.* San Diego, CA: Author.

Ifinedo, P. (2009). Information technology security management concerns in global financial services institutions is national culture a differentiator? *Information Management & Computer Security, 17*(5), 372–387. doi:10.1108/09685220911006678

Industry Canada. (2003). *Privacy and the information highway, regulatory options for Canada* (Ch. 6). Retrieved September 5, 2003, from http://strategis.ic.gc.ca/SSG/ ca00257e.html#6

International Association of Chiefs of Police. (2005). *Local Law Enforcement's Response to Identity Theft Crimes.* Retrieved May, 4, 2011, from http://www.theiacp.org/ Portals/0/pdfs/WhatsNew/IdentityTheft.pdf

International Organization for Standardization (ISO). (2005). *ISO/IEC 27002:2005: Information technology -- Security techniques -- Code of practice for information security management.* Retrieved from http://www.iso.org/ iso/catalogue_detail?csnumber=50297

International Organization for Standardization (ISO). (2008). *Introduction to ISO 27002.* Retrieved from http:// www.27000.org/iso-27002.htm

International Organization for Standardization. (1987). *ISO/IEC 7816: Electronic identification cards with contacts, especially smart cards 15 minus 1 Part Series.* Geneva, Switzerland: International Standards Organisation (ISO) and the International Electrotechnical Commission (IEC).

International Organization for Standardization. (2000). *ISO/IEC 14443: Proximity cards (PICCs) 4 Part Series.* Geneva, Switzerland: International Standards Organisation (ISO) and the International Electrotechnical Commission (IEC).

International, S. R. I. (n. d.). *Event Monitoring Enabling Responses to Anomalous Live Disturbances (EMERALD).* Retrieved from http://www.sdl.sri.com/projects/emerald/

Ippolito, L. J. Jr. (2008). *Satellite communications systems engineering: atmospheric effects, satellite link design and system performance.* New York, NY: Wiley. doi:10.1002/9780470754443

Ishida, K. (2008). Extracting spam blogs with co-citation clusters. In *Proceedings of the WWW 2008 Conference.*

ISO/IEC. (2000). *Information Technology – Code of practice for information security management, ISO/IEC 17799:2000.* Geneva, Switzerland: Author.

ISO/IEC. (2005). *Information Technology – Code of practice for information security management, ISO/IEC 27002:2005.* Geneva, Switzerland: Author.

IT Governance Institute (ITGI). (2006). *IT Governance Global Status Report - 2006.* Rolling Meadows, IL: Author.

IT Governance Institute (ITGI). (2008). *Aligning COBIT 4.1, ITIL V3 and ISO/IEC 27002 for Business Benefit.* Rolling Meadows, IL: Author.

IT Governance Institute (ITGI). (2008). *IT Governance Global Status Report.* Rolling Meadows, IL: Author.

IT Governance Institute. (2007). *Control Objectives for Information and Related Technology (COBIT) 4.1.* Rolling Meadows, IL: Author.

ITU-T. (2005). *ITU-T recommendation X.509/ISO/IEC 9594-8: Information technology. Open systems interconnection - The directory: Public-key and attribute certificate frameworks.* Retrieved from http://www.infosecurity.org.cn/content/pki_pmi/x509v4.pdf

Jackson, M. (2001). *Problem frames.* London, UK: Addison-Wesley.

Jacobson, I. (1992). *Object-oriented software engineering: a use case driven approach.* Reading, MA: Addison-Wesley.

Javelin Strategy and Research. (2008). *Consumer Survey in Data Breach Notification.* Retrieved July 25, 2010, from http://www.tawpi.org/uploadDocs/Data_Breach_survey.pdf

Javelin Strategy and Research. (2010). *2010 Data Breach Prevention and Response: Causes, Consumer Consequences, and Tools for Layered Defense.* Retrieved July 20, 2010, from https://www.javelinstrategy.com/uploads/1016.R_2010%20Data%20Breach%20Prevention%20and%20Response%20Sample%20Report.pdf

Javelin Strategy and Research. (2010). *2010 Identity Fraud Survey Report.* Retrieved July 10, 2010, from https://www.javelinstrategy.com/research/Brochure-170

Jewell, M. (2007). *TJX breach could top 94 million accounts.* Retrieved from http://www.msnbc.msn.com/id/21454847/ns/technology_and_science-security/

Jindal, N., & Liu, B. (2007, May 8-12). Review Spam Detection. In *Proceedings of the WWW 2007 Conference,* Banff, AB, Canada.

Johnson, D. B., & Maltz, D. A. (1996). Dynamic Source Routing in Ad-Hoc Networks in Mobile Computing. In Imielinski, T., & Korth, H. (Eds.), *Mobile Computing* (pp. 153–181). Dordrecht, The Netherlands: Kluwer Academic Publishers. doi:10.1007/978-0-585-29603-6_5

Jones, D. W. (2005). *Threats to voting systems.* Paper presented at the NIST Workshop on Threats to Voting Systems, Gaithersburg, MD.

Jones, V. E., Ching, N., & Winslett, M. (1995, August 22-25). Credentials for privacy and interoperation. In *Proceedings of the New Security Paradigms Workshop* (pp. 92-100).

Jubin, J., & Tornow, J. D. (1987). DARPA Packet Radio Networks. *Proceedings of the IEEE, 75*(1), 21–32. doi:10.1109/PROC.1987.13702

Juran, J., & Godfrey, B. (1999). *Juran's quality handbook* (5th ed.). New York, NY: McGraw-Hill.

Jurjens, J. (2003). Developing safety-critical systems with UML. In P. Stevens, J. Whittle, & G. Booch (Eds.), *Proceedings of the Sixth International Conference on the Unified Modeling Language,* San Francisco, CA (LNCS 2863, pp. 144-159).

Kahn, R. (1978). Advances in Packet Radio Technology. *Proceedings of the IEEE, 66,* 1468–1496. doi:10.1109/PROC.1978.11151

Kang, D.-H., Kim, B.-K., Oh, J.-T., Nam, T.-Y., & Jang, J.-S. (2006). FPGA based intrusion detection system against unknown and known attacks. In Z.-Z. Shi & R. Sadananda (Eds.), *Proceedings of the 9th Pacific Rim International Workshop on Agent Computing and Multi-Agent Systems* (LNCS 4088, pp. 801-806).

Kantarcioglu, M., & Clifton, C. (2004). Privacy-preserving distributed mining of association rules on horizontally partitioned data. *IEEE Transactions on Knowledge and Data Engineering, 16*(9), 1026–1037. doi:10.1109/TKDE.2004.45

Kaosar, M. G., Paulet, R., & Yi, X. (2011, January 17-20). *Secure two-party association rule mining.* Paper presented at the Australasian Information Security Conference (AISC 2011), Perth, WA, Australia.

Kapron, B., Malka, L., & Srinivasan, V. (2007). A characterization of non-interactive instance-dependent commitment-schemes (NIC). In *Proceedings of the 34th International EATCS Colloquium on Automata, Languages and Programming* (pp. 328-339).

Karig, D., & Lee, R. (2001). *Remote denial of service attacks and countermeasures* (Tech. Rep. No. CE-L2001-002). Princeton, NJ: Princeton University.

Katashita, T., Yamaguchi, Y., Maeda, A., & Toda, K. (2007). FPGA-based intrusion detection system for 10 gigabit ethernet. *IEICE Transactions on Information and Systems*, *90*(12), 1923–1931. doi:10.1093/ietisy/e90-d.12.1923

Katos, V., & Patel, A. (2008). A Partial Equilibrium View on Security and Privacy. *Information Management & Computer Security*, *16*(1), 74–83. doi:10.1108/09685220810862760

Kenny, S., & Korba, L. (2002). Adapting digital rights management to privacy rights management. *Computers & Security*, *21*(7), 648–664. doi:10.1016/S0167-4048(02)01117-3

Kim, B.-K., Heo, Y.-J., & Oh, J.-T. (2006). Design and implementation of FPGA based high-performance intrusion detection system. In S. Mehrotra, D. D. Zeng, H. Chen, B. M. Thuraisingham, & F.-Y. Wang (Eds.), *Proceedings of the IEEE International Conference on Intelligence and Security Informatics* (LNCS 3975, pp. 724-725).

Kirk, J. (2007). *Google calls for global online privacy standard*. Retrieved from http://www.infoworld.com/article/07/09/14/Google-calls-for-global-online-privacy-standard_1.html

Klein-Berndt, L. (2001). *A quick guide to AODV routing*. Retrieved from http://www.antd.nist.gov/wctg/aodv_kernel/aodv_guide.pdf

Knuth, D. E. (1997). The art of computer programming: *Vol. 2. Seminumerical algorithms* (3rd ed.). Reading, MA: Addison-Wesley.

Kocher, P., Jaffe, J., & Jun, B. (1999). Differential power analysis. In M. J. Wiener (Ed.), *Proceedings of the Workshop on Advances in Cryptology* (LNCS 1666, pp. 388-397).

Kohnfelder, M. (1978). *A method for certification (Tech. Rep.)*. Cambridge, MA: MIT, Laboratory for Computer Science.

Kohno, T., Stubblefield, A., Rubin, A. D., & Wallach, D. S. (2004). Analysis of an electronic voting system. In *Proceedings of the IEEE Symposium on Security and Privacy* (pp. 27-40.)

Kolari, P. (2007). *Detecting Spam Blogs: An Adaptive Online Approach*. Unpublished doctoral dissertation, University of Maryland, Baltimore County.

Kolari, P., Java, A., Finin, T., Oates, T., & Joshi, A. (2006). Detecting Spam Blogs: A Machine Learning Approach. In *Proceedings of the AAAI 2006 Conference.*

Krishna, P., Vaidya, N. H., Chatterjee, M., & Pradhan, D. K. (1997). A cluster-based approach for routing in dynamic networks. *ACM SIGCOMM Computer Communications Review*, *27*, 49–65. doi:10.1145/263876.263885

Ku, L., Liang, Y., & Chen, H. (2006). *Opinion Extraction, Summarization and Tracking*. Menlo Park, CA: American Association for Artificial Intelligence.

Kulak, D., & Guiney, E. (2000). *Use cases: requirements in context*. New York, NY: ACM.

Laboratoire Spécification et Vérification. (n. d.). *Orchids Real-Time Intrusion Detection System (IDS)*. Retrieved from http://www.lsv.ens-cachan.fr/Software/orchids/

Lainhart, J. W. (2000). COBIT: A methodology for managing and controlling information and information technology risks and vulnerabilities. *Journal of Information Systems*, *14*, 21–25. doi:10.2308/jis.2000.14.s-1.21

Lainhart, J. W. (2001). COBIT: An IT assurance framework for the future. *The Ohio CPA Journal*, *60*(1), 19–23.

Lamsweerde, V., Brohez, S., De Landtsheer, R., & Janssens, D. (2003). From system goals to intruder anti-goals: attack generation and resolution for security requirements engineering. In *Proceedings of the 2nd International Workshop on Requirements Engineering for High Assurance Systems*, Pittsburgh, PA (pp.49-56).

Laredo, V. G. (2009). PCI DSS compliance: A matter of strategy. *Card Technology Today*, *20*(4), 9. doi:10.1016/S0965-2590(08)70094-X

Latif, A. A., Din, M. M., & Ismail, R. (2010). *Challenges in adopting and integrating ITIL and CMMi in ICT division of a public utility company*. Paper presented at the 2nd International Conference on Computer Engineering and Applications, Bali, Indonesia.

Law, Y. W., Hoesel, L., Doumen, J., Hartel, P., & Havinga, P. (2005). Energy-efficient link-layer jamming attacks against wireless sensor network MAC protocols. In *Proceedings of the 3rd ACM Workshop on Security of Ad hoc and Sensor Networks*, Alexandria, VA (pp. 76-88).

Lee, C. C. (2001). *User authentication schemes for mobile communications*. Unpublished doctoral dissertation, Chaoyang University of Technology, Taiwan.

Lee, C. C. (2007). *Mobile users' privacy and authentication in wireless communication systems*. Unpublished doctoral dissertation, National Chung Hsing University, China.

Lee, J. W., & Marshall, V. A. (1994, October). Maximum capacity prediction and anti-jamm performance analysis for commercial satellite communication systems. In *Proceedings of the IEEE Military Communications Conference (MILCOM 94)*, Fort Monmouth, NJ (pp. 506-510).

Lee, T. F., Chang, S. H., Hwang, T., & Chong, S. K. (2009). Enhanced Delegation-Based Authentication Protocol for PCSs. *IEEE Transactions on Wireless Communications*, *8*(5), 2166–2171. doi:10.1109/TWC.2009.070032

Lee, W. B., & Yeh, C. K. (2005). A new delegation-based authentication protocol for use in portable communication systems. *IEEE Transactions on Wireless Communications*, *4*(1), 57–64. doi:10.1109/TWC.2004.840220

Li, J., & Wang, S. (2007). New efficient proxy blind signature scheme using verifiable self-certified public key. *International Journal of Network Security*, *4*(2), 193–200.

Lin, C.-H., Huang, C.-T., Jiang, C.-P., & Chang, S.-C. (2006). Optimization of regular expression pattern matching circuits on FPGA. In *Proceedings of the Conference on Design, Automation and Test in Europe*, Leuven, Belgium (pp. 12-17).

Lin, L., Nuseibeh, B., Ince, D., & Jackson, M. (2004). Using abuse frames to bound the scope of security problems. In *Proceedings of the 12th IEEE International Requirements Engineering Conference*, Kyoto, Japan (pp. 354-355).

Liu, L., Yu, E., & Mylopoulos, J. (2003). Security and privacy requirements analysis within a social setting. In *Proceedings of the 11th IEEE International Conference on Requirements Engineering* (pp. 151-161).

Liu, J., Xiao, Y., Chen, H., Ozdemir, S., Dodle, S., & Singh, V. (2010). A survey of payment card industry data security standard. *IEEE Communications Surveys & Tutorials*, *12*(3), 287–303. doi:10.1109/SURV.2010.031810.00083

Li, Y., & Wei, J. (2004). Guidelines on selecting intrusion detection methods in MANET. In. *Proceedings of the Information Systems Education Conference*, *21*, 1–17.

Luftman, J. N., & Brier, T. (1999). Achieving and sustaining business-IT alignment. *California Management Review*, *1*, 109–122. doi:10.2307/41166021

Luftman, J. N., Lewis, P. R., & Oldach, S. H. (1993). Transforming the enterprise: The alignment of business and information technology strategies. *IBM Systems Journal*, *32*(1). doi:10.1147/sj.321.0198

Luo, Y., Zhao, Y., & Le, J. (2009). A survey on the privacy preserving algorithm of association rule mining. In *Proceedings of the 2009 2nd International Symposium on Electronic Commerce and Security (ISECS '09)* (Vol. 1, pp. 241-245).

MacDonald, D. (1999). Elephants. In MacDonald, D. (Ed.), *The encyclopedia of mammals*. Oxford, UK: Oxford University Press.

MacQueen, J. B. (1967). Some Methods for classification and Analysis of Multivariate Observations. In *Proceedings of 5th Berkeley Symposium on Mathematical Statistics and Probability* (pp. 281-297).

Mahoney, T., Kerr, P., Felstead, B., Wells, P., Cunningham, M., Baumgartner, G., & Jeronim, L. (1999, October 31-November 3). An investigation of the military applications of commercial personal satellite-communications systems. In *Proceedings of the IEEE Military Communications Conference (MILCOMM 1999)* (Vol. 1, pp. 112-116).

Malman, S. (2000). Memes and corporate identities in the telecommunication sector. In *Proceedings of the XIII Biennial Conference of the International Telecommunications Society (ITS 2000)*. Retrieved from http://www.its2000.org.ar/conference/malman.pdf

Mandala, S., Ngadi, M. A., & Abdullah, A. H. (2007). A survey on MANET intrusion detection. *International Journal of Computer Science and Security*, *2*(1), 1–11.

Manoj, B. S., & Baker, H. (2007). Communications Challenges in Emergency Response. *Communications of the ACM*, *50*(3), 51–53. doi:10.1145/1226736.1226765

Martin, J. (1973). *Security, Accuracy, and Privacy in Computer Systems*. Englewood Cliffs, NJ: Prentice-Hall.

MasterCard. (2011). *Merchant levels defined.* Retrieved from http://www.mastercard.com/us/sdp/merchants/merchant_levels.html

Matulevicius, R., Mayer, N., Mouratidis, H., Dubois, E., Heymans, P., & Genon, N. (2008). Adapting secure tropos for security risk management in the early phases of information systems development. In E. Dubois & K. Pohl (Eds.), *Proceedings of the 20ᵗʰ International Conference on Advanced Information Systems Engineering*, Montpellier, France (LNCS 5074, pp 541-555).

Mayer, N., Rifaut, A., & Dubois, E. (2005). Towards a risk-based security requirements engineering framework. In *Proceedings of the International Workshop on Requirements Engineering for Software Quality, Foundations of Software Quality* (pp. 89-104).

McAllister, N. (2009). *Developers should learn from the Palm Pre's privacy mistakes.* Retrieved from http://www.infoworld.com/d/developer-world/developers-should-learn-palm-pres-privacy-mistakes-529

McDermott, J. (2001). Abuse-case-based assurance argument. In *Proceedings of the 17ᵗʰ Annual Computer Security Applications Conference*, New Orleans, LA (p. 0366).

McDermott, J., & Fox, C. (1999). Using abuse case model for security requirements analysis. In *Proceedings of the 15ᵗʰ Annual Computer Security Applications Conference*, Phoenix, AZ (p. 55).

McGraw, G. (2006). *Software security: Building security.* Upper Saddle River, NJ: Pearson Education.

Mead, N. R. (2007). *How to compare the security quality requirements engineering (SQUARE) method with other method* (Tech. Rep. No. CMU/SEI2007-TN-021). Pittsburgh, PA: Software Engineering Institute, Carnegie, Mellon University.

Meckley, J. (1998). *Definition - Smartcard.* Retrieved from http://searchsecurity.techtarget.com/definition/smart-card

Melnyk, S. A., Stewart, D. M., & Swink, M. (2004). Metrics and performance measurement in operations management: Dealing with the metrics maze. *Journal of Operations Management, 22*(3), 209–218. doi:10.1016/j.jom.2004.01.004

Micali, S., & Shamir, A. (1990). An improvement of the Fiat-Shamir identification and signature scheme. In S. Goldwasser (Ed.), *Proceedings of the Workshop on Advances in Cryptology* (LNCS 403, pp. 244-247).

Miller, G. (1995). WordNet: a lexical database of English. *Communications of the ACM, 38*, 39–41. doi:10.1145/219717.219748

Milne, G. R., & Culnan, M. J. (2004). Strategies for reducing online privacy risks: Why consumers read (or don't read) online privacy notices. *Journal of Interactive Marketing, 18*(3), 15–29. doi:10.1002/dir.20009

Mishne, G. (2006). Multiple Ranking Strategies for Opinion Retrieval in Blogs. In *Proceedings of the TREC 2006 Conference.*

Mishne, G., & Carmel, D. (2005). Blocking blog spam with language model disagreement. In *Proceedings of the AIRWeb 2005 Conference.*

Mølmann, R. A. (2003). The Human Factor – Taxonomy for classifying human challenges to information security. In Kufås, I., & Mølmann, R. A. (Eds.), *Informasjonssikkerhet og innsideproblematikk. Institutt for produksjons- og kvalitetsteknikk.* Trondheim, Norway: NTNU.

Moores, T. T., & Dhillon, G. (2003). Do Privacy Seals in E-Commerce Really Work? *Communications of the ACM, 46*(12), 265–271.

Morshed, M. M., Ko, F. I. S., Lim, D., Rahman, M. H., Mazumder, M. R. R., & Ghosh, J. (2010). Performance evaluation of DSDV and AODV routing protocols in mobile ad hoc networks. In *Proceedings of the IEEE Conference on New Trends in Information Science and Service Science*, Dongguk, South Korea (pp. 399-403).

Motorola. (2001). *C2000 The Netherlands Digital Radio Networks for Public Safety.* Retrieved from http://www.motorola.com/governmentandenterprise/contentdir/en_GB/Files/CaseStudies/c2000.pdf

Moulton, R., & Coles, R. S. (2003). Applying information security governance. *Computers & Security, 22*(7). doi:10.1016/S0167-4048(03)00705-3

Murthy, C. S. R., & Manoj, B. S. (2004). *Ad Hoc Wireless Networks: Architecture and Protocols.* Upper Saddle River, NJ: Pearson Education-Prentice Hall.

Murthy, S., & Garcia-Luna-Aceves, J. J. (1996). An efficient Routing Protocol for Wireless Networks. *Mobile Networks and Applications, 1*(2), 183–197. doi:10.1007/BF01193336

Musa, A. (2010). Information security governance in Saudi organizations: An empirical study. *Information Management & Computer Security, 18*(4), 226–276. doi:10.1108/09685221011079180

Nadkarni, K., & Misra, A. (2004). A novel intrusion detection approach for wireless ad hoc networks. In *Proceedings of the IEEE Wireless Communications and Networking Conference* (pp. 831-836).

Nam, C., Song, C., Lee, E., & Park, C. (2006). Consumers' Privacy Concerns and Willingness to Provide Marketing-Related Personal Information Online. *Advances in Consumer Research. Association for Consumer Research (U. S.), 33*(1), 212–217.

Newman, A. (2009). *Regulating personal data in the global economy*. Ithaca, NY: Cornell University.

News, B. B. C. (1998). *Floods in Worcestershire*. Retrieved from http://news.bbc.co.uk/1/hi/uk/

News, B. B. C. (2004). *BT Manchester Tunnel Fire*. Retrieved from http://news.bbc.co.uk/1/hi/england/manchester/

News, B. B. C. (2007). *Floods in Herefordshire and Worcestershire*. Retrieved from http://news.bbc.co.uk/1/hi/uk/

News, B. B. C. (2009). *China Earthquake*. Retrieved from http://news.bbc.co.uk/1/hi/in_depth/asia_pacific/2008/china_quake/default.stm

News, B. B. C. (2009). *Earthquake L'Aquila, central Italy*. Retrieved from http://news.bbc.co.uk/1/hi/world/europe/

Ngugi, B., Dardick, G., & Vega, G. (2009). Lessons from computer intrusion at TJX. *The CASE Journal, 3*(2).

Ngugi, B., Vega, G., & Dardick, G. (2009). PCI compliance: Overcoming the challenges. *International Journal of Information Security and Privacy, 3*(2), 54–67. doi:10.4018/jisp.2009040104

Nguyen, M.-H., & Vadhan, S. (2006, May 21-23). Zero knowledge with efficient provers. In *Proceedings of the Thirty-Eighth Annual ACM Symposium on Theory of Computing*, Seattle, WA (pp. 287-295).

Nilsson, M., Adams, A., & Herd, S. (2005, April 2-7). Building Security and Trust in Online Banking. In *Proceedings of the CHI 2005 Conference*, Portland, OR (pp. 1701-1704).

NIST. (2005). *Developing an analysis of threats to voting systems: Preliminary workshop summary*. Gaithersburg, MD: NIST.

Norden, L., Kimball, D., Quesenbery, W., & Chen, M. (2008). *Better ballots*. Retrieved from http://www.brennancenter.org/content/resource/better_ballots

Nowak, R. M. (1991). Elephants. In Nowak, R. M. (Ed.), *Walker's mammals of the world* (5th ed.). Baltimore, MD: The Johns Hopkins University.

NS2. (2011). *The network simulator*. Retrieved from http://www.isi.edu/nsnam/ns

Ntoulas, A., Najork, M., Manassee, M., & Fetterly, D. (2006). Detecting Spam Web Pages through Content Analysis. In *Proceedings of the WWW 2006 Conference*, Edinburgh, UK.

OASIS. (2001). *Security Services Markup Language (S2ML)*. Retrieved August 1, 2009, from http://xml.coverpages.org/s2ml.html

OASIS. (2004). *Application Vulnerability Description Language (AVDL)*. Retrieved August 1, 2009, from http://www.oasis-open.org/committees/avdl/

OASIS. (2004). *Intrusion Detection Message Exchange Format (IDMEF)*. Retrieved July 20, 2009, from http://xml.coverpages.org/idmef.html

OASIS. (2005). *OASIS eXtensible Access Control Markup Language (XACML)*. Retrieved August 1, 2009, from http://www.oasis-open.org/committees/xacml/

OASIS. (2006). *OASIS Emergency Management*. Retrieved August 1, 2009, from http://www.oasis-open.org/committees/emergency/

OASIS. (2008). *Security Assertion Markup Language (SAML)*. Retrieved August 1, 2009, from http://xml.coverpages.org/saml.html

Office of the Attorney General- State of UTAH. (2011). *Identity Theft Reporting Information System (IRIS)*. Retrieved from http://www.idtheft.utah.gov/iris.html

Ohio Secretary of State. (2003). *Direct recording electronic (DRE), Technical security assessment report*. Retrieved from http://www.sos.state.oh.us/sos/upload/everest/01-compuware112103.pdf

Ohta, K., & Okamoto, T. (1990). A modification of the Fiat-Shamir scheme. In S. Goldwasser (Ed.), *Proceedings of the Workshop on Advances in Cryptology* (LNCS 403, pp. 232-243).

Oliver, D. J. (2003). A Selective Approach to COBIT. *Information Systems Control Journal, 3*.

Ong, S., & Vadhan, S. (2007). Zero knowledge and soundness are symmetric. In M. Naor (Ed.), *Proceedings of the 26th Annual International Conference on Advances in Cryptology* (LNCS 4515, pp. 187-209).

Open Security Foundation. (2010). *Data Loss Statistics.* Retrieved July 20, 2010, from http://datalossdb.org/statistics

Open Security Foundation. (2010). *State-by-State Listing of Data Loss and Freedom of Information Legislation.* Retrieved July 10, 2010, from http://datalossdb.org/us_states

Open Security Foundation. (2011). *DataLoss Database.* Retrieved January 3, 2011, from http://datalossdb.org/download

OpenNLP. (2010). *Home.* Retrieved from http://opennlp.sourceforge.net/

Oracle. (2010). *Java Card platform specification 2.2.2.* Retrieved from http://java.sun.com/javacard/specs.html

Oracle. (2010). *Smart Card overview-Chip comparisons.* Retrieved from http://www.oracle.com/technetwork/java/javacard/documentation/smartcards-136372.html#chart

Oritz, C. E. (2003). *An introduction to JAVA Card technology – Part 1.* Retrieved from.

Ouyang, W., & Huang, Q. (2006). Privacy preserving association rules mining based on secure two-party computation. In *Intelligent Control and Automation* (LNCIS 344, pp. 969-975).

Oz, E. (1994). Barriers to international data transfer. *Journal of Global Information Management, 2*(2), 22–29.

Paillier, P. (1999). Public-key cryptosystems based on composite degree residuosity classes. In *Proceedings of the Advances in Cryptology Conference (Eurocrypt 1999)*, Prague, Czech Republic (pp. 223-238).

Palmer, J. W. (2002). Website usability, design and performance metrics. *Information Systems Research, 13*(2), 151–162. doi:10.1287/isre.13.2.151.88

Pardue, H., Landry, J., & Yasinsac, A. (2009). A risk assessment model for voting systems using threat trees and Monte Carlo simulation. In *Proceedings of the First International Workshop on Requirements Engineering for E-voting Systems*, Atlanta, GA (pp. 55-60).

Parker, D. B. (2006). Making the case for replacing risk-based security. *ISSA Journal*, 6-9.

Patel, A. (2010). Concept of mobile agent-based electronic marketplace – Safety measures. In Lee, I. (Ed.), *Encyclopedia of e-business development and management in the digital economy* (*Vol. 1*, pp. 252–264). Hershey, PA: IGI Global.

Pathak, J. (2003). Internal audit and e-commerce controls. *Internal Auditing, 18*(2), 30–34.

Patwardhan, A., Parker, J., Joshi, A., Iorga, M., & Karygiannis, T. (2005). Secure routing and intrusion detection in ad hoc networks. In *Proceedings of the 3rd International Conference on Pervasive Computing and Communications* (pp. 191-199).

Payne, S. (2006). *A Guide to Security Metrics- SANS Security Essential GSEC Practical Assignment Version 1.2e.* Retrieved November 5, 2010, from http://www.sans.org/reading_room/whitepapers/auditing/guide-security-metrics_55

Pedley, P. (2002). Data protection for intranets and web sites. *Business Information Review, 19*(3), 41. doi:10.1177/026638202401093608

Peltier, T. R. (2001). *Information security risk analysis* (2nd ed.). Boca Raton, FL: Auerbach.

Peña, D. (2002). *Análisis de datos multivariantes.* Madrid, Spain: McGraw-Hill/Interamericana de España.

Peng, T., Leckie, C., & Ramamohanarao, K. (2007). Survey of network-based defense mechanisms countering the DoS and DDoS problems. *ACM Computing Surveys, 39*(1). doi:10.1145/1216370.1216373

Personal Data Privacy and Security Act of 2009, 111th Congress, S.1490 Cong. Rec. (2009).

Peslak, A. R. (2006). Internet privacy policies of the largest international companies. *Journal of Electronic Commerce in Organizations, 4*(3), 46–62. doi:10.4018/jeco.2006070103

Peyret, P. (1995). *Which Smart Card technologies will you need to ride the information highway safely?* Retrieved from http://www.gemalto.com/gemplus/index.html

Phillips, R., Freeman, E., & Wicks, A. (2003). What stakeholder theory is not. *Business Ethics Quarterly*, *13*(4), 479–502.

Pollard, C., & Cater-Steel, A. (2009). Justifications, strategies, and critical success factors in successful ITIL implementations in US and Australian companies: An exploratory study. *Information Systems Management*, *26*, 164–175. doi:10.1080/10580530902797540

Posthumus, S., & von Solms, R. (2004). A framework for the governance of information security. *Computers & Security*, *23*, 638–646. doi:10.1016/j.cose.2004.10.006

Potts, T. (2008, November 5). *Fire guts Patton store, forces change of polls*. Retrieved from http://www.tribune-democrat.com/local/local_story_310012455.html

Powers, C. S., Ashley, P., & Schunter, M. (2002). Privacy promises, access control, and privacy management - Enforcing privacy throughout an enterprise by extending access control. In *Proceedings of the 3rd International Symposium on Electronic Commerce* (pp. 13-21).

Pratt, J., & Conger, S. (2009). Without Permission: Privacy on the Line. *International Journal of Information Security and Privacy*, *3*(1), 30–44. doi:10.4018/jisp.2009010103

Privacy Commissioner -Canada, & Information & Privacy Commissioner-Alberta. (2007). *Report of an Investigation into the Security, Collection and Retention of Personal Information at TJX*. Retrieved from http://www.scribd.com/doc/47024592/TJX-Investigation-Report-P2007-IR-0061

Provos, N., McNamee, D., Mavrommatis, P., Wang, K., & Modadugu, N. (2007). The Ghost in the Browser Analysis of Web-based Malware. In *Proceedings of the 1st Conference on Hot Topics in Understanding Botnets.*

Puttini, R., Percher, J., Me, L., & Sousa, R. (2004). A fully distributed IDS for MANET. In *Proceedings of the IEEE Symposium on Computers and Communications* (pp. 331-338).

Puttini, R., Percher, J., Me, L., Camp, O., & De Souza, R. (2003). A modular architecture for distributed IDS. In V. Kumar, M. L. Gavrilova, C. J. Tan, & P. L'Ecuyer (Eds.), *Proceedings of the International Conference on Computational Science and its Applications* (LNCS 2669, pp. 91-113)

Quisquater, J. J., Quisquater, M., Guillou, L., Guillou, M., Guillou, G., Guillou, A., et al. (1990). How to explain zero-knowledge protocols to your children. In G. Brassard (Ed.), *Proceedings of the Workshop on Advances in Cryptology* (LNCS 435, pp. 628-631).

R Development Core Team. (2009). *R: A language and environment for statistical computing*. Vienna, Austria: R Foundation for Statistical Computing.

Radosavac, S., Benammar, N., & Baras, J. S. (2004, March 17-19). Cross-layer attacks in wireless ad hoc networks. In *Proceedings of the Conference on Information Sciences and Systems,* Princeton, NJ.

Raghani, S., Toshniwal, D., & Joshi, R. C. (2007). Distributed certification authority for mobile ad hoc networks – A dynamic approach. *Journal of Convergence Information Technology*, *2*(2), 10–20.

Ranganathan, C., & Ganapathy, S. (2002). Key Dimensions of Business-to-Consumer Websites. *Information & Management*, *39*(6), 457–465. doi:10.1016/S0378-7206(01)00112-4

Rausch, H. (2006). Jamming commercial satellite communications during wartime: an empirical study. In *Proceedings of the 4th IEEE International Workshop on Information Assurance* (pp. 109-118).

Raymond, E. S., Relson, D., Andree, M., & Louis, G. (2004). *Bogofilter*. Retrieved from http://bogofilter.sourceforge.net

Rice, H. G. (1953). Classes of recursively enumerable sets and their decision problems. *Transactions of the American Mathematical Society*, *74*, 358–366. doi:10.1090/S0002-9947-1953-0053041-6

Richmond, R. (2009). *More Scamming and Spamming on Twitter.* Retrieved from http://gadgetwise.blogs.nytimes.com/2009/06/11/more-scamming-and-spamming-on-twitter/

Ridley, G., Young, J., & Carroll, P. (2004). COBIT and its utilization: A framework from the literature. In *Proceedings of the 37th Hawaii International Conference on System Sciences.*

Rivest, R. L., Shamir, A., & Adleman, L. (1978). A method for obtaining digital signatures and public-key cryptosystems. *Communications of the ACM, 21*(2), 120–126. doi:10.1145/359340.359342

Rizvi, S. J., & Haritsa, J. R. (2002, August 20-23). Maintaining data privacy in association rule mining. In *Proceedings of the 28th International Conference on Very Large Data Bases*, Hong Kong (pp. 682-693).

Roesch, M. (1999). Snort: Lightweight intrusion detection for networks. In *Proceedings of the 13th USENIX Conference on System Administration* (pp. 229-238).

Romanosky, S., Telang, R., & Acquisti, A. (in press). Do data breach disclosure laws reduce identity theft? *Journal of Policy Analysis and Management.*

Romero, C., Garcia-Valdez, M., & Alanis, A. A. (2010). Comparative Study of Blog Comments Spam Filtering with Machine Learning Techniques. In *Studies in Computational Intelligence* (Vol. 312, pp. 57-72).

Ross, R., Katzke, S. W., Johnson, L. A., Swanson, M., Stoneburner, G., & Rogers, G. (2007). *Recommended security controls for federal information systems.* Retrieved from http://csrc.nist.gov/publications/nistpubs/800-53-Rev3/sp800-53-rev3-final.pdf

Rostad, L. (2006). An extended misuse case notation: including vulnerabilities and the insider threats. In *Proceedings of the Conference on Requirements Engineering: Foundation for Software Quality*, Luxembourg (pp 33-43).

Rouached, M., Sallay, H., Ben Fredj, O., Ammar, A., Al-Shalfan, K., & Ben Saad, M. (2010). Formal analysis of intrusion detection systems for high speed networks. In *Proceedings of the 9th Conference in Advances in E-Activities, Information Security and Privacy* (pp. 109-115).

Rouached, M., Ben Fredj, O., Sallay, H., Ammar, A., Al-Shalfan, K., & Ben Saad, M. (in press). Lightweight RESTful IDS communication model for high speed networks. *Journal of Computer Science and Technology.*

Rowlingson, R., & Winsborrow, R. (2006). A comparison of the payment card industry data security standard with ISO17799. *Computer Fraud & Security*, 16–19. doi:10.1016/S1361-3723(06)70323-2

Roy, J., Barik, M. S., & Mazumdar, C. (2004). ESRML: A Markup Language for Enterprise Security Requirement Specification. In *Proceedings of the IEEE INDICON 2004 Conference*, Kharagpur, India (pp. 509-512).

Rumbaugh, J. (1994). Getting started: using use cases to capture requirements. *Journal of Object Oriented Programming, 7*(5), 8–23.

Rushby, J. (1994). Critical system properties: Survey and taxonomy. *Reliability Engineering & System Safety, 43*(2), 180–219. doi:10.1016/0951-8320(94)90065-5

Ryker, R., Lafleur, E., McManis, B., & Cox, K. C. (2002). Online Privacy Policies: An Assessment of the Fortune E-50. *Journal of Computer Information Systems, 42*(4), 15–20.

Saeednia, S. (1997). Identity-based and self-certified key-exchange protocols. In *Proceedings of the 2nd Australasian Conference on Information Security and Privacy,* Sydney, Australia (pp. 303-313).

Saeednia, S., & Ghodosi, H. (1999). A self-certified group-oriented cryptosystem without a combiner. In *Proceedings of the 4th Australasian Conference on Information Security and Privacy,* Sydney, Australia (pp. 192-201).

Saeednia, S. (2003). A note on Girault's self-certified model. *Information Processing Letters, 86*(6), 323–327. doi:10.1016/S0020-0190(03)00203-5

Sahami, M., Dumais, S. D., Heckerman, E., & Horvitz, A. (1998). Bayesian approach to filtering junk e-mail. In *Proceedings of the AAAI Workshop on Learning for Text Categorization.*

Sahibudin, S., Sharifi, M., & Ayat, M. (2008). Combining ITIL, COBIT and ISO/IEC 27002 in order to design a comprehensive IT framework in organizations. In *Proceedings of the 2nd Asia International Conference on Modelling & Simulation* (pp. 749-753).

Salem, O., Vaton, S., & Gravey, A. (2010). A scalable, efficient and informative approach for anomaly-based intrusion detection systems. *International Journal of Network Management, 20*(5), 271–293. doi:10.1002/nem.748

Sallay, H. (2009). An efficient secure manageable P2P Framework. In *Proceedings of the 5th International Computer Engineering Conference*, Cairo, Egypt.

Sallay, H., & Al-Shalfan, K. (2010). A standard-compliant integrated security framework. *Saudi Computer Journal, Applied Computing & Informatics, 8*(1).

Sallay, H. (2011). Towards an integrated intrusion detection monitoring in high speed networks. *Journal of Computer Science, 7*, 1094–1104. doi:10.3844/jcssp.2011.1094.1104

Sallay, H., Al-Shalfan, K., & Ben Fredj, O. (2009). A scalable distributed IDS architecture for high speed networks. *International Journal of Computer Science and Network Security, 9*(8), 9–16.

Saygin, Y., Verykios, V. S., & Elmagarmid, A. K. (2002). Privacy preserving association rule mining. In *Proceedings of the 12th International Workshop on Research Issues in Data Engineering: Engineering E-Commerce/E-Business Systems (RIDE'02)*, San Jose, CA (p. 151). Washington, DC: IEEE Computer Society.

Saygin, Y., Verykios, V. S., & Clifton, C. (2001). Using unknowns to prevent discovery of association rules. *SIGMOD Record, 30*(4), 45–54. doi:10.1145/604264.604271

Schiller, J. (2003). *Mobile Communications* (2nd ed.). Reading, MA: Addison Wesley.

Schneier, B. (1996). *Applied cryptography: Protocols, algorithms, and source code in C* (2nd ed.). New York, NY: John Wiley & Sons.

Schneier, B. (1999). Attack trees. *Dr. Dobb's Journal of Software Tools, 24*, 21–29.

Schneier, B. (2000). *Secrets & Lies: Digital Security in a Networked World*. Indianapolis, IN: John Wiley.

Schnorr, C. P. (1990). Efficient identification and signatures for smart cards. In G. Brassard (Ed.), *Proceedings of the Workshop on Advances in Cryptology* (LNCS 435, pp. 239-251).

Schnorr, C. P. (1990, March 14-16). Key distribution system using ID-related information directory suitable for mail systems. In *Proceedings of the SECURICOM'90 Conference,* Paris, France (pp. 115-122).

Schuff, D. L., Choe, Y. R., & Pai, V. S. (2007). Conservative vs. optimistic parallelization of stateful network intrusion detection. In *Proceedings of the 12th ACM SIGPLAN Symposium on Principles and Practice of Parallel Programming* (pp. 138-139).

Schweitzer, J. (1987). How security fits in — A management view: Security is essential for quality information. *Computers & Security, 6*(2), 129–132. doi:10.1016/0167-4048(87)90083-6

Scott & Scott. (2010). *State Data Breach Notification Laws*. Retrieved June 20, 2010, from http://www.scottandscottllp.com/resources/state_data_breach_notification_law.pdf

Sengupta, A., & Mazumdar, C. (2010). ESRML 2.0: A Markup Language for Expressing Requirements for Information Security Governance. In *Proceedings of the 1ˢᵗ International Conference on Management of Technologies and Information Security (ICMIS 2010)*, Allahabad, India.

Sen, S., & Clark, J. A. (2009). Intrusion detection in mobile ad hoc networks. In Misra, S., Woungang, I., & Misra, S. C. (Eds.), *Guide to wireless ad hoc networks* (pp. 427–454). London, UK: Springer. doi:10.1007/978-1-84800-328-6_17

Sepura. (2005). *Sepura Case Studies – Lancashire Fire and Rescue*. Retrieved from http://www.sepura.com/case-studies-detail.php?caseid=9

Sepura. (2005). *Sepura Case Studies – Shropshire Fire and Rescue Service*. Retrieved from http://www.sepura.com/case-studies-detail.php?caseid=11

Sepura. (2005). *Sepura Case Studies – West Yorkshire Police.* Retrieved from http://www.sepura.com/case-studies-detail.php?caseid=12

Shah, J., White, G., & Cook, J. (2007). Privacy Protection Overseas as Perceived by USA Based I.T. Professionals. *Journal of Global Information Management, 15*(1), 68–81. doi:10.4018/jgim.2007010104

Shamir, A. (1984). Identity based cryptosystems & signature schemes. In *Advances in Cryptology: Proceedings of CRYPTO '84,* Santa Barbara, CA (pp. 47-53).

Shao, Z. (2005). Improvement of threshold signature using self-certified public keys. *International Journal of Network Security, 1*(1), 24–31.

Sindre, G. (2007). A look at misuse case for safety concerns. In *Proceedings of the IFIP International Federation for Information Processing, Situational Method Engineering: Fundamentals and Experiences* (Vol. 244, pp. 252-266).

Sindre, G., & Opdahl, A. L. (2001). Capturing security requirements through misuse cases. In *Norsk Informatik Konferanse,* Tromso, Norway.

Sindre, G., & Opdahl, A. L. (2005). Eliciting security requirements with misuse cases. *Requirements Engineering, 10*(1), 34–44. doi:10.1007/s00766-004-0194-4

Singh, S., Cabraal, A., Demosthenous, C., Astbrink, G., & Furlong, M. (2007, April 28-May 3). Password Sharing: Implications for Security Design Based on Social Practice. In *Proceedings of the CHI 2007 Conference,* San Jose, CA (pp. 895-904).

Singleton, T. W. (2006). COBIT- A key to success as an IT auditor. *Information Systems Control Journal, 1.*

Smith, H. J., Milberg, S. J., & Burke, S. J. (1996). Information Privacy: Measuring Individuals' concerns about Organizational Practices. *Management Information Systems Quarterly, 20*(2), 167–196. doi:10.2307/249477

Smith, S. W. (2003). Humans in the Loop: Human-Computer Interaction and Security. *IEEE Security & Privacy, 1*(3), 75–79.

Solms, S. H. V., & Solms, R. V. (2009). *Information Security Governance.* Berlin, Germany: Springer. doi:10.1007/978-0-387-79984-1

Sommerville, I. (2003). *An integrated approach to dependability requirements engineering.* Paper presented at the 11th Safety-Critical Systems Symposium, Bristol, UK.

Spivey, J. M. (1992). *The Z Notation: A reference manual.* Upper Saddle River, NJ: Prentice Hall.

Stahlberg, M. (2000). Radio jamming attacks against two popular mobile networks. In H. Lipmaa & H. Pehu-Lehtonen (Eds.), *Proceedings of the Helsinki University of Technology Seminar on Network Security and Mobile Security.*

Stakhanova, N., Basu, S., & Wong, J. (2006). *Taxonomy of intrusion response systems* (Tech. Rep. No. 06-05). Ames, IA: Iowa State University.

Stallings, W. (2002). *Wireless Communications and Networks.* Upper Saddle River, NJ: Prentice-Hall.

Stallings, W. (2003). *Cryptography and Network Security.* Upper Saddle River, NJ: Pearson Education-Prentice Hall.

Stephens, D. O. (2007). Protecting personal privacy in the global business environment. *Information Management Journal, 41*(3), 56–59.

Sterne, D., Balasubramanyam, P., Carman, D., Wilson, B., Talpade, R., Ko, C., et al. (2005). A general cooperative intrusion detection architecture for MANETs. In *Proceedings of the 3rd IEEE International Workshop on Information Assurance* (pp. 57-70).

Stiglitz, J. E. (2003). *Globalization and its discontents.* New York, NY: W. W. Norton.

Stoneburner, G. (2001). *Underlying Technical Models for Information Technology Security* (Tech. Rep. No. 800-33). Gaithersburg, MD: National Institute of Standards and Technology.

Stoneburner, G., Goguen, A., & Feringa, A. (2002). *Risk management guide for information technology systems.* Gaithersburg, MD: National Institute of Standards and Technology.

Strong, D., & Lee, Y., W., & Wang, R., Y. (1997). Data quality in context. *Communications of the ACM, 40*(5), 103–110. doi:10.1145/253769.253804

Su, C., & Sakurai, K. (2008). A distributed privacy-preserving association rules mining scheme using frequent-pattern tree. In C. Tang, C. Ling, X. Zhou, N. Cercone, & X. Li (Eds.), *Advanced Data Mining and Applications* (LNCS 5139, pp. 170-181).

Sullivan, R. J. (2010). The changing nature of U.S. card payment fraud: Issues For industry and public policy. In *Proceedings of the Workshop on the Economics of Information Security*.

Sun Microsystems. (1997). *Java Card 2.0 reference implementation user's guide Java Card 2.0 programming concept.* Retrieved from http://www.it.iitb.ac.in/~satish/phd/smartcard/usinix_99/javacardapi21/jc2ri-users-guide.pdf

Sundt, C. (2006). Information security and the law. *Information Security Technical Report, 11*, 2–9. doi:10.1016/j.istr.2005.11.003

Tan, P. N., Steinbach, M., & Kumar, V. (2006). *Introduction to Data Mining.* Upper Saddle River, NJ: Pearson Education.

Tari, F., Ozok, A. A., & Holden, S. H. (2006, July 12-14). A Comparison of Perceived and Real Shoulder-surfing Risks between Alphanumeric and Graphical Passwords. In *Proceedings of the Symposium On Usable Privacy and Security (SOUPS)*, Pittsburgh, PA (pp. 56-66).

Technorati. (2008). *State of the Blogosphere.* Retrieved from http://technorati.com/blogging/state-of-the-blogosphere/

Telsis. (2004). *Critical Role for Telsis in 02 Airwave Network.* Retrieved from http://www.telsis.com/0218.htm

Telsis. (2005). *Telsis wins emergency services network expansion contract.* Retrieved from http://www.telsis.com/0297.htm

The President's Identity Theft Task Force- United States. (2008). *President's Identity Theft Task Force Report.* Retrieved from http://www.idtheft.gov/reports/IDTReport2008.pdf

Thompson, K. (1984). Reflections on trusting trust. *Communications of the ACM, 27*(8), 761–763. doi:10.1145/358198.358210

Tijssens, M. (2003). *Implementation of GRN's in Europe.* Retrieved from http://www.euro-police.com/pdf/tijssens.pdf

Tipton, H. F., & Henry, K. (2007). *Official (ISC)2 guide to the CISSP CBK.* Boca Raton, FL: Taylor & Francis.

Tseng, Y. M., & Jan, J. K. (1999). A group signature scheme using self-certified public keys. In *Proceedings of the 9th National Conference Information Security,* Taichung, Taiwan (pp. 165-172).

Tseng, Y. M. (2007). A heterogeneous-network aided public-key management scheme for mobile ad hoc networks. *International Journal of Network Management, 17*, 3–15. doi:10.1002/nem.603

Turner, C. W., Zavod, M., & Yurcik, W. (2001, November). Factors that affect the perception of security and privacy of e-commerce web sites. In B. Gavish (Ed.), *Proceedings of the 4th International Conference on Electronic Commerce Research (ICER-4),* Dallas, TX (Vol. 2, pp. 628-636).

Turner, M. J., Oltsik, J., & McKnight, J. (2009). *ISO, ITIL, & COBIT together foster optimal security investment.* Retrieved from http://www.thecomplianceauthority.com/iso-itil-a-cobit.php

U.S. Department of Homeland Security. (2008). *One Team, One Mission, Securing Our Homeland: U.S. Department of Homeland Security Strategic Plan Fiscal Years 2008-2013.* Retrieved from http://www.dhs.gov/xlibrary/assets/DHS_StratPlan_FINAL_spread.pdf

Udo, G. (2001). Privacy and security concerns as major barriers for e-commerce: a survey study. *Information Management & Computer Security, 9*(4), 165–174. doi:10.1108/EUM0000000005808

Umbria. (2005). *Spam in the blogosphere.* Retrieved from http://www.umbrialistens.com/consumer/showWhitePaper

United States General Accounting Office. (2002). *Critical Infrastructure Protection: Commercial Satellites Should Be More Fully Addressed.* Washington, DC: Author.

Vadhan, S. P. (2004). An unconditional study of computational zero knowledge. In *Proceedings of the 45th Annual IEEE Symposium on Foundations of Computer Science* (pp. 176-185).

Vaidya, J., & Clifton, C. (2002). Privacy preserving association rule mining in vertically partitioned data. In *Proceedings of the 8th ACM SIGKDD Conference,* Edmonton, AB, Canada (pp. 639-644). New York, NY: ACM.

Vallentin, M., Sommer, R., Lee, J., Leres, C., Paxson, V., & Tierney, B. (2007). The NIDS Cluster: Scalable, stateful network intrusion detection on commodity hardware. In C. Kruegel, R. Lippmann, & A. Clark (Eds.), *Proceedings of the 10th International Symposium on Recent Advances in Intrusion Detection* (LNCS 4637, pp. 107-126).

Valsmith, A. C. (2008). *Inside the Malicious world of Blog Comment Spam.* Retrieved from http://www.offensivecomputing.net/?q=node/800

Victorian Government, Department of Human Service. (1999). *Information Privacy Principles.* Melbourne, VIC, Australia: Author.

Vigna, G., Gwalani, S., Srinivasan, K., Belding-Royer, K. E., & Kemmerer, R. (2004). An intrusion detection tool for AODV-based ad hoc wireless networks. In *Proceedings of the 20th Annual Computer Security Applications Conference* (pp. 16-27).

Von Solms, B. (2001). Information security – A multidimensional discipline. *Computers & Security, 20,* 504–508. doi:10.1016/S0167-4048(01)00608-3

Von Solms, S. H. B. (2005). Information security governance- Compliance management vs. Operational management. *Computers & Security, 24,* 443–447. doi:10.1016/j.cose.2005.07.003

Walker, J., Cam-Winget, M., Housley, R., & Wagner, D. (2003). Security flaws in 802.11 data link protocols. *Communications of the ACM, 46*(5), 35–39. doi:10.1145/769800.769823

Wallhoff, J. (2004). *Combining ITIL with COBIT and 17799.* Retrieved from http://www.scillani.se/assets/pdf/Scillani%20Article%20Combining%20ITIL%20with%20Cobit%20and%2017799.pdf

Wan, T., Kranakis, E., & van Oorschot, P. C. (2004). Securing the destination-sequenced distance vector routing protocol (S-DSDV). In *Proceedings of the 6th International Conference on Information and Communications Security* (pp. 358-374).

Wand, Y., & Wang, R. (1996). Anchoring data quality dimensions in ontological foundations. *Communications of the ACM, 39*(11), 86–95. doi:10.1145/240455.240479

Wang, K., Parekh, J. J., & Stolfo, S. J. (2006). Anagram: a content anomaly detector resistant to mimicry attack. In D. Zamboni & C. Kruegel (Eds.), *Proceedings of the 9th International Symposium Recent Advances in Intrusion Detection* (LNCS 4219, pp. 226-248).

Wang, H., Lee, M., & Wang, C. (1998). Consumer Privacy Concerns about Internet Marketing. *Communications of the ACM, 41*(3), 63–70. doi:10.1145/272287.272299

Wang, R. Y., Storey, V. C., & Firth, C. P. (1995). A framework for analysis of data quality research. *IEEE Transactions on Knowledge and Data Engineering, 7*(4), 623–640. doi:10.1109/69.404034

Wang, R. Y., & Strong, D. M. (1996). Beyond accuracy: What data quality means to data consumers. *Journal of Management Information Systems, 12*(4), 5–33.

Warren, S., & Brandeis, L. (1890). The right to privacy. *Harvard Law Review, 4*(5), 193–220. doi:10.2307/1321160

Webb, S., Caverlee, J., & Pu, C. (2007). Characterizing Web Spam Using Content and http session Analysis. In *Proceedings of the 4th Conference on Email and Anti-Spam.*

Weier, M. (2009, July 20). Wal-Mart change hints at data-driven marketing. *InformationWeek,* 10.

Wei, Q., & Patel, A. (2009). A secure and trustworthy framework for mobile agent-based e-marketplace with digital forensics and security protocols. *International Journal of Mobile Computing and Multimedia Communications, 1*(3), 8–26. doi:10.4018/jmcmc.2009070102

Weka. (n.d.). *Weka 3: Data Mining Software in Java.* Retrieved from http://www.cs.waikato.ac.nz/ml/weka/

Weldemariam, K., & Mattioli, A. V. (2009). Experiments and data analysis of electronic voting system. In *Proceedings of the 4th International Conference on Risks and Security of Internet and Systems,* Toulouse, France.

Wenbao, J., Shuang, H., Yiqi, D., & Tinghua, L. (2006). Load balancing algorithm for high-speed network intrusion detection systems. *Journal of Tsinghua University, 46*(1), 106–110.

Westin, A. (1967). *Privacy and Freedom*. New York, NY: Atheneum.

White, M. D., & Fisher, C. (2008). Assessing our knowledge of identity theft: The challenges to effective prevention and control efforts. *Criminal Justice Policy Review*, *19*(1), 3–24. doi:10.1177/0887403407306297

Whitman, M., & Mattord, H. (2005). *Principles of Information Security* (2nd ed.). Boston, MA: Course Technology.

Whitten, A., & Tygar, J. D. (1998). *Usability of Security: A Case Study* (Tech. Rep. No. CMU-CS-98-155). Pittsburgh, PA: Carnegie Mellon University.

Whitten, A., & Tygar, J. D. (1999, August 23-26). Why Johnny Can't Encrypt: A Usability Evaluation of PGP 5.0. In *Proceedings of the 9th USENIX Security Symposium*, Washington, DC.

Wikipedia. (n.d.). *Search engine optimization.* Retrieved from http://en.wikipedia.org/wiki/Search_engine_optimization

Williams, P. (2001). Information Security Governance. *Information Security Technical Report*, *6*(3), 60–70. doi:10.1016/S1363-4127(01)00309-0

Wilson, J. (2005). *The Next Generation of Wireless LAN Emerges with 802.11n*. Santa Clara, CA: Intel.

Wilson, W. (1887). The study of administration. *Political Science Quarterly*, *2*(2), 197–222. doi:10.2307/2139277

Wood, C. C., & Banks, W. W. (1993). Human Error: An overlooked but significant information security problem. *Computers & Security*, *12*(1), 51–60. doi:10.1016/0167-4048(93)90012-T

World Wide Web Consortium. (W3C). (2003). *Extensible Markup Language (XML)*. Retrieved July 27, 2009, from http://www.w3.org/xml

Wugmeister, M., Retzer, K., & Rich, C. (2007). Global solution for cross-border data transfers: Making the case for corporate privacy rules. *Georgetown Journal of International Law*, *38*(3), 449–498.

Xie, Z. X., Quirino, T., Shyu, M. L., Chen, S. C., & Chang, L. W. (2006). A distributed agent-based approach to intrusion detection using the lightweight PCC anomaly detection classifier. In *Proceedings of the IEEE International Conference on Sensor Networks, Ubiquitous, and Trustworthy Computing* (Vol. 1, pp. 446-453).

Xu, M., Lin, C., & Chen, Q. (2008). A multiple keyword fusion scheme for P2P IDS alert. In *Proceedings of the First International Conference on Intelligent Networks and Intelligent Systems* (pp. 317-320).

Xu, W., Trappe, W., Zhang, Y., & Wood, T. (2005). The feasibility of launching and detecting jamming attacks in wireless networks. In *Proceedings of the 6th ACM International Symposium on Mobile Ad Hoc Networking & Computing,* Urbana-Champaign, IL (pp. 46-57).

Xu, W., Grant, G., Nguyen, H., & Dai, X. (2008). Security breach: The case of TJX Companies, Inc. *Communications of the Association for Information Systems*, *23*(1).

Yang, H. K., Choi, J. H., & Ann, Y. H. (1996, November 26-29). Self-certified identity information using the minimum knowledge. In *Proceedings of the Digital Signal Processing Applications Conference (IEEE TENCON)*, Perth, WA, Australia (pp. 641-647).

Yao, A. C. (1982). Protocols for secure computations. In *Proceedings of the 23rd Annual Symposium on Foundations of Computer Science*, Chicago, IL (pp. 160-164). Washington, DC: IEEE Computer Society.

Yasinsac, A., & Bishop, M. (2008). The dynamics of counting and recounting votes. *IEEE SandP Magazine*, *6*(3), 22-29.

Yasinsac, A., & Pardue, H. (2010). Voting system risk assessment using threat trees. In *Proceedings of the Conference on Information Systems Applied Research*, Nashville, TN.

Yasinsac, A., Wagner, D., Bishop, M., Baker, T., De Medeiros, B., Tyson, G., et al. (2007). *Software review and security analysis of the ES&S iVotronic 8.0.1.2 voting machine firmware, final report*. Tallahassee, FL: Security and Assurance in Information Technology (SAIT) Laboratory, Florida State University.

Ye, E. Z., Yuan, Y., & Smith, S. (2002). *Trusted Paths for Browsers* (Tech. Rep.). Hanover, NH: Dartmouth College, Department of Computer Science. Retrieved from http://www.cs.dartmouth.edu/~pkilab/demos/spoofing

Yi, X., & Zhang, Y. (2007). Privacy-preserving distributed association rule mining via semi-trusted mixer. *Data & Knowledge Engineering*, *63*(2). doi:10.1016/j.datak.2007.04.001

Yu, F., Dai, X., Shen, Y., Huang, H., & Zhu, M. (2005). Intrusion detection and simulation for high-speed networks. In *Proceedings of the International Conference on Services Systems and Services Management* (Vol. 2, pp. 835-840).

Yurcik, W., Sharm, A., & Doss, D. (2002, March). False Impressions: Contrasting Perceptions of Security as a Major Impediment to Achieving Survivable Systems. In *Proceedings of the IEEE/CERT/SEI 4th Survivability Workshop*, Vancouver, BC, Canada. Washington, DC: IEEE Computer Society.

Zaki, M. J. (2000). Scalable algorithms for association mining. *IEEE Transactions on Knowledge and Data Engineering*, *12*, 372–390. doi:10.1109/69.846291

Zhang, L., Zhu, J., & Yao, T. (2004). An evaluation of statistical spam filtering techniques. *ACM Transactions on Asian Language Information Processing*, *3*(4), 243–269. doi:10.1145/1039621.1039625

Zhang, X., Sakaguchi, T., & Kennedy, M. (2007). A cross-cultural analysis of privacy notices of the Global 2000. *Journal of Information Privacy & Security*, *3*(2), 18–36.

Zhang, Y., Lee, W., & Huang, Y. (2003). Intrusion detection techniques for mobile wireless networks. *Wireless Networks*, *9*(5), 545–556. doi:10.1023/A:1024600519144

Zhong, S. (2007). Privacy-preserving algorithms for distributed mining of frequent itemsets. *Information Sciences*, *177*(2), 490–503. doi:10.1016/j.ins.2006.08.010

Zhou, J., & Stgtlhane, T. (2004). A framework for early robustness assessment. In *Proceedings of the 8th IASTED Conference on Software Engineering and Application*.

Zuckerman, A. (2001). Order in the courts? *World Trade*, *14*(9), 26–29.

# About the Contributors

**Hamid Nemati** is an Associate Professor of Information Systems at the Information Systems and Operations Management Department of The University of North Carolina at Greensboro. He holds a Doctorate from the University of Georgia and a Master of Business Administration from The University of Massachusetts. Before coming to UNCG, he was on the faculty of J. Mack Robinson College of Business Administration at Georgia State University. He also has extensive professional experience as a consultant with a number of major corporations. Dr. Nemati is the Editor-in-Chief of *International Journal of Information Security and Privacy* and the Advances in Information Security and Privacy (AISP) Book Series. His research specialization is in the areas of decision support systems, data warehousing and mining, and information security and privacy. His research articles have appeared in a number of premier journals. He has presented numerous research and scholarly papers nationally and internationally.

\* \* \*

**Khalid A. Al-Shalfan**, BEng, M.Sc, PhD in computer vision, (computer science) from the University of Bradford. Recently He is assistant professor at the college of computer and information sciences, Al-Imam Muhammad Ibn Saud Islamic University. His research activities are in information security and computer vision. He is the leader of the IT research program of the Saudi IT research plan in Imam Mohammad Ibn Saud University.

**Adel Ammar** is an assistant professor at college of computer science and information systems in Imam University, Riyadh, Saudi Arabia. In 2008, He received his PhD degree in computer science from Paul Sabatier University, Toulouse, France. His research interests include machine learning, pattern recognition, statistical modeling, and intrusion detection.

**Oluwasefunmi Tale Arogundade** is a PhD student at Academy of Mathematics and System Sciences, Graduate University of Chinese Academy of Sciences, Beijing China. She received a B.Sc. degree in computer science from the University of Ado-Ekiti, Ekiti State, Nigeria. She had the M.Sc. degree in computer science from the University of Agriculture, Abeokuta, Nigeria. Her current research interests include requirement engineering, reuse, ontology, business /IT alignment and information management science. She had published many articles in journals and conference proceedings. Adio Akinwale is an associate professor and researcher at University of Agriculture, Abeokuta Nigeria. His research interest encompasses Management Information System, Query Algorithms Optimization and cybernetics. Adio holds Master degree in Cybernetic and Computer Science and PhD degree in Economic Informatics all from Oskar Langer University, Wroclaw, Poland. He had published many articles in journals and conference proceedings.

**Hussein Fakhry** is the Assistant Dean of the College of Information Technology at the University of Dubai. He received PhD in Intelligent Control Systems from the University of Waterloo, Canada. His research interests are in Information Systems Research using Systems Dynamics, Information Systems Security, E-Commerce and E-Business, Decision Support Systems, Applications of Artificial Intelligence, and Assessment of Academic Programs. His research appeared in international journals and conferences such as Review of Business Information Systems, IETECH Journal of Information Systems, An International Journal of Information & Security, The Journal of Mathematical and Computer Modeling, Communications of the International Information Management Association (CIIMA), Proceedings of the IEEE International Conference on Information and Communication Technologies, and Proceedings of the IADIS International Conference on Information Systems.

**Ouissem Ben Fredj** received his PhD degree in computer science from Evry Val d'Essonnes University, France in 2007. He worked as an assistant professor at college of computer science and information systems in Imam University, Riyadh, Saudi Arabia. Since September 2011, he is an assistant professor at College of computers and Information Systems in Taif University, Saudi Arabia. His research interests include parallel and distributed systems, high-speed networks, Network and information Security, and voice over IP.

**Laleh Golafshan** received her B.S. from Islamic Azad University, Iran in year 2005, and her M.S. degree in (Computer Science) from Universiti Kebangsaan Malaysia (UKM), Department of Computer Science in 2011. Prior to her Masters degree, she ran a Private IT Training College in Shiraz. Her research interests are data mining, optimization and classification; and undertaking research in software engineering and computer security in collaboration with Prof. Dr. Ahmed Patel. Currently, she teaches computer engineering and IT courses as an instructor in Islamic Azad University Fars Science and Research Branch and also performs researcher at this university.

**Ling He** is currently an Associate Professor in the Department of Accounting, College of Business and Management at Saginaw Valley State University. Dr. He received her MS and PhD in Decision Information Systems from the University of Florida. Her research interests include accounting information systems, managerial accounting, database management systems, information security, electronic commerce, and PAC learning theory. She has published papers in *Decision Support Systems*, *Journal on Computing* and *Journal of Database Management*.

**Min-Shiang Hwang** received the B.S. in Electronic Engineering from National Taipei Institute of Technology, Taipei, Taiwan, ROC, in 1980; the M.S. in Industrial Engineering from National Tsing Hua University, Taiwan, in 1988; and the Ph.D. in Computer and Information Science from National Chiao Tung University, Taiwan, in 1995. He also studied Applied Mathematics at National Cheng Kung University, Taiwan, from 1984-1986. Dr. Hwang passed the National Higher Examination in field "Electronic Engineer" in 1988. He also passed the National Telecommunication Special Examination in field "Information Engineering", qualified as advanced technician the first class in 1990. He was a chairman of the Department of Information Management, Chaoyang University of Technology (CYUT), Taiwan, during 1999-2002. He is currently a professor of the department of Management Information System, National Chung Hsing University, Taiwan, ROC. He obtained 1997, 1998, 1999, 2000, and 2001 Outstanding Research Awards of the National Science Council of the Republic of China. He is a member of IEEE, ACM, and Chinese Information Security Association. His current research interests include electronic commerce, database and data security, cryptography, image compression, and mobile computing. Dr. Hwang had published 140+ articles on the above research fields in international journals.

**Zhi Jin** received the MS degree in computer science and the PhD degree from the Changsha Institute of Technology, China, in 1987 and 1992 respectively. She is now a professor of computer science in the Academy of Mathematics and System Science, Chinese Academy of Science. Her current research is on software requirements engineering and Knowledge Engineering. She has published more than 90 referred papers in the area of requirements engineering and knowledge-based software engineering.

**Kenan Kalajdzic** received his BSc degree in Electrical Engineering and his MSc in Telecommunications and Computer Science from University of Sarajevo, Bosnia and Herzegovina. His interests span a wide range of topics in the area of operating systems and computer security. He is currently working as a lecturer at the Center for Computing Education in Sarajevo, and as an external visiting researcher with Prof. Ahmed Patel at the Universiti Kebangsaan Malaysia. He has published 4 papers. He is a reviewer of papers for Computer Standards & Interface Journal.

**Md. Golam Kaosar** is at the final stage of completing his PhD from the School of Engineering and Science, Victoria University, Australia. Before he starts his PhD, he used to work as an engineer at Research Institute (RI) in King Fahd University of Petroleum and Minerals (KFUPM), Saudi Arabia. Prior to that, he got his MS in Computer Engineering and BSC in Computer Science and Engineering from KFUPM, and Bangladesh University of Engineering and Technology (BUET), Bangladesh at the years 2006 and 2001 respectively. As a young researcher, he has a good research background. He has published number of conference papers including IEEE and some good quality journals. His area of research includes but not limited to Private computation, Privacy Preserving Data Mining, Ubiquitous Computing, Security and Cryptography, Ad-hoc sensor network, Mobile and Wireless Network, Network Protocol, etc.

**Douglas M. Kline** is Associate Professor of Information Systems in the Cameron School of Business, UNC Wilmington. His research interests include security technologies, neural network methodologies, and software architecture. His research has been published in *IEEE Transactions on Neural Networks*, *Neural Computing and Applications*, *OMEGA*, *International Journal of Data Modelling, Mining, and Management*, and *Journal of Information Systems Applied Research*. He works extensively with students in UNC Wilmington's unique MS of Computer Science and Information Systems.

**Sathish Alampalayam Poru Kumar** obtained his PhD in computer science and engineering from the University of Louisville, Kentucky in 2007. He also completed his MBA from the University of Louisville in 2001. Currently he is working as Senior IT Architect in US and as an Adjunct Faculty at the Department of Computer Science, California State University, Los Angeles. Sathish has more than 15 years of industry, teaching and research experiences in US. Also, he has more than 10 publications in refereed journals and conferences at the international level. His current research contributions are in the areas of mobile ad-hoc networks, in particular, the security architectures and algorithms for this type of networking.

**Cheng-Chi Lee** received the B.S. and M.S. in Information Management from Chaoyang University of Technology (CYUT), Taichung, Taiwan, in 1999 and in 2001. He researched in Computer and Information Science from National Chiao Tung University (NCTU), Taiwan, Republic of China, from 2001 to 2003. He received the Ph.D. in Computer Science from National Chung Hsing University (NCHU), Taiwan, in 2007. He was a Lecturer of Computer and Communication, Asia University, from 2004 to 2007. From 2007, he was an assistant professor of Photonics and Communication Engineering, Asia University. From 2009, he is an Editorial Board member of International Journal of Network Security and International Journal of Secure Digital Information Age. From 2010, he is now an assistant professor of Library and Information Science, Fu Jen Catholic University. His current research interests include information security, cryptography, and mobile communications. Dr. Lee had published over 60+ articles on the above research fields in international journals.

**I-En Liao** received the BS degree in Applied Mathematics from National Cheng-Chi University, Taiwan, in 1978, and both the MS degree in Mathematics and the PhD degree in Computer and Information Science from the Ohio State University in 1983 and 1990, respectively. He is currently a professor and chair in the Department of Computer Science and Engineering at National Chung-Hsing University, Taiwan. His research interests are in data mining, XML database, and wireless networks. He is a member of the ACM and the IEEE Computer Society.

**Jafar Mana** has been teaching in the Sawyer Business School department of Information Systems and Operation Management at Suffolk University for eleven years. As an entrepreneur, Dr. Mana is a co-founder of Analytic Development (ADI) Inc., which provides computer solutions and data analysis to a variety of corporate clients. He is also a co-founder of the software development company Yafa Software, Inc., which produces specialized software applications for the real estate industry. His research interests are in the areas of product development methodology, modeling and design of processes, software engineering, Security issue, and knowledge discovery and data mining.

**Chandan Mazumdar** is now heading the Department of Computer Science and Engineering of Jadavpur University, India. He is also the Coordinator of the Centre for Distributed Computing. His research interests include enterprise information security modeling, fault tolerance, and disaster management information systems.

**Benjamin Ngugi** is an associate professor in the information systems and operations management at the Sawyer Business School, Suffolk University in Boston. He received his PhD in information systems from New Jersey Institute of Technology and his bachelors in electrical and electronics engineering from University of Nairobi, Kenya. He conducts his research in the areas of behavioral biometrics, cyber security & compliance, business intelligence and technology adoption. Ben brings over eleven years of professional experience initially as a system engineer and then as a Technical Director in charge of technical sales, Installations and training in computer networks, security systems and satellite systems. He has published his research in journals including Decision Support Systems, Journal of Organizational and End User Computing, Fordham Journal of Corporate and Financial Law and the ACM Journal of Data quality.

**Mathew Nicho** is an Assistant Professor in the College of Information Technology at the University of Dubai. He obtained his Master's degree and PhD from the School of Computing and Mathematical Sciences of Auckland University of Technology, New Zealand in 2004 and 2009 respectively. He started his career in the computer hardware and software industry in 1990 before moving to academics in 1995 lecturing on Computer Science and IS subjects. He also trains students and computer professionals on ethical hacking and defense technologies. He is certified in CEH, RWSP, SAP, and, has published papers on IT audit and governance, enterprise systems, and IS security in international journals and conference proceedings.

**Ahmed Patel** received his MSc and PhD degrees in Computer Science from Trinity College Dublin (TCD) in 1978 and 1984 respectively, specializing in the design, implementation and performance analysis of packet switched networks. He is a Professor in Computer Science at Universiti Kebangsaan Malaysia. He is visiting professor at Kingston University in the UK. He has published over two and ten hundred technical and scientific papers and co-authored several books. He is currently involved in the R&D of cybercrime investigations and forensic computing, intrusion detection & prevention systems, cloud computing autonomic computing, Web search engines, e-commerce and developing a framework and architecture of a comprehensive quality of service facility for networking protocols and advanced services. He is a member of the Editorial Advisory Board of the following International Journals: (i) Computer Standards & Interface, (ii) Information Management & Computer Security and (iii) Cyber Criminology.

**Murthy Rallapalli**, an executive architect (security and privacy) at IBM, specializing in customer solutions and enablement in the area of security and business analytics. He has authored several red books in the area of architectures, security and privacy, and presented many papers on security and privacy at several international conferences. He is a certified CISSP (Certified Information Systems and Security Professional) by ISC2 organization. Mr. Rallapalli is currently pursuing his PhD from Stevens Institute of Technology in the area of privacy and Service Oriented Architectures. He is also an adjunct faculty at Stevens Institute of Technology at School of Systems and Enterprises (SSE). Mr. Rallapalli holds two patent filings by IBM in the area of data privacy and security.

**Mohsen Rouached** is an assistant professor at college of computers and information systems in Taif University, Saudi Arabia. He received his PhD degree in computer science from Nancy University in France. His research interests include service oriented computing, wireless sensors networks, security, privacy and forensics management. He has published more than 30 papers in various journals and conference proceedings. He has served as program committee member and session chair in several conferences.

**Majdi Ben Saad** received his engineer degree in networks and telecommunication from the Institut National des Sciences Appliqués et Technologie, Tunisia, 2007. He has more than three years of experience in Sagem Software and Technologies, as a real-time embedded software engineer. He joined, in March 2010, the amansystem research group at Al-Imam Mohammed Ibn Saud Islamic University. His research interests include real-time embedded systems, network and system security and network forensics.

**Hassen Sallay** received his PhD degree in computer science from Nancy University in France. He worked as an assistant professor in the dept. of computer science and information systems, Imam Mohammad ibn Saud Univ. Since 2011, he is serving as a Security Consultant in the Deanship of Information Technology - Imam University. His research interests include Network and information Security Management, Security forensics, Service Oriented Computing, Network Management and Multicast services. He also served as the leader of AMAN security research team.

**Lydia Segal** is associate professor of business law and ethics at Suffolk University's Sawyer Business School in Boston. With degrees from Harvard Law School and Oxford, her specialty is organizational stewardship and integrity. Her latest book is Battling Corruption in America's Public Schools (Harvard University Press).

**Anirban Sengupta** is pursuing his Ph.D. (Engineering) from Jadavpur University, India. After serving in industry, he joined the Centre for Distributed Computing, Jadavpur University where he is now Principal Research Engineer. His research interests include enterprise information security modeling, and risk analysis methodologies.

**S. Srinivasan** is a Professor of Information Systems and Chair of the Division of International Business and Technology Studies at Texas A & M International University. He joined TAMIU in Fall 2010. He was at the University of Louisville for the prior 23 years. His research interests are in Information Security. He has published several papers in both Mathematics and Computer Science. He led the InfoSec program development at the University of Louisville, which was designated a National Center of Academic Excellence by the National Security Agency and the Department of Homeland Security. Currently he concentrates his teaching in Information Security and Databases. He volunteers his time extensively for public education causes.

**Nice Mona Taghavi**, a.k.a. CMT, received her B.Sc. degree in Information Technology from Parand Islamic Azad University of Iran in 2007. Besides her involvement in several Iranian national ICT research projects, she had worked for an IT consulting and project managing company which was responsible for overseeing and preparing some of the technical reports for the Supreme Council of Information and Communication Technology (SCICT) of Iran programme. Currently, she is pursuing her MSc in Information Systems at Universiti Kebangsaan Malaysia and undertaking research in cooperation with Prof. Dr. Ahmed Patel in advanced secure Web-based information systems and Secure Mobile Agent-based E-Marketplace Systems. She has published 4 papers. She is a reviewer of papers for Computer Standards & Interface Journal.

**Xiaoguang Yang** is a full professor at Institute of System Sciences, Academy of Mathematics and System Sciences, Chinese Academy of Sciences (CAS). He is currently the director of key laboratory of management Decision and Information system (MADIS), CAS. Prof. Yang research interests include risk management, operation research, network optimization, social network, decision support systems for macro-economics. He is associate editor of Journal of Systems Science and Complexity, Acta Mathematicae Applicatae Sinica, System Engineering Theory and Practice (in Chinese) and Operations Research and Management (in Chinese). He had published many papers in both domestic and international journals. He has long years of working experience both as an academics and practitioner.

**Ulku Yaylacicegi** is an Assistant Professor of Information Systems at Cameron Business School, University of North Carolina at Wilmington. She obtained her Ph.D. from the University of Texas at Dallas. Her research interests span information communications technologies, telecommunications policy, information security, IT productivity, health-care IT, quality management, and innovative education. Her research has appeared in, or is forthcoming in, *Technology in Society, Industrial Management and Data Systems, Journal of Information Systems Applied Research,* and *International Journal of Innovation and Learning.*

**Xun Yi** is an Associate Professor in the School of Engineering and Science, Victoria University, Australia. His research interests include applied cryptography, privacy-preserving data mining, computer and network security, mobile and wireless communication security, and intelligent agent technology. He has published about 100 research papers in international journals, such as IEEE Trans. Knowledge and Data Engineering, IEEE Trans. Wireless Communication, IEEE Trans. Dependable and Secure Computing, IEEE Trans. Circuit and Systems, IEEE Trans. Vehicular Technologies, IEEE Communication Letters, and conference proceedings.

# Index

## A

abuse case 202-203, 205, 207-208, 211, 213, 215, 219, 224
accuracy 19-20, 30-31, 67, 83, 149, 226, 230, 233, 237, 240, 243, 245-248
Ad hoc On Demand Distance Vector (AODV) 170
Ad-Hoc on Demand Routing Protocol (AODV) 8
anchor texts 21-23, 25
ANOVA 58-59
APDU (Application Protocol Data Unit) 135
Apriori technique 83
assets 103-104, 106-109, 112-119, 159, 161, 183, 190, 194, 203, 206, 240
Association rule mining (ARM) 83-84
attacks
desynchronisation 35-36, 39, 42-43, 46, 49
dictionary 35, 37, 48-49
replay 35-37, 47, 49
authentication phase 37-46, 48

## B

B2C 105, 195, 197, 200
blog spam 16, 19, 32-33
detection 19
Body (B) Component 249
bootstrap interval 59-60
Brain-Trunk Feet (B-T-F) Component 246
browser lock 76, 79

## C

CC protocol 40-43, 45-46, 48
certificate-based scheme 125
Chess Grandmaster Problem 140
Chi-square test 56
comment spam 15-20, 23-24, 31-33
Common Criteria (CC) 204
complement number 86

## completeness

completeness 115, 166, 222, 226, 230, 232, 234
consistent representation 226, 230, 237
consumer behavior 70, 73, 75
control chart 171-174
control list 107, 114-115, 117, 119
Control Objectives for Information and related Technology (COBIT) 120, 177
correspondence analysis 56, 62
cryptography 14, 100, 124, 129, 131-132, 136, 145-147
cryptosystems 83, 101, 124, 129-130
customer relationship management (CRM) 83
cybernetic attacks 241

## D

data breaches 177, 179-181, 225-226, 228-229, 233-234, 237, 239
Data Breach Notification Act (DBNA) 233
data mining 33, 82-84, 86, 100-102, 175, 196, 242, 248, 251
data quality 225-226, 228-229, 237-238, 240
data theft 177, 181
denial of service 35-36, 39, 49-50, 163, 171, 174-175, 212, 215, 217
Destination Sequenced Distance Vector (DSDV) 163, 171
Destination Sequenced Distance-Vector (DSDV) 7
digital certificate 71, 74, 76, 78-80, 199
direct recording electronic (DRE) 149, 162
dynamic source routing (DSR) 8

## E

ease of manipulation 230-231
e-commerce 1, 53-54, 66, 68, 72, 81, 83, 100, 102, 110, 193, 195, 197-200
electrically erasable and programmable read only memory (EEPROM) 136
electronic communication 1